BEACH BOYS vs Beatlemania:

Rediscovering Sixties Music

by

G A De Forest

Booklocker.com, Inc.
2007

ACKNOWLEDGMENTS:

Thanks most of all to my best friend, John Barnett-Goodman, whose unstinting support for twenty-three years (so far) for what threatened to be an imaginary writing career sustained me through the rotten times; to Angela Hoy of Booklocker.com in Bangor, Maine, USA for giving me the opportunity to publish—and on the best writers' terms anywhere; my sister Colette Shields, who patiently typed my first novel; Peter Shields (shields@ihug.co.nz) for lending computer assistance above and beyond, even for a brother-in-law. To Fred Vail, legendary Beach Boy promoter and manager, for graciously agreeing to write the Foreword to this book, his encouragement and recollections of the Sixties group scene—I'm almost sorry I beat you to it, Fred. To Italian rock journalist Aldo Pedron for his early offer to publish a review; and same to Val Johnson-Howe and Andrew G Doe of the UK Beach Boys fan scene. To Kie Miskelly of Blueboarders and Metro, Scotland and Brett Hayhoe of Q magazine in Australia, who similarly lent kind help to a total stranger. And to Bob Gill of New York for his perseverance in delivering me extra chart statistics for the Beach Boys.

DEDICATED TO:

Brian, Mike, Dennis, Carl & Al—for working miracles against the odds—and Dave, Bruce and Glen for being there

ALSO IN PROGRESS BY G A De FOREST:

A QUIRKY LOOK AT EARLY CINEMA (3 vols)

THE LAST WARRIOR (screenplay on Maori chief Hone Heke)

THE WHALE WARS (a novel of war over conservation)

TALES FROM THE PENINSULA (collection of short stories)

CONTENTS

FOREWORD by Fred Vail

When Steve Moon (born three years before the Beach Boys' last hit single, 'Kokomo') e-mailed me that there was a new book coming out on The Beach Boys, my first reaction was: not another one! What more could be written about the band that had not already been written? Then, when I read about Gary's unusual approach, The Beach Boys vs. Beatlemania: Rediscovering Sixties Music, it made perfect sense.

For the first time that I recall, someone—other than me—was thinking about the two legendary groups as opponents. And, in a sense, during those crazy mid-60s, they were. Some of the books on the Beach Boys have exploited the negative side of the group, particularly Denny, but the best books—the ones that caught the true spirit of the individual members of the band— have always been written by people who were, in the final analysis, fans of the boys.

Over the years I've repeatedly been asked about my take on The Beatles and I've often replied that I was never that 'into' the group during their heyday. Sure, I thought they were unique when they first came out—they wore neat outfits on stage, their accents were cool—and those first singles were quite catchy. But I really didn't have time to dwell on them. After all, I was working with The Beach Boys, America's #1 band, and The Beatles—at least to me— were the 'enemy.'

No, it wasn't a war in the conventional sense, but there certainly was competition between the two groups nevertheless. Throughout the mid-60s the two groups vied for radio airplay, television appearances, promotion and marketing dollars from Capitol and EMI Records, newspaper articles, album reviews and concert ticket sales. If merchandise had been popular back then—baseball caps, teeshirts, sweatshirts and the rest—they would have been competing for that market too.

And don't forget: being on the same record label in the US and UK, they were also vying for the attention of record label personnel. There were those in the Capitol Tower who were huge Beatles supporters, while others, like the boys' dear friend Karl Engemann, were behind The Beach Boys 110%. In fact, if it wasn't for "Beach dad" Murry, the boys would not have gotten as much attention from Capitol as they did. While Murry has been villainized in a number of books over the years, he certainly deserves our eternal thanks for promoting—dare I say 'fighting' for—the group during those early years.

While the two groups continued to battle each other through the 60s, we all know who ultimately won out: The original Beach Boys—Brian, Dennis, Carl, Mike and Alan—outlasted The Beatles by nearly fourteen years; after the tragic death of DW in December of '83 the rest of the band, including Bruce, outlasted The Beatles by sixteen more years. Now, if you include Mike, Bruce, Chris and the current touring Beach Boys they've outlasted The Beatles by an amazing thirty-eight years!

While it's not always been rosy for either group—both have had their share of tragedy—perhaps 1970 summed it up best. It was the final year of the 'Fab Four' and it was also the year that *Sunflower* was released on Brother/Reprise Records, distributed by Warner Brothers Records.

The first single was 'Add Some Music To Your Day'. It was a perfect record as to timing. After all, it was the 'peace and love' era in American music and culture. The lyrics tapped in on that theme and all of us working in The Tomb (as I called it) on Ivar Avenue in Hollywood thought we had a smash.

As Brother Records' sole representative I was on the road for over seven months in 1970, meeting with Warner Brothers sales, promotion and marketing executives, setting up press interviews for the band, and attending radio and records trade conferences in New York City, Washington DC, Los Angeles and Atlanta. Getting airplay for The Beach Boys in 1970 was not as easy as it had been in the early and mid-60s. They were no longer an automatic add at radio stations and nothing summed up that fact more than my visit to WFIL Radio, Philadelphia, in the late winter of 1970.

WFIL was not only one of the top radio stations in America, its television affiliate was the home of *American Bandstand*. In the 1950s I remember rushing home from school each afternoon to catch Dick Clark and the Bandstand Buddies as they danced to the hottest new tunes. WFIL Radio was indeed legendary. Some of the great deejays of "Boss" Radio were on the air there: guys like "Doctor" Don Rose, George Michael and Jim Nettleton. I knew that if "FIL" added the single dozens more stations up and down the East Coast would also add it to their playlists. We would certainly get our 'bullet' in Billboard Magazine!

Jay Cook, the program director of the station, was known for his good ears and for occasionally taking chances on new releases and obscure singles. I needed Jay and WFIL to help break the single and as I was escorted into his office I could not help but be impressed by the numerous Gold albums and singles that adorned his walls. Since I was the manager of The Beach Boys I was given every courtesy at most stations. They would often keep the record men waiting outside in the lobby while the program directors and music directors chatted with me about Brian and the boys.

Jay was no exception. He immediately started out by asking what the group was up to; how Brian was doing; and stressed the fact that he felt The Beach Boys were one of the most talented groups ever. "I've enjoyed playing Brian's music since my deejay days in radio," Jay said. And, of course, he also said those three magic words I'd heard so many times before: "Brian's a genius, Fred." I couldn't agree more, I responded.

After twenty or so minutes of chit-chat it was time to do what all salesmen do: call for the order. I asked Jay if he would add the single. I just knew—after spending the past 20 minutes talking about Brian and the group—that this was going to be a slam dunk. "I can't add the single, Fred," Jay calmly said. "But why, Jay? You've just told me how great the group is and how much you enjoy their music." "I know, Fred, but The Beach Boys aren't hip anymore," he replied. I was devastated.

But now, when I retell that story, a smile will come to my face, tears will often well up in my eyes. It's been nearly thirty-eight years since that meeting at WFIL. The WFIL of old is a memory—probably broadcasting all news or all talk nowadays; Jay Cook has passed on, as have my two dear brothers-in-spirit, Dennis and Carl. The Beatles are also gone. Even The Beach Boys, as we knew them, are no longer. But the music—which has always been at the heart of the group's success—lives on. And on any given day, at any given moment, someone, somewhere, is playing or listening to a Beach Boys song.

Yes, I think it can be said with absolute certainty: In the case of "The Beach Boys vs. Beatlemania" the Beach Boys have, indeed, won the war.

Fred Vail
Treasure Isle Recorders, Inc.
October 26, 2007
Nashville, TN—"Music City, USA"

PS—November 9, 2007

As I was putting the finishing touches on the Foreword to Gary's book he requested that I say a few words about my dear friends Denny and Carl. Those of you who know me know the great friendship that I enjoyed with both of them during their all-too-brief time on this earth.

I have often referred to them as my 'brothers-in-spirit' and that is no exaggeration. DW and CW died far, far too young and even though they left us a rich musical legacy—to say nothing of their sons and daughters—their tragic passing left a gap in me that will never be filled.

I'm often asked what they were "really like" and I must say that what they personified on stage—Carl's warm and passionate vocals, Denny's enthusiasm and energy on the drums, were much like their personalities off stage. CW was the most unchanged of any of the boys. He always had time for the fans, who would often wait hours for an autograph or a handshake. And he rarely had anything but good things to say about others.

DW was much the same way, particularly with the fans. He enjoyed posing for pictures, signing autographs, and hanging out late into the night in the hotel lobby or lounge as if he wanted to milk every last waking minute out of the day. Denny would give you the shirt off his back—and often did.

But when you get right down to it all of the boys had their individual key roles. Call it divine intervention. Call it timing and luck. I'd prefer to think of The Beach Boys as God's gift to all of us. Each member had a role. Without any one of the individual members of the group it simply would not have had its enormous success and lasting impact: Brian, the soul of group; Denny the spirit; Carl the compassion; Mike the cheerleader; Al the loyal friend. The core of the group was family and the catalyst was the music. It's as simple as that.

When I was thinking about what to add to the remarks I'd already put down on paper it dawned on me that there is one thing that The Beach Boys and The Beatles did have in common. It was the early and tragic deaths of two of each of the groups' members. John and George. Dennis and Carl. We can be thankful what time they did spend on this earth was in making our lives a lot richer and enjoyable by their unselfish contributions.

Editor's note: Fred Vail, a legend in Beach Boy circles, from age 18 promoted some of the best and most famous acts of the Sixties. He was the Beach Boys' first 'advance man', hired the night of their Sacramento concert, May 24th 1963. It was his idea to record a live album, taken from their concert in the same city, produced and emceed by him, Dec 21st 1963. This became their first #1 album and first Gold one—the first major live album in rock history. One afternoon early in 1966 he happened to be with Brian Wilson—in the booth, as he mastered *Pet Sounds*. And he arranged for the Beach Boys to play that summer 1983 concert for the Reagans at The White House, six months before the death of his good friend Dennis Wilson.

PREFACE

The fully creative rock group—writing songs, arranging and playing backing music, producing recordings, performing them on the road—was unknown until the Beach Boys started doing just that in 1962. Producing remained outside the scope of all but one of the Beatles, arranging until Paul McCartney wrote his symphony at the end of the millennium. Pop (unlike folk) acts had been vocalists without instruments, or instrumentalists backing a star. Now a family gathering melded into a unit, developing a unique group sound while each as lead vocalist added distinction to a song— something else the Beatles couldn't match.

Their group has been condemned for lightening the shade of rock'n'roll, yet this was a trend set in train long before they arrived by earlier white artists—by the Everly Bros, Buddy Holly (note the over-dainty accompaniment on 'Every Day', 'It Doesn't Matter Anymore'), and then Elvis Presley with his switch from rock to teen idol schmaltz. It was this placid side of Holly and Presley that the Beatles ('Words of Love'), Hollies and numerous other British acts were most impressed with, judging by the evidence.

From the start, early in 1962, the Beach Boys acted to *reverse* this blight with rock'n'roll classics 'Surfin' Safari', '409' and 'Surfin' USA'. The raw and vital attack of these recordings, rejecting the teen idol mush dominating the era (that was embraced by the Beatles) hadn't been heard in white rock since the Elvis of the Fifties. Venturing hard against the mainstream of the day, their playing on these, often disparaged as "rudimentary", is marvelous in achieving the most with least. Their guitar solos strike to the heart of rock'n'roll: crisp, fluid, controlled yet played with apparent wild abandon, exciting in juxtaposing seemingly discordant notes; and above all concise—all in the space of 15 seconds. All was enhanced by drumming—and later other percussion—perfectly attuned to the requirements of the song, explosive with imaginative touches or subtly weaving under the surface texture.

Many well-informed commentators believe the Beach Boys were the greatest musical force to come out of the Sixties—greatest in originality, in breadth, in depth. The more convinced of these greet with incredulity the relative neglect the group has endured— a stupefaction recurring whenever EMI, with assiduous absence of imagination, reissues the same twenty to thirty tracks, in a different order, in its latest "summer music" compilation.

A clear picture of "Beach Boys vs Beatles" has been thickly fogged by almost 44 years of propaganda. Neither has it been helped by the overly humble perspective of most of the Beach Boys themselves, with the exceptions of Dennis Wilson and Mike Love. Beach Boys creator Brian Wilson has gone from supremely confident in his position, at least until the early Seventies fully aware of his contribution to Twentieth Century music, to on one occasion in the new millennium conceding on balance the overall supremacy of the Beatles—which says it all about his continuing confused state of mind.

Despite personal setbacks and industry obstacles designed to frustrate their independent spirit they won world acclaim as the most popular American group of the Sixties—but without ever matching the unconditionality of Beatle worship. From the start they bucked the powers of the music industry by making their own music their own way and were repaid as supreme independent producer Phil Spector was—radio bosses simply stopped playing their records.

At peak their impact was blunted by three insurmountable facts:

* The British Invasion, which until 1967 featured new fashions over and above new music. Its prime representatives, the Beatles, so famous so suddenly after years in obscurity, cry out for debunking.

* The resurgence of black artists held back three years by the invaders—and the conformist white Counter Culture—rebounding politically on the 'whitest' of major rock groups, the Beach Boys.

* The Beach Boys' refusal to cater to trends or join cliques in a Sixties scene dominated by snobberies.

So who were the Sixties' real rebels?

This book is by a Southern California/Hawaii exile. Home has been ten thousand kilometres away—Auckland, New Zealand— since a year before the Beach Boys formed. So how can I assess their career having 'missed' it? The fact is they are a living world entity half a century on. The month of writing this, February 2007, I have heard 'Trader' (1973) and 'Lonely Sea' (1962) on Radio NZ, and full reviews featuring songs famous and obscure. Controversial antinuclear prime minister the late David Lange and film star Sam Neill hailed the Beach Boys as their favorite group.

Their California exists in the imagination. Seeing them from a foreign culture allows winnowing out the surf music chaff of hangers-on that they seem forever burdened by in their own. And, as a young eyewitness, I was not tainted by the American Beatle phenomenon—a catered media event. True, I experienced the Beatles second hand. My eldest sister skipped school to see them, then restyled me from a ducktail to a mop and scarab-beetle string tie. The Beach Boys I've seen a few times. There was their 1970 performance at Auckland Town Hall; I almost met them at their reception the evening before— if a 14-year-old standing dumbstruck and thrusting a torn page in front of Carl and others to autograph counts; '78 when they filled Auckland's Western Springs Stadium; and Brian Wilson's *Smile* concert nearing Xmas 2004. It remains to be seen how much their November 2007 concert will resemble a classic Beach Boy performance.

'Down Under' the Beach Boys were no superstar fixation, more part of the environment—the outdoor, car-loving, beachgoing lifestyle mirroring that of Southern California. I vividly recall 'Surfin' Safari', 'In My Room' and 'Fun Fun Fun' as radio favorites but my idols were New Zealand sports figures, miler Peter Snell, pacer Cardigan Bay and rugby's All Blacks. I noticed no Beach Boy theme until 'California Girls'—drummed into me before school by my sisters.

When the Beatles reached New Zealand in the northern spring of 1963 the Beach Boys met them head on mounting the hit parades. Maybe the most popular record of the era (and my first) was the 'Twist and Shout' e.p.—four Beatle songs for not much more than the price of two. Then came the American frenzy over a group we had loved for nine months.

The figures speak for themselves: The Beatles wrote and performed more pieces that pleased more people than anyone else—and still do, adding such gargantuan successes as their compilation *1* to the history. But then, a chocolate box painter—by averaging out audience expectations, homogenising and reproducing them as 'art'—could say the same thing to Munch or Leonardo. In bulk sales they are in the same class as (Bing Crosby and) Elvis Presley, depending on whose fans you believe. Beatle fanatics claim a billion sales—exactly three times the number estimated by Beatle *scholars*. Both plumbed every audible nook and cranny in eking out and maximising product: rock and roll, pop, Latin American, operetta, straight balladeering. For the Beatles, add English Music Hall, Euro-Merseyside, classical and French Provincial off the top of my head.

It is not a biography, nor chronology. Recountings of life events in isolation read like buckets of spare nuts and bolts without a blueprint. It might be called an historio-critical appreciation. I try to back up my opinions—though when I listen today I am still touched by the magic of both groups, without reasoning. Obviously, it is a rebalancing: How with any justice could I not redress the distortion to taste brought by acts whose real distinctions were fluffy hair and half-English, half-Mississippi accents? After years of piecemeal progress I was spurred to complete it by pure practicality. I wanted a reference and there were none in bookshops, while lining Borders shelves were two dozen books on every possible aspect of the Beatles… *but their music*: spouses, groupies, offspring, Lennon 'philosophy'. Early in 2006 good fortune struck: My hard drive crashed and I was thrown back on a draft two and a half years old, enabling a focused, "versus" approach.

Why the Beach Boys? Because I like them. Humble and cocky at the same time, always aware of their roots pounded into them by a relentlessly levelling father-manager, they are the least calculating of acts. The Beatles wore their working-class status as badges while hobnobbing with the élite of class-bound English society—cosily elevated as pets through social strata. Adoption by the English upper classes through the persons of Brian Epstein and George Martin, and approval by the Royal Family, guaranteed their place in history. The Beach Boys' insecurity translated into an engaging awkwardness in the spotlight. Seen in tv spots, they *know* they're out of place in showbiz with its artifices, but persevere in entertaining audiences eager to listen. The Beatles always showed that on stage, charming people, was where they belonged. But, beginning recording, they recognized the Beach Boys as their one and only rivals, and secretly, their models?

And, because they are *not the Beatles*, not celeb royalty, Hollywood A-list. Dennis Wilson, the original beachboy: "The Beach Boys are not a superstar group. The music is the superstar." There is that redressing. Histories promote the Beatles as the soul of Rock's most important decade, prime of few remnants worth serious interest. A student delving into the literature today could be forgiven for writing a thesis on the development of Rock that starts with Elvis (influenced by nameless black singers), proceeds through a revival by the Beatles/Dylan/Stones, mixed with elements of black Soul and on 'up' to the Jacksons, the Bee Gees and Disco, with a sideline to Punk, thence to the culmination of sixty years of Rhythm & Blues, its gift to civilisation: Rap.

Beatle fans must forgive my 'attack' on their heroes—which is, anyway, futile. The media drivers who create and maintain reputations have shown for over forty years that nothing short of a mass frontal lobotomy, extensive rewiring and intensive retraining— maybe by timely, well-placed rabbit punches with Heimlich Manoeuvre chasers—will snap them out of their mesmerism. Questioning of Beatle primacy still brings on genuine reactions of hurt from many who don't consider themselves over-the-top fans; the enquirer is seen to wantonly blaspheme against a fundamental truth held with fundamentalist zeal. And because two of the Beatles have died before their times, the first by fan murder, the second's death probably hastened by an earlier knife attack by one, they are martyrs to the devout. Delving into things the Beatles admitted to is all the more a crime, like a Rottweiler disembowelling a submissive puppy. This protective halo belittles or obscures many real artists of quality of the time—who deserve their own books.

This comes from someone once immersed in Beatlemania who holds them in considerable nostalgic affection. But what else is an iconoclast to do to icons? It is enough to say that both groups are the ones I consider worth putting myself out to write about, prioritising this over other projects I consider important.

If The Who and the Stones are the greatest-ever rock bands, they give way to the other two overall. The Stones have transmuted past the millennium by a bizarrely successful Emperor's New Clothes act. In a time when youth is admired above all these visibly *old* geezers, by a strategy of arrested maturity, remain bankable as thoroughly tamed icons of rock rebellion: near-billionaire businessman Mick Jagger off and on with supermodel wives; Bill Wyman and his attaché case retiring at 60 with child-bride in tow; and Keith Richards damaging the remnants of his brain by falling out of coconut trees and reportedly snorting his father's ashes. Having succeeded in selling this youthful rebellion 40 years past its use-by date to what can only be called a gullible public, the Stones have aped soul and reggae (according to one of them interviewed at the start of their September 2002 tour) as well as twenties-style rotgut blues—without ever becoming important to any genre. They are a commercial corporation obviously willing to do anything to prolong their profitability. Curiously, stories are legion of the particular admiration in which Mick Jagger, no less than the Beatles themselves, held the Beach Boys, and how McCartney, Jagger and Townshend admire Wilson, consistent with the aphorism about talent instinctively recognising genius.

Of the four recognised great Sixties groups the Beach Boys are sole American representatives and so the authentic torch-bearers from Fifties rock'n'roll, an idiom as purely American as jazz. Fittingly, they integrated not only Jazz but a tincture of genuine down-home folksy Americana into their music. More than tinges of Gershwin and

Tchaikovsky are found in their body of work. So how far did they *transcend* rock'n'roll? My focus in this volume is their Sixties career, as they came to grips with alien forces attempting to take over American music.

G A De Forest

1. THIS WHOLE WORLD

Rock is a fickle mistress. While some rock stars go on decade after decade on mediocre talents even the great ones of the Sixties—by consensus Rock's greatest decade—seemed to be here and gone in a heartbeat. And while other great ones of arts and entertainment—actors, filmmakers, painters, even composers—carve out careers over a generation or two the two world-shaking acts of the Sixties, the Beatles and Beach Boys, each had half a dozen years or so of world fame to make marks which have lasted. It is little short of a miracle that many young musicians still revere Brian Wilson (and to a growing extent, Dennis Wilson) as creative figures worth aspiring to emulate.

The Beach Boys are "the golden boys of rock'n'roll" (Nikki Corvette's Rock'n'Roll Heaven", 1997)—all the more remarkable because it is an image made from their music, without the hype lavished on the Beatles by the record company they had in common, Capitol-EMI. Perhaps better than any other performers in 20th Century show business they thrived through the ordeal of being overshadowed by a new dominating name so soon after starting. What music historian today places the names of Rudy Vallee or Russ Columbo alongside Bing Crosby's, though both were once as big as he?

They had been on the scene a year and a half, had reached the top, when the Beatles—in many ways similar in essentials—arrived with a jolt to world consciousness, threatening to obliterate any valid place the Beach Boys had in pop culture. A total eclipse was the reward for many pop acts who had served their apprenticeship, built a body of work, and now found themselves irremediably out of fashion. If the Beatles' breakthrough had happened as attempted a year earlier the Beach Boys might exist today in the history of popular culture as a tiny footnote the size of Jimmy Gilmer & the Fireballs'. Instead, they enhanced their career geometrically and staked an enduring claim in the pantheon of pop.

Brian Wilson & the Beach Boys matching the Beatles makes one wonder at other confluences: Botticelli, Leonardo, Michelangelo and

1

Raphael; Bach vs Handel; Mozart vs Beethoven. Does one inevitably feed off another to make oneself greater? In such doublings-up of artistic brilliance it is as if one artist existed to fill out the possibilities missed by contemporaries—whether of style, technique or emphasis. For, given that true artists might be unconsciously influenced by their fellows but above all must follow their own inclinations, each must expand the sum of artistic knowledge—rather than merely duplicating the work of someone more talented as lesser 'artists' do. In the context of the Sixties, having the Beach Boys, why need we ever listen to Jan & Dean, the Hondells, the Turtles or the Cowsills, except in the occasional mood for nostalgia? And having the Beatles, would accidentally wiping the entire stock of tapes stored at Oldiesrepository.com of Gerry & the Pacemakers, Billy J Kramer, Freddie & the Dreamers, Herman's Hermits and a large chunk of the Bee Gees' and ELO's repertoires be such a loss?

But it is not destined to be, and the general rule of life being that quantity is preferred to quality, we can look forward to another decade or two of readily hummable ditties from Sixties imitators recycling from every source available into every orifice accessible.

THE BEACH BOYS... THE NAME CONJURES VISIONS to those unborn at the time of their last big hit, though for a long while the span across no.1s, 1964-88, was an all-comers record. We are reminded of it by bands who crib on their name for recognition value—the Beastie Boys vying with the closest yet, Scandinavian group the Bitch Boys. A New Zealand guitar jazz group goes under the name of Surfin' USSR. And then there are the Butthole Surfers.

Their personal story, centered on the mercurial, self-destructive personalities of Brian & Dennis Wilson, after a series of tv movies and documentaries, lives in the popular imagination as vividly as that of any show business phenomenon from any time. And in the creative struggle, if there is anything today to match the emotional turmoil of Beethoven or Van Gogh, this must be it. While many from recent generations know little of their music, others know they were led by an eccentric who "spent years lying in bed," as the legend goes; or that they were the band that spent heaps perfecting their recordings; or they were around at the same time as the Beatles, yet their music sounds somehow fresher.

In speaking of Brian Wilson, the Beach Boys' leader, few if any have noted similarities to Elvis Presley, the embodiment of rock'n'roll. At first sight it is hard to reconcile Carl Wilson's assertion—and father Murry has been credited with similar—that his big brother "could have been Elvis Presley if he'd wanted to." Not only was Brian not the world's greatest sex symbol, as Elvis was to fans, Brian during his sexual peak was afraid of women. Elvis dissed them, it has been suggested (by biographer Albert Goldman), in reaction to his momma's boy cum good ole boy complex. Both could take the best from contemporaries and absorb their essence, though Brian could also from classical music, twenties jazz... Anyone who has listened to Beach Boys 1964-65 knows he could duplicate the vocals of Elvis, his beloved Four Freshmen and Phil Spector's girl groups.

Elvis and Brian had kindred spirits of a naïf: children at heart, searching for fun things to stave off ever-threatening depression, addicted to junk food and falling prey to the spiritual pursuits of Sixties LA. Both had self-indulgent, self-obsessed private lives. Apart from a common proclivity for self-absorption, Brian, though three inches taller, as he grew heavier came to bear a resemblance at a glance to the later fattening Elvis. Coincidentally, Brian would for some years in the Sixties also share Elvis's exclusive street address— Bellagio Road, Bel Air, Beverly Hills.

While Elvis hid his unconventional side alternately behind a macho veneer in private and a polite Southern Gentleman public persona, Brian surrendered at the most basic level to his impulses, until spontaneity was taken from him by repeated breakdowns and he was reprogrammed in the early Eighties by a therapist. Brian clung to his childlike vulnerability—the better to free his creative spirit from ego-driven concerns.

In following their 'authentic selves', Wilson showed more stickability than Elvis, who seems to have been readily manipulated when threatened by loss of his stardom—by the Colonel or movie studio bosses. Early associates at Sun studios have said he wanted nothing more than to become a second Dean Martin. If there's even a tiny kernel of truth in this it is obvious that post-army he was far more malleable to showbiz dictates and was no longer offering himself as any kind of rebel or candidate as King of Rock'n'Roll. Did Elvis abdicate at the behest of Frank Sinatra, who detested rock as amoral jungle music, in order to regain his high footing on the showbiz ladder via appearances in a Sinatra tv special? Was this his priority— to win the stamp of approval from the showbiz bigwigs? The question can as easily be put to the Beatles, who inherited his mantle.

Both Elvis's and Brian's psyches took temporary batterings at the onset of the Beatles. That said, the Beach Boys and Beatles had more in common than any other two groups who gained world fame in the Sixties (aside from the Beatles and Bee Gees, superficially). Both rock-harmony groups were blessed, and cursed, with strong personalities dragging in different directions. In one, the strain eventually destroyed the group. In the other, though each of the three Wilson brothers embarked on solo careers, breaking from the family fold proved impossible. For the most part, for listeners, the diversity in both was a good thing—so much variety that you might search across the dozen next best groups for a similar creative span.

Based partly on the fact that they were similarly universal, to many Sixties survivors—dedicated followers of fashion—the Beach Boys were passé once the Beatles were embraced by the world in 1964, and further out of it when Bob Dylan became fashionable the year after that, then Jimi Hendrix…. To today's cynical Oldies Radio programmers they are just another niche act loaded at random on a neverending tape loop for a living. These middlemen who market music still refer to Beach Boys 'surf' or 'summer' music, not having the wit or imagination to appreciate it out of that context. Surf was rarely mentioned in their songs after mid-1963, summer post mid-1965. Eclectic works 'Wouldn't It Be Nice?' and 'Good Vibrations' are referred to today with circular logic as surf music simply because they're Beach Boy songs. It's as if the pioneering, transcendent *Pet Sounds* and the "Smile" Era, and the seventies never happened—like the Beatles would have ended up if defined by what they did in their first two years of stardom, from *Please Please Me* to *Beatles For Sale.*

EVERYONE, IT SEEMS, KNOWS THE BEACH BOYS sound. Music lovers revere them as legends despite appearing on lowbrow tv (*Full House, Home Improvement, Baywatch, T J Hooker*), or as rheumatic middle-agers cavorting with siliconed beach bunnies in a choreographed nightmare for the 'Kokomo' video. On tour they lowered themselves as "... featuring John Stamos" as if the actor in *Full House* (and producer of a miniseries on the group) not only replaced the late Dennis Wilson but was the star of the group.

In 1995 I was browsing in a West Auckland public library, half-aware of three boys in the next aisle, aged no more than twelve. One burst forth at a real find, surreal as it sounded: "The Beach Boys!" They had released one new album in fifteen years and peaked in popularity another fifteen before that—*20 years before this boy was born*; the youngest Beach 'Boy' was nearing fifty. I tried to think of a parallel in history. Did boys of the Sixties crave Glenn Miller? Al Jolson? Bing Crosby? Or today react the same to, say, the Beatles? The Beach Boys may be unique in creating a timeless sound, able to attract the young as readily as nostalgia buffs, their work through the Sixties and their neglected seventies career acknowledged by today's serious music critics, rock's middle-aged statesmen and by hot new bands as maybe the strongest of all influences.

This is surely the supreme test of a work of true art—that it not only impresses experts and musical peers but withstands the erosion of time and communicates to the broadest audience on a fundamental level, continuing to touch people's emotions regardless of changing tastes and fashions. Pinning Wilson's music down, some have called it a cross between Tchaikowsky and the Four Freshmen. If you imagine the melodies arranged for and played on harpsichord (hear his solo original of 'Wonderful' for *Smile*) they are virtually the only pieces in Rock that translate effortlessly back to the Classical Era. That is reckoning without group influences from rock'n'roll (Carl), blues

(Dave), r&b (Mike), folk-Americana (Al), Wagner (Dennis), Doo-Wop and Jazz—Brian; classical/jazz/Easy Listening—Bruce.

It has been described as "the happiest sound in rock music." But this is forgetting the melancholy, the angst, the elemental power, all conveyed through the music. What is meant is their music is exuberant, the opposite of clinical, listless Abba. Classic Beach Boys music of the Sixties might be called deeply enjoyable—like rare great films you want to re-experience, reflecting every emotion, unlike the bulk of rock music and movies, which tread water safe at the shallow end. Its profundity is sensed through sheer gut feeling.

A good word for the group's treatment of music is spirited: Whatever the mood of a piece or its attached lyrics, it came from the soul and was delivered sincerely, in true spirit. Bee Gee Maurice Gibb, speaking not long before he died, might have captured it: The Beach Boys were "great at soul music—not black soul, but music from the soul, from the heart."

The sense of goodwill engendered in the listener is matched by the transparent delight of the performers. No major rock act took themselves less seriously, or their work more seriously. Their histrionic power was considerable: Dennis said that the Wilson father, Murry—a tough nut to crack by all accounts—was at times so affected by their singing as to dissolve in tears. The Wilson brothers repeatedly described music as a "holy" thing. As one would imagine Michelangelo doing before setting out on a demanding work for the Pope, they prayed for the ability to make *Pet Sounds* the greatest ever album—and succeeded. Like all great music it explores the gamut of human feeling, unlike modern rock with its heavy beat and volume belted out with zero finesse. The musical intricacy of chord progressions and subtlety of timbre required are simply beyond the creative nerve or ken of today's pop/rock writers and performers.

The Beach Boys are mistakenly but duly credited with mega surf-and-hotrod hits 'Surf City' and 'Little Honda', both written, arranged and part performed by Brian Wilson but issued by other acts—and 'Little Old Lady from Pasadena' because performed in obvious imitation. Their style was appropriated by contemporaries and has been misappropriated by hack soundalikes for tv and radio jingles ever since. Their music should not be confused with the likes of the soundtrack of *Back to the Beach* with Frankie Avalon & Annette Funicello (Paramount Pictures 1987)—a superficial facsimile and typical travesty arranged with harmony lines added at random and none of the emotional substance.

Beach Boy music is outgoing, inclusive, speaks directly to the listener on the same level. Unlike the conspicuously indoor Beatles, who cultivated more and more an intellectual veneer, all but Carl had been athletes, Mike distinguishing himself in track, Brian a quarterback and baseballer, maddening his coaches by dumping sport for music. Al was up for selection by colleges as a running back. Carl started out unashamedly fat, Brian meeting him halfway through inactivity. Dennis, lean, surfer-muscled, excelled at everything he took up. Almost too good-looking, he hardly seemed one of the family: "If there wasn't the Beach Boys and there wasn't music, I would not even talk to them. But through music I fell in love with my brothers." It turned out he was most like his chunky human dynamo of a father in restless temperament.

Their visage was outdoorsy, father-manager Murry struggling to keep Denny's and Dave's sprouting peroxide tops within bounds and Mike's shoes on and shirt tucked in. Older tv-watchers and fans of classic compilation videos see them lined up on stage as fresh-faced kids in the trademark candy-cane shirts and white surfer dungarees (chinos, in Southern California vernacular); matching baby faces of Brian and Carl atop Fender guitars alongside compact sandy-haired Al Jardine, ditto, at stage left. The lean, handsome Mike Love of the receding hair is on mike on the right, and athletic Denny back on drums—the real surfer and bona fide box-office sex symbol, from summer '64 growing his wayward surfer hair into a not-quite-beatlesque thing.

The playful anarchy that connected one to another on stage and in the studio—heightened by family tensions—transmitted a psychic-musical energy to audiences. This contrasted with the sterile Osmonds, that other scrubbed-white vocal group of brothers occupying American tv screens, the darlings of *The Andy Williams Show* from late 1962. Fabricated with their careful choreography, glowing teeth and cloying sentimentalizing of a rewritten Americana, the brethren from Utah revived a tradition that had died with Vaudeville over thirty years before but has since carried on through an endless stream of over-drilled fivesomes, as 'boy bands' and 'girl bands' playing no instruments but overperforming carnie style, dancing and singing in unison: something resembling not too distantly a trained animal act.

A Beach Boy tv image transmogrified naturally. From their first appearance summer '62 in Pendleton lumberjack shirts, propelling 'Surfin' Safari' live, they were seen early '63 seated as reluctant choir boys lip-synching four-part harmony *a capella*, not quite believable as an angelic, apprentice barbershop quartet— untamable, husk-voiced Dennis watching from behind his drum kit. At the height of fame they donned leather jackets as hotrodders leading the Rockers of the world against the threat of effeminate Mods in back-combed hair and frills; and convincingly imitated a gang of beach toughs intimidating ho-dads Bob Hope and Jack Benny.

Far from Swinging London hyping the latest Carnaby Street fashion, unsophisticated suburbanite Brian Wilson "created an industry—but that's not what he meant to do." The words are Terry Melcher's, leading Los Angeles record producer of the Byrds and r&b's Paul Revere & the Raiders who would move in and out of the Beach Boy scene, son of Doris Day, world's no.1 box-office movie star through the early Sixties. As songwriter and arranger for his group, and producer of their records, the eldest Wilson brother— inspired by Dennis's rebellious, physical exploits—defined a new setting for them in a creative environment where they could explore new bounds of mind and soul; and as a by-product depicted an enhanced, larger-than-life California for those unable to experience the intimacy of his work. His dual vision, largely fulfilled, was a parallel world in which his music took on a spiritual existence.

The spinoffs were immeasurable. Few of the major recording companies had bothered to keep offices in LA. Soon the movie capital would boast a parallel claim in recorded music, Wilson paving the way for the Byrds, Turtles and the Mamas & the Papas —LA's branch of San Francisco flower children. (The connection revived in the next generation via Wilson-Phillips, a female trio cooing three no.1s: daughter of Papa John & Mama Michelle Phillips and the daughters of Brian Wilson, the elder Carnie latterly a tv talkshow queen.) The westward momentum created by the early seventies was such that Motown left Detroit in the lurch to resettle in Los Angeles.

Serious music critics not fooled by the unworldly exterior would come to refer to Brian Wilson as an *auteur*—as in the tradition of French filmmakers, the 'author' of his work. If a film director conceived a new movie genre, researched his subject, scripted his screenplays, placed the cameras, played the main characters and chose the rest of the ensemble cast, edited and completed post-production solo, then gave roadshow performances there would be grounds for comparison. His Sixties peers the Beatles, Stones and The Who use everyday superlatives to describe him.

By temperament and upbringing they rebelled against the puffery of show business injected into the ego-driven pretence that enables superstars to swallow their own hype. Their innate humility and loyalty to their public was such that Mike Love, vilified for many things but always a stalwart for the group, once performed with a strep throat and 104° temperature. In stark contrast to the Beatles' awareness and sanguine acceptance of an exalted destiny, when audiences started screaming for the Beach Boys they looked around in alarm. Dennis: "We thought there was a fire." Yet, as they grew up, evolved more complex music and pined for the innocence the world had lost, they lost their fairweather fans because they weren't 'fun' anymore; but they never were remotely the lightweights the undiscerning took them for. Those who couldn't keep up settled for the Hollies or Tremeloes.

The Beach Boys represented the California lifestyle and the hopes and dreams of teen America in facing the English hordes. They were the one major pre-Beatles act to thrive on the competition, their artistic reputation enhanced and fame reinforced worldwide as a bulwark of resistance to all things 'fab'. Not reaching their world pinnacle until three years after B-Day, for a year they surpassed in popularity the Beatles in both the US and UK, most of continental Europe, Russia and Japan: virtually the known rock world. It was their tragedy that the fine balance of elements that barely allowed their success against the odds was turned on its head. Henceforth they were adored the world over for their real musical achievements but scorned as walking anachronisms in their home country for lack of a sociopolitical stance or Afro hairstyle.

The sound, not any superstar *cachet*, is what made them famous and sustains them in the world's consciousness. In the Sixties the Beach Boys had just thirteen Billboard top ten songs—but 22 taking in other US charts; plus another six that made the UK and other major top tens. In August 2002 Capitol claimed they had "earned some 35 top ten singles... over the course of four decades." In total they have garnered hit status for more than eighty songs in charts around the world (see Appendix I). In a chameleon-like decade they weren't matched for consistency. For almost five years, 1963 to late 1967, every single issued in America made Billboard's top twenty. And for their first ten years every Hot 100 entry—36—refused to settle for the bottom quarter of the chart: Every song that kicked in kicked on. But, fought head to head to a standstill by the Beatles, chart trivia barely hint at the full story.

THEIR DETERMINED NAÏVETE MADE THEM TARGETS. The Sixties abounded in Austin Powers *poseurs*—hangers-on more than musicians. The fashion industry, especially in Britain, was a hotbed of bitchiness dictating *the* 'correct' look, and very quickly, the one correct, latest sound. The Beach Boys, who had perfected their style before British rule, were therefore not even in the race and were short-changed as artists for their unpretentious, single-minded focus on their art. Serious musicians knew better. Bob Dylan, Robert Zimmermann of small-town Minnesota reinventing himself after pastoral Welsh poet Dylan Thomas, Fifties darling of culture vulture America—saw fit to perform with Brian Wilson. But ruling were acolytes—satellites reflecting the lights of Dylan, Beatles, Stones, Simon & Garfunkel, Donovan, poet-guru Leonard Cohen....

This self-serving elitist element championed nonsensical upper middle class rebellion—an inbreeding ingroup boring the pants off those wanting truth in music, seducing the pants off wannabe-intellectual coeds. These disciples heard music best through clouds of hashish and faded fast as charmless antiques of their era. Dopeheads mellowed out beyond feeling are its only legacy. Today necrophiliac groupies idol-worship self-destructive late-Sixties performers—Jimi Hendrix, Janis Joplin, Jim Morrison, not for their genuine, sensuous music but as icons of junkie lifestyle, keeping t-shirt and toilet-mat printers in business for forty years.

As a natural development, Brother Records was born—the first independent label founded by artists to promote the lesser known, two years before Apple was hailed as just another first by the Beatles in their effortless makeover of Western Civilization. By that time if the Beach Boys were mentioned at all by mass media it was for draft-dodging, adhering to Transcendental Meditation teachings of a scandalized Maharishi Mahesh Yogi, or bankruptcy; or for the too-adventurous Dennis, buddying up with nascent mass murderer Charles Manson.

These disasters through the late Sixties decimated their career. Carl, a sworn pacifist and physically the least likely to be of use as a soldier, was harassed by the Draft Board for five years, hampering the group's work as unmatched pop ambassadors. The group bowed out of the key Monterey Pop Festival that introduced Jimi Hendrix (a former US Marine but hip), Joplin and Otis Redding and took years to live it down. Months later they were written off as a creative force by hugely influential Rolling Stone magazine to the advantage of the Beatles; a recent generation of Rolling Stone critics voted 'Good Vibrations' best song of the Twentieth Century. Two developments to the long-term good were Wilson's collaboration with Van Dyke Parks, producing underrated gems 'Heroes & Villains', 'Surf's Up' and 'Sail on Sailor', and brother Dennis working with outsiders too, embarking on his lasting musical achievements. At the time both of these enormous gifts were overlooked or discounted.

In the Maharishi controversy the Beatles got credit for 'exposing' him, leaving the Beach Boys again looking like sad old-timers in something that wasn't cool anymore now the Fab Four rejected it. The barbaric Manson Family—murderers of Sharon Tate, pregnant wife of *avant garde* film director Roman Polanski, and her dinner guests—

also victimised Dennis and Terry Melcher for blocking their leader's aspirations to be a rock star. Brian, acting for Brother Records, rejected fledgling stars Three Dog Night and maybe in frustration Dennis, Carl and Brian too had been tempted to make records with Manson instead.

Unjustly, while the Beach Boys as individuals condemned the Vietnam War in the most personal way, in danger of being dragged into it as cannon fodder and rejecting the Draft, their lack of corporate propaganda *a la* the Beatles hurt their cred with youth in the era of Protest: much better to sit in bed naked like John & Yoko in the cause of Peace or spend your days showering flower petals around Haight-Ashbury, San Francisco with the Hippies. Given the obstacles loaded in their path an intelligent view can only conclude that their music succeeded *despite* the powers that be. It's a near-miracle it hasn't been buried under the mountains of corporate-driven, Grammy-fed dross that has passed for quality popular music over the past quarter-century and more.

The time the Beach Boys lived on their personal Olympus—the five middle years of the Sixties, fall 1962 to the *Fall* of 1967—saw great convulsions become the norm. Anything called cool ruled. Through the middle two years two imperatives directed pop: 1) The Beatles strained to produce American music; 2) White Americans strained to be Beatles. And the infatuation lingers.

In a strange way the career of the Beach Boys combines the tragedies of two Los Angeles forebears. D W Griffith was the world's celebrated pioneer of film technique—and led others to the new creative center as Brian Wilson did for recorded music a half-century later. Griffith's career slowly imploded as his worldview was overtaken and his special genius was deemed passé by the industry—though his films were popular with the public for some years more. His protégée Mary Pickford was the great interpreter of the new art of film acting, playing a girl in ringlets who never grew up, so identified as 'America's Sweetheart' that she was rejected as anything else by the public that made her a superstar— doomed to retread the same ground into middle age.

The Beach Boys, based on an image encrusted in amber, long past their prime were dubbed "America's Band" by an adoring public— and exist in the same constricting mold to this day. Against all odds they remained in their prime as artists as long as they flew in the face of public tolerance, daring to wander according to multifaceted talents. It is their Peter Pan collective persona, their eternal boyishness as a group that enabled them to survive repeated scandals over the years—generations. Having built a post-Brian body of work that continues to move fellow musicians, in stark defiance of market expectations they have depths yet to be discovered by music buyers.

2. CATCHING A WAVE

The mercurial launch of the Beach Boys to hit-making in four months contrasts with other hopefuls' gritty struggles. The Beatles, Four Seasons and Supremes—their rivals—all paid dues through a five-year lead time. The Four Tops took ten years—from generations of pop prior at the dawn of the Doo-Wop Era, when the influential Drifters were stars.

Dennis recalled fifteen years later to Disc it was 1955 that his father drove the Wilson kids home from his work in the pickup as they sang 'Smokey Joe's Café', r&b from Jerry Leiber & Mike Stoller who also created 'Riot in Cell Block No.9', a Beach Boy concert favorite. More street-wise, sexually-charged narratives came from the same five voices, piano, drums, bass and guitar— the Robins morphing into the West Coast's top black group, the Coasters. In summer 1959 the big r&b hit from Leiber-Stoller was 'There Goes My Baby' performed by Ben E King & the Drifters.

And in that last Fifties summer Denny, not yet 15, sized up the waves at his local haunt, Manhattan Beach, dogged by cousin Mike hassling him to get musically grounded brother Brian to form a band. It wasn't until two springs later that things began coalescing, Brian coaching them in precise Four Freshmen harmonies, favorite among favorites. In the Wilson home, going-on-19-year-olds Brian and Al Jardine, his alarmingly little (5ft-5) grid-iron buddy from the Hawthorne High Cougars, recruited youngster Carl, who gave saxophone over to Mike for Chuck Berry guitar riffs. Mike's predominantly black former school, Dorsey High, gave him a headstart in close-up interpretation of rhythm & blues singing, and the Wilson-Love clan were imbued with r&b broadcast incessantly by LA stations. It was Dennis, dropout from high school drumming lessons, who inspired Brian and Mike to write about surfin'; in another two months, again finessed by Dennis, they had that recording contract.

The California they would come to represent around the world — then with only a fraction of its 40 million population—was emerging as the Golden Age of Hollywood movie studios passed and television invaded every living room. The USA's West Coast seemed ripe for revolution. Those who held the purse strings over movies, TV and the big radio networks were still in New York, the center of American entertainment for two centuries. A geographical rebalancing was overdue. Pop music needed a local guiding genius to buck the powers.

As if sprinkled from a cloud of pixie dust, it would be Brian, the teenage but already eccentric creative leader of the Beach Boys, who created California Music; not Phil Spector, the savvy New Yorker transplanted to LA who at 17 had played at being a native Californian by forming the gently cooing teen trio the Teddy Bears ('To Know Him Is to Love Him'); nor Lou Adler, Liberty Records producer soon to marry tv starlet Shelley Fabares; nor producer-trumpeter Herb Alpert, boss of brand new A&M Records and wedding Lani Hall, Sergio Mendes & Brasil 66's vocalist.

Settlers were attracted to this land famous for its resources—the native population early dispossessed—plundered by Spanish conquistadors and Gold Rush '49-ers. Few stars originated here. The movies came to Los Angeles, not sophisticated San Francisco, for its equable weather offering filming year-round. The Arizona wilds of Flagstaff and Tucson had been tried—a little closer to Civilization, that is, the founding colonies Back East. By the Twenties the Hollywood Hills were circled by the screen industry. As the prosperous, ultra-conformist Fifties passed, Hollywood liberals blacklisted in the McCarthy Era were allowed back, secretly. Kansas president "I like Ike" Eisenhower was better known as a war hero and golfer; his vice-president, LA's Richard Nixon, a commie-hunter. When handsome intellectual cum touch-footballer JFK was chosen in LA at 1960's Democratic Party convention to run as the first-ever president born in the 20th Century the time was ripe for a new breed of local go-getters—young and competitive, confident, even cultured, energized by an invigorating outdoors spirit. The Beach Boys saw LA grow into a metropolis, then exiled themselves as the inevitable decay set in.

World events seemed to barely touch the lives of the Disney-raised kids. April 1961, Soviet cosmonaut Yuri Gagarin was first in space, and Kennedy flunked his first real test when he allowed a CIA plan to go ahead for an invasion of Cuba from the US by expatriates; face was saved two months later by ballet master Rudolf Nureyev defecting to The West. In the tit-for-tat propaganda war, on August 13th East German border guards strung barbed wire along Berlin's East-West boundary, now a menacing frontier. September 18th Swedish diplomat Dag Hammarskjold, secretary-general of the UN, was assassinated—his plane shot down en route to peace talks with a Congo dictator. That month London's Ban the Bomb protest march ends in a thousand arrests.

LABOR DAY WEEKEND, SEPTEMBER 2-3 1961, SEVEN months into the Kennedy Era: Brian, Dennis & Carl Wilson, Mike Love and Al Jardine, now at community college with Brian, rehearse their first hit-to-be at the Wilson home in blue-collar subdivision LA—the corner of grandly named Hawthorne Boulevard & 119th Street, five miles from the Pacific Ocean. They attract neighborhood throngs and a squad of police, but it's a party atmosphere, just a bunch of South Bay kids whipping up a rock'n'roll storm. Within two years there would be two hundred garage bands around LA playing gigs. Arrest and trial comes with the Wilson parents' return from a business trip to Mexico City, astonished that the emergency money they left their sons, along with additional finance from Al's mother, is swallowed up to rent instruments. After bristling father Murry—a physical disciplinarian when frustrated—pushes ringleader Brian up against the wall and threatens the others, and gentling mother Audree calms everyone, the group performs a nerve-racking audition.

Murry and Audree—and her brother, Mike's father—were brought as children post-World War I to the Promised Land, as it was called in the parched and rugged Midwest according to all expectations, to end up settling among other economic refugees on Huntington Beach, a locale that would only take on a romantic aura in song a generation later, in the lyrics of their first iconic hit.

They were used to hard times—and hard, make-or-break saving, young Murry coming from rural Kansas preempting the Dust Bowl exodus of the Thirties Depression, and Audree of Swedish stock from Minneapolis, Minnesota. The Loves were evidently as tough. The Wilsons and Loves stayed close, bolstered by musical get-togethers when Murry on piano and Audree on organ were augmented by the kids' voices—until well into their teens, to the point when one of the Love girls was almost a Beach Boy. Like Ike Eisenhower, Murry nourished a Kansas conservatism destined to clash constantly with Hollywood-liberal sons. On the other side of the family coin, the rugged commonsense and integrity shown by their elders would often prove the firm base the boys could turn to.

Murry, sucking sagely on his pipe, that end-of-summer day for once forcing himself to listen to rock'n'roll, grudgingly accepts that here is something special: "I never did like that song ['Surfin"]... it's so rude and crude, you know?" But on songs Murry liked, "They sang like the Four Freshmen, but with a younger, sweeter sound." Having struggled to get a few of his own songs published, he's struck gold and takes his boys under a smothering wing. Ambivalence about Brian's success, and a proprietorial attitude to the group, would make inevitable the implosion of a time bomb planted with the domineering upbringing of his sons.

Though his songs tended sub-Stephen Foster to Lawrence Welk, Murry was an avid Cool Jazz follower who exposed Brian early on to jazz piano 'feels'. He would later make his musical presence tangible in *The Many Moods of Murry Wilson*, recorded by Capitol to placate the Beach Boys' ubiquitous stage father: one of those Easy Listening sixties albums that was anything but easy listening, especially in what he did to his son's 'Warmth of the Sun'. Life with father was hardly harmonious. At one point in his boyhood, rebelling against Murry's physical regimen directed at Dennis, especially, and himself (young Carl retired quickly from the battlefield), Brian is said to have "dumped" on a plate and served it up for dad's dinner, compliments to the chef not recorded.

Alan, leader of a semipro folk group at Hawthorne High but enticed by Brian & Carl singing "kind of sophisticated" duets at a talent show, had played stand-up bass at that first command performance and now advanced the group through his contacts song-publishers Hite & Dorinda Morgan. 'Surfin'' was conceived by surf-crazed Denny, backing Brian and Mike into a corner by bluffing the Morgans that the song already existed, ready to record. Reluctant surfers taught the lingo by Dennis, they took a melody written by Brian for a 12th grade 'F' (his teacher wanted a sonata). An October 3rd recording session led to release late in November through the Morgans' tiny X label and then on Candix organized for mass pressing and distribution.

If it wasn't recorded in a garage, with Brian beating on a garbage can lid for a snare drum—as once reputed—the debut hit sounded like it: raw r&b. The lineup, as reported by Carl in 1965: Mike singing lead (and wanting to play saxophone for a Coasters sound but the rest of the group forbidding it); Al on (still-rented) standup bass; Carl, basic chords on guitar; and Brian—who took off his shirt to lay it over and beat on an actual snare drum. Lack of a recording studio was a minor inconvenience—a movie-dubbing studio doing just as well for their purposes, to get a record out. They sang all the vocals together through one microphone.

O ctober: The nucleus of English group the Beatles— John Lennon & Paul McCartney—are in Paris celebrating John's 21st birthday. Together four years with a good lead guitarist and now a steady drummer their group has in the past year or so tripped twice to Hamburg—the Reeperbahn district, a hotspot of sleazy showbiz where many Liverpool acts find better paid work. Paul, especially, is into fashion—and he and John get their hair styled anew by friend Jurgen Vollmer, now a French resident, in the mode of Parisian art students, ungreased and combed forward. Astrid Kirscherr had already done this in Hamburg for boyfriend Stu Sutcliffe, in the group only on the strength of being John's friend. On the way home they stop in London's fashion district in Chelsea, and buy pointy-toed slip-on shoes. Posterity will hail 'Le Beatle' hairstyle and Beatle boots.

Peter Eckhorn, manager of the Top Ten Club, Hamburg, where the Beatles had played for four months up to July: "The interesting thing about the Beatles was that people liked them more for their engaging personalities, their onstage antics, and smart remarks than for their music. Their music sounded very much like all the other English groups, but as performers they were unique" (Pritchard & Lysaght, 1998).

While there the band was signed for Polydor as Liverpool teen idol Tony Sheridan's backing group—by bandleader/A&R man Bert Kaempfert of huge American success 'Wonderland By Night', and recorded in a school hall by him. A Merseybeat version of the old standard 'My Bonnie (Lies Over the Ocean)' by Sheridan & the Beat Brothers emerges. The Beatles receive session fees. John's art school friend Stu Sutcliffe, who has grappled with bass guitar without ever coming close to taming it, leaves the group just before recording to take up a scholarship. Those who have seen them play say the Beatles have lost their most charismatic member: apart from Paul, good playing was somehow irrelevant to this act. The best looking one— most popular with girl fans—remains for now, but Pete Best refuses the Beatle haircut: one more factor separating him from the others.

Back in Liverpool the Beatles have resumed a casual residency doing lunchtime shows at the Cavern Club. Unlike other groups— immaculately turned out in florid dinner suits modelled on the Shadows, the no.1 UK group—the Beatles sustain their round-the-clock Hamburg timetable and at first turn up in the attire they woke up in. It is a bohemian image cultivated by John Mayall's Bluesbreakers and soon capitalised on by the Rolling Stones, much to the fury of John Lennon, who gives in to the Establishment.

Local editor Bill Harry starts 'Mersey Beat' with a John Lennon article on the Beatles. Week by week he favors the engaging characters so much other groups complain. "Beatlemania" won't be coined by the British press for another two years but in Liverpool it has been part of the scene since returning from their first Hamburg trip, Xmas 1960—but shared with mob scenes for the Flamingos, Searchers and others. Eventually overtaking Rory Storm & the Hurricanes, the Big Three, Gerry & the Pacemakers and the Fourmost, the Beatles will become most popular of 350 working bands —more than there are in London.

By November 1961, after more than four years playing and composing together, Lennon & McCartney finally believe enough in two of their songs to introduce them to their setlist, 'P.S. I Love You' and 'Love Me Do'. Orders for 'My Bonnie' catch the eye of records division manager and heir of NEMS stores, Brian Epstein, and assistant Alistair Taylor, who persuade Polydor to press it in the UK; it will only puncture the bottom of the chart at #48 on the momentum of growing Beatlemania a year and a half later. Epstein, a frustrated actor and dropout from the Royal Academy of Dramatic Arts, follows his bent as theatrical entrepreneur. Visiting a show at the Cavern, his reaction is typically couched in English diplomatic-speak: "They had a very honest and unrehearsed sound. I thought that if I liked it and all those teenagers liked it, then there was something worth exploring." Alistair Taylor: "There was this very scruffy band on stage in black leather and black T-shirts. They were fooling about and they weren't very good musicians. But it was the most phenomenal experience I've ever gone through... They had Ingredient X... So we signed the boys and nobody wanted to know about them"(Pritchard & Lysaght, 1998).

But after cleaning up—nice suits, no smoking or drinking onstage—they are on their way to the big time. John got moody, but there was no real rebellion from the rock'n'rolling Teddy Boy. Soon Epstein's proudest boast was that he had got the Beatles a gig for 15 pounds ($36 then)—unheard-of heights for a Liverpool group. London might as well be on another planet. Like the Beach Boys they will be hindered by recording brains who say guitar-and-drum vocal groups are on the way out.

Events are shaping the modern world—the first US military observers are posted to Vietnam in December; King of Rock'n'Roll Elvis Presley has not made a personal appearance for nine months (and won't until the end of the decade)—but the Beach Boys' immediate concern is their new record, revelling in its primitive origins. It is none the less picked up as phone-vote favorite on the platter-rack at popular KFWB the week after Xmas, its first airing causing the Wilsons uncontrollable excitement. Denny: "Brian ran down the street screaming 'We're on the radio!' Carl threw up."

Constantly distracted, Dennis is only now let into the group at Audree's insistence. It means a step up from his dollar-a-day chore sweeping out Murry's workshop and free-flowing girls on stream— though all the boys (but late developer Brian, at 22) would be married by 21, Mike by 'shotgun'.

KFWB, their favorite station for its r&b, took minor vocal groups the Olympics ('Hully Gully'), Passions, Skyliners and Fireflies to the top of the LA charts regardless of national trends, plus instrumental groups Johnny & the Hurricanes, the Fireballs and the Spacemen, and paid ongoing respect to rock'n'rollers Bo Diddly, Fats Domino, Johnny Burnette and the Bill Black Combo past their commercial prime. Black vocalists Richard Berry, Etta James, Della Reese and Sarah Vaughan got a look in here better than other mainstream outlets across the country. Ray Charles, the Jive Five, Ike & Tina Turner, Lee Dorsey, the Drifters, Chantels, Jackie Wilson, Jimmy Reed ('Bright Lights, Big City'), Van McCoy and Mary Wells were others punching above their weight. Local youths the Jaguars, among others, featured on playlists—encouraging the new boys. Now there was one more reason to like the Warner Bros station, for breaking their group into local fame.

'Luau', written by the Morgans' son, best described as rhythmic in a simple hip-hop way, was put on the B-side. 'Barbie (Barbie, Queen of the Prom)'/'What is a Young Girl Made Of?', a falsetto dirge backed with a bouncy ditty—provided by Hite Morgan— were released too, luckily invisibly by tiny local label Randy under Kenny & the Cadets, said to be Brian, Audree and Al. Reflecting on these, recorded under obligation—duds at the time, and all happily lost to history—must have taught Brian a valuable lesson not to rely on the creative ability nor the business judgment of others.

Candix, making up for the Z-material the group was lumbered with, chose a new name for their green clients. On the new 45 under 'Surfin'' they print "The Beach Boys"—maybe inspired by 'Beach Boy Blues' on Elvis's new *Blue Hawaii* album. There had briefly been a Beach Boys two years before on Kapp, and a Beachcombers singing sedate pop in the Fifties would soon convert to surf rock on Dot. There would turn up, too, a Beach Girls recording act. Posing a potent image of smooth confidence, decadent rebellion, danger to unwary beach girls, the name wiped memories of doo-wop style Carl & the Passions (used by Brian to lure Carl into the group) and Pendletones, Mike's play on Washington State's Pendleton lumberjack plaid shirts popular for winter surfing.

Brian preferred the old corny tags of Fifties vocal combos—luckily in vain. The right name, with an edge to it, all the better separated them from the insipid Lettermen, emerging that fall in the top ten with smooth ballads 'The Way You Look Tonight' and 'When I Fall in Love', 1961's incarnation of the all-American Four Freshmen/Aces/Lads/Preps format that had ruled white harmony groups: a schmaltzy Ivy League varsity tone of age-old glee clubs, ragtime raccoon coats, crewcut jocks and cheerleading nerds upheld by Disney teen comedies (*The Absent-Minded Professor, Son of Flubber*): It would see a brief revival 1966-8—the Association, Harper's Bizarre, Sandpipers, Arbors—but was a tune very far from the driving rock'n'roll and Soul ballads the boys played.

Carl was taking lessons from John Maus, later of the Walker Bros, joined by over-the-road neighbor kid Dave Marks, two years younger but also a pal of Denny. The barely pubescent Marks, of Pennsylvania Italian-Jewish descent, reproduced B.B. King licks precisely and Carl showed equal fidelity to Chuck Berry's blues-tinged rock'n'roll guitar. They soaked up the Southern California *milieu* too—the Ventures' guitars used as background for filmmaker Bruce Brown's surfing documentaries (*Endless Summer*). Months later had come Dick Dale, whose Lebanese background lent interesting melodic overtones to his staccato machine-gun guitar and other unique effects evoking the sound of waves. With the growth of the music, surfing came to graduate from a cult interest to a widespread sport.

The Marketts' 'Surfer's Stomp' and 'Surfin'' on a fast rise up KFWB-LA's top 30, January 19th 1962: Leaping from #29, the Hawthorne teens made the biggest jump on the sales survey in living memory.

1. The Twist — Chubby Checker
2. Surfer's Stomp — the Marketts

3. Duke of Earl—Gene Chandler
4. The Wanderer—Dion
5. Peppermint Twist—Joey Dee & the Starlighters
6. Surfin'—the Beach Boys
7. Can't Help Falling in Love—Elvis Presley
8. Let There Be Drums—Sandy Nelson
9. The Lion Sleeps Tonight (Wimoweh)—the Tokens
10. I Know—Barbara George

IT WOULD BE A WHILE BEFORE SURF GAVE THE TWIST a run: This top ten were big national hits—all but the surf tunes. But surfing culture was spreading with branchlets up the Pacific Coast, in Florida and the upper Atlantic Seaboard. That first Xmas-New Year would prove portentous for the Beach Boys. Absorbing more widely than any other group of the Sixties, they also took their local environment to heart, remaking 'There's No Other', the debut for Phil Spector's Crystals; 'Let's Go Trippin'', Dick Dale's instrumental classic; and traditional folk song 'Cotton Fields' by the Highwaymen, an enduring favorite of Al's. Other local hits they amplified in their concerts were Richard Berry's 'Louie Louie' and (sic) the Lettermen's 'Silly Boy'.

Their later technical polish absent in spades, the group's first record's raw simplicity moved "up to 250,000 copies", going beyond the usual regional hit to make the group's name as far afield as Italy and Sweden. Whatever the final tally the bulk were unpaid-for due to Candix's delaying tactics, presaging the group's later troubles collecting royalties due. The label went under six months after release, the pretenders to the princedom of pop having received the unprincely sum of $990, equivalent to payment for shipping 50,000 at the standard two cents per copy—topped up to $1000 by Murry, then split five ways.

Instantly on registering on one station's playlist they were an attraction and were called to make their official public bow on New Year's Eve for a Richie Valens Memorial Concert, Municipal Auditorium, Long Beach, in tribute to the Hispanic native of Los

Angeles—hero of aspiring rockers, of 'La Bamba' and 'Donna' fame, killed at 17 in the same small-plane crash as Buddy Holly and the Big Bopper nearly three years before, February 3rd 1959. They followed Ike & Tina Turner, who'd scored national hits, notably million-selling 'A Fool in Love'. The black temptress in her early twenties was far from the leggy legend that would only grow with age. Backing singers the Ikettes had entered the charts too, the day before with 'I'm Blue (The Gong-Gong Song)', an r&b classic (*Hairspray*, 1988). The Beach Boys' fee: $300—not stupendous but a stratosphere above what a brand new band could expect for a 15-minute gig, and they were hardly worth it: Having a repertoire of three including 'Bermuda Shorts', a California hit by the Delrays from four years before, they played an unrequested encore of 'Surfin'' to fill out their spot.

Things were moving at a more than hectic pace. Reportedly (by Carl) the evening of the concert they were also booked to play at a local radio station. Hardly begun playing, Murry was already referring to the group's 'career'—so it was with split-second timing that, three days before, he had bought Brian an electric bass with amplifier. Brian learnt to play in time and Dennis, said by his high school music teacher to be a fast learner, had already mastered drums adequately. Once stage fright, suffered by both at their official debut, eased, shows were greeted with growing enthusiasm. As Murry willed it, a career materialized.

*T*he *Beatles are Liverpool's no.1 group, voted by the readers of Mersey Beat—not surprising since they are lent the lion's share of coverage. New Year's Day they are in London, a recording audition for UK Decca. It is a step further than the Beach Boys get with the Los Angeles branch of the same company, but the Beatles too are rejected—Brian Poole & the Tremeloes, auditioning that same day, are signed for their better presentation tape and their handiness as Londoners. To Dick Rowe, Decca's boss who wins notoriety as "the man who turned down the Beatles", their versions of such American hits as 'Twist & Shout', 'Money' and others on the audition tape are no better than covers by any number of other British acts, that is, imitative and ordinary. Rowe was given a second* *chance a few months later, and on a tip—from Beatle George Harrison—signed the Rolling Stones.*

Another London label to reject the Beatles, this time without even listening, is Pye—the company later to sign the Searchers and the Kinks. The leap the Beatles would have to make to conquer London is about as likely as the Beach Boys storming New York City.

The Beach Boys in their first year or so played ballrooms, frat parties and private clubs. One poor reception early on came from a tiara-and-toupée-topped audience. Their first out-of-town gig was intermission at a surfing movie showing in San Diego. After a three-day residency at plush Santa Monica Hotel the cream was school hops around greater LA supporting guitar hero Dick Dale and often with the Surfaris, a group reluctant to stray from school studies based on the outskirts of a spreading suburban wasteland at Glendora, 30 miles inland from Hawthorne en route to San Bernardino. They did tv slots for Wink Martindale—DJ and biblical philosopher ('Deck of Cards')—and comedian Soupy Sales.

Studies were something the Beach Boys wouldn't have to worry about much longer. While Brian and Al persevered for a time, Dennis had been expelled from Hawthorne High for fighting. Carl would be ejected too at 16 either for "fucking up his grades, unlike Brian and Dennis," or on the pretext that he neglected to raise his hand to go to the toilet. There had been static from at least one teacher irked at being outshone by a star in the class. Mike had been thrown out of home by his mother, another sternly made Wilson—and was working at a gas station to support his wife and child on the way.

As 1962 opened the Cold War was threatening an outbreak of thermo-nuclear heat. The American government confiscated the passports of its communist citizens while U-2 pilot Francis Gary Powers, shot down over Russia months before, was returned in a spy swap. International intrigue was being made glamorous by big-screen versions of Ian Fleming's adventures of James Bond, and ludicrous by *Mad* magazine's 'Spy vs Spy'.

Space travel was invented. February saw astronaut John Glenn the hero of the Western World as the first American to orbit the earth in his Mercury module—months after Russian cosmonaut Yuri Gagarin was celebrated by socialist countries as first man in space. More profoundly for Californians, striking to their souls, the classic, ostentatious tailfins of the "Yank Tank" had disappeared from Cadillacs and Chevies alike after ruling for five years, to reappear mid-decade on tv's Batmobile.

By March the runner-up sales success in LA of their 45 warranted a quarter way up and six weeks on Billboard's Hot 100, America's tablet of overall popularity instituted four years before; Dale made it a little higher, but it was his biggest ever hit. It was the Beach Boys, celebrating in graphic detail the joys of the sport, that attracted attention in the music scene and made the city the center of surfing—helped by actor Cliff Robertson's surfboard business that could count on movie star clients to publicize what was growing into a Southern California pastime.

Their first song had broken the ice but they urgently needed a stronger follow-up—the critical point for any new act to escape ending up a one-hit wonder. A total of 210 million 45s would be bought and sold in the US in 1962. Some 200 to 300 new A-sides were pressed and issued each week but most radio stations didn't have enough programming time to introduce more than 15-20 of them, said an RCA spokesman. Of the fraction of these that made it as local hits a tiny proportion would break nationally.

Since the late Forties LA had been host to a thriving r&b scene, with such famous 'indie' labels as Imperial, Specialty and Aladdin setting up. To the coast they brought the Coasters and Ike & Tina Turner, and impresario Lester Sill, manager of the Coasters and associate of Leiber & Stoller and Phil Spector. Many settled in the slums fringing Hollywood while the golden turf was reserved for the likes of major white-pop label Capitol, formed the first year of America's entry into WWII during the Big Band Era. It was a power that would loom large in the career of the Beach Boys. White artists weren't yet accepted as r&b specialists though it wasn't long before local duo the Righteous Bros made inroads via the Moonglow label. Five white boys from Hawthorne might have been sorely tempted to go with one of their hometown indies known for black r&b, but more likely would have ended up at white, mainstream Arwin owned by Doris Day or fledgling A&M.

Realistically, only a major label—in LA this meant Decca, Capitol, Liberty or Dot—had a good shot at wangling enough airplay to ensure another placement on Billboard's Hot 100. From there sales tended to look after themselves through self-advertising. According to Tom Noonan, Billboard's research director at the time, "For every step a record goes up our charts the manufacturer can count on an additional 2,000 sales."

All but one Beach Boy were determined to crack one or the other label. After graduating from Hawthorne High, Al and Brian had taken up where they left off, in the university's music room trying out arrangements and vocal patterns. To further the group, Brian threw in his psychology and music theory courses to focus on his vocation— creating *new* music via piano, leaving his Fender Precision bass for performing. Al, though a group co-founder, was always conscious of his precarious position outside the family, but his status as full participant was never challenged. Carl, turning 15 just as 'Surfin'' broke, was most accomplished instrumentalist, so lead guitar on the Fender Jaguar Murry had bought him. Al filled in rhythm guitar chording to Carl's confident lead, adapting his folk strumming to rock via a classic Fender Stratocaster, and his excellent voice was extremely malleable, able to take on at will a Wilson timbre. Dave, virtually matching Carl on gutsy guitar strokes, had been tolerated around the house but disqualified from official recognition by his youth; and his voice, with Denny's, was considered only average. Dennis, the elemental one experienced beyond his years and imbued with the rhythms of the pounding surf, pounded on Gretsch drums, later replaced by a treasured new Rogers set. Mike, seeing that he couldn't be a convincing lead singer otherwise, ditched his saxophone except for rare occasions. The saxophone smacked of old rhythm & blues, detracting from the new rock'n'roll sound they wanted. His sister Maureen would contribute celestial sounds on the harp (the introduction to 'In My Room') when needed on recordings.

Now came the first shock. Al bailed out in early February, according to legend to go to dental school, disheartened at what must have felt—to a California kid with the world at his feet—like a long five months' grind since Labor Day, and no sign of a major label offering a steady income. His parents had moved back to the Midwest, and Al wondered whether it was too late to take up Pepperdine U's offer of a football scholarship.

Early February demos of 'Surfer Girl' (written by Brian up to two years earlier according to Dave) and 'Surfin' Safari' featuring Brian, Dennis and Al were recorded by Hite Morgan, crude prototypes recognizable on compilation anthologies cut-and-pasted in the '70s by budget labels. It is hard to believe Al left not recognising the quality of the songs, or that he didn't factor in Murry's determination born of paternal instinct and unrequited ambition to fight to success. The impression he gave to Dave, "He didn't see it going anywhere," sounds like the calculated offhandedness of someone wounded.

Mrs (Virginia) Jardine, part-financier of the group, much later came forward with another explanation that made more sense of Al's toing and froing between California and the Midwest over the next year and a half. Bitterly sticking in his craw was an unrepaid $800 loan to Brian's new collaborator, Gary Usher—Al's life savings. Reportedly, the money was used by Usher to record, with Brian, a dance tune—'The Revo-lution'. He was also disenchanted with the group's reliance on Chubby Checker tunes, and tried to rekindle his folk group the Islanders with lifelong friend Gary Winfrey.

Brian reluctantly resorted to Carl and Dennis's friend Dave, all of 13 and a half. Marks had ambitions beyond his tender years, and had not so secretly longed to join them, barred from official rehearsals but watching through the Wilson living-room window from the street. The remaining Beach Boys, forced into a corner, popped the question. Dave took Al's place.

T   *he Beatles have a date in nearby Manchester March 8th
to record their first ever radio-played numbers, aired on BBC the next day—a leap for a band from the provinces. "Auntie BBC", as it is derisively called, is making a rare concession to English youth—who are expected to be seen and not heard. The brief program is called condescendingly 'Teenagers' Turn'. Private radio*

stations are still two years away, and among many American records UK radio's government department bans is 'Monster Mash', for being offensive—to monsters....

Numbers already written by Paul McCartney—'When I'm Sixty-Four', 'Like Dreamers Do', 'I'll Follow the Sun', etc—are thought not good enough for a national audience. Another Lennon & McCartney have hopes for, 'Hello Little Girl', is recorded, then nixed. The Beatles, into their fifth year, are introduced to the nation as a covers band with versions of Roy Orbison's current 'Dream Baby', the recent Marvelettes hit 'Please Mr Postman' and Chuck Berry tearjerker 'Memphis'.

Twice when drummer Pete Best is ill George calls on his mate Richie Starkey a.k.a. Ringo Starr of Rory Storm & the Hurricanes to stand in. Pete's mum, Mona, runs the Casbah club, a good fallback gig for the Beatles. During Pete's two years in the group they have grown into a tight unit—he thinks—living together and going through two grueling residencies in Hamburg. But George and Paul have their own ideas about Pete's future.

In mid-April the Beatles and Brian Epstein fly to Hamburg to take up their third contract, to open the prestigious Star-Club. Told of Stu Sutcliffe's death the day before from brain haemhorrhage, John breaks down. The Beatles are paid $400 a week for this engagement—a big pay rise, but they will earn every penny playing eight hours a night. Playing alongside the Big Three and Kingsize Taylor & the Dominoes, they will learn most watching international stars including Ray Charles.

Horst Fascher, manager of the Star-Club: "The Beatles watched Little Richard, Fats Domino, Jerry Lee Lewis, and all those names very carefully to see what they were doing onstage. The Beatles were behind the curtains or backstage, taking in all the moves and performance tricks and trying to copy them. I think that had a lot to do with their success later."

Little Richard: "I thought they were a very good group... but I never thought they were a hit group. I was offered 50 percent of them by Brian Epstein, and I didn't take it. I always thought Paul would make it... but I didn't think the group would do it." Richard befriends

Paul, and gives him tips on perfecting his imitation of the original rock'n'roller, copying his technique in minute detail.

Three weeks later, 9th May, George Martin, Parlophone A&R head looking to sign a pop group, is introduced to Brian Epstein looking for a recording contract.

Martin: "He was undoubtedly a tremendous influence in making them a hit. When Brian played me the disc ['My Bonnie'] in my office, I wasn't terribly knocked out by it. In fact, I thought it wasn't very good. But there was some indefinable quality of rawness. And when we did meet... well, it was just love at first sight. I thought they were super" (Quotes from Pritchard & Lysaght, 1998).

Renting time at pokey Studio 3 of Western Recorders on April 19th, producing themselves and engineered by Chuck Britz, a valued assistant over the next five years, 'Safari' takes its final form. New lyrics are injected and it is slicked up in a vastly improved production reminiscent of Chubby Checker's recording of 'The Twist', a no.1 twice in the previous two years and later named by Billboard as Rock's biggest-ever hit. The resemblance is more apparent at its original speed, but Murry, ever conscious of his boys' image, insists on increasing 'Surfin' Safari''s tape speed fractionally to make the recording pitch higher and the group sound younger. Heard for the first time are the clear youthful harmonies set in counterpoint against Mike Love's strident masculinity—a conjunction that becomes the most famous feature of the Beach Boys' vocal style.

Content for their music to speak for them, the group begs Murry to make the rounds of the majors first. The "big shots" refuse to even see him at Dot, Decca and Liberty. It seems their efforts have been wasted too on the powerhouse '409' from the same recording session, about the 409-cubic-inch-motored Chevy that had come on to the market the year before. Loads of special features were celebrated in the song, which Mike delivered in his best sassed-up tone in the style of Billy Guy of the Coasters on 'Searchin''. A similarly paced r&b rocker, it was immaculately honed lyrically and sonically to sound even tougher than 'Surfin' Safari', including motor-revving taped in a late-night session with co-writer Gary Usher outside the Wilson home that woke the neighborhood.

THUS, ACCORDING TO THE LEGEND "REJECTED BY every other label in town" the Beach Boys finally find a home when both songs are snapped up on first hearing by Capitol A&R man Nick Venet, a young singer just retired from the scene with an ear for hot new Rock. He plays it cool for Murry and then *runs* down the hall to play them both to vice president Voyle Gilmore. The record is pronounced a double-sided hit pre-release. Venet later claimed 'Surfin' Safari' was "probably the best record I heard that year. Sensation. They produced it, Brian and the guys, and it was a-fucking-terrific" (Tom Nolan, 1972).

By Murry's accounting the entire cost of launching nationally — presumably including Capitol's input—was $7,600. He passed on official status as producer of this rock'n'roll outfit to Venet, but as manager he made an indelible mark. The overpowering persona of Wilson Sr grew legendary in LA-Hollywood showbiz circles and was later the subject of colorful anecdotes around London from those intent on retaining 'good form' who judged him gauche. Murry prided himself on being pushy, the scourge of the execs perched at the top of the Capitol Tower and anyone else who might sell his boys short.

Venet has been recorded in Beach Boy lore as anything from peripheral/irrelevant (Brian) to misrepresentative (Murry and Carl). Visiting the UK at the height of the British Invasion, he was well liked in the industry, even in dark glasses and presenting himself larger than life but suitably as a Nick the Greek character. Undoubtedly, kudos go to him for even listening, for his ear, then apparently sticking his neck out—at a company reputedly of nine-to-fivers almost completely lacking in enterprise. By his testimony, he threatened to resign and promote the Beach Boys himself if vice president Voyle Gilmore wouldn't play fair by them; in fact he did resign for other reasons a year later. Also, he advised at that first meeting that the boys should start their own publishing company, ensuring a much bigger take of the cake. This contrasts sharply with

31

the workhouse deals done on the Beatles' behalf by their own manager, Brian Epstein, though some UK insiders of the time, upholders of the class system, argue that the heavily loaded terms were standard for the local industry.

On the strength of their two latest tracks Brian Wilson's group is signed on an attractive starting rate of a 5% cut of gross sales, fifteen to twenty times what the Beatles would get. The endearing story told by Capitol president Alan Livingston—creator of label mascot Bozo the Clown and husband of big-screen great Betty Hutton—has Murry ratcheting up the asking rate at his boys' urging as their first big hit grew steadily bigger. Livingston could only have been pleased from reports from Gilmore, who called the new record "a smash", and Venet: "I knew that song was going to change West Coast music." Denny, Carl and Dave, as minors, sign in court under California's Coogan law—to avoid the fate of silent movie child star Jackie Coogan, remorselessly picked clean of four million in earnings (when the average wage was $10 a week) by his mother.

Fellow teen Sacramento high-schooler Fred Vail arranges that May for Smokey Robinson & the Miracles, Jan & Dean, Bobby Freeman ('Do You Wanna Dance') and Johnny Crawford of tv's *Rifleman* to play at his school assembly. Meeting the Beach Boys a year later, he goes on to be a key element of their touring success, his one regret not offering to manage them for a modest cut of 5% (Vail, 2002). Co-manager by the end of the decade, he helps them out of a deep career hole.

Issued 4th June '62 is the Beach Boys' independent creation—a 45 rpm 7-inch vinyl record with two hit songs self-written, arranged, performed and produced. In an unprecedented snub of corporation by artist, Capitol, as part of a major worldwide business conglomerate that is EMI, is required only for publicity and record distribution, functions they will perform patchily over the next seven years. The starlets are out of their skins—freshfaced kids in glamorous Hollywood, acing the best job interview of their lives, their photo taken symbolically mounting the steps of Capitol Tower—hoisted straight away to a major company's no.1 vocal group. It was a dream come true about to turn sour. Strain in this loveless marriage of convenience is soon obvious after the buffer that is Nick Venet removes himself. Another source of disquiet, looming just around the corner, will be the UK-owned EMI's insistence on pushing their prize British act to the detriment of Capitol's other clients.

J une 6th the Beatles are back from Hamburg just in time to meet George Martin, Parlophone's recording boss, to perform an artist's test in London's Abbey Road studio. After recording engineer Norman Smith completes makeshift repairs on their heavily worn amplifiers he records the group playing "the old standards... and I think we had a couple of original pieces that didn't set the whole world alight. So, to sum it up, the artist's test The Beatles did was not impressive. I don't think we were expecting anything, really. I don't think EMI was expecting anything exciting from them. It was solely because of their personalities"(Pritchard & Lysaght). Chris Salewicz reported more detail from the engineer: "I thought their music was pretty dreadful on that day... the only one who could really play was Paul; John just stood there knocking out chords, George's solos were not that impressive, and any average drummer could have done just as well." The Beatles' engineer, later an EMI producer, would in 1966 introduce Pink Floyd to recording and in the early seventies have a career as vocalist "Hurricane" Smith producing his own records (scoring a US no.1 with 'Oh Babe, What Would You Say?'), displaying a not inconsiderable individual talent.

George Martin: "It wasn't a question of what they could do, because they hadn't written anything that was great at that time, but they had great personalities. They had a great way with them, and they charmed me a great deal. They knew I was the guy who made all the Peter Sellers records, and they were all fans." Martin, who thinks 'Love Me Do' would "make a good B side", searches frantically through London's Tin Pan Alley and looks up song publisher Dick James (singer of tv theme 'Robin Hood') for a hit A side. And, having no understanding of beat groups, he wonders which one he should make the star, out front singing the songs, like Elvis Presley or Cliff Richard.

In June songwriter Bob Dylan is playing a four-day Montreal gig for a total of $125. Formerly a backup musician for Bobby Vee, he has been a professional solo performer for over a year and is preparing to record his first album. It won't chart, but some of his songs take off.

Frequent co-stars the Surfaris would be signed a year later by two of the labels who rejected the Beach Boys, Dot and then Decca. Liberty took the Marketts franchise, starting as a session group, a fivesome from Hollywood High taking over for live dates. They were gathered by former Candix producer Joe Saraceno, who— taking DJ Russ Regan's suggestion—had renamed the Beach Boys. In '63 Liberty would sponsor too, with a hefty push from Brian Wilson, a new career for LA's Jan & Dean; and later pluck Gary Lewis & the Playboys from a regular gig at Disneyland's soundshell to raise them to fleeting heights of teeniebopper stardom.

Disneyland had grown with Walt Disney's expanding television schedule and the Wilson boys, spoilt by Murry and Audree with toys and treats (according to Dave Marks), had enjoyed occasional trips across town to the huge amusement park. Like millions of American kids they were brought up on tv's Mickey Mouse Club, its Mouseketeers and Disney's version of Davy Crockett, spawning seven million sales of the theme song and even more coonskin caps. It is said Brian Wilson found a spark of inspiration in Jiminy Cricket, the little conscience of Pinnocchio, whose 'When You Wish Upon a Star' led, when roughed out on piano, to the chord progression of 'Surfer Girl'.

Equivalent in the Beatles' world were the rundown amusement arcades, pinball machines and *Punch & Judy* shows of Blackpool Pier up the Lancashire coast. Just being in a band or otherwise part of the pop scene was an escape from humdrum daily lives for thousands of Liverpool youths. Of course, everything American was bigger, flashier, and therefore better in the eyes of the chronically 'skint' Beatles, whose growing ambitions daren't stray even in their dreams to the possibility of any great success in the skewed Land of Opportunity.

Capitol—against the Beach Boys' advice—markets '409' as A-song: What did record-buyers know about surfing? The label was already seeking to define them by topical matter, but would soon change its stance 180 degrees, irrevocably, to *pro*-surfing—as if its very life depended on the beach theme. Did the label execs dream of signing a baseballin' band—to thus capture the hearts of the whole country at once and forever? The flip, after two weeks left on its own, breaks through in the sinus-drying heat of Phoenix, then an oasis of 650,000 hardy souls in the Arizona Desert. There any mention of an ocean of water over the airwaves must have made for a sado-masochistic pleasure/torture experience for parched listeners longing for a cool, refreshing drink of raw and vital rock'n'roll after years of teen idol mush and middle-aged serenades dominating mainstream radio.

So in June 1962 the people of Phoenix are first in the world to learn there's nothing quite like waking up to the Beach Boys in spring or early summer—via Top 40 Radio on the family phonogram, feeling the first rays of the morning on your face and stumbling to the cornflakes that sponsor the breakfast show. And Murry, Brian and Mike made sure, before they ever left the studio, that in the playback booth their new sound reproduced perfectly from a monaural (mono) recording through the single-speaker pocket transistor radios that kids carried with them. Such attention to detail was beyond the interest of the Beatles, who according to Norman Smith (in Salewicz) refused to even wear headphones to hear how their playing was coming across in the control booth. Anyway Brian, virtually deaf in one ear, couldn't comprehend the stereophonic system that was just coming into its own.

Arizona, including Tucson, sustained its liking for the group, soaking up all the music they could send through the decade and beyond. For now they were busy with local commitments, including the graduation dance for UCLA (University of California in LA). Maybe the oldest surviving document of their step-up to fame is the June 23rd top 60 survey of Canton, Ohio taken by station WHOF, showing 'Surfin' Safari' entering at #38—going on to take up top five placings in larger state centers Cincinnati, Columbus and Dayton. By the fourth of July they were featuring in top thirties from San Diego to Birmingham, Alabama. When the group starts on a 40-date six-week tour of the Midwest late that month their songs have paved the way as spearheads of vocal 'surf' and 'hotrod' music. Den mother Audree kept an eye on them; Murry stayed home taking care of business and paid Dave Marks' father Elmer to act as tour manager accompanying her.

Their vibrant grassroots appeal grabbed Audree's hometown, Minneapolis, with its twin city St Paul rising a million and a half, hoisting them after a long haul to no.1. Over the next five years the Beach Boys would boast 25 Twins top-ten songs, all but a half-dozen reaching the top four—typical of Heartland USA's love affair with their music.

'409' was co-hit everywhere but New York City, in some spots still received as the 'A'. Crossing the arid Southwest, it was Dallas, Texas's hit of the year in KLIF's official sales survey—so evocative of teen lust for that model of Chevrolet that the company jumped at the chance to sponsor Beach Boys tours.

Problem #1: According to Nick Venet (in Tom Nolan, 1972), as the company wallahs celebrated their twentieth anniversary in Hollywood, he was at this time the only one of Capitol's management aged under 62; the others are therefore older than Bing Crosby, Capitol's most famous client among a roster of legends but now retired golfing at Palm Springs. Among numerous investments that would make him almost as rich as his pal Bob Hope, he went into tv production (*Hogan's Heroes*).

From the current generation, just to get on the rock'n'roll bandwagon, scouting and auditioning of hundreds of prospects in 1956 had netted Gene Vincent & his Blue Caps. But Gene was long gone to the UK where he was hero-worshipped, and hadn't been replaced —unless the pretend "rock and roll" of Tommy Sands counted ('Teenage Crush', 1957). LA's top r&b performer, Johnny Otis ('Willie and the Hand Jive', 1958), had trouble crossing over to the pop market. Country chanteuse Wanda Jackson remodelled herself into a rock'n'roller—'Let's Have a Party'—and added young glamor to the Capitol lineup through the sixties. While replicating the gruffer side of Brenda Lee she never managed top twenty, switching back to country and still releasing on Capitol into the seventies.

So, far removed from the priorities of youth, tuned out from rock music and the special requirements of the Beach Boys, Capitol bosses were heavily committed to a mature market for such prestigious 'young' artists in their portfolio as Frank Sinatra, Dean Martin and Nat 'King' Cole—all just one generation adrift in their mid-forties— and the spritely Al Martino, 35, ten years later awarded a comeback in *The Godfather* by Marlon Brando making an offer that couldn't be refused. Capitol's jazz greats Judy Garland and Peggy Lee were entering middle age and still popular with the veteran audience but, established for more than twenty years, could hardly be called promising prospects. There was nothing the Beach Boys could do apart from Murry's constant cajoling to get the company's attention, short of severing the head off Bing's putter for some big shot's bed.

It must have been all these seniors could do to pretend any kind of empathy even with the straight, collegiate-style Four Freshmen & Preps and Lettermen already on Capitol's books. What relationship they could find with their most popular young incumbents is anyone's guess: folk group the Kingston Trio, prone to left-wingish social statements in the tradition of Woody Guthrie, the Weavers and other proletarian, people's troubadours—of whom Peter, Paul & Mary were the latest, but on Warner Bros. The Kingstons—hailing from Hawaii and Southern California but named after Jamaica's capital of Calypso Folk—had in the spring just past celebrated their biggest hit in three years, 'Where Have All the Flowers Gone?'—and would have three top forty hits in 1963 plucked from popular albums.

Bing, the most successful recording star of the quarter-century from 1930, and the biggest box-office star in movies through the middle of that period, had come to Capitol when his hit-making days were over, other than drives, chips and putts; he would die on a golf course in Spain. Lowlights he had to look forward to in 1962 were a return of his 'White Christmas', which had sold 30 million—but on Decca—and a minor Xmas outing next year for Capitol, 'Do You Hear What I Hear?', much later remade by Mike Love in solo career.

But, as Capitol would advertise on the dust-slips of Beach Boy albums through the Sixties, Bing remained one of the label's prides along with acts as diverse as recently deceased thespian Charles Laughton, operetta show-tune belter Gordon McRae, Pasadena parodier Stan Freberg, Soul crooner Lou Rawls, black and soulful Nancy Wilson and Ketty Lester, jazzman Cannonball Adderley, country & western stars Sonny James and Buck Owens, and the orchestra of Carmen Dragon, musical director at the Hollywood Bowl and father of Daryl Dragon, later to feature prominently as a session man for the group, a collaborator with Dennis Wilson and the husband and Captain of Tennille.

In other words, the Beach Boys were not exactly the single-minded focus of this major label that wanted to be all things to all listeners. Capitol tended to poach established stars, and many former staffers from the sixties have been scathing about the company's lack of insight in picking quality in new performers. As one put it, as one might expect from a company represented by Bozo the Clown, "They threw stuff at the wall to see what would stick." New York vocal group the Tokens, coming from their one huge hit, were hired by Capitol early in 1962 as *producers* on a one-year contract. Learning to produce as they went along, all ten demo recordings they submitted were rejected including the last, a lively r&b number which they got the Chiffons to record independently on Laurie. Having been knocked back on this song by other labels, a simple rejection letter wasn't enough for Capitol and the Tokens were treated to a full description by Voyle Gilmore memo of just "how bad it stunk", according to Token Phil Margo who played drums on the record. 'He's So Fine' became the most durable no.1 of 1963, and copying the melody for 'My Sweet Lord' landed Beatle George Harrison in trouble years later.

Of the middle-agers Frank Sinatra had recently founded his own label, Reprise, breaking out of a long fallow period that wasn't bringing many residual sales for Capitol. "Old Blue Eyes"'s bestselling albums from the fifties, including *Come Fly With Me*, would wait for a new millennium to be certified gold. Hollywood-Las Vegas "Rat Pack" buddy Dean Martin followed him from Capitol.

Near-namesake Martino stayed a company man sharing in the middle-aged market: 'I Love You Because', 'I Love You More Everyday', 'Spanish Eyes', 'Mary in the Morning'—as did Cole: 'Ramblin' Rose', 'Those Lazy-Hazy-Crazy Days of Summer', until cut down by cancer early in '65.

None—young, old or in between—could live in the same ballpark as the Beach Boys: rookies of the year promising a third-base hit every time up at bat, thickly peppered with high-flying homers. The softening of the way for later rock groups arriving at Capitol — including the Beatles—might be jotted under "Beach Boys: runs batted in". Capitol's runner-up harmony act, the Lettermen, whose pristine but low-energy sound was already spacing their top 40 hits out three years apart, couldn't compete. The Four Preps, popular on campuses for their satirical revues, had started strong with the almost rock'n'roll "I was a 'Big Man' yesterday—but boy you oughtta see me now" amid gentler fare. Now they were noted for satirical parodies 'The Big Draft', and to come, 'A Letter to the Beatles'.

From the day they signed it was obvious, if only to Nick Venet at Capitol, that the Beach Boys would be the most important thing to happen to the company for the foreseeable future—i.e. over the next year or so. He disdained their youthful cockiness though only 23 himself, and at the time even he doubted their durability. But Capitol had nothing to lose and everything to gain by going all out on the group. It didn't happen that way.

BOBBY DARIN, ROCK'N'ROLLER ON 'SPLISH SPLASH' and 'Queen of the Hop', switching to crown prince of the teen idols with 'Dream Lover', had restyled himself as a junior Sinatra by redoing classics 'Mack the Knife', 'Beyond the Sea' and 'Up the Lazy River' in a swept-up jazz style, not even the so-called rock and roll beloved of teenieboppers. In late summer '62 came his biggest hit for some time, the self-penned ("Thinkin' about") 'Things', and Capitol lured him from home of Drifters/ Coasters r&b, up-and-coming Atlantic where creative conditions were right to make all Darin's hits. Capitol must have suspected they didn't have the producing scope to match Atlantic and his star dimmed within a year.

The time and energy they spent on Bobby went to waste though Venet, seeing the Beach Boys handle themselves in the studio, relished his time in New York recording him. Bobby would return to Atlantic when it had grown into a major. For the burgeoning career of the Beach Boys it meant just one more distraction for their new record label they couldn't afford.

Hard up against Motown, girl groups, the Beach Boys and Four Seasons, the time for crooners was over. They were slow to get the message from young record buyers, insulated by continuing high play by radio stations as a hopeful alternative to rock'n'roll. Yet by late 1962 Fifties survivors Pat Boone and Paul Anka disappeared from even Billboard's top twenty, Darin following in another six months— the most youthful, Ricky Nelson, reprieved for a further semester.

There would be little recognition from the management of the fact that within a year of the group joining Capitol the company was boosted from lowly eighth place to second in singles sales figures (Murry Wilson in Tom Nolan). 1963 would see it overtake such industry giants as RCA, Decca, Philips, Mercury, Warners and ABC-Paramount and drive clear of hungry youth specialists Atlantic, Motown, Cameo-Parkway and Philles—thanks to the Beach Boys' seven songs in and around Billboard's top twenty that year: exactly half of Capitol's biggest hits.

The prior claims of the sedate, white vocal quartets signed by Gilmore and Venet (who had to sneak even the unchallenging Lettermen in through the back door) explains why Capitol repeatedly through the Sixties attempted to tone down the Beach Boys' rock sound—by eliminating the instrumental grunt from the group's recordings by electronic processing, sanitising them into pale reissues, resembling as far as practicable the old-styled groups' mannered, almost monastic harmonies. Murry later (Tom Nolan) colorfully told the story of how Brian, who actually produced the recording sessions, came to him in early '63 boo-hooing, "They're changing our sound.": a situation not wholly remedied by 'going independent' in the middle of that year; Capitol still owned the master tapes. It was the opposite of what they did for the Beatles, beefing up the volume and other rock-enhancing effects. Listeners always had to tweak up the volume knob on a gramophone to even hear the Beach Boys. Aside from consistently castrating the drums and bass, and boosting the treble-scale giving them an anaemic 'whitebread' taint, the most notorious specific example of wanton interference has to be hacking off the ending, the climax, of 'Fun Fun Fun' as heard on the Brian Wilson-produced single, his wailing falsetto refrain backed up by Dennis's thumping-good drum flourishes: mindlessly deleted and not restored until the 1990s.

If not exactly cultural vandalism ranking with drawing a moustache on the Mona Lisa, such interference in an artist's work can hardly have had a parallel since the Renaissance. Did 18th Century sheet music salesmen 'improve on' Haydn or Mozart scores for publication? The attitude would worsen—undoubtedly a factor in the Beach Boys being written off in many circles as lightweights: a speeded-up version of the insipid offerings that proved readily acceptable to Middle America from Capitol's college glee club foursomes. But, come to that, they *were* white, with whatever advantages (and later disadvantages) that brought.

C apitol didn't displease everyone by its contribution. The Beatles were thrilled with what the company did with the original Parlophone recordings produced by George Martin and engineer Norman Smith—modifying the American pressings to be louder and bringing up the rhythm section. At the Abbey Road studio the group constantly implored Smith to emulate the sound of American records.

Smith: "We were always very conscious, both The Beatles and myself, that we weren't coming out with the sort of sound we would like... You see, the thing is, we were always basing our sounds on certain American records, and each time they came into a session with me, they would say, 'Norm, have you heard so-and-so American record? Have you heard the bass sound or the drum sound or whatever?' Of course, I was very aware of that... It was the start of the recording development at Abbey Road. All I can say is that we were striving to emulate the American records at that time and certainly the Americans set standards for us" (Pritchard & Lysaght).

While Motown and the girl groups have received their due as early recording influences on the Beatles, the Beach Boys—the only major act in the world then recording rock'n'roll—have gone unrecognised at this formative stage of the Beatles' recording career though what rock'n'roll the Liverpool group was doing was much closer to 'Surfin' Safari', '409' and 'Surfin' USA' than to Motown. Paul McCartney: "I listened to a lot of different bass players—mostly Motown records. They were great and the bass player, who I found out later was James Jamerson, was an influence. So smooth, melodic, and solid... And, of course, I've always liked Brian Wilson all the way through The Beach Boys" (1969, reproduced by Pritchard & Lysaght).

In July the Beach Boys are filmed singing 'Surfin' Safari' apparently by chance by a documentary film crew at one of their LA gigs. Six weeks later on 22nd August the Beatles were filmed playing at the Cavern Club by Granada, the new North of England regional channel—deliberately as part of a documentary on Liverpool's fast growing music scene.

It was obvious to producer George Martin on first meeting him in June that Pete Best was not a personality boy like the others— "very much the background boy. He didn't say much at all. He just looked moody and sullen in the corner." Best had good reason to be moody, apart from innate shyness—he had been hearing rumors for some time from others in the Liverpool scene that he was out. Shrewdly, it is only after the recording audition, on 16th August, that George and Paul put to it to Epstein that Pete must be dismissed (in quaint English phraseology)—outsiders would draw the obvious conclusion that he is inadequate for recordings. Martin, for his part, made it plain that Best's playing wasn't up to recording standard—just as he and Epstein seriously considered bringing in specialist musicians to replace or supplement the other Beatles. Best could still easily have remained in the Beatles to play live, according to Martin, but this wasn't an option for Harrison in particular, who had a replacement in mind.

Accounts of the quality of Best's drumming vary widely, from inadequate through average to the distinguishing attraction of the *band. Strangely, this phase of their career, pre-recording and playing nonstop Hamburg gigs—when Best was playing with them —is when the Beatles without dissent said was their best performing period. Evidently Pete Best was the most popular with the girls— obviously judging from photos the most virile looking of the band —and Paul McCartney and George Harrison wanted him out, in favor of George's pal Richie Starkey. After using him for two years the band left manager Brian Epstein, who was for keeping Pete for all but recording, to do the dirty work. Two weeks later Paul and John were at a Butlin's holiday camp where Rory Storm & the Hurricanes were playing, offering their drummer 'Ringo Starr' a new job. Then, when George Martin substituted session drummer Andy White for Ringo on 'Love Me Do' (September 4th and 11th), the new boy was left wondering if the group was "doing a Pete Best" on him too. At the session the Beatles are still suffering from bruises and abrasions, George Harrison a black eye, dealt out at a recent Cavern gig by Pete Best fans who knew what the score was.*

For the first five years of their career the Beach Boys presented on-stage as sort of electrified, rocking, 'fun' Kingstons. Even before meeting folk fan Al Jardine, Brian had bought and studied all the Trio's albums. Murry thought their music should be the model, as 'more serious' than rock'n'roll. Brian resisted, thankfully for the history of rock. Famous for 1958's Grammy-winning ("Hang down your head") 'Tom Dooley', in '61 the Trio were Most Played Vocal Group on radio and received four Gold Discs for albums; in another four years their l.p. sales would total 18 million (details from Murrells)—massive for those days. Maybe as a concession to Murry's outdated commercial instinct, Brian and Mike went along with the Kingstons' open-necked warm-weather Hawaii/ California attire that had also served crewcutted all-Americans the Four Freshmen and Kennedy liberals the Four Preps. But to usurp the Trio's position as Young America's touchstone of rock-solid sincerity, and to emulate their authenticity in an artistic interpretation of Americana and at the same time far surpass their popularity worldwide... These feats were as yet undreamt as the group struggled to survive through mid-1962.

' SURFIN' SAFARI' IS PASSED OVER IN BIOCLIPS AS the song that "entered the top 20 and brought them national attention." This doesn't nearly cover it. The Beach Boys' first classic broke nationally on July 14th and doused the country in surf fever till February 1963 when it finally left playlists in the snowbound Twin Cities of Minneapolis-St Paul, hugging either side of the confluence of the Minnesota and upper Mississippi Rivers. Conquering climatic and lifestyle extremes of desert and snow country, rural and as urban as it gets, they proved with one song that the appeal of their music had little if anything to do with surf or even California. In fact, to listen to the reverse snobbery of today's instrumental surf groups the Beach Boys are a blight on 'real' surf music.

As the Beach Boys led by Brian, overseen by Nick Venet and Murry, complete recording material in mid-August to go on their first album, 'Surfin' Safari' is shaping as top seller across LA's urban sprawl, for two weeks at KRLA. September 19th it jumps to second on premier New York City station WMCA's sales survey in *Go* magazine, coming to rest almost as high at WBCB-Philadelphia. Through mid-October it settles fifth in greater Chicago for three weeks, and was on its way to #3 San Francisco. Taking America's megalopoli by storm, it would top too in New England, Dallas (November), San Diego and the Twin Cities (Xmas). Through their first extended stay on the airwaves—a sweeping nine-month run—the group is adopted universally as the trend-setters of vocal surf music, as distinct from but associated in the public mind with twangy-guitar instrumentals. The Beach Boys were suddenly vastly influential: The Ventures, from cold, rainy Washington state a thousand miles up the West Coast, switched their titles to surfing themes to be the world's best-selling instrumental group (20 million discs US; 10 million Japan). Thanks to the Beach Boys 'surfing music' was gaining widespread commercial credibility by the month.

Sales surveys of the two biggest markets in America, by WMCA and WLS-Chicago for, respectively, the week ending 19th September and the week beginning 29th September 1962:

NEW YORK CITY	CHICAGOLAND
1. Sherry — Four Seasons	1. Let's Dance
2. Surfin' Safari	2. Venus in Blue Jeans
3. Let's Dance — Chris Montez	3. Monster Mash
4. A Wonderful Dream — Majors	4. Sherry
5. Green Onions — Booker T & MGs	5. Surfin' Safari
6. Monster Mash — Bobby Pickett	5a. 409
7. Ramblin' Rose — Nat King Cole	6. Patches — Dickey Lee
8. Do You Love Me? — Contours	7. Ramblin' Rose
9. The Loco-Motion — Little Eva	8. Do You Love Me?
10. Beechwood 4-5789 — Marvelettes Break a Heart — Gene Pitney	9. Only Love Can
	10. Hully Gully Baby Dovells

Rising no.10 in Cash Box, America's foremost chart of weekly sales, 'Surfin' Safari' set a personal best run of 21 weeks (broken by 'Rock and Roll Music' in the stagnant Seventies). In the nation's top twenty compiled by UPI (United Press International), published out of Chicago by newspapers across America and overseas, it scored September 24th to December 17th: 16-13-out-20-10-12-7-5-8-12-16-10-17. And it staked a claim as their first international chart-topper— for four weeks on the national survey of Sweden's Radio 3. Shrewdly buying the rights to publish and distribute the disc in Sweden was Stig Anderson, later to handle Abba. A California garage band had in one stroke taken on the world.

Superficially, Billboard's lowly rating at no.14 compares with Beatle contemporary 'Love Me Do' in the UK. Yet in any chart 'Surfin' Safari' would have peaked close to top had it risen and ebbed across the country in a few weeks like 99% of hits. According to Brian Wilson's autobiography *Wouldn't It Be Nice?* it rang 900,000 cash registers during its chart run—this after the rush for Rock'n'Roll in its first years had died down. 1960 had shown a dip in US sales and recovery was slow through '61 and '62, the culprit the tiny new

Japanese transistor radio that allowed repeated listens to a favorite song without forking out the steep 75 cents to buy it. Of all places, it quickly broke Capitol sales records in New York City. And long-term, the NBC network station there, 66-WNBC, one of America's dozen premier Top 40 stations, rated it over the next fifteen years the Eastern Seaboard's 7th most popular 1962 song after two monster hits by homies the Four Seasons.

Far beyond the grudging 'attention' of downplayers, this state-ment of youth power brought them iconic stardom, a devoted fan base of rockers (and wannabe surfers) around the world, and has been a defining signature tune ever since, a rock music standard featured in Lucasfilm's retro *American Graffiti* (1973), tv's *Happy Days* and umpteen documentaries epitomizing the joys of a beach lifestyle. It was all done under their own steam, without the mass-media campaign backing up pop stars that was soon mandatory. In fact it could be justly claimed the recording succeeded regardless of Capitol's efforts, and directly against the wishes of other powers connected to the Los Angeles radio business who actively "put it down" according to Nick Venet.

Once the sport of kings in Hawaii, surf-riding had been reduced by Hollywood to a vehicle for movie star Sandra Dee in *Gidget* (1959) and to present Columbia studio contractees Cliff Robertson and James Darren without ever suggesting the authentic lifestyle of surfers. The nationwide media, seeing the sport as a niche interest, gave the music curt mention, instead feteing hot East Coasters the Four Seasons, whose 'Sherry' and 'Big Girls Don't Cry' offered teen romance appeal and instant ear-catching gratification, ideal fodder for the *Bandstand* network tv show. Their novel delivery, continuing on 'Candy Girl' and 'Peanuts'—Frankie Valli's frantic falsetto contrasted against a comic dimwit bass voice—grabbed listeners immune to any deeper quality from pop music.

The Beach Boys briefly adopted 'Sherry' into their act, with passing novelty 'Monster Mash' by Bobby 'Boris' Pickett & the Crypt Kickers, involving a suitable piece of live theatre: green lights shone on Mike Love's face as he did an admirable audio-visual Boris Karloff take.

IF ANY YEAR CAN BE CALLED THE SEMINAL YEAR OF Sixties rock, 1962 would be. Maybe it was the emphatic New Year return to no.1 of Chubby Checker's smokin' remake of Hank Ballard's 'The Twist' that sparked it off. Three mainstream strands of rock'n'roll styling were rapidly evolving: Soul music, developing from r&b and Gospel; Motown's brand of commercialised soul, increasingly popular with the white audience; and Phil Spector's and other girl groups, also popular across the racial divide but to prove shortlived. And three white groups across the broad "rock and roll" idiom, including one to be imported from Liverpool, England—who would wage war for fans through the Sixties—had their first sizable hits that autumn: the Beach Boys, the Four Seasons and the Beatles, all three drawing heavily from black music. The Rolling Stones, formed in July, were parroting Chicago Blues in London's clubs. Bob Dylan, newly recording, would be considered a folk music writer until three years later he followed the Byrds and electrified folk's gentle guitars and put a solid drum beat behind them.

The movement that was the Beach Boys started as a reaffirmation of original, American music. In Italy, where they had already scored twice, there was no doubt about the derivation of Sixties music. Piero Scaruffi: "The Beach Boys started the fire: they fused the four-part harmonies of vocal groups like the Four Freshmen with Chuck Berry's rock'n'roll and a new genre was born. The Beatles, the Byrds and countless others copied the idea and the history of popular music would never be the same again" (Scaruffi's *History of Rock Music* internet site).

Country & Western had waned since its Fifties heyday. Latin music via Herb Alpert & the Tijuana Brass returned late in '62, introducing too the Baja Marimba Band and Sergio Mendes & Brasil '66 in the mid-Sixties on A&M. Aretha Franklin hadn't found her *metier*, and another leading light of Sixties Soul, Otis Redding, was years away too from breaking into the white market.

Premiering on tv in September as the Beach Boys, Four Seasons and Beatles made their leaps into destiny were the Beverly Hillbillies and the Jetsons. CBS reporter Mike Wallace went into world

47

syndication with *Biography*. Bugs Bunny and the Flintstones began their third year. Classic westerns *Wagon Train* and *Maverick* gave more ground to horse operas *Bonanza*, and now *The Virginian*, Universal's 90-minute tv-movie series that would see off the last of the B-Westerns playing in theaters. Clint Eastwood carried on in *Rawhide*. The 1958-style glamor of Warners' *77 Sunset Strip* and *Hawaiian Eye* was congealing under the compelling realism of *Naked City* and *Route 66*. *The Fugitive, Gilligan's Island*, Mel Brooks' *Get Smart*, and *Star Trek* were one, two, three and four years away. In musical variety *The Ed Sullivan Show* started its eighth year, *Bandstand* its sixth, and *The Andy Williams Show* premiered. On the way out was Steve Allen, comedian and former host of the long-running *Tonight Show*, who had made derisory fun of Elvis, Gene Vincent and anyone else who performed real rock'n'roll and didn't spout 'culture' with a capital 'C' or wear a MENSA badge.

The teen stars of the sister Warner series were Ed 'Kookie' Byrnes and Connie Stevens, believed to be the coolest things on television, each celebrating a string of pop hits to go with the image. Ed's co-star Roger Smith, later to marry Ann-Margret, had a hit too, 'Beachtime'. On the big screen were Sandra Dee, a top ten box-office star, and Connie's tv co-star Troy Donahue, Sandra's boyfriend in *A Summer Place*, a tawdry soap opera that made a mint. In real life, Sandra's wedding to Bobby Darin cemented them both in youth culture. But the Beach Boys, filled with pent-up rock'n'roll energy back in the garage that was Studio 3 at Western Recorders, threatened to turn Hollywood's treacle-laden summer image on its head.

War films *The Longest Day* (Zanuck/20th Century-Fox) and *Lawrence of Arabia* (Columbia) were the two big movies of New Year 1962-63. Darryl F Zanuck's all-star overkill—50 international names—found roles for teen idols Paul Anka (who wrote the theme tune) and Fabian, as well as Tommy Sands and Sal Mineo, actors who'd had pop hits five years before. The teen idol was an adaptable breed until the greased Elvis pompadour, its defining club badge, was replaced by the fluffy Beatle cut.

Disney's Hayley Mills, too, made hit parades with bouncy 'Let's Get Together'—"Yeah yeah yeah". Daughter of stoic screen Brit John

Mills, she was the world's favorite screen waif—her coltish appeal working for tomboys, and boys up to 12, after which Sandra Dee's pliable lips and thrusting *décolletage* were bound to win out. The British-made James Bond (*Dr No*) was brawny Scot Sean Connery— in successive years to be outgrossed only by musicals *Mary Poppins* and *The Sound of Music*. Both starred Julie Andrews, yet another performer who by 1964 helped escalate an English accent and chronic chirpiness to high fashion and almost a prerequisite for showbiz superstardom.

Coming up strong in the all-American stakes alongside blonde nymphet Sandra (who ditched *Gidget* and succeeded Debbie Reynolds in the *Tammy* franchise) was graduate mouseketeer Annette Funicello—Disney's reply for 1963's teen market, featuring a nicely expanded bustline putting Minnie Mouse to shame. Paired with teen idol Frankie Avalon for a series of "Beach Party" musical comedies, they invaded, or rather sabotaged, the Beach Boys' turf, bringing the beach theme into derision. The group would only just escape in critics' minds the charge of being "plastic"—a mass-produced, cheap product, the hallmark of such American icons as Disney movies and pop groups the Osmonds, Monkees, even Beatles—according to many. The Beatles had nerve enough to retaliate with titles *Rubber Soul* and the Plastic Ono Band.

TWO GENUINE 20TH CENTURY CULTURAL ICONS WHO have transcended all since were lost in 1962. As the Beach Boys record for the first time at Capitol studio on the midsummer morning of August 5th, barely five miles from where Dennis would drown at Marina del Rey, some way up Santa Monica Boulevard at her modest, unstarlike Brentwood bungalow, Marilyn Monroe's body was found, so the official story goes, by her paid companion-maid, somehow neatly laid out on her bed nude and face down, arms by sides, the apparently staged victim of suicide or accidental drug overdose. The emphatic embodiment of sex on the screen for ten years, recently the lover of President Jack Kennedy, then of attorney-general Robert Kennedy and, much more debatably the man she nominated as world's sexiest—Albert Einstein— she touched a great many men in her lifetime and has moved many beyond.

A liaison with Einstein, touted by some, seems ludicrous on the face of it. Marilyn, who'd called him the world's sexiest man for his intellect, was virtually unknown outside Hollywood until 1952, certainly to Einstein's rarefied circle, when the genius was an ailing 73-year-old man three years short of death. Did the absent-minded eccentric die in ecstasy, uncovering another of the world's natural wonders? Marilyn, apart from frequent freebies granted powerful men for career favors, in a free spirit of sexual largesse cast her net far wider than her eight-times-married rival Elizabeth Taylor, who restricted herself to fellow exhibitionists from showbiz or wealthy conspicuous consumers. Amid a legion of males out of the public eye who swore their undying love for her, all-time-great Yankee baseballer Joe DiMaggio, and of equal status in their fields, playwright Arthur Miller and ageing movie hunk Clark Gable (who settled for surrogate fatherhood) all fell under Marilyn's spell of vulnerability.

Apart from the shattering effects on Marilyn's fellow Angelenos her demise left Liz Taylor, Brigitte Bardot and Sophia Loren, up to now all overshadowed by Marilyn, to vie for the mantle of world's sexiest-woman-with-talent, a title none would wear convincingly; apart from her bodily allure 'Norma Jeane' was to stage/film master Elia Kazan "one of the three most talented people I ever met", to acting master Lee Strasberg "out of hundreds and hundreds of actors" one of "two that stand out way above the rest", with Brando. Liz and Sophia had recently won Best Actress Oscars (Marilyn the Golden Globe as the world's most popular star though she hadn't released a film in a year and a half), more in amazement that glamor girls with such luscious natural boobies had any other talent at all; Brigitte's other major talent, it was agreed by male observers, was in her celebrated, eloquent *derriere*. Hollywood's "world's most beautiful woman" crown had passed to Liz in 1958 via Ava Gardner from Hedy Lamarr, in a succession from the thirties—mainly for her striking, violet eyes. But her 5ft-2 frame had run to plumpness and Liz, currently married to nightclub crooner Eddie Fisher filched from

Debbie Reynolds—and conducting a very public affair with Richard Burton on the *Cleopatra* set— would emerge a pale victor only as media fodder, much later as inspirational mentor to Michael Jackson in how to generate public sympathy in the face of outrageous superstar self-indulgence.

And the world of rock'n'roll, less visibly but just as traumatically, lost its favorite son, Elvis Presley, just 27 but sunk as an authentic idol under the dross of evermore anti-rock movies. The current *Blue Hawaii* and *Follow That Dream* were two of the better vehicles lined up by manager 'Colonel' Tom Parker, released lucratively in a stream by film majors Paramount, MGM, Fox and United Artists—thrilling Elvis fans and taxing critics' patience three times a year. Later, cut-rate companies Allied Artists and National General would ensure worse films and, through participation deals, much bigger cuts for Parker and Presley, in that order.

Elvis had been discharged from the army after his two-year stint and come back from Germany with a simper where his sneer used to be—but bigger than ever for abruptly severing his rock'n'roll roots. Before repatriation he had worried out loud whether his place in fans' hearts had been taken by Fabian. Frank Sinatra, anxious to convert Elvis from despised rock'n'roll, sent comely daughter Nancy (later to marry Elvis lookalike Tommy Sands) to meet him at the airport—at once introducing her to youth music straight in at the top and obligating Elvis to him. Elvis was one who understood loyalty. From his hard rock released while on duty—'Hard Headed Woman', 'King Creole', 'I Got Stung', 'One Night', 'A Big Hunk of Love'—he went straight to soppy ballads and pretend rockers dumbed down to self-parody: 'Little Sister', 'Devil in Disguise'….

He now appealed to an undiscerning wider audience, and pleased his domineering mother figure, the Colonel. Sentimental ballads 'It's Now or Never', 'Are You Lonesome Tonight?' and Euro-pap 'Wooden Heart' and 'Surrender' were super-sellers around the world. But record-buying kids in America didn't want another Dean Martin and his number ones soon declined in favor of Chubby Checker, newly emerged as the real deal. Though his movie fans would keep Elvis in the box-office top ten—by sheer bulk of product—appalled rock fans deserted in droves and late '62 saw his last topper for seven years, 'Return to Sender'. Rock'n'Roll devotees saw that, like his friend and rival Pat Boone, a $half-million-a-movie contract (at a time when admission was 50 cents and Elvis's biggest hit grossed $10 million domestically) could tame the sneeringest hepcat into a toothless lapdog. Aggravated by the traumatic death of his mother and the consequent victory of gladhanding, backslapping Colonel Parker's influence over him, he recognized the commercial imperative of moneymaking movies—after trying the other kind several times. The sight of a lovesick Elvis plunking on a ukulele and crooning 'Can't Help Falling in Love', 'Hawaiian Wedding Song' and 'Rock-a-Hula Baby' to fake-dusky South Seas maidens was one rock'n'roll fans would cringe from for the rest of the Sixties.

A space was opening up for a candidate to replace Elvis as The Great White Hope of Rock'n'Roll. It might have been that if he hadn't abdicated as "The King" he would have been dethroned. It seemed that something or someone was out to get rock'n'roll and there were few contenders offering their heads on a platter for what might be a 90-day reign. Website *Pop Culture Madness* in mid-2007 rated the three Beach Boy hits thus far among the current forty most popular from 1962—equalling Elvis with three from that year. In retrospect, the Beach Boys did inherit his Rock'n'Roll crown. But the powers that be at EMI HQ in London were soon formulating other plans and the way the Sixties turned out would be under an entirely different scenario.

A S THE BEACH BOYS EMERGED AS A WORLD NAME October 1962 many wondered if the world, never mind surf music, would last out the month. Discovering, from U-2 spy plane photos, missile silos installed 90 miles from Florida by strongman Fidel Castro, Kennedy ordered a naval blockade and issued an ultimatum to Soviet Premier Khruschev to withdraw the weapons. The Cuban Missile Crisis kept the world in suspense 13 days, pondering if this would be the final brink in the brinksmanship played through the Cold War. On this occasion, fortunately for all living things, the charismatic gurus of Capitalism and Communism would survive long enough to start arms limitation.

'Surfin' Safari' entered Billboard's top 20 October 5th and that weekend the Beatles released their first single, 'Love Me Do'/'PS I Love You'—unheard in the USA for the next 18 months. Andrew Loog Oldham, an ambitious 19-year-old publicist just out of a private school—soon to be the Rolling Stones' formative manager— takes the Beatles around London introducing them to influential press people, hoping to inflate them from a regional phenomenon into a national one.

For now the Beach Boys, Southern California youths led by a young man three months out of his teens, rumble with four streetwise New Jerseyites shaping as top contenders for the title of world champion group. Propelled on to the international scene before they realized it, there was something substantial about these musical prodigies, even before release of their first album that screamed they were here to stay. On October 27th they played their first gig at the Hollywood Bowl with Debbie Reynolds the biggest name, just 30 and a veteran of MGM screen musicals and still top box office. Also on hand were Shelley Fabares and Paul Petersen, the kids from *The Donna Reed Show*, both also high on the charts, the Beach Boys' friends the Rivingtons ('Papa-Oom-Mow-Mow'), and girl group the Castells.

The Four Seasons, named after a bowling alley nitespot they played, hailed from the tough "Little Italy" Jersey side of metro New York, then famous for its real-life mafia depridations and later for *The Sopranos* of tv infamy. In 1956 they had enjoyed a one-off recording success locally, suitably lounge-lizard style as the Four Lovers. Now as older family men in their mid-twenties, but under the expert tutelage of impresario/ex-teen idol Bob Crewe, they impressed with Frankie Valli's striking voice popping from baritone to a piercing shriek of a falsetto. They were buoyed too by young recruit (from the Royal Teens—'Short Shorts') Bob Gaudio's songwriting ability and keyboards as the quartet's second tenor. Nick Massi (singing and playing bass, soon replaced by Joe Long) and Tommy De Vito (first baritone and guitar) made the Neapolitan flavor unanimous. More a supper-club act live, but looking like Scorsese mean-streets movie characters, they came to spearhead Italo-American pop with Dion (DiMucci)—now without his Belmonts ('Teenager in Love') and famous for solo classics 'Runaround Sue', 'The Wanderer' and 'Ruby Baby'—all hitting the top or near it into 1963. A few months later Dion's 'Donna the Prima Donna', with multiple layered dynamic counterpoint harmony—a Space Age advance on traditional Doo-Wop—sounded very much like the direction the Beach Boys would later take.

In '63 Dion was outsold for singles only by the Beach Boys, and followed by the Four Seasons, then Ray Charles. The Seasons' recordings, though dubbed Schlock Rock by their detractors for their deliberately crafted teen feel, were imaginatively and immaculately produced over some of the slickest arrangements and studio musicians heard anywhere. Helmed by Crewe, learning a lesson or two from fellow New Yorker Phil Spector, the quartet had started with twin sensations 'Sherry' across September-October, shifting a quarter-million copies the day after the disc was spun by Dick Clark on *American Bandstand*, its six weeks at #1 unequalled in 1962; and 'Big Girls Don't Cry', topping five weeks—then 'Walk Like a Man' into 1963, barely slowing. In six years they would move more than 50 million discs US, 90% of them 45s.

Breaking down the vocal parts, the East-West Coast rivals were not dissimilar. Both featured a cool Sixties mid-range lead that owed something to jazz, Frankie Valli stronger on dramatic expression, Mike Love on rock-drive; immaculate harmony back-up; a falsetto—Brian Wilson more genuinely expressive than Valli, who must have inspired the Newbeats' comic 'Bread and Butter'; not to forget the 'dumb' Fifties bass voice used as song punctuation by the Coasters, employed now by Mike Love and Joe Long.

Lyrically, they were *simpatico* in essaying a hedonistic male-dominated world, though bluffing half the time. Both played the role of the boy's answer to the girl groups, strident in asserting his rights but on the B-side Brian Wilson backed away, emotionally vulnerable. The Seasons bluffed on 'Big Girls' but 'Walk Like a Man' contained the memorable Crewe-Gaudio lines "Soon you'll be cryin' on 'count of all your lyin'—Oh yeah, just look who's laughin' now!" and "No woman's worth crawlin' on the earth!—so walk like a man, my son." The proto-masculist sentiments might have influenced John Lennon/Beatle songs on *A Hard Day's Night* and *Beatles for Sale*, if not Bob Dylan's bitter, paranoiac expressions of betrayal a year later.

Crewe in his collaboration with the Four Seasons exerted magnificent control over the recording booth in converting r&b into Sixties pop. Few recordings that year could compete for sheer dynamic modernism with 'Walk Like a Man' and its crackling baion-beat guitar rhythm—entering the top 20 in the US the same weekend (2nd February '63) as the George Martin production 'Please Please Me' did in England, and as the Beach Boys completed recording 'Surfin' USA'.

The Beach Boys had only cracked the top ten of the hit parade at national level—and were soon faced with challenges from two other harmony groups who both sold well with self-penned hits, but fleetingly as it turned out: the Cascades ('Rhythm of the Rain') from San Diego and Philly's the Tymes ('So Much in Love'). It was figured by industry insiders of the time that a top ten hit buoyed a career for a year and a half, so they had ample time with the pressure off for experimenting in the studio.

California might afford them a marginal career. Metro LA was overtaking Chicago's seven million market. San Francisco-Oakland on the upswing had three million—four with San José. There were San Diego's million, and Sacramento's and San Bernardino's half-millions. Beach Boy fever also went with generic surf music up the West Coast to Portland (750,000) and Seattle (one million) but surf affiliation was barely an entrée to their longevity at East Coast surfer spots Miami, New York and Boston. And soon they were bigger than that too. It was Dick Dale, the Challengers, Bob Vaught & the Renegades, the Lively Ones that dominated LA's top five albums with surfer l.p.s early in '63; *Surfin' Safari* that sold nationwide and overseas.

Warner Bros' KFWB with KRLA and KHJ, owned by Capitol in the late sixties, were the big LA stations. But the Beach Boys' backyard, ranking as entertainment Mecca with New York, thrived on suburban stations reflecting micro variations in taste via local record stores—KBLA-Burbank, KACY-Oxnard, KEZY-Anaheim, KLFM-Long Beach... up the coast KIST-Santa Barbara. KFXM-San Bernardino ruled the "Inland Empire" north to KYNO-Fresno, Sacramento (KROY, KXOA); and KKIS-Pittsburg surveyed sales in what is now Silicon Valley. KEWB and then KYA ruled the San Francisco Bay area, challenged by KFRC, and KLIV-San José. San Diego, hugging the Mexican border, divvied up its loyalties among KDEO, KCBQ and KGB with its Boss 30.

California accounted for one in nine stateside record sales, New York State one in seven—Buffalo a city of a million-plus before decline, Rochester, Syracuse and Capital (Albany) tri-cities all supported by dynamic Top 40 stations. Pittsburgh, Cleveland and St Louis each had 1.8 million people, larger than Dallas or Houston, twice as big as Miami, Atlanta or New Orleans. Boston was a major market of 2.5 million ahead of Washington DC. Inland cities perched in and around the Rockies—Salt Lake City, Denver, Phoenix—and across the flatland eastward—Minneapolis-St Paul, Milwaukee, Omaha—some of a million people, are the overlooked heroes of the Beach Boys story along with the farflung towns they toured, Butte and Billings, Fargo, Sioux Falls and Des Moines, which supported them through the lean times that inevitably came.

About fifty stations located in the two dozen biggest-selling cities (that accounted for 54% of US sales) were considered 'primary', including many of these: KQV-Pittsburgh; WRIT and WOKY in Milwaukee; WIXY (with a top 60), WHK and WKYC in Cleveland and elsewhere in Ohio—then the sixth biggest record-buying state—WSAI-Cincinnati and WCOL-Columbus; Louisville's WAKY, "one of the most influential secondary market stations", and WKLO carving up "Kentuckiana" between them.

Out of the dozen or so premier Top 40 stations across the nation those of New York City, especially WABC that charted a reliable survey of sales across the land's largest megalopolis (then 15 million), carried nationwide sway making hits—overseas hopefuls a specialty. Beyond coincidence, it was precisely those Beatle songs New Yorkers weren't overboard crazy about—'Ticket to Ride', 'Nowhere

Man', 'Yellow Submarine', 'Lady Madonna'—that weren't all-out no.1s nationally. WNBC-New York of the giant NBC network, with its multi-media resources, kept a tag on ongoing sales across the Northeast and later proved the enormous, secret appeal of Beach Boy records into the seventies, at their lowest ebb of media exposure—so far out of fashion as to be virtually nonexistent to radio stations across America.

It was reckoned by Chapple & Garofalo (1977) that a song backed by WABC sold at least an additional 50,000 automatically, and backed by a major chain could count on extra sales of "several hundred thousand". The ABC chain also included highly influential WLS-Chicago and KQV-Pittsburgh with sister stations in New York, Los Angeles, San Francisco and Detroit. The RKO chain had WRKO-Boston, KFRC-San Francisco, WOR-New York, and later LA's KHJ, to grow as powerful as WABC.

Stations that didn't keep strict sales surveys underestimated massive Beach Boys sales—illustrated by their consistently better performance on the strictly audited chart of WABC-New York than at rival WMCA. If a song got old it was demoted at WMCA and like stations around the country for the sake of freshness. Group standing was affected, many of their later hits suffering from inordinately low national placings—made up not only from sales reports but local station reports of airplay. (For more on airplay biases see stations instituting Bee Gee-less days c. 1980.)

THE BEACH BOYS WERE SHOWING AS A CULTURAL force over the Four Seasons, stamping their unique image with huge l.p. sales, averaging nearly two and a half million per international release through the next eighteen months as rock'n'roll albums began to stake a foothold around the world almost through their efforts alone. Each featured signature tunes hailing themes strongly identified with by teenagers and other idealists the world over. Defying the norm, much of their early so-called 'album filler' grew familiar through high requested airplay.

The music travelled well, helped by youth-oriented themes but hardly reliant on them around the English-speaking world where

Southern Californian idiom was a foreign language, even less so across continents where the nearest thing to a surfboard or woody was a canoe or rickshaw. The excitement was in the music itself, an elemental force. According to the Beach Boys Fan Club Italiano, 'Surfin'' had been a hit in Italy—but evidently solely by airplay, given lack of distribution overseas. As so often in their European career, a cover, in this case by Peppine di Capri, one of Italy's biggest stars, was bound to be the bigger hit. It was bettered by 'Surfin' Safari' in a market where few English-language songs apart from Twist dance recordings ever saw a turntable. No less than Elvis Presley was caught recording love songs specially in Italian in response to commercial demands—that is, apart from 'It's Now or Never' and 'Surrender' cribbed from the original Italian and wringing every bit of Latin emotionalism out through them.

'Surfin' Safari' had topped in Sweden in November just passed and registered in Germany. In France, inevitably, performers co-opted Beach Boy music as part of French pop culture. The *Surfin' Safari* album would reach top six in Japan, their first of thirty to breach the upper dozen there over the next fifteen years: their most consistently appreciative audience, absorbed as it was in all things American, and by far the most important outside the USA.

And the quality was abundant: '409' was as good as its A-side, starting a norm of double winners. To date only Elvis, Ricky Nelson and the Everlys had regularly featured Bs. The Four Seasons had their share, but their best early Bs 'Connie-O', 'Marlena' and 'Peanuts' were merely passably good pop tunes, later improving with two Bobs Crewe & Gaudio songs that would find fame when replicated by British Invasion groups, 'Silence is Golden' and 'The Sun Ain't Gonna Shine Anymore'.

The Seasons served up more waste on their A-sides too—some adrift at the stone cold end of the Hot 100 or missing entirely. From June '62 to Xmas '64 they issued twenty-three 45s to the Beach Boys' eleven, just pipping them in bulk domestic sales of 45s but lagging far behind in albums. The key emphasis on Doo-Wop—lately re-popularised by Maurice Williams & the Zodiacs ('Stay') and the Marcels ('Blue Moon')—and the fact that they were associated with the first major black-owned label, Vee Jay, gave them big crossover appeal to black record buyers (their first three no.1 pop hits also scored no.1 on the r&b chart), obviously attracted by such close stylistic imitations and excited by updated instrumental backing. How black the Four Seasons sounded to the untutored was illustrated by a brazen showbiz coup. On missing the plane for a tour of the mother country, big Italy, the Seasons' icy-nerved promoter at the other end hired a quartet of black singers as imposters, leaving Roma fans apparently none the wiser.

In the US the Four Seasons were identifiably "Eyeties"; in Italy they were Americano, black or not. It was a matter of perception marking American icons the world over. Regional or ethnic distinctions meant the earth in the US market. Overseas fans saw American celebrities through a glossy veneer, genetically coated with a glamor lent by Hollywood, New York, Las Vegas or Nashville; Yankee knowhow equated to slickness. To the rest of North America the Beach Boys were Southern Californians first; to English star Elvis Costello on first sight they simply "looked very, very American." Eventually, to the world, they would come to represent a better America.

On October 1ˢᵗ the Beatles sign a new contract with Brian Epstein, to run for five years. The terms, to become generally known on Epstein's death just short of expiry, will be a subject of marvel to envious managers in show business, and can only be compared to Colonel Parker's exploitation of Elvis Presley. Parker tried to justify it by saying Elvis was his sole client. Epstein could argue he devoted the bulk of his business, and personal, time to the Beatles —to the neglect of his many other clients, they could justly retort.

From the Beatles' first recording session at Abbey Road, actually handled by George Martin's assistant Ron Richards, emerges 'Love Me Do'/'PS I Love You'. Norman Smith: "[The editing by Martin] took a long time. Quite honestly, by the time it came out I was pretty sick of it—I didn't think it would do anything" (Salewicz). And it didn't—not for more than two months when it appeared in the UK charts on December 15ᵗʰ, fuelled by Brian Epstein buying 10,000 copies himself. While Martin and many others think 'Love Me Do' would have been better as a B-side, it pushes up to #17 with Epstein's secret help, selling 116,227. Even this moderate success nationally prompts their first appearance on Manchester television (Granada), singing on the 'People and Places' program. In the judgment of Record Mirror's Peter Jones the A-side "drags a bit" but he thinks the group have potential.

Ten thousand kilometres away in Los Angeles Capitol A&R man Dave Dexter receives the usual EMI box lot from Britain of recent releases on the conglomerate's UK labels Columbia, Parlophone and HMV. Listening to 'Love Me Do', John Lennon's mouth organ jars: "I didn't care for that harmonica sound because I had grown up listening to the old blues records and blues harmonica players, so I nixed the record instantly. I told EMI to peddle it somewhere else."

Capitol president Alan Livingstone sums up: "We don't think the Beatles will do anything in this market." 'Love Me Do' is not released in the US and in Canada, where other English acts are taking off, sells 140 copies (Paul White, EMI A&R man for Canada).

November, the Beatles are introduced to Dezo Hoffmann, international photographer to the stars. Over the next three years he becomes an integral element in the Beatle publicity and image-making machine, saturating the media with tastefully taken images devoted to making them a "photographic phenomenon".

R ECORDS AT THIS STAGE EARN THE WEST COAST champs just a supplementary income. *Surfin' Safari* begins a nine-month run in November to lower top 30, then an impressive debut for a rock'n'roll band—youths generally couldn't afford l.p.s. Album-buyers were Easy Listening fans, now including Elvis Presley on their shopping list. *Blue Hawaii*, a year old, is the first so-called rock album to top a US million (eventually 1.5). On his new soundtrack those coming closest to highlights are laid-back 'Return to Sender' and a hash of the Coasters' earthy, comic 'Girls, Girls, Girls'. Purveying real rock—risky in these times—the Beach Boys will soon have durable top ten l.p.s that accumulate a US million or so.

'Ten Little Indians' was picked by Capitol as a 45 to keep its young milchcow prodigies spotlighted, and hit a week after its album, December 1st. The traditional song was adapted to a rock format with added love lyrics and denouement "The squaw didn't care if he never did a thing 'cos she loved the tenth Indian boy." Though nothing to rest a career or reputation on, it was upbeat and catchy in its counterpoint harmonies but fared badly, barely top half of the Hot 100, bought in numbers only in isolated parts of the Midwest— Pittsburgh, Des Moines, Oklahoma City, Minneapolis, where it met up with long-lived 'Surfin' Safari' and '409' in the top ten January 12th 1963. Chicago, Dallas and Toronto treated it respectably but here too it was overwhelmed by feisty surf'n'hotrod music. It was remade as a single, far less successfully, five years later by British invaders the Yardbirds.

Cash Box listed 'Surfin' Safari' 31st best-seller in its "Top 100 Singles of 1962" after six Adult Contemporary and seven dance songs—four Twist, two Mashed Potato, one Loco-Motion. 'Ten Little Indians' provided the Beach Boys with their third hit in Europe, again at Radio 3, Sweden. As usual it was covered in France. But this song's comparative failure Stateside taught Capitol one dodgy, Orwellian lesson: "Surf music good, other music bad." These guys called themselves beachboys, let them stick to songs about the beach!

From this moment the Capitol execs' collective brain can be heard ticking over up and down the profit column. They had their prime product pegged and would shun anything dicey from them —i.e. non-surf/youth oriented—that might end up a debit in the corporate accounts. In this the Beach Boys must qualify as the most straightjacketed true artists in the history of show business. Even a medieval court buffoon might have been allowed to vary his act before he got pissed on. To radio bosses and other media wallahs the group manifested in a visitation as a giant dollar sign with its feet nailed to a surfboard. It might as well have been two big-kahuna surfboards in the shape of a cross that the Beach Boys would have to bear past the millennium, all but their peers and the best-informed critics taking years to catch up with progress—for which the group had to fight every step of the way.

Although the tag would hogtie them into singing about fun in the sun, for now it was their inclination. Having navigated an often dispiriting first year of what were then accepted rip-offs by radio stations and promoters up and down the West Coast, as later told by Mike Love, the Beach Boys were highly sought after live performers clearing $3,000-plus per show at a time when concert tickets were typically $1.50.

Murry, revving into overdrive wherever his boys were concerned, has described (Tom Nolan, 1972) how a whizzkid from the group's bookers the William Morris Agency told him December 17th that the Beach Boys would never be bigger than supper club act Ruby & the Romantics, pulling down $3,500 for a seven-day week. Taking it as a taunt beyond enduring, Murry sprang into action, personally booking five dates Christmas Eve to New Year's, two at Santa Monica Civic Auditorium 27th/28th, for gross receipts of $26,684. The group took 60%. Later claiming up to 75% on occasions, they had already overtaken Las Vegas headliners Pat Boone, Eddie Fisher and Bobby Darin clearing the personal appearance top scale of $40,000 a week flat, 14 shows.

Wary of swelled-headedness and the flipside of the showbiz big time spoiling his kids, Murry proudly recounted how he "held them back" from the public spotlight for nine months after release of their first big hit—until their first network tv date, *The Steve Allen Show*, March 2nd 1963. He grounded them in grassroots gigs, calling on college freshman Fred Vail to promote their first headliner concert produced by Murry at Sacramento Civic Auditorium on May 24th. Young enough to be a member of the group, Vail becomes a particular friend of Dennis's.

Lacking surf songs though littered with images from a California excursion, their first l.p. was rudimentary. Apart from the four hits a routine remake of Eddie Cochran's 'Summertime Blues' with Carl and Dave singing lead lifted it above the mediocre. The raw sound was that of a rowdily youthful live band, that would inspire the favoritism of The Who drummer-to-be Keith Moon, who looked and played like Gene Krupa on speed—a surf music fan in those early Beach Boy days fed by discs imported to England and destined to be a hellraising soul brother of Denny Wilson, both marked for early booze-assisted death. Libido-driven 17-year-old Dennis's prank on tour of painting his penis green—in a lewd concession to inexperience—and walking it through a hotel lobby would have impressed Moon.

And there were takers. On their first big tour in summer '62 Elmer Marks had to put nearly $300 of gate takings towards paying for VD shots to clear up infections several of the boys had contracted—but from prostitutes rather than eager groupies. Accorded a lead vocal— "Little girl still in your teens, You're my Miss America" co-written by Herb Alpert—Dennis was beginning to make little girls' hearts quicken with his moves on stage too. Opportunity for recording leads was limited by his voice coinciding exactly with Mike Love's preferred range; and the fact that his nervous energy didn't allow him to stay in the studio long enough for multiple takes.

Beach Boy albums were never the uniform entities Beatle l.p.s were—a fact of differing approach held against them. McCartney-Lennon-Martin would in 1964 make all songs on an album sound related, sometimes to the point of monotony; Brian Wilson was far too mercurial a talent to impose one technique throughout. Consistent with his belief that he was guided to write each song by a higher presence, each was treated as an individual creation with its own soul.

For now Capitol's hands were tied by the absence of 'Surfer Girl' and 'In My Room', sitting idle until Brian could wrest full control of recording conditions. Always the leader and musical director, at 20 he was careful to allow Murry to save face—until the phony 'control panel' rigged for him was exposed, to crushing humiliation. Brian was assisted with technical problems by Western Recorders engineer Chuck Britz, whom he would utilize at up to six studios over the next few years—Capitol's studio a last resort. Nick Venet was corporate liaison, artists and repertoire—A&R man in showbiz parlance. Brian Wilson was already the leading up-and-comer in West Coast rock recording, challenging the major players in the pop music industry still concentrated in the old eastern centers New York and Philadelphia; for blues, jazz and country— Chicago, St Louis, New Orleans, and emerging Detroit, Nashville and Memphis.

THE BEACH BOYS—vs Beatlemania

IT WAS SHORTLY INTO 1963 THAT THE BEACH BOYS remet established LA duo Jan Berry & Dean Torrance, med students and part-time pop stars for the past five years. Jan was the driven one, putting together a super-abundance of echo and other effects for teen-idol style hits in his home studio/garage under their Bel Air bachelor pad. Brian sang them a song he'd written in November and recorded as a demo, 'Surfin' USA', based on Chuck Berry's 'Sweet Little 16' but speeded up, modernised to a rock beat and with surf lyrics. Basic as the presentation was, Brian accompanying himself on piano, they craved it with a passion. To universal dismay he sacrificed 'Surf City', Torrance describing how the Beach Boy went through this one, starting "Two girls for every boy… I bought a '34 wagon and we call it a woody…" With this cast-off, number one written all over it, he handed them on a plate their biggest hit. Yet, compared to the adopted Jan Berry production, 'Surfin' USA' as it turned out has a unique freshness and rock credibility.

They milked from him, contributing varying levels of participation, several more—In fact in their revived career they would have only two sizable hits not directly dependent on Brian: 'Honolulu Lulu' ("Queen of the surfer girls") and 'The Little Old Lady from Pasadena'. Much more, their whole new sound came from the Beach Boys and casual listeners couldn't tell them from the real thing. In a text book case of showbiz superego that seems loopy to those acquainted with the facts of who's indebted to whom, Dean has ever since told an unintentionally amusing story that they were flattered that the Beach Boys copied *their* sound— based on a resemblance of the background "bop-bop" chant of 'Surfin'' to their contemporaneous hit version of the ancient Hoagy Carmichael Tin Pan Alley standard 'Heart and Soul'!

Not only did they convert Jan & Dean from outdated schlock to modernised rock'n'roll, and lend them their performance style, but supported them backing, instrumentally and vocally, their cuts of 'Surfin'', 'Surfin' Safari' and 'Little Deuce Coupe', kick-starting their Beach Boy-soundalike career. Taken under their young mentors' wings, they would open several Beach Boys shows. Murry reacted to the appropriation of 'Surf City' by dubbing them "song pirates"—at which Jan turned up to a Beach Boy recording session in improvised buccaneer rig ready to "steal" more songs, provoking Murry to fury and breaking up Brian in tears of laughter. Jan used this vein of mild satire on record (and film) and, though lacking the talent at musical parody or wit of the Coasters or Four Preps the duo carved a niche as "the clown princes of rock'n'roll" helped by mentor Lou Adler and other key figures.

The eager young songwriter continued to share his creations with largesse, as with another pair—over a year later to materialise as a double-sided hit, 'Little Honda'/'My Buddy Seat', for the Hondells, a group purpose-made by Brian's Hawthorne buddy Gary Usher. So it was that the Beach Boys became overlords of surf music, emphasised by Brian sharing lead vocals on 'Surf City' with Jan—and Carl playing his rocking-good guitar licks on the track—and Brian reportedly a lead voice too on the Hondells' 'Little Honda'. Dennis too teamed with Usher to write, produce and perform 'RPM'/'My Stingray', both popular enough locally to earn and lose Denny, in a drunk-driving crash, a Chevy Corvair sports car.

They met a new surf duo, Bruce Johnston and Terry Melcher, to have a West Coast hit with Brian's ("Check my") 'Custom Machine', later as part of Sagittarius—with Glen Campbell and Usher added, a remake of 'In My Room'. Bruce & Terry, as they were billed, formed the nucleus of the Rip Chords ('Hey Little Cobra') and stayed in the Beach Boys circle through the Sixties and beyond. KFWB radio DJ Roger Christian, recruited to the cause by Murry on hearing him analyzing the lyrics of '409' on air, quoted hotrod jargon for 'Shut Down' and 'Little Deuce Coupe'. Rarely were Brian's early writing partners more than technical, apart from Usher credited as tutor in co-composing 'Lonely Sea' and 'In My Room'; Christian on 'Don't Worry Baby'. Brian and Mike, still on the same wavelength and in amicable mood, were the most commercially rewarding team.

WHILE *SURFIN' SAFARI* KEPT BEACH BOY FANS around the Pacific Rim and beyond enthused through the first half of '63, instrumental groups on the local Dot label—the

Chantays from Santa Ana ('Pipeline', going to #4) and the Surfaris ('Wipe Out', #2) plundered the top of the hit parade. The Surfaris' driving performance made famous the drumming of Ron Wilson (no relation), *the* test for aspiring teenage garage-band beaters the world over. And he won a solid following for his nasal vocal on the humorous flipside, 'Surfer Joe'. They cut a minor hit in 'Point Panic' at the end of summer and later covered the Beach Boys' 'Karen' and 'Don't Hurt My Little Sister', but their one remaining success of any note would be a top ten reentry of 'Wipe Out', out of place in a distant summer three years into the future.

Late in January the Beach Boys recorded 'Surfin' USA' with full regalia and paired it with a hotrod song to follow up '409'— 'Shut Down'. Issued as a double-shot March 4th, three weeks later they formed with medium-tempo girl tributes 'Farmer's Daughter' and 'Lana' the basis of a new album. The car songs were intended for the vast hinterland centered on Chicago, bordered in the north by Toronto and Montreal, in the south by Dallas and Houston. Here they were greeted like shamans that might bring the sunshine back from the depths of winter. Ironically a holdout in this Bermuda Shorts Triangle where all Beach Boy offerings were voraciously sucked up by a vortex, the Motor City buffered itself against outside acts that might be passing fancies. Its high density of black record buyers stayed faithful to gritty r&b—uneasily absorbing its lightened-up homegirls the Supremes, then coming home to Soul girl Aretha Franklin. Detroit lapped up Beach Boy albums as elsewhere, but fully relaxed its reserve only as the boyish cherubic visage wore off and they proved themselves in a tougher groove as the Sixties wore on.

One last gesture to small beginnings—a backward glance and maybe a wistful wave by Brian, who had won some acceptance from officialdom singing solo out front of school assemblies—was playing the Hawthorne High School Valentine's Day Dance. It was no real loving gesture to an institution that had been more of a juvenile penitentiary to Dennis and Carl, and that Brian had long outgrown, enduring ridicule from meathead jocks discomfited that he had given up football for falsetto.

That month, Capitol took on Dick Dale too as a client. Unfortunately the prophet of surf music never captured his Rendezvous Ballroom vitality on record—his career limited from the outset. The Beach Boys, in introducing surf-and-hotrod music to the world, set about confirming their hegemony over what would be the most popular genre of American music for the next indeterminate number of decades: rock'n'roll.

The Beatles, after a couple more trips to the Star-Club in Hamburg over November-December supporting American instrumental group Johnny & the Hurricanes, complete a short tour the first week of February 1963 supporting their country's top female star, Helen Shapiro. In between they have cut ultimately epochmaking discs in the studio thanks to their Parlophone team. Within two weeks high-flyer Shapiro will be in Nashville recording in front of the Jordanaires, Elvis Presley's backing vocalists—but in a typical move corruptive of American music the sessions are produced by Cliff Richard mentor Norrie Paramor. It is a sharp lesson for the Beatles, whose UK recordings are saved by American engineers at Capitol injecting them with concentrate of rock'n'roll.

In a rush to avoid having 'How Do You Do It?'—another track recorded with 'Love Me Do' three months before—put out as their second single by George Martin, John Lennon has roughed out a tune. Disappointed by the considerable catalogue of songs Lennon and (mainly) McCartney have written over five years in music, Martin picks the best of what he considers a poor bunch. In changing it here and there and speeding up John's Roy Orbison-like ballad, he gives 'Please Please Me' back to the group to record, on January 11th. That evening the group makes its nationwide tv debut on 'Thank Your Lucky Stars' singing the song, which is released across the UK the following day. As insurance Martin signs to his label a Manchester fivesome, the Hollies—of more practised, professional musicianship. To Martin, new to recording pop music, the field is littered with dubious talent. But whichever group comes out top he is wedded to the Beatles' winning personalities.

Aired on the UK's number one rating tv show, 'Please Please Me' is a (disputed) no.1. 'How Do You Do It?' makes it, topping for four weeks—but as recorded by another Liverpool group in the Brian Epstein stable, Gerry & the Pacemakers, just as hot in the UK. A month after their second 45 they record their first album on February 11th, taking a day off touring. Only Paul, beginning to act as musical director for the group, takes an interest in what goes on in the control booth over the 13-hour stint. In March the Beatles begin a tour starring visiting teen idols Tommy Roe ('Sheila') and Chris Montez ('Let's Dance'). Outmania-ing the US stars, they are switched to headliners.

At KFXM-San Bernardino April 12th, the day 'From Me to You' is released in Britain as their third single, 'Surfin' USA' is at no.1 for its third week and its album too is tops. 'Please Please Me' by "The Beattles" heads "The Wax to Watch" below top 40 then disappears. They sell an audited US total of 7,310 copies with an additional 180 in Canada (Paul White in Pritchard & Lysaght). Pushing them is Vee-Jay, a thriving black-owned label out of Chicago. Huge in r&b, its stars are Gene Chandler ('Duke of Earl'), Jerry Butler ('Moon River', a Grammy-winning recording acclaimed by its writer Henry Mancini), Betty Everett ('The Shoop Shoop Song—It's in His Kiss') and the world's currently hottest group, the Four Seasons. Attaining their third number one, 'Walk Like a Man', introducing a tougher, genuine rock sound, the Seasons reach a career goal and retire to the Mecca of 'adult' live performance: a nightclub season at New York's ritzy Copacabana.

Capitol of Canada, issuing 'Love Me Do' in early February to stark indifference, pores over British EMI singles passed on by its US overlord, Capitol in LA. In the past six months it has begun releasing Frank Ifield, Helen Shapiro and now Cliff Richard, all British EMI artists ultimately rejected by America. Now in spring 1963 Capitol of Canada takes on a mounting invasion of British acts. Gerry & the Pacemakers, Freddie & the Dreamers and Billy J Kramer & the Dakotas all chart north of the border before the Beatles (Encyclopedia of Music in Canada), the Brits' growing familiarity contributing to the eventual conquest of North America. The Beatles *benefit enormously from this back door diplomacy into the huge US market—after more persistent and much greater efforts spent on their behalf tips the scales in their favor.*

Performing at the New Musical Express Poll Winners Concert on April 21ˢᵗ, the Beatles take in the show at the Crawdaddy Club and meet the resident band, the Rolling Stones. A week later the Stones will meet Andrew Loog Oldham here, the young go-getter who will create their image of sneering offhandedness and make them the envy of John Lennon. The Beatles are well ahead in the showbiz stakes, on May 13ᵗʰ second to Del Shannon on the bill at London's Royal Albert Hall for broadcast by the BBC.

*S*URFIN' USA WAS A LIGHTNING STRIKE FOR THE Beach Boys, for rock'n'roll, for popular music and for youth everywhere—the first value-for-money album since Elvis went AWOL from rock three years before. The title song, like its predecessor, appealed by romanticising the lifestyle of a specific time and place: circa 1962, the Southern California coast—from Rincon and the Ventura County Line at Santa Barbara in the north, on to Pacific Palisades through LA's Malibu, Manhattan and Redondo, and Haggerty's turning east past Long Beach and Sunset, then south again along "Surf Route 101" past Laguna, Doheny, Trestles and as far as San Diego County's San Onofre, Del Mar and La Jolla almost astride the Mexican border. They catered for the international audience: The previous summer's safari had taken in Hawaii and Peru, replacing the original demo's South Africa, and now there were Waimea Bay in Hawaii and Australia's Narrabeen. Youth around the world couldn't visualise juarachi sandals but loved the sound of them, and envisioned a bushy blonde hairdo on the girl next door.

Unlike the Beach Boys' previous big hit, it didn't offer surfing as simply an engrossing hobby but as an ideal, tonic lifestyle remedy for almost all that ails you. Together, their first two signature tunes found a lofty place in posterity, chosen in 1997 by Rolling Stone magazine's critics' 48 greatest songs of the Sixties. Beyond 'Surfin' Safari' written and first recorded a full twelve months before in the mode of Chubby Checker r&b, 'Surfin' USA' struck out into something new, two steps past the old Fifties rock'n'roll. It positively rumbled with Brian's pounding bass and Carl's confident rampage on lead guitar — right from his crackling intro, with Dave filling in twitchy strokes most audible at the end. Maybe best of all were Denny's imaginative snare and tom-tom variations, perfectly attuned to the recording's frantic pace and mood and performed better than Hal Blaine could have; his throbbing bass-drum beat propelled the track from start to finish. The middle instrumental break went further too, led by a high-pitched organ assertive and confident into a gutsy guitar solo. All were buoyed by Mike's high-school-dropout vocal kicking sand in the face of authority— the teacher—to go surfin'.

It had more touches of sheer music magic than any song that year. Openly adapted from Chuck Berry's 'Sweet Little Sixteen' melody—not a straight copy, as always insisted by Brian—it was radically redesigned from an old-fashioned countrified shuffle to a quickened rock beat and sustained by a jinking rhythm guitar pattern instead of Berry's simple strumming. It was 'black' enough to post #20 on Billboard's r&b chart. So, rearranged as it was from a tame, even quaint ditty, the new song justly garnered immortality way beyond the original—a rock anthem that continues to sell and ring bells on the radio for generations of listeners. Berry sued to, ludicrously, become sole credited writer, taking some of the glory and all of the royalties—when instead he should have thanked Brian Wilson for breathing everlasting life into a limp original. (On this basis Berry should have given full credit to Wynonie Harris for 'Reelin' and Rockin''—rendered by Berry almost word for word and note for note from 1945's 'Around the World', and Dave Bartholomew all royalties from 'My Ding-a-Ling', hardly adapted from 'My Bell'. Bereft of the creative imagination expected of one of rock's all-time greats, Chuck's upcoming 'No Particular Place to Go' was identical, but for new lyrics, to his previous 'School Day'.)

The quantum-updated production made an art of recording in a way that hadn't been conceived before, developing parallel with Phil Spector's studio work. Previously, apart from experiments with 'echo' and other isolated sound effects, a faithful reproduction of a performance was the most that could be hoped for. Now, over and above Spector's aspirations, the spirit and pace of rock'n'roll was injected into the mix to concoct an infectious cocktail and effectively kick off a new modern genre.

'Surfin' USA' rose to #1 and stayed there in LA, San Francisco and California's secondary centers Sacramento, Bakersfield, San Bernardino; Philadelphia, Boston and elsewhere in the Northeast—Hartford, Syracuse and the Scranton tri-cities area; Dallas, Toronto (CKEY). In places where it was a weekly runner-up it was still one of the year's biggest hits—Miami, Montreal (CKMG). In all-important New York City it made #5 (probably why it didn't quite make top nationally) and spent a career best fifteen weeks in the top 30 of WABC's sales chart; #3 at Chicago's WCFL, but muted across Midwest expanses in favor of the preferred flip. Nationwide it was rivalled by teen crush 'I Will Follow Him' and 'Puff (the Magic Dragon)'—Peter, Paul & Mary, on May 17th winning kudos at the first Monterey Folk Festival with Bob Dylan, Joan Baez, Pete Seeger and the Weavers.

At the end of the year the Beach Boys were assessed by Billboard to have outsold these and some twenty other songs that topped the magazine's weekly charts, second only to Jimmy Gilmer & the Fireballs' sub-bubblegum 'Sugar Shack'; this and 'Hey Paula' by Paul & Paula were reputed to be the only single *sides* to sell over a US million in depressed 1963. Taken with its B-side the Beach Boy 45 was supreme, confirmed by prominent columnist Earl Wilson the following year. Other sources today put it top too, especially taking into account its long stay in the Capitol catalogue, reissues and sales via Capitol's hyperactive record club. It had climbed to no.2 in Music Vendor, the third big national chart, one place lower in Billboard (which gave it an extra week in the top hundred, 17) and Cash Box. According to Brian, 'Surfin' USA' was Capitol's *fastest* seller up to the Beatles' 'I Want to Hold Your Hand'. On American radio through the years since it has amassed more than two million plays—double those of 'Sugar Shack' and 'Wipe Out'.

The 45 was launched lip-synchronized on Steve Allen's show two days before release, showcased in a hopeful studio mock-up of beach picnics, surfer stomping in a row as mature gals twisted in fringed, one-piece bathing suits—not at all the bouncing, gyrating bikini-clad jailbait called for, that would be supplied for its *TAMI* outing a year and a half later. The juxtaposition with *a capella* dirge 'The Things We Did Last Summer', a recent tiny hit for Shelley Fabares but pitched at the older market *a la* the Osmond Bros, muddied a clear message that here were the new leaders of rock... rock... Rock!

The Beatles' debut album is Please Please Me, *recorded in a one-day session straight, playing as they would live. The album sells 300,000, the title track the same—about half as many as Beach Boy B-side 'Shut Down'. On this small scale America is oblivious to the fact that in their own country the Beatles are all conquering. American progress is limited to 'Please Please Me' appearing in the first week of May one-third the way up the KNUZ-Houston top 50, with 'Shut Down' near top.* Please Please Me *the album stays in the UK top 10 for 62 weeks—their longest residency ever, later almost matched by the Beach Boys—including a 30-week stay at top, only relinquished when its successor* With the Beatles *takes over.*

Beatle manager Brian Epstein, a thwarted theatrical talent, becomes an ambitious theatrical impresario, taking on more top Liverpool groups including Gerry & the Pacemakers, the Big Three and the Fourmost, songstress Cilla Black and a number of complete unknowns. Brian Sommerville, the Beatles' PR man hired by Epstein: "Brian Epstein was charming, pleasant, and shallow: a delightful man, but there was no substance to Brian whatsoever. He was constantly shifting his ground because he was unsure of himself in nearly all his dealings and, of course, in his personal relationships. He would be very involved with someone for a while, but then didn't want to know them"(Salewicz).

On top of John Lennon's secret marriage last year, Epstein's immediate problem seems to be how to keep Paul McCartney's new steady girlfriend, Jane Asher, a secret. It was a truism of the day that male stars must be kept "available" to their female fans.

' SURFIN' USA' UNFORTUNATELY IMPACTED TOO ON the crass sensibilities of pop culture. Just as it arrived in April cheapo movie studio American International announced production of a flick celebrating the beach-loving lifestyle, to star teen smoothie Frankie Avalon and former Mouseketeer Annette. *Beach Party* was bearable fun in itself—and hooked Beach Boys in to appear—but started a desultory trend that culminated in Z-grade horror *The Beach Girls and the Monster*. The world's number one rock'n'roll group was thus associated with this less than exalted new genre of cinema art. It wasn't the American way to shun goofy *kitsch* if it broadened your exposure—it smacked of elitism or snobbishness, even a radical rejection of the capitalist system. But they can be imagined swallowing hard at this choice three years later when wanting to be taken seriously.

A leap up the Hollywood scale, the biggest spring releases were *Cleopatra,* alias Elizabeth Taylor, making a statement in forked asp-tongue eye-liner copied by trendy young things around the world; Alfred Hitchcock's *The Birds*, starting a new mass phobia after *Psycho*'s shower scene; and the second James Bond, *From Russia With Love*—an annual event until Sean Connery tired of it. *Cleopatra* was a lesson in Hollywood *chutzpah*, Fox spending five times what it had on *The Longest Day* to prove to itself it could still create movie magic—the epic that ended epics for a generation. Screen rebels Paul Newman (*Hud*), Steve McQueen (*Great Escape*) and Shirley MacLaine (*Irma La Douce*) entered the box-office top ten stars, paralleling the anti-hero appeal of Jean-Paul Belmondo in France. June 3rd brought the death of Pope John XXIII, and on the 18th cosmonaut Lieutenant Valentina Tereshkova voyaged into space—a quarter century before a semblance of gender equality was bestowed on American women.

Reinforcing the popularity of new instrumentals, the Tornadoes, an English group, latched on to the surf theme and introduced themselves to the American charts two weeks after 'Surfin' Safari' peaked with 'Bustin' Surfboards'. Their Joe Meek-produced Polynesian-rhythmed 'Telstar' emerged the same day, the biggest UK recording in America to date, no.1 for three weeks. Elvis Presley, perched flat-footed on a studio surfboard for *Blue Hawaii*, had already popularized the theme somewhat, and 'Kon-Tiki' (hitting the

UK chart the weekend the Beach Boys formed) by the Shadows, Bill Justis's 'Tamoure' and the Beach Boys' 'Hawaii' followed Polynesian theme and rhythm. The Shadows, stopping just short of Hawaiian guitars, had ruled Blighty charts since 1960 parallel to the Ventures Stateside—giving the lie to the myth that 'surf music' and the music of the Beach Boys are indivisibly linked. 'Pipeline' had impacted and it would be late summer before the Beach Boys made it in the UK—barely top 30 in the New Musical Express alongside 'Surf City' and 'Wipe Out'. Brits showed stiff resistance to the Americans, home acts easily outselling them: Shadows surf-sound instrumental 'Atlantis', the Dakotas' (minus vocalist Billy J Kramer) 'The Cruel Sea' and Billy Fury's crooner 'In Summer'.

Because of *Surfin' USA*'s five instrumentals detractors have chorused "Filler!" with some justice—it wasn't as if voiceless tunes were the band's selling point. Yet it seemed only right to pay obligatory nods to Dick Dale and Bill Doggett, even if they were more like guitar exercises. In comparison, Carl's high-energy, frantic 'Surf Jam' would be a driving force on any album with Dennis the uninhibited surfer in full flight rampant on the skins, whooping it up, Mike punctuating the rhythm with power chords on sax. Forty years later it would feature over an extended soldier-crabs-versus-tide sequence in BBC-TV nature series *Time After Time*. The other self-penned instrumental, Brian's 'Stoked', comes over better too than the three remakes.

While again the two hits bear the main thrust there is real quality in other vocals. 'Lonely Sea', revamped from its demo a year earlier, is a plaintive ballad prefiguring Skeeter Davis's 'End of the World' with its spoken intimate passage. Trite—not surprisingly, written within hours of Brian Wilson and Gary Usher first meeting, but the first of Brian's confessional introspection, achieving a haunting atmosphere. The girl tributes 'Lana' and 'Farmer's Daughter' are sweetly upbeat, the latter rated highly by many, remade by Fleetwood Mac. Minus two of the cover instrumentals the album still had enough in a different world (1969) to rechart.

As 'Surfin' USA' peaked ('Shut Down' trailed by seven weeks) Brian was showing a reluctance to tour—then a gruelling experience and especially for an individual so finely balanced, driving up to 800 miles per leg in a crammed car, youthful hormones trying to run wild, and all under Murry's thumb—enforcing a stern regime of fines for what he deemed misbehavior. Al Jardine, at Brian's appeal, was drafted back into the band, making for an awkward shuffle of instruments and personalities as he took over bass for now, leaving Dave Marks on rhythm guitar. This lineup played through the second week of June on a Hawaiian tour, also backing Dee Dee Sharp— whose current hit was dance song 'Do the Bird' —and Jackie De Shannon, who they took along with them. Amid growing tensions arising mostly from Murry, Marks, just turning 15, was the inevitable casualty and was gone in a few months before release of the third album.

Two events in July confirmed their new status as *the* leaders of Rock. In the first week *Surfin' USA* glided to runner-up spot, staying for a second week on its way to top-selling rock album of the year. Two weeks later Brian's composition and co-vocal 'Surf City' was no.1, moving 1,250,000 copies US. To many radio listeners who never knew the name Jan & Dean it was another Beach Boy hit— coming thick and fast.

Capitol's only number one in 1963 (in fact, since the Kingston Trio's 'Tom Dooley' five years before) was Kyu Sakamoto's 'Sukiyaki', actually 'Ueo Muite Aruko', "Walk with your chin up" — its chosen name catchier by far to Anglo-American record buyers. It too sold a million-plus, eventually, ranked 13th in Billboard's annual sales list, a decile above 'Surf City'. Few singles had been so certified by the RIAA since the inauguration of Gold Discs in 1958. There was only one act Capitol would regularly submit for auditing, the Beatles.

In Canada the double reached the top, as in the equable climes of Australia and New Zealand, where it was a perennial favorite and the whole beach-and-car lifestyle was taking off enhanced by a backdrop of Beach Boy music. It enhanced their name on the Continent— France, Italy, Holland, Sweden; in West Germany it was hit of the year in Rheinland-Pfalz state bordering Luxembourg.

Not only the landlocked Midwest identified with Beach Boy car songs, as Mike Love's rationalisation goes. 'Shut Down', pitting

Denny's new fuel-injected Stingray against a "413", was treated as the A-side in Chicago with four weeks at #3 (WLS) and across Ohio. But also on its own along the coasts it made #5 LA, #8 Miami, the first car song to rev up New York City—#14 at WABC. On the Great Lakes it was #2 in Toronto; in Buffalo, NY one of the ten top hits of the year. The same in Dallas and Houston, the two Texas centers adopting the Beach Boys as faves. It enjoyed a four-month run in the Cash Box sales chart—longer than its A—and in the UPI nationwide survey, after a tour as B in April-May, rose to no.8 on June 24th. Similar in feel to its flip with its dynamic Denny drumming, Carl's fluid solo again gave Mike a chance to blast chords on his saxophone. The song featured ten years later in a piece of filmic sleight of hand in George Lucas's autobiographical first hit about outgrowing school days in the Central Valley, *American Graffiti*: As MacKenzie Phillips (Papa John Phillips' daughter) and Paul LeMat cruise mainstreet wrestling for control of the car radio knob, 'Surfin' Safari' is magically replaced on air by the car song. The girl concludes "The Beach Boys are boss!"

The Beatles' third single, 'From Me to You', is a still bigger UK success, sells 660,000—continuing a pattern of more-than-doubling the previous 45's sales—and tops for seven weeks May-June. A 'Twist & Shout' e.p. moves another 720,000—an unheard-of figure. Their phenomenon prompts North American trade magazines to feature items on the group, marking a high tide in initial interest in the Beatles. The single still stiffs—just not quite as badly as the previous two: 21,126 US and some 240 in Canada (Paul White in Pritchard & Lysaght). It pushes into Billboard's "bubbling unders" for three weeks from August 3rd—this alone indicating greater airplay than its sales warrant—selling most in LA, where it falls short of top 40 as 'Surfer Girl' leaps to the top. Vee-Jay is fatally discouraged, turned down for airplay even locally by the two big Chicagoland Top 40 stations, WLS and WJJD.

For good reason, 'From Me to You' is their last single on Vee-Jay—until the Beatles are manoeuvred to superstardom. Strangely, as the record that did best on its merits, it will be their only pre-Invasion

45 not to make good the second time round riding on their fame. American star Del Shannon, who tours the UK with the Beatles, has commandeered 'From Me to You' for a minor hit, rationalising that they stole his falsetto so this is payback.

The Beatles receive their first big press notice in June from London's Daily Mirror: *John has seriously injured Bob Wooler, Liverpool's top compere and The Cavern's DJ. A big booster of the group, Wooler's misdemeanor is to crack suggestive jokes at a party about John and Brian Epstein's recent vacation together. In the English lad culture gays including Epstein are only tolerated closeted—and homosexual aspersions cast at yourself, not at all. In the next two years Lennon will make an amazing turn around, coloring himself as the intellectual liberal of the group*

The Beatles are big enough at home to call the shots—the exception in British teen culture, with their own BBC radio show named 'Pop Go the Beatles' in that cutesie literary-punning style that will become so familiar around the world. Broadcasting weekly with eight or nine songs, times 15 weeks through summer, the Beatles are able to introduce—and thrash—their own songs to a captive audience in the millions: Private radio is still nine months away and the BBC is the only game in town. How can the Beatles not overwhelm the competition from this vantage point?

Moving on from what they meant as a convenient song-hanger, not a genre—surf—the Beach Boys had made car songs (if another label was needed) so popular that there were demands for a reissue of '409' too. Capitol shrewdly piggy-backed on the group via an anthology dedicated to auto culture, named after their second B-hit but released without their knowledge. The label's habit of springing pleasant and unpleasant surprises alike would one day run awry; already the boys were being lumbered with excess baggage. *Shut Down*, containing by the group only the two car songs, was 'credited' to the "Beach Boys & various"—so in the way of show business any mud flung at the project would stick to the only real stars associated with it. The compilation celebrated such unsung deeds as movie star Robert Mitchum's rendering of 'Thunder Road', the theme song from his cult fatal-crash movie some years before; and four car-tracks by a make-up group called the Superstocks, featuring a youngish Glen Campbell and Leon Russell, heavyweight session musicians who would become much more famous singly later on.

In contrast to this tribute to car worship, which under Capitol's push sold almost as well as the real thing, *Shut Down Vol 2* would be solely a Beach Boy effort and only ostensibly about cars. Their early spring release next year, stuck with a deadend series title but containing some of their best early songs, it would be swamped by a growing tsunami reminiscent of that created by the eruption of Krakatoa—powerful enough to travel around the world three times through the Sixties under the name the British Invasion.

B Y THE TIME OF RECORDING *SURFER GIRL* IN JUNE-July Brian's composing, arranging and producing talents were too obvious even for staid Capitol to deny, and this time he, not Nick Venet, was credited on the label. Venet had left by the time of release, so this was probably less than a change of heart by the company. Brian has described this group move as *leaving* Capitol, which it was in all but name, involving Murry's intercession: "I fought Capitol for four and a half months, straight," resulting in a new contract allowing the group to record their work in independent studios, and accordingly having to pay for studio time and all the extra technical paraphernalia necessary to perfect the sound they wanted.

'Surfer Girl' and 'In My Room', both written years before, were duly revealed by Brian, now able to ensure the right sparkling setting. Emerging a slim ten months after their first album, the title track of their third would be their last surf title, leaving the field free for bandwagon imitators—usually real surfers or hotrodders with all the accoutrements down pat and expecting a creative imagination to flow from that. They would try their damnedest to be Beach Boys for the next three years and never come close to the essence—most missing the point completely.

The 'Surfer Girl' melody remains among Brian's favorites and many others'. Its latest mass airing might be in *Charlies Angels 2*

(2004), for which it was played in its enirety. 'In My Room', according to Usher, was written after a baseball game within an hour. It was the only song they remade for a foreign-speaking market, i.e. the German one: 'Ganz Allein' ('All Alone')—never released.

The two key tracks are sung by Brian—six-beats-to-the-bar blues-style harmony ballads, much in the mode of 'My True Story', the Doo-Wop no.1 r&b hit at the time the Beach Boys formed two summers before, sung by black group the Jive Five. 'Little Deuce Coupe' is Mike singing about his own 1930s model Ford, and 'Catch a Wave' sounds like Dennis with a typical throaty cockiness but it's Mike in hoarse r&b voice. There is similar confusion over 'Hawaii' though 'Surfers Rule' is undoubtedly a Dennis lead with its closing taunt to their rivals: "Four Seasons, you better believe it!"—Brian's falsetto trailing off imitating Frankie Valli's wailing line on 'Walk Like a Man'. The Seasons replied with a send-up B-side, 'No Surfin' Today' about a surfer mourning his lost beach girl. 'Our Car Club' was recorded in tribute to another competitor, at the new Gold Star LA studio employed by Phil Spector, using engineer Larry Levine and Hal "Drummer Man" Blaine. Blaine, a highly respected jazz drummer who would become the most recognisable session instrumentalist in California pop, played on the final cut of 'Surfer Girl', doubled with Dennis on 'Little Deuce Coupe' and would play on many more regardless of Dennis's skills and confident individual style. Blaine in turn would be discarded by Spector, who preferred Earl Palmer's "better time" (Richard Williams, 1972).

Surfer Girl's relatively uncluttered recording schedule—given that the group was averaging an album every four months and would sustain that pace for another three years—allowed for more thoughtful production. The result was a greater variety of treatments accorded to individual songs than on the two previous albums, in reality escaping the surf music idiom altogether. In fact, the emotional songs alienated the hard-assed surfer vote. Mike Doyle, the reigning superstar of surfing, recounted how he and his bros had a good laugh over 'Surfer Girl''s tenderness. The song obviously transcended this Yahoo element to a much broader, enduring audience than your typical surfer's stomp or the do-it-yourself, unplugged Jack Johnsons or Donavan Frankenreiters.

In *Surfer Girl* a wider listenership discovered this tutorial in modern music reproduced sounds of the ocean. The ingeniously realised 'Catch A Wave' musically evoked the sound of surf, right down to Denny's drum intro rendered concisely with four simple raps in standard rock time—three tom-tom, one snare—vividly conjuring an image of a breaking wave impacting. Later, a cymbal crescendo unmistakably represents a pristine, smoothly cresting wave. The album has accrued status as their "best" album overall up to mid-1964, allowing for justly argued preferences otherwise. British critics have tended to argue this way mainly because their literary approach frustrated them at not being able to relate to the immersion in California/surf culture of the first two albums. Admittedly, also, the constant twangy guitar sound of standard surf music comes to grate as much as any similarly narrow style would on those who aren't died-in-the-wool fans. Britons didn't get to decide for themselves on this l.p. until its release almost four years later; nor on the hotrod songs on the forthcoming album, *Little Deuce Coupe,* its issue two years off at the height of the Dylan era.

Summer's end brought the Dave Marks debacle. The way he tells it today the split was mutual. His mother, miffed at Dave's relatively small performing pay (though he got a full share of recording royalties from Capitol), had suffered repeated run-ins with Murry. Wilson Sr., to the chagrin of the band—though Brian and Mike had shown impatience with the boy's immaturity—took advantage of an outburst of temper from Dave, holding him to his "I quit!" uttered in the heat of the moment on tour. Anyway sickening of Murry's references to him as "the little Jew" (he was taller than Murry by this time) and other casual insults, he went into a better job, as he tells it—boss of his own group, Dave Marks & the Marksmen, recording as the only rock'n'roll group on A&M. Murry, from his side, seemed to have no problem with Brian marrying into a Jewish family, or Carl into a Hispanic family for that matter. From Marks' perspective later he credited Murry's acumen in helping to produce 'Surfin' Safari'/'409'. In a television interview soon after Brian said he liked

Dave "as an artist" but that his attitude needed work. And Murry went on to mentor/exploit Dave's new band, while Dave occasionally returned for Beach Boy dates into 1964, singing some leads on stage including 'Louie, Louie' and 'Kansas City'. At home, he and Carl continued their schooling with morning classes at the Hollywood school for showbiz brats, and met sisters Diane and Marilyn Rovell there—soon two thirds of girl group the Honeys. Marilyn, 15, was attracted to Carl as boyfriend material but all too soon would be Mrs Brian Wilson.

Cultural Note: *The upfront-and-personal confrontation between Murry and Dave—frank and over in a minute, leaving the door open for continuing relationships—contrasts with the cloak-and-dagger Pete Best episode, handled by the 'polite' English approach, on the eve of the Beatles' recording career, leading to lasting bitterness (see August 1962).*

By August 1963 Parlophone's sister company under EMI in America, Capitol, has rejected outright the opportunity of releasing all three of the Beatles' singles so far—'Love Me Do', 'Please Please Me' and 'From Me to You'. Senior A&R man Lee Jollet condemns them as "terrible" in the face of mounting pressure from EMI and Brian Epstein in Britain. The first has been discarded entirely in the United States and the second and third, licensed out to Vee-Jay (where Bob Crewe and the Four Seasons are thriving as independents under contract), bombed so badly the company lost money just starting up presses.

Vee-Jay does its best by the group, packaging Introducing the Beatles *for the American market. Their debut US album sells 80,000 or so copies in five months: not at all bad first time up but hardly the breakthrough hoped for. It is not enough to hit the Billboard Top 200 or make a passing name for them in the States.*

With three 45s already judged unlovable it must be a company with an edge that takes on the next Beatle single for release, 'She Loves You'—though it sets a UK record of 1,500,000 shipped to stores in five months, maintaining their more-than-double rule. In the US it is leased out to Philadelphia's Swan Records, part-owned by showbiz heavy Dick Clark. But again, with all Clark's muscle in the industry, "Swan couldn't give it away. I don't think they sold more than a couple hundred copies, which is fewer than you send out to the radio stations for promotion. So the Beatles were pretty well stone-cold dead in the US marketplace" (Dave Dexter, Capitol A&R man).

Murray "the K", New York's star DJ at WINS, after 'She Loves You' comes third out of five in a spin-off judged by audience votes: "Regardless of that, because of the hype that was given to me about this group from England, I played their record for about two and a half weeks, and nothing. No reaction. Absolutely nothing" (both quotes from Pritchard & Lysaght). Neither Dexter nor Kaufman could have predicted the forces marshaling to ensure the Beatles' success in defiance of the public's standing judgment.

In far-flung corners of the British Commonwealth including India, Malaysia, Australia and New Zealand the Beatles' Parlophone records have been highly popular since 'Please Please Me'. Finally in Canada, dominated by the entertainment sphere of influence of its giant neighbor, news of the Beatles' conquest of the home country has filtered through and a fan club started based on their personality cult. Record buyers now go wild over 'She Loves You', and pressing begins seven days a week to catch up with demand. Back in Blighty a nationally distributed fan magazine, this one officially devoted to the Fabs, 'The Beatles Book', has begun printing in August and will continue for years.

Unlike Dave Marks, Al Jardine's ongoing friendship with Brian would see him treated as an equal, though placed on salary, contributing his fair share to the harmonies, and lead vocals on records after a year. Later a serious music scholar, who would castigate Carl for not developing his guitaring prowess, Marks claimed in 1998 to have been "on their first five albums." He is pictured on four, but must have played a very minor role on the fourth— mainly recorded the week after he left—and fifth. But for decades to come he would average $15,000 a year in performers' royalties for what he did play on, still receiving a full fifth. To punish Al for perceived disloyalty to the 'family', Murry until his death divvied up what was once Dave's share of recording royalties between the four blood-family members of the group.

No more than a gentle swirl on the surface of troubled waters showed as the Beach Boys completed their second summer schedule of touring, stretching to an unbroken run over the next 44 years (from Mike Love's point of view, a sole original Beach Boy this millennium). Through September they crisscrossed the country from a fair in chronically depressed West Virginia to small-town Wisconsin, via LA's "Show of Stars" and then back to Sacramento and on to San Francisco's Cow Palace.

At the end of summer the land was abuzz with the news that a 13-year-old "genius" had topped the Hot 100, r&b and album charts simultaneously—the first time ever. Little Stevie Wonder, a blind boy named by a carnival barker, took personal inspiration from Ray Charles, another r&b legend who had just celebrated his own no.1 album. The next that would be heard from the young Motown sensation, apart from a couple of minor hits, was an album a year later, *Stevie at the Beach*, inspired by you know who. It was a recourse a surprising number of black artists would turn to: it was American, it was modern rock'n'roll, and it wasn't as if they could shake their mops to turn on audiences.

THE DOUBLE TAKEN FROM THE NEW BEACH BOYS album repeated the impact of the last, but started a rocker/ballad strategy giving listeners the best of both worlds on one 7-inch slab of vinyl. According to David N Howard in *Sonic Alchemy: Visionary Music Producers and Their Maverick Recordings* (2004), on hearing even Brian's demos from Western Recorders the Capitol execs were "flabbergasted" at the quality. His "triumph of creative independence was not only a personal victory, it was an achievement that would wield a tremendous effect on a whole new crop of young, up-and-coming producers. Within five years, an entirely new breed of California producers would come to the forefront, an explosion that would not have been possible without Wilson's fiercely determined independence"—resulting in Los Angeles becoming the "true" centre of recording, taking over from New York.

'Surfer Girl' stayed #5 for three weeks in Cash Box's national sales chart. Billboard rated it two places lower on its airplay-affected listing and #18 r&b—the Beach Boys' best recognition by black radio stations so far. Their most durable #1 in Los Angeles (four weeks, and three runner-up), at San Francisco Bay's KEWB it was a knockout, six weeks at top. Halfway across country it was the biggest song of the year too in Dallas-Ft Worth, with potential surfers and surfer girls gazing longingly at desert sand dunes. Non-surfers around Delaware Bay made it the group's biggest ever song on legendary WFIL-Philadelphia. On the rocky shores of Boston and New England, 'Surfer Girl' was second to 'Wipe Out' that year. It went close to top in Canada's big centers, Toronto and Montreal (where French sensibilities took its album to no.1), high too in the Twins and Pittsburgh, PA—helped by sidewalk surfers? —and the deserts of Tucson (KTKT), Wichita (KWBB) and West Texas: that ocean-and-bikini imagery working its magic again.

'Surfer Girl''s last week at peak in Cash Box, October 5th 1963:

1.   Blue Velvet—Bobby Vinton
2.   Be My Baby—the Ronettes
3.   Sally, Go Round the Roses—the Jaynetts
4.   My Boyfriend's Back—the Angels
5.   Surfer Girl—the Beach Boys
6.   Then He Kissed Me—the Crystals
7.   Heat Wave—Martha & the Vandellas
8.   Cry Baby—Garnet Mimms & the Enchanters
9.   Busted—Ray Charles
10.   Sugar Shack—Jimmy Gilmer & the Fireballs

It suffered from a less than spectacular reception in Chicago (#7) and a mild one indeed in New York (#15), though given its rave reception almost everywhere else hardly enough—one would have thought—to drag it down nationally. The UPI nationwide survey rated it 4-7-11-6-8-4-3-4-5 from August 19th to October 13th, peaking behind the Ronettes and Jaynetts.

Facing divided loyalties of record-buyers and radio-listeners over the sides, preventing both songs from reaching the nation's top spot, 'Surfer Girl' was pipped by heavily one-sided girl-group hits with throwaway flip sides—all but 'Then He Kissed Me', which the Beach Boys would adapt two years later. The vagaries of split airplay and sales frustrated Brian and infuriated a constantly uptight Murry in the quest for a US Number One.

Sales of each side of a double-sided hit continued to be scored separately in the US until late in 1969 after George Harrison's 'Something' had stalled for three weeks on the edge of the top ten before curiously leaping to #3 where it rested for two weeks; B-side 'Come Together' had peaked at #2, then fallen to #7. Billboard obligingly lumped them together the following week to give the Fab Four another *two* chart-toppers out of nothing: one innovation the Beatles were indisputably responsible for.

'Little Deuce Coupe', transparently r&b rock and a cousin of the Coasters' 'Young Blood' but less black, placed in the national r&b 30 too. Their only flip to make Billboard's pop 20, it drove higher in the UPI, no.6 on one national pop chart (an EMI source, 1973)—and their first to claim a million sales, moving well anywhere kids dreamed of hotted-up cars, driving into Australasian and Parisian top tens alike— 20th biggest of French hits in 1963. Stateside it went to #1 in San Francisco (KYA, two weeks) and Hartford, Connecticut; first runner-up St Louis and Louisville; same Dallas and Miami, in the year's twenty top hits in both regions, and Boise, Idaho. Cruising to #5 Washington DC and Montreal (CJMS), #7 in Chicago, 'Deuce Coupe' would with 'In My Room' join that select group in broadcast music history of Bs played on American radio stations more than a million times.

It might have been in Australia, in whose masculine culture surfing was seen as something mystic and girls as something remote, that 'Surfer Girl' began to take on its spiritual quality. A Beach Boy concert wouldn't seem complete without it, and decades later Brian Wilson would liken its cosmic love appeal to Paul McCartney's 'Let It Be'.

With a liberal president came great expectations from 'Negro' citizens, and targeting of the Kennedy brothers by archconserva-tive interests. In August Martin Luther King led the civil rights rally in Washington DC and gave his "I Have a Dream" speech. September, three members of hate group Ku Klux Klan—the last not convicted until May 2002—bombed the 16th Street Church in Birmingham, Alabama, killing four girls. Two months afterward President JFK himself would be murdered. It was a fertile time for political activists, not least for popular folk songwriters and musicians protesting against current events.

The Beach Boys kept their music stubbornly apolitical in favor of the spectrum of human experience. Even personal politics, reliving private enmities soap-opera style that Bob Dylan and the Beatles got into, were shunned for raw emotion: *primal weeping*, a therapy in music. Beach Boy imitators avoided human relations entirely for the mechanics of male pastimes. LA inbreeding meant that Gary Usher, Roger Christian, Jan Berry, Terry Melcher, Bruce Johnston, Randy Newman (tv theme *Monk*) and team P F Sloan & Steve Barri recycled most surf and hotrod music over the next two years in roles as writers and/or producers/performers. Usher performed on and produced for the Surfaris and Hondells. Melcher, Johnston and Christian were just as ubiquitous. Johnston had been in bands with Phil Spector and Jan & Dean in the late fifties and in 1963, going on 19, was leader of his own recording band (details from Timothy White).

September, and the Beatles win a Variety Club award as their country's top vocal group. October 13th the Beach Boys' new car album has been in shops six days—and the Beatles appear on UK tv's popular 'Sunday Night at the Palladium' to a bigger captive BBC audience than ever—15 million. Shrieking over them ascends to a new magnitude that can only be called Beatlemania. In France too, where observers have been puzzled about talk of the Beatles' 'new' hairstyle, their records begin to take off. Two weeks after the Palladium event America's favorite Englishman of the moment, Anthony Newley, a middle-aged Broadway star, issues his (thankfully) inimitable Cockney version of 'I Saw Her Standing

There', about seduction of a 17-year-old girl. The Beatles return from their first publicized overseas tour, of Sweden. At the airport Beatlemania in full screech is witnessed by showbiz czar Ed Sullivan and wife. Knowing nothing of their music, he knows hysteria in any language is good box-office and determines to book them for his huge weekly tv variety show as one of his foreign curiosities from Continental culture along with the usual Italian puppeteers, French mime artists, Cossack dancers, Bavarian lion tamers, Bohemian tumblers, Slovenian spinning-plate balancers....

Paul McCartney is now established in London society, living with teenage Jane Asher and her well-to-do family including older brother Peter—both well-known juvenile actors. Writing songs for Liverpool acts Cilla Black and Billy J Kramer & the Dakotas, McCartney is in the social whirl attending their recording sessions and concerts to lend moral support, and be seen. Gifted to the Rolling Stones is their first big hit, 'I Wanna Be Your Man', co-written to order after bumping into them one evening by John and Paul, in ten minutes— which doesn't even begin to convey its banal ineptitude.

The Beatles line up 4ᵗʰ November in the Royal Variety Performance, an English institution crowning the Music Hall and Pantomime season. They ooze personality and, playing to the Royal Box, John boyish-charms the upper crust in the audience—and thus the rest of this class-bound kingdom—by cheekily urging "Those of you in the cheap seats clap your hands, the rest of you just rattle your jewellery." They are cuter than ever but this goes down in Beatle mythology as a daring piece of social rebellion with the wit of a Peter Sellers thrown in. That day Bob Dylan, now hailed as a supreme folk artist worthy to take over the ailing Woody Guthrie's mantle, plays New York's hallowed Carnegie Hall. Few screams are heard.

TO CASH IN ON THE WANING SURF SEASON CAPITOL has issued a new auto-themed l.p. just three weeks after Beach Boy fans were first treated to *Surfer Girl*, accordingly halting in its climb of sales lists on hitting top ten—a marketing strategy hardly designed to showcase the group's best new music or enhance their career. It is one of many occasions that Capitol crowds major releases within a month. This one was what Carl Wilson and others have called the first concept album, years before becoming *de rigueur* as a Beatle brainchild. *Little Deuce Coupe*'s recycling of title track and yet again of '409' and 'Shut Down' paid off for the label at the expense of what would have been a good double in 'Catch A Wave'/'Hawaii'—neither issued even as Bs. Now there opened up a yawning five-month gap between singles. To Capitol's satisfaction the car album—Brian anxious for it to extinguish memories of *Shut Down*—sold even quicker than *Surfin' USA*, indicating skyrocketing numbers in the album-buying public in the seven months since. It did well enough in under two months to claim 6th spot on Billboard's end-of-year list (closing at the end of November) of biggest-selling rock l.p.s.

"The latest 'hot rod' fad in music is nothing more than rock'n'roll rhythm with the beat in the exhaust. Even so it's much better than some of the junk passed off on the record-buying public for many years but not quite as imaginative as surf music. Leading purveyors of hot rod are The Beach Boys, who offer a number of good selections in LITTLE DEUCE COUPE (Capitol ST 1908)"—UPI release from New York, November 24th 1963, William D Laffler, 'Latest Fad is Rock'n'Roll'.

Little Deuce Coupe had little if any filler. 'Cherry Cherry Coupe', written as 'Land Ahoy' the previous year, was of single standard while 'Custom Machine' recorded by Bruce & Terry, 'No Go Showboat' by the Timers (Brian again on vocal support), and 'Car Crazy Cutie' *were* issued as 45s, the last in disguise under the name 'Pamela Jean' by the Survivors, a lineup concocted by Brian. The weepy 'Spirit of America', a love song addressed to Craig Breedlove's land-speed-record-breaking jet-powered car that tore up the Utah salt flats like a grounded X-15 rocket plane, would a decade later front a highly successful compilation album. 'Ballad of Ole Betsy' lamented a love gone horribly wrong: "She may be rusted iron, but to me she's solid gold..." And James Dean's fatal car crash was remembered in the *a capella* 'A Young Man is Gone' to the tune of 'Their Hearts Were Full of Spring', a song showing off their live vocal prowess for years to come. It was spiritual-cum-kinky listening but cloaked in appealing Americana. Only later in a cynical era did people ask what the album's creator "was on".

Capitol's recycling of songs has been the subject of complaint from modern commentators obviously ignorant of the accepted practices of the time in the US recording industry. Brian attempted to delay 'Little Deuce Coupe' and 'Our Car Club' for the appropriate car album but the company saw no problem in just repeating them. An extreme example was the policy of Phil Spector's Philles label in 1963. Out of the three Crystals albums issued in the space of a year 'There's No Other', 'Uptown' and 'On Broadway' were on *every* one. Fans who'd somehow missed out could find 'Da Doo Ron Ron' and 'He's A Rebel' for their third outing too on an instant follow-up compilation before the end of the year. The fourth releases of all these songs had thus come within months of their issue as 45s.

The policy materially affected Beach Boy 45 sales, fans seeing they could get the songs on the album instead. At the other extreme it would be Rolling Stones policy by their own admission *not* to include tracks issued as 45s on albums, as a deliberate strategy so fans would have to buy both. The Beatles, painted as nicer than the Stones, did the same but drew a happy face on the practice saying they didn't want to cheat their fans by doubling up on vinyl space—so made them buy all their albums and all their 45s to obtain the full Beatle catalogue.

Brian's other romantic gem preserved from his fertile teenagerhood, 'In My Room', was recorded as a brilliantly moving ensemble vocal featuring the Wilsons replicating the three-part harmonies (now double-tracked for resonant, doubled beauty) Brian had drilled them in years before in their three-way shared room before lights-out. Issued as the next flipside, it became a bestseller internationally. Nationally, it was the highest-flying chart entrant for its week, matching their three A-sides to date. Rising to the fringe below the Billboard twenty on 21st December, it had been no.17 in the nation on December 2nd said UPI. Played as the hit it did best across WRKO-Boston's New England catchment—#1 and 4th biggest record of the year after 'Wipe Out' and the previous two Beach Boy 45s; also topping in San Francisco (KEWB), Seattle (two weeks at KJR);

in the ten in Houston, Minneapolis, Vancouver, Columbus, Pittsburgh. Its success did no justice to its place in Wilson's personal testament or its special identification among fans and non-fans alike. Given orchestral treatment it could have slotted on to *Pet Sounds* three years later as a featured hit. Guessers, like Graham Nash and David Crosby on one occasion, usually gauge its era c.1965— indoctrinated like others to think music so advanced must surely be *post*-Beatles by the later media-led switch-round of who led whom.

An energised, much denser re-recording of parochial 'Be True to Your School' from *Little Deuce Coupe*, an infectious conformist jocks' fight song, was deemed A-side over 'In My Room' by America's 'positive-thinking' national psyche. Now it was propelled by a marching-band bass drum and punctuated by cheerleading shouts from the Honeys. A thrilling, whistling mellotron solo was added, followed by the obligatory guitar break. All was keyed marvelously to conjure the atmosphere of a senior high school or varsity sports fest, and must be seen as Brian Wilson's first super-special production for its complexity—every effect geared to heighten excitement. Used for propaganda purposes, this stirring accompaniment would outdo that of a Nuremburg rally. LA-San Diego hailed it number one (three weeks at KFWB). Proud as Brian was of "capturing the spirit of competition", it caught Texas's national psyche in spades, going top four in Dallas (KBOX)—and San Francisco, Pittsburgh, Montreal (CKMG), Toronto (CHUM); one lower in Miami.

But it also had the distinction of being shunned by irked New York 'sophisticates' and Detroit r&b snobs—who must have thought its theme far too corny and all-American, lasting just one week top twenty in either city. In some coincidence it leapt twelve places in New York up to #11 on December 24th before wiping out days later on the city's discovery of the Beatles. There was no room in Big Applers' hearts for two groups challenging its Four Seasons. In fact, as the Beach Boys would be in LA, the Seasons were relegated to an afterthought in their home megalopolis. 'Be True to Your School' was popular enough elsewhere to average out to #6 in Billboard the week before Xmas and almost match 'Surfer Girl' in UPI's chart survey for the press: November 18th to January 13th, 10-12-14-8-4-5-10-10-13.

On November 22nd, the day President Kennedy was assassinated, the Beach Boys by audience demand went ahead with a scheduled concert in northern California and their rivals-to-be released their second album, With the Beatles, *recorded over four months. It would go on in the UK to be the first million-selling album, its tracks juggled, deleted and supplemented by Capitol for issue in the US as* Meet the Beatles. *The Royal Command Variety Performance has brought the fancied foursome to the forefront of British show business, and their American dreams are primed to come true. Brian Epstein and George Harrison (visiting his sister) have made research trips to America. New York promoter Sid Bernstein had already, a year before, booked them into Carnegie Hall for February 1964. A spot opens up in the same week on Ed Sullivan's show, taped at the CBS center in the same city.*

In Britain the Beatles have saturation media coverage—the first teen act to be front page news just reporting on their movements. In late November, a month before its issue in the USA, 'I Want to Hold Your Hand' is released and moves a million copies in its first three days. As pets of the Royal family—after their cordial exchange with them—it would be a surprise if it hadn't, as with Elton John's 1997 retread of 'Candle in the Wind' for Princess Di. The group now embodies all that is classy about Britain, and on Fleet Street that means glossy magazine cover-feature material. Their latest hit takes over top spot from 'She Loves You'—their biggest sellers ever for the home audience.

Capitol in the US is prevailed upon for the first time to release a Beatle record, and with way-over-the-top ballyhoo. It's a decision heavied by EMI in the UK. Quality experts, in the form of Capitol's recording engineers, are required only to improve the record they are presented with.

THE AMERICAN FAVORITES BROUGHT THE HOUSE down with their performances, shown by a wild reception for their December 21st show at Sacramento's Civic Auditorium, its taping culled for *The Beach Boys Concert*, comprising a selection of their first two years' of hits and tributes to other acts: Chuck Berry's 'Johnny B Goode', current Southern California r&b hit 'Papa-Oom-Mow-Mow' by the Rivingtons, and Dennis's rendition of Dion's 'The Wanderer' (Brian taking drums more than competently) hyping his image: "Well, I'm the type of guy who'll never settle down. Where pretty girls are, well you know that I'm around. I hug 'em and I squeeze 'em 'cos to me they're all the same..." From this concert comes the treasured Fred Vail intro of the group to his hometown: "And now [pause for something approaching quiet], from Hawthorne, California [a rising buzz from the crowd], to entertain you tonight [rising still] with a gala concert [a lull, catching breath] and a recording session [shrieks]—The fabulous [half a beat for effect] Beach Boys!", followed by incredible screaming of 5,300 fans. The California state capital, a day's drive from the nearest surf beach, had kept 'Surfin' USA' at top seven weeks and stayed a happy hunting ground for them.

Closing the year, 'Little Saint Nick' was a fanciful song about Santa's souped-up sled akin to 'Little Deuce Coupe' but with its shuffle beat laid back. It deservedly found favor—#3 on the nation's Xmas shopping list, Billboard's new hushed, less-than-festive chart. Still in mourning for the president, the media deemed there was to be subdued good cheer this year so seasonal airplay was much reduced across the country—until the Beatles arrived the day after Christmas with the release of 'I Want to Hold Your Hand'; then it was open slather. The Beach Boys played in Kentuckiana's upper five, ten in Los Angeles, San Diego and Sacramento, and Seattle and Vancouver at the colder end of the West Coast, fringing the twenty in the Twins, Miami and Houston. It returned for years and in the last decade of the millennium listed in Billboard's fifty all-time seasonal songs. An internet Yuletide songs sales site lists it just below the thirty top songs and 'Snoopy's Christmas', and above the collective discs by Eartha Kitt and Madonna of 'Santa Baby', indicating one more unofficial million-seller for them.

They were supreme in North America, Japan, Australasia, Scandinavia. France was showing as their best large European audience, the cultural impact so great that local acts drained much of the Beach Boys' commercial potential. Gallic soloists, bands and girl groups had covered all their hits but 'Be True to Your School'—a very foreign concept to a youth *societé* concerned with *l'amour*, *couture* and *cuisine* as points of honor. Remakes had been released of such unlikely cultural orphans as 'Surfin'' and '10 Petits Indiens'— one of teen idol Lucky Blondo's biggest ever hits. 'Surfin' Safari' was done by Les Fingers. A girl-group foursome of Connie Francis/Brenda Lee/Helen Shapiro lookalikes, the Gams, covered 'Shut Down' as 'Attention! Accident!', and a feminine treatment of 'Surfer Girl' was rendered as 'Ne pleure pas' by a group coyly called Les Celibataires (the Virgins). There came covers of 'Little Deuce Coupe' by both Les Champions and Les Lionceaux, a suave but rebellious (posed cigarette-smoking) five-piece Twist group still with a following this side of the millennium. French-bred but California-styled duo Ron et Mel filled Jan & Dean's shoes— 'Deux Filles pour un Garcon', Brian Wilson's macho rally cry "Two Girls for Every Boy".

Los Angeles was over its first infatuation with its most famous homeboys. A rush of music from actual surfers had come in an irresistible wave but broke by May. To the disgust of many surfers 'Surfin' USA' hit the top (KFWB & KRLA) though *Surfin' USA* spent a sole week top 5 locally, vanquished by Dick Dale & the Deltones and various-artists albums compiled of instrumentals by KFWB. By midyear surfers had been replaced by knockoffs— 'Soul Surfer', 'Surfin' Hootenanny', 'Our Surfer Boys' by LA girl group the Surf Bunnies. Of surf bands only the Surfaris and the Astronauts ('Baja') had big LA hits in the second half of the year. *Surfer Girl* missed and *Little Deuce Coupe* made for one week the top 5 albums.

Others attempted to carry on where the Beach Boys left off, churning out anything related to the latest music-consumer fad: 'California'. Jan & Dean took a sharp S-bend, switching a hitch from the trailblazers' surf board to their running board with 'Drag City', 'Dead Man's Curve'. Bruce Johnston & Terry Melcher incarnated into the Rip Chords with 'Hey Little Cobra', a no.4 million-seller. Marketts instrumental 'Out of Limits' went one higher; the Trashmen's 'Surfin' Bird' and Rivieras' 'California Sun'—no more than raucous caricatures—top five. And California Girl Robin Ward strained to sound like Brian Wilson's now famous falsetto in a female reply song thanking her guy for "the most 'Wonderful Summer' in my life"—a horrendous off-key take on 'Surfer Girl', surely Dot's revenge for the young group being passed up on Murry's approach a year and a half before and making a runaway success of themselves anyway.

These one-off opportunists were lumped together as surf music — a product brand the greedy were making into a full-fledged movement, homogenising the style so that the average punter couldn't pick the nuggets from the slurry. In the year-end roundup at Miami's top-rated WQAM the two biggest Beach Boy hits did not quite as well as 'Wonderful Summer' and 'Surf City', a little better than Frankie Avalon's *Beach Party* theme. Glimpsed behind the scenes are Brian's vain efforts to escape close association. Naïvely, he played along with the gag for a time because it was fun and he never saw it as a genuine *genre* in the first place. As he broke new ground and his group branched out into broader territory unconditional love was hard to come by. And there was an unforeseeable threat that was to change their world and the whole face of show business.

Instead of hailing Beach Boy music as a unique synthesis of rock that would guide many through the decade and far beyond, undiscerning media wallahs lumped it in with their piggy-backees and stowed it under belittling labels that crushed analysis. Lack of precedent set the starmakers' brains a-reeling. What mold to squeeze these kids into? And anyway, come to think of it, isn't this stubborn independence a dangerous trend to set under a major label and shouldn't it be stopped?

The corporate collective beast rarely thinks past the next fiscal year. They'd got away with it up to now but these Beach Boys would fizzle out by themselves in that time like 99% of youth acts, so why worry? If they lasted beyond that, eventually the Anti-Rock Establishment and multifarious radio interests would clobber them as they had Elvis (the Beatles would be much more cooperative). So Capitol showed all the confidence in them that had been shown Philadelphia's *American Bandstand* generated stars by their network producers: Frankie Avalon its first tv season, Fabian/Freddie Cannon the next, then Bobby Rydell, until Chubby Checker challenged the mold—the trick to switch them as a ceaseless line of products groomed to show as much variety as the choice from Malibu Barbie to Prom Barbie, the primary purpose of their music being to fill shelves and pick teens' pockets. When Capitol started pushing the Beatles in December it didn't know if they would last beyond next summer either, so rammed them home to the hilt.

At the end of their first two years Beach Boy fans had a choice of four albums—forty or so songs for every occasion and mood including eleven chart hits. 1963 was surf music's year. In its December 28th issue the record business's Cash Box placed, after topper *Surfin' USA*, the Ventures' *Surfing* 4th in sales, followed by *Shut Down*. Across metro New York NBC network would rank, long term, 'Surfin' USA', Wipe Out', 'Surf City' and 'Surfer Girl' the year's four biggest records. New England, as far away as you could get from Southern California geographically and culturally and still be in the old forty-eight states, shuffled the order, and 'In My Room' pipped 'Surf City'. Up and down California, Texas, Pennsylvania, Florida, Beach Boy records were the most popular on aggregate. In American sales of 45s five unassuming youths from suburbia had boosted Capitol to runner-up to Columbia.

Postscript: In mid 2007 the Pop Culture Madness website, whose business it is to measure ongoing popularity through requests and plays, rates 'Surfin' USA', 'Little Deuce Coupe', 'Surfer Girl' and 'Be True to Your School' ('Surf City' just below them) all in the current top two dozen 1963 songs—way ahead of their nearest challengers, the Crystals and Miracles, each with two listed in the top forty. Elvis has none. The Beach Boys match the durability of their 1962 songs and have truly superseded him. And yet...

John Lennon and Paul McCartney had got together in July 1957 and were joined seven months later by George Harrison to form the nucleus of the Beatles. Through distraction, inaction—18 months when they didn't have any professional gigs—and a series of dissolute sojourns to the fleshpots of Hamburg, it wasn't until the end of 1960 that they built up a visible following in their native Liverpool— but were still just one of many local groups wanting to make good.

Their desultory journey from Tin Pan Alley roots planted by parents and cherished by the genteelly raised John, and Paul, through the skiffle music of Lonnie Donegan—and finally something like real rock'n'roll, has been described in Paul McCartney: Many Years from Now *by Barry Miles (1998). Pre-recording career the Beatles included in their act such fawning showbiz standards as 'Falling in Love Again' and 'Till There Was You', and a version of the Shirelles' sentimental 'Soldier Boy'. Their rock side was represented by a jam on Ray Charles' 'What'd I Say', played at Liverpool's Cavern Club along with the old favorites, depending on what the audience wanted to hear that night and what John, Paul and George had in their piecemeal record collections.*

It wasn't until Brian Epstein, heir to the largest record retailing chain in the north of England, took them in hand as manager, and then George Martin, head of the Parlophone division of EMI, became their recording mentor, that they made any strides towards wider success. And now, with these two brilliant show business minds behind them, and seemingly all the luck in the world falling right in their lap at just the right points in time, world adulation was virtually assured.

The Beatles first met with and tested for George Martin 6th June 1962—coincidentally the 18th anniversary of the original D-Day and two days after the Capitol division of EMI had released 'Surfin' Safari' in the States. Their debut album, Please Please Me, *came out in Britain near the end of March 1963—the same week that* Surfin' USA *was issued in America. If it wasn't apparent that the Beach Boys were being dogged by unseen forces on the opposite side of the Atlantic, by New Year of 1964 it certainly was.*

Walter Shenson, producer of the two Beatlemania movies, A Hard Day's Night *and* Help!: *"I was an American living in London and felt*

The Beatles' music was typical copycat stuff. Elvis Presley had been doing it and The Beach Boys and so forth. I didn't recognize the nuances and the brilliance of The Beatles until I got to know them and work with them." The Fab Fours' personalities strike again—in spite of unstriking music.

As the Beach Boys made the cover story in Cash Box (January 4th) and having just recorded what would be their biggest seller to date, Capitol has switched to superhyped promotion of a sister-label's act from England, Liverpool to be exact. On a directive from chairman Sir Joseph Lockwood to push export product to America, EMI movers and shakers had lined up the Beatles to replace the Beach Boys, like the network bosses had with the *Bandstand* acts. Only, the American band didn't know when to lie down. Overnight the Beach Boys were relegated to a backup product useful as long as it continued to dominate 'summer' music. The new promotional campaign for the thrice-tried Beatles, to erase the faint traces made by their previous North American failures and set them on the track of acclaim, would cost a sum unheard-of in pop.

In a plea to Capitol and others to stop pigeon-holing his group to maximise exploitation, Brian Wilson announced, "Surfing music is dead. It was just a summer craze for kids on the beach." That summer was two seasons past for the Beach Boys heading into 1964, but the rest of the world, for the next half-century, would have other ideas.

All that was in an undreamt-of, unimaginable future.

3. TWIST'N'SURF! FOLK'N'SOUL!

As the world bleached itself blonde, daydreamed of waxing ironing-boards or bikini lines to go surfin', hitched up its collective swimsuit and pondered on converting the family runabout into a woody or hotrod, the Beach Boys hung ten over a cauldron of pop sounds. The vocal surf sound they invented superseded both Elvis Presley and "The Twist" that had ruled under the perpetual-motion hips of Chubby Checker.

By the time the sizzling Twist tempo simmered down to a 'Mambo Twist' and 'Twistin' USA' those with an ear knew it was time to move on; just as Capitol wouldn't know when surf music passed its prime. By summer '63 when the Beach Boys had left the field Chubby had moved on too—but to 'Surf Party'; and the Isley Bros from 'Twist and Shout' to 'Surf and Shout'. Rock iconoclast Frank Zappa conquered and held the Mexican charts most of that year with 'Tijuana Surf'. For the next four years, as he sustained his creative momentum, the world would not catch up to—but for an idealistic minority, did not want to catch up to—Beach Boy leader Brian Wilson. It had new champions in the Beatles, much better at keeping pace with even the slow, retro-inclined audience.

FATS DOMINO WAS SOLE ORIGINAL ROCK'N'ROLLER to make it with a hit catalogue to the end of 1963. Then he faded, ironically to forge a comeback in the late Sixties showing up the Beatles with raunched-up takes on 'Lovely Rita' and 'Lady Madonna'. Chuck Berry and Little Richard both revived in 1964 after five years of relative obscurity—still with old-style rock'n'roll, as a direct result of imitations by the Beatles.

Shunning the sappy teen idolatry of the Frankies and Fabians, white rock'n'rollers Gene Vincent and Eddie Cochran, were too rebellious to be tolerated by the Establishment though continuing popular in the UK, and especially France, just catching up with the play. Here they were treated as current, even after Cochran was deceased, shown by their huge chart success into the mid-sixties. Closest in toughness—but judged marshmallow enough for vulnerable American teens—were Del Shannon and Dion (DiMucci). Del was far less consistent in the States but, unlike Dion, hugely appreciated in Britain, where he passed as an almost-leather-clad rocker touring there over the Beatles in 1963. His lukewarm cover of 'From Me to You' that introduced Beatle music to America was a comedown after 'Runaway', a couple of soundalikes and his latest, 'Little Town Flirt'. Reduced to remakes, 'Keep Searchin'' kept him alive a year into Beatletime.

Coming from Italian-American Doo-Wop humming on Bronx street corners, Dion by '63 was the most respected of all teen idols in Elvis's trail. 'Runaround Sue'—like Bobby Darin on speed— and even better his convincing r&b growling on 'The Wanderer' and 'Ruby Baby', set new marks for white singers. The complex cyclical harmony-and-percussion of 'Donna the Prima Donna' was an exciting arrangement the Beach Boys would later use. He then attempted Chuck Berry's 'Johnny B Goode'—in too-direct competition with British groups, who had (apart from the Beach Boys) cornered the market on Berry refrains.

While English groups from London, Liverpool, Manchester, Birmingham and Newcastle—and West Coast US groups from Seattle, Portland, San Francisco and LA—merely extrapolated on old forms of r&b and blues, black artists were developing a new form, "Soul", often as African as the original Blues and Gospel. Black singers and musicians in distinctive African form were rarely given the limelight, James Brown & the Famous Flames being the shining exception—in America, not Britain, which has forever cherished its tuneful pop, Beatle music coming to serve as its epitome. A new strength was showing in black music in 1963, building on a base created by Curtis Mayfield & the Impressions, their former lead singer Jerry Butler (often coupled with Betty Everett) and Gene Chandler at Vee Jay and the Isley Bros. All of these were habitually successful on the r&b charts but only fitfully on the pop charts. A whole array of talent at Atlantic/Stax so far undiscovered by the white audience but for instrumental group Booker T & the MGs, and a new direction in girl groups and male vocalists (notably Marvin Gaye and Smokey Robinson) headed by Motown, would change all that. Brown and 13-year-old Stevie Wonder were even now rising to the very top of mainstream pop with hard-out r&b—an initiative effectively stifled and set back years by the Brit conquest of America.

Barred from contributing to black music for obvious reasons, the Beach Boys took r&b rock in a divergent direction over several years, from garage-band rock to psychedelia. The white world of 1963 in which they infused their music was an ill-fitting one dominated by tv's *Bandstand*, the first teen-oriented pop show. Given the setting of their songs' images their music was inevitably dubbed white and therefore middle-class, avoiding any deeper thought on the subject. Chubby Checker, a protégé of Dick Clark (and named by Mrs Clark), the most popular performer in rhythm & blues— was the first 'colored' rock'n'roller to come anywhere near Elvis Presley, dominating the Twist as Elvis had original rock'n'roll. He was made all the more important by Elvis deserting rock for balladeering. Grooving on a rhythm similar to the dormant Little Richard, Chubby was arguably the biggest contemporary influence on the Beach Boys in their formative stage.

'The Twist' was huge in America and after 'Let's Twist Again' it came back even bigger. In Britain the four big twist tunes (including the watered-down 'Twisting the Night Away' and 'Peppermint Twist') hit in a bunch early '62, leaving Frankie Vaughan and Petula Clark to carry on with minor entries. Afterward Chubby was hardly heard from there, bowing to Pat Boone's milksop twister 'Speedy Gonzales'. In fact, Chubby's genuine 'Twist' had been considered far too raucous for English ears on first release and missed top ten on re-release. No wonder English reviewers had no taste for 'Surfin' Safari'—they couldn't recognise r&b authenticity when they heard it. The Brits preferred their own diluted covers of Twist songs, and their r&b groups were still infatuated with long-gone Lonnie Donegan and rockabillies Gene Vincent and Eddie Cochran. It was fitting as per the cyclical nature of pop culture that, after Cash Box named his 'Limbo Rock' top hit of '63 and then years in rock'n'roll revival shows, Chubby returned with a version of 'Back in the USSR', written by Paul McCartney for the Beatles, but sounding like the Beach Boys.

The American group's special aspirations were later summed up by Chapple & Garofalo in *Rock'n'Roll is Here to Pay* (1977): "The surfing music that appeared in the early sixties should not be seen as just another fad that softened rock'n'roll. Rather it was a precursor to the psychedelic and underground progressive rock of the sixties. Several of the important people involved in surfing music—especially the Beach Boys ('Surfin' Safari', 'Surfin' USA', 'Surfer Girl') and Lou Adler, one of the first producers of Jan & Dean, became central figures in sixties rock. Surfing music represented an authentic West Coast rock'n'roll culture that differed in one important way from earlier rock'n'roll produced by urban blacks and Southern rockabillies: it was made by middle-class whites." The Beatles and other British groups of the mid-Sixties attempted to reproduce the earlier rock'n'roll.

Bandstand's update of teen idols—in light of the turn away from solo vocalists to groups wielding their own instruments, a development toward independence diametrically opposed to what the industry wanted—was the Four Seasons, Dick Clark's new favorites from just down the New Jersey turnpike. Modelled on doo-wop vocal quartets and stopping short of adding a drummer meant they didn't qualify as a rock'n'roll band and so appealed to the conservative music industry bosses of 1962-63 as a half-way stop; still desperately seeking an alternative to rock'n'roll, for a while they thought they'd found it in folk music. Self-determining like the Beach Boys, the Seasons recorded in their choice of studio, or rather producer Bob Crewe's—in New York—and did a pressing, distribution and promotion deal with Chicago's Vee-Jay for 16 cents per single—about 21%, around sixty times what the Beatles were now getting from their songs licensed to the same label. One estimate of Four Seasons career sales is 175 million worldwide.

Under Crewe they showed just the right combination of toughness and sophistication in the studio, described as "technically brilliant" by an English reviewer who visited them, though in person up against laddish English *boys* came across as overly mature squares though hardly older than the Beatles or, especially, Stones. It was an image that would hamper them all too soon, considering the assets they drew together to offer Pop, combining modern r&b —hear departing member Nick Massi's vocal arrangement of 'Ain't That a Shame'— with Tin Pan Alley, often employing composers Denny Randell & Sandy Linzer ('Let's Hang On', 'Working My Way Back to You', 'Opus 17'). Their arranger, Charles Calello, incorporated classical touches on piano and harpsichord to add Noo Yawk class. Keyboard player Bob Gaudio was sole or main writer of breakthrough no.1 'Sherry', 'Marlena', 'Dawn (Go Away)', 'Big Man in Town' and 'Beggin'', and created with Crewe 'Big Girls Don't Cry' and 'Walk Like a Man', 'Save It for Me', 'Ronnie', 'Rag Doll' (their biggest gobally) and 'Bye Bye Baby', later blanded out by the Bay City Rollers.

F EW SOLO STARS—THOUGH THE SEASONS' FRANKIE Valli was distinctive and well enough known to be a teen idol, and did issue solo discs—continued strong into 1963. Bobby Vee, come from an association with Buddy Holly, from whom he continued the trend of orchestrated pop, was little seen after 'The Night Has a Thousand Eyes' early in the year. Brian Hyland ('Itsy Bitsy Teenie Weenie Yellow Polka Dot Bikini', 'Sealed With a Kiss') returned at four-year intervals: 'The Joker Went Wild' and remaking the Impressions' 'Gypsy Woman'; Lou Christie, emulating Frankie Valli's shrill falsetto and now in the last intake of idols with 'The Gypsy Cried' and 'Two Faces Have I', every three years—'Lightnin' Strikes', 'Rhapsody in the Rain'— then 'I'm Gonna Make You Mine'. Bobby Rydell ('Wild One'), counting as almost a major star for four years, pegged out with 'Forget Him' late '63, as did Johnny Tillotson ('Poetry in Motion', 'Judy, Judy, Judy'), a prolific but minor 'idol', with 'Talk Back Trembling Lips'. Rick Nelson, a rock'n'roll stylist cum teen idol who featured top-notch backing musicians, bowed with a bossa nova treatment of 'Fools Rush In'.

Urban-Italian-sweet Connie Francis ('Everybody's Somebody's Fool', 'My Heart Has a Mind of Its Own', 'Where the Boys Are', etc) and country-Georgia-sassy Brenda Lee ('Sweet Nothin's', 'I'm Sorry', 'Dum Dum') remained top teen princesses, each mounting nearly twenty top 20 US hits—and then their head-to-head contest came to a dead halt. While '63 was a great year for Brenda—two international multimillion-sellers in 'All Alone Am I' and 'Losing You', the belter 'My Whole World Is Falling Down'—her last real big one, 'As Usual', was leaving the charts as the Beatles landed. That was really the end. Connie treaded water in beach movies (*Follow the Boys*), and Brenda—succeeding Connie—retained her Cash Box world's top female vocalist crown for two more awards, but it was only the wan impact of their British equivalents that enabled the two to stay recognised names, just submerged under the new group scene.

Connie Stevens and Annette Funicello, recording actresses, were their runners-up in popularity polls. Precocious acting talent Patty Duke, with her own teen sitcom, would succeed them in the pop market and last four hits. Big for a while in '63 were Marcie Blane's 'Bobby's Girl', Skeeter Davis's 'End of the World' and melodramatic 'I Will Follow Him' ("wherever he may go") emoted by Little Peggy March, all following up award-winning 'Johnny Get Angry' from Joanie Sommers the year before. All were one-shots until Lesley Gore ('It's My Party', 'Judy's Turn to Cry', 'You Don't Own Me') made the teen girl vein her own.

Virtually all teen idols, female and male, were gone *before* the arrival of the Beatles—thanks to the dominating presence of the Beach Boys and Four Seasons driving the pop industry away from sometimes puerile, often sentimental, mush into a much tougher group-oriented scene. In the new world of male groups, alternately male rights were demanded and male longing for "the right girl" was openly expressed. All had melted away, that is, but for the resistant strain of Bobby Vinton, in America; and Gene Pitney, more popular ex-USA.

Pitney hit through movie themes *Town Without Pity* and *The Man Who Shot Liberty Valance*, ending '62 in 'Only Love Can Break a Heart', a no.2, backed by jukebox favorite 'If I Didn't Have a Dime'—as big as he ever got in America though through '63 he continued to define Sixties pop: 'True Love Never Runs Smooth', 'Half Heaven, Half Heartache', upbeat 'Mecca' and signature tune 'Twenty-four Hours From Tulsa'. All fell short of top ten but by now a superstar in Britain he switched to suit the market from the

Bacharach-David writing team to big ballads 'I'm Gonna Be Strong' and 'Looking Through the Eyes of Love' from Spector favorites Mann-Weil. His pseudo-operatic pleading style hit a chord worldwide. Spending a deal of time in the UK with publicist Andrew Loog Oldham and thus the Stones and other new figures at the centre of the industry, he came to adopt, and was adopted by, the British Invasion with trans-Atlantic sounds 'It Hurts to Be in Love' and 'Last Chance to Turn Around'. But while staying a fixture there—'Princess in Rags', 'Backstage', etc—he also sank with the Brits.

The new Bobby had only been around a year ('Roses Are Red') but dominated second-half-of-'63 charts: 'Blue on Blue', 'Blue Velvet', 'There! I've Said it Again' all reaching top and spanning into Beatletime. Sticking to slow, melodious Easy Listening as a sort of white Johnny Mathis, he went all the way again with 'Mr Lonely' (hear the dire rehash c. 2005) but stuck fast in glutinous remakes thereafter. Like Mathis, he defied the trends— and uniquely for a teen idol scored better in sales than in airplay. But the fact that the Brits ignored him made him an anachronism, never figuring in the development of Sixties Music.

Vinton's sentimental sweetness and total lack of rock impetus— a male Patti Page—kept sleepy Middle America in the Fifties, though strangely well in tune with the sentimental Beatle ballads everpresent through the Sixties. Of Middle European extraction, nicknamed the Polish Prince, his Polka-paced melodies brought out the Old World tradition the Beatles were so fond of. Vinton's album *Tell Me Why* revealed his affinity with many Lennon-McCartney tunes. He carried the stream of comfortable-sweater Bobbys to Bobby Goldsboro mid-decade, on to *Shindig* resident Bobby Sherman—Las Vegas style, not hinting even at the cleaned-up version of "rock and roll" but successfully passed off as such.

F RUSTRATING REAL ROCK'N'ROLL FANS, SICKENING from the milk-sop diet served up by their elders, lounging in the way of energetic, progressive sounds on the radio were single-shots Steve Lawrence ('Go Away Little Girl'), Japanese torch singer Kyu Sakamoto ('Sukiyaki'), proto-bubblegum 'Sugar Shack' (Jimmy

Gilmer) and sanitised brother-and-sister acts Nino & April, Dale & Grace and pretend siblings Paul & Paula. Novelties that went all the way to the top included comedian Allan Sherman's 'Hello Muddah, Hello Faddah' and 'If You Wanna Be Happy', so-called "calypso-soul". Public inertia had proven immovable by Chubby Checker, already fading, and would be by any but the most attractive figures to the most buyers, sporting unprecedented novelty value and covering all genres, primed and detonated by industry powers. Namely, in one package, the Beatles.

From on high descended a world phenomenon as the first contender, monopolising the six weeks from Kennedy's assassination to the Beatles' second coming. 'Dominique' was a folk song rendered entirely in French by "The Singing Nun", who also wrote it, a.k.a. Belgian Sister Luc-Gabrielle, a.k.a. Soeur Sourire. She might have been sent by God but her message came in a foreign language utterly meaningless to America. Conspicuously garbed as a sacred image, could the Catholic sister, if properly promoted, have been the savior Americans were looking for on the recent death of Pope John XXIII and the destruction of their own spiritual leader, JFK? Her later suicide suggested depths never explored by the media. Instead, turned into a circus act by entrepreneurs, she was soon extinguished by another impresario-driven European novelty, a rock and roll group who had thought up their own cute name that would go down in history but were called "The Mopheads" by those who would make fortunes off them.

It was certain Elvis wasn't looking like himself—his single sales down more than a third on 1962. His biggie, 'Devil in Disguise', sounded like a movie-filler but no movie promoted it and it sold only 700,000. Movie songs did worse: 'One Broken Heart for Sale', and 'Bossa Nova Baby'. Album sales were hit harder, down to about 300,000 for each US release (figures Peter Guralnick). All but his most faithful Brit fans too were turning away. 'Devil' won a solitary week at top but it was his sole entry in the ten—a steep comedown from the year before when all four singles scored among career best. The first quarter his English counterpart Cliff Richard and the Shadows held top for ten weeks. For the rest of the year Elvis was decimated by the Beatles and Gerry & the Pacemakers—30 weeks at top between them. The best thing about his movies lately was Ursula Andress, Hollywood's latest continental sex goddess coming clinging-wet out of the surf for James Bond to turn Elvis on in *Fun in Acapulco*. No longer considering demanding roles, his manager and the studios colluded in giving his fans all they wanted in Elvis: songs and hokum, nonstop.

A few genuine rock artists found room to bloom, showing through the morass of carnie attractions by creating their own music and/or determining how it was recorded, including Elvis's Texas buddy Roy Orbison. 'In Dreams' from early 1963 had a timeless feel about its production, so endured. Orbison's generosity saw each side of his singles grooved with a classic performance. An unlikely looking star, his trademark dark glasses hid myopic, beady eyes in the middle of anything but chiseled features, like two raisins looking out of a suet pudding. Stock still, gently strumming his guitar, he delivered drama on stage solely through a distinctive voice often reminiscent of Elvis's low down—but quavering, purring and soaring to the heights. 'Dream Baby', that the Beatles had sung on the BBC the year before because 'When I'm Sixty-Four' and 'I'll Follow the Sun' weren't up to it, perfected his distinctive style of country pop tinged with r&b. Months later he put out 'Working for the Man', and B-side 'Leah' was the bigger hit. 'Mean Woman Blues' was one more in his string of million-sellers—not quite as mean as Elvis's and held back by the attention given to great ballad 'Blue Bayou'. He was the only country singer to retain superstardom in 1964—because less country than ever. 'It's Over' could have been done (less dramatically) by Jim Reeves, but 'Pretty Woman' was pure rock.

Johnny Cash was probably best of all: the genuine article, far more convincing as a people's troubadour than Bob Dylan because he'd lived life and sang about it in the simplest, most straightforward way, didn't intellectualize it. Singing from well springs as deep as they come, he was a charismatic performer who happened to choose country & western as his medium of soul-to-soul communication. "The Man in Black" came up with 'Ring of Fire' summer '63, atypical for him in its Tex-Mex feel. Writing in the first person as a spokesman of the unwanted, identifying with a hard-bitten persona, he was mainly silent—maybe dumbfounded— through the upbeat, gimmicky Brit years, to make a comeback at decade's end. By then the Beatles were hailed for writing and recording genuine folk songs about real people—something Cash had been doing since the mid-fifties, and better. Others silenced after the height of that Indian summer were Grammy winners with affecting country ballads, George Hamilton IV ('Abilene') and Bobby Bare ('Detroit City').

Over the radio, on records and from diner jukeboxes distinctive styles grabbed attention. Real artists like Patsy Cline ('Crazy', 'I Fall to Pieces')—the Queen of Country killed in a plane crash in March 1963 (with Cowboy Copas, a boyhood hero of Carl Wilson) —and Loretta Lynn, rarely broke the pop fifty. This in the face of foreign novelties selling a quick million: Anglo-Aussie Frank Ifield and 'I Remember You', the Springfields' 'Silver Threads and Golden Needles' and Aussie Rolf Harris's 'Tie Me Kangaroo Down, Sport'. Facing a growing stranglehold from producer pop, the biggest country-flavored homegrown sellers were Ned Miller's 'From a Jack to a King' and from gingham-pleated songstress Skeeter Davis—but 'End of the World' was disowned by Country Music authorities as too pop.

Like Orbison and a select few others, the Every Bros had a five-year career at the top in America before carrying on in Britain. And here they had been knocked down a peg or two when outmaniaed on tour by their support act, the Beatles. They had not so much influenced the Beatle sound as determined it right down to their tone of vocal harmony, guitar rhythm and lead guitar licks, and the format of Simon & Garfunkel and English duos Peter & Gordon, Chad & Jeremy, David & Jonathan....

IN A NATIONWIDE SURVEY OF US TEENS BY GILBERT Youth Research at the end of 1963 Folk Music was by far the most popular of musical tastes—the participatory, singalong aspect being the decider according to Eugene Gilbert: it only took a campfire to start things off, and the last thing to worry about was individual voice quality. This was the route Ringo Starr took to introduce himself as occasional lead singer with the Beatles. Enquiring who was the most popular singer of westerns in America, he was told Buck Owens, and so set about learning his songs.

Pete Seeger of the Weavers had served his country in World War II and, though frequently banned by America media for raising controversial issues like civil rights, inspired the Kingston Trio and was influencing sixties folkies. The Highwaymen had released *the* massive world hit of 1961 in 'Michael (Row the Boat Ashore)'—a ready standard for Christian-educated school children everywhere. By bringing folk music into fashion they made possible new folk groups Peter, Paul & Mary and later the Seekers, both sustaining huge popularity around the world while remaining acoustically pure when everyone else was plugging in his guitar.

The Kingstons returned with Seeger's protest about the dead of wars, 'Where Have All the Flowers Gone?', and stood against corporate America: "I don't give a damn about a 'Greenback Dollar' —spend it fast as I can. For a wailing song and a good guitar's the only thing that I understand." In May 1963 'The Reverend Mr Black' went up against 'Puff the Magic Dragon', 'Surfin' USA', and in the UK the Beatles' 'From Me to You' and the Pacemakers' 'How Do You Do It?'.

The big new artists, Peter, Paul & Mary, had closed '62 with a stirring rendition of 'If I Had a Hammer'. This and other decent folk songs were coopted and dumbed down by singalongster Trini Lopez: 'Lemon Tree', 'Michael' and more, all to the same pace, for bigger hits: the Johnny Rivers of Hispania—a double whammy out of LA. 'Puff', written by Peter (Yarrow), was huge around the world despite rumors it was a drug fable instead of a children's one. They borrowed from Dylan: 'Blowin' in the Wind' and 'Don't Think Twice'—"It's all right", their last big hit for some years. Others in '63 folk style were 'Walk Right In' (the Rooftop Singers) and 'Green, Green' "on the far side of the hill"—the New Christy Minstrels with Barry McGuire and Kenny Rogers and sounding like the Kingstons.

Peter, Paul & Mary set a tone against show business excess, for musical integrity. And they celebrated Americana: 'This Land is Your Land' from Woody Guthrie. Enough of the hard-working self-discipline and grassroots Americanism of this, and the other trio, the Kingstons, rubbed off on the Beach Boys to make them an anachronism in the trendy era just around the corner. The female-male vocal blend was duplicated by another Greenwich Village folk group, the Mamas & the Papas, to go Hollywood when they got to California.

Folk songs emerging in New Year '64 would be swamped by a first wave of Britons—and pure folk strangled in one stroke as the mainspring of American music. The Beach Boys—'Sloop John B', 'Cottonfields'—would attempt to revive it in rock form. Recognized as standards around the world but hardly fitting the new Top 40 diktats were Tom Paxton's 'Marvelous Toy' recorded by the Chad Mitchell Trio and Pete Seeger's 'Little Boxes'. The year would see just two big folk hits, the Serendipity Singers sounding like the Minstrels on 'Crooked Little Man' ('Don't Let the Rain Come Down'), and New Zealand-born Gale Garnett's declaration of sexual freedom, 'We'll Sing in the Sunshine' ("and I'll be on my way"), astonishingly going all the way in Cash Box; no.4 in Billboard, deferring to much greater airplay given Brit acts. The Beatles had taken over with Boy-Girl Lite.

'Go Tell It On the Mountain' from P, P & M was as telling a performance as ever but stalled under a swarm of Beatle tunes. At the Invasion's height 'Early Morning Rain' barely made the hundred; at its end they must have got some satisfaction in 'I Dig Rock & Roll Music', parodying the Beatles' voices and contrived recording effects. 'Leaving On a Jet Plane', as the Beatles broke up, finally gave them a no.1.

From blonde, full-lipped, wide-hipped, chicly casual Mary Travers came the model for female folk singers—half intellectual, half earth mother; more sensual, less didactic than Joan Baez, admired as much for their poise as their voices. Hers rose to the heights of intensity as the pivot of the group sound. The trio headed the Folk Establishment when Dylan was booed off the stage at 1965's Newport Folk Festival on switching to electrics— "selling out" to Beatleism and a Byrd brainchild.

THE GIRL GROUP SOUND—AND THERE COULD BE NO wider social, economic and musical gulf—was everywhere in 1963. Folk had neglected 'Negro' music evolving into regional styles of Blues: Chicago, St Louis, Memphis, Mississippi Delta, Harlem.... Artists like acoustic bluesman Huddie "Leadbelly" Ledbetter ('See See Rider', 'Cottonfields') had been forgotten by all but a few. Black performers were excluded from recognized forms of Country and Folk and barred from the teen idol club. Girl groups, overwhelmingly African-American, represented an essential outlet.

This shortlived, early-Sixties rage inhabited two-minute singles while it lasted; folk music filled half-hour l.p.s. It was accessible to young teens' budgets, unlike the folk popular with older, upper middle class youth who were after an instructive experience maybe even more than a musical one. And the guarded intellectual independence of the socially conscious folk artist was anathema to the strict (read 'control freak' for Phil Spector) management setup governing the girl groups. Ponderous intellect was banned altogether from the genre for hormone-driven, teenage emotions. On disc The Girl alternately pleaded for mercy from a boyfriend or otherwise strutted in triumph, and always purred in self-absorption.

Nurtured and then pushed by Eastern labels, impressionable teens in a once-innocent after-school pastime came to be molded to appeal to fans their own age. The creative units that were the Shirelles, Bobettes, Chantels and Marvelettes—composing, writing and arranging vocals for their own songs—were taken over by professional writers, producers, corporate middle-men and retailers, who took the lion's share of returns on the 'product'. While most scored a string of hits, one-hit wonders followed up with a soundalike that spelt their doom. Striking one-offs on DJs' platter-racks came from up-and-coming record entrepreneurs, producers taking over the reins of pop. These mavericks used artists as conduits to creative and business ends. With such a cavalier attitude taken to their careers, it was rare for group members to make it as real stars. Those who did could be counted on three fingers—Diana Ross, Martha Reeves, Gladys Knight. The rest, used as interchangeable makeweights by producers who could swap personnel among established groups at will for purposes of cutting a 45, were anonymous to record buyers and to rub in their employee status were usually paid per hour of studio time on a union scale.

The '62-63 girl groups owed nothing to passive fifties sweeties the McGuire Sisters ('Sugartime') and Chordettes ('Mr Sandman', 'Lollipop'). The Chantels ('Maybe'), whose soaring gospel tones had set the standard, inspired New Jersey's Shirley Owens to call her group the Shirelles—and to also write their own hits. For more than two years it was a two-horse race until late in 1960 with 'Will You Love Me Tomorrow?' the Shirelles were snatched up by the big time—Brill Building Pop and composer Carole King. Black girl groups took off as an industry, though it took almost a year for other major acts to arrive: the Marvelettes and self-penned 'Please Mr Postman', and the Crystals, 'There's No Other'. These were remade by the Beatles and Beach Boys. Not merely paying tribute to current American culture, with 'Boys', 'Chains' and 'You've Really Got a Hold On Me', the Beatles adopted it.

The Shirelles reigned for two years as *the* top group, male or female—manager Flo Greenberg owned Scepter Records—continuing with 'Dedicated to the One I Love' (remade by the Mamas & the Papas), 'Baby It's You' (Beatles) and 'Soldier Boy', a Beatle live favorite. But as black rock'n'rollers they were unacceptable to network tv, the most racist of the mass media. People had prejudices about whom they "invited into their living rooms". Through '63 the Shirelles gave ground to the sounds of Phil Spector and then to big media machinery—EMI, backing Britain. They were last seen in the US top fifty the very week the Beatles arrived in America. Months later their 'Sha La La' flopped only for Manfred Mann to run strong with it. In fact, *all* existing girl groups—but the strongly supported, highly drilled and adaptable Motowners—would be wiped out by the Brits.

Hot on the heels of Spector's Philles in exploiting a girl group sound was Philly's Cameo-Parkway, Dee Dee Sharp and the Orlons —launching them with '62 dance crazes 'Mashed Potato Time' and 'Wah-Watusi'. And there was 'The Loco-Motion' intended by Goffin

& King for Dee Dee but passed on to Leiber & Stoller protégée Little Eva.

Small labels who knew how to improvise and innovate often incorporated male voices to broaden the two-minute dramas. The Orlons (also 'Don't Hang Up', 'South Street') and Exciters ('Tell Him', United Artists) had a male voice in their lineups; Sensations ('Let Me In' on Argo), Ruby & the Romantics (Kapp) and the Essex (Roulette) a female lead backed by males. The Essex was comprised of off-duty US Marines—a fun, semi-professional element was still essential to the entertainment business.

Soloists were produced to sound like groups by backing singers or double-tracking the lead's voice: Mary Wells'/Motown's 'My Guy'. Before that Detroit sister Barbara Lewis was (like homegirl Aretha Franklin) claimed by Atlantic, creating the highly attractive self-penned 'Hello, Stranger'. Shirley Ellis from New York City was on small indie Congress: 'Nitty Gritty', 'The Name Game'. Branching out from the Four Seasons, Bob Crewe took one more New Jerseyite to the top—a double-tracked Lesley Gore and her pleas to boyfriend Johnny, declaring independence in 'You Don't Own Me'—blocked from no.1 by the Beatles in their first sales rush. Darlene Love was a member of LA's Blossoms but as a freelancer was used anonymously by Spector as one of the Crystals— lead voice on 'He's a Rebel' and 'He's Sure the Boy I Love' before stamping her mark with 'A Fine Fine Boy' and 'Christmas (Baby Please Come Home)', now a perennial on *The Late Show*.

In twenty months up to the end of '63 thirteen acts recording in girl group mode reached no.1. Dee Dee Sharp's and the manbait Ronettes' were disputed chart toppers, as was 'Sally Go Round the Roses' by the Jaynetts—a highly advanced theme (insanity over love loss) and sound released by tiny Tuff. The Chiffons (Laurie), the Essex based in North Carolina and New Jersey's Angels (Smash) ruled for multiple weeks in a fickle year.

The Crystals—whether using Lala Brooks or Darlene Love as lead—and the Chiffons from The Bronx and Upper Manhattan with personality-plus, were now the top girl groups, though hardly long enough for a reign. Between them they defined the genre in 'Da Doo

Ron Ron' and 'Then He Kissed Me'—and 'He's So Fine', a five-week no.1 through April, and equally famous classic 'One Fine Day', 'Sweet Talkin' Guy' sneaking in three years later. At Motown the Marvelettes ('Playboy', 'Beechwood 4-5789') lay fallow through '63 but revived fitfully through the Brit era with 'Too Many Fish in the Sea' and more. New girls Martha & the Vandellas had a similarly patchy stardom: 'Come and Get These Memories', then true classic 'Heat Wave'. A year later they and Motown's house band delivered a shining milestone, 'Dancing in the Street', then 'Nowhere to Run'—but again at the height of the British Invasion their impact was blunted.

The Ronettes, unlike the Crystals, survived into 1964, but were unceremoniously pushed to the margins. New girl group releases went begging: the Secrets' 'The Boy Next Door' and 'When the Lovelight Starts Shining Through His Eyes' by the chronically ignored Supremes—laboring under the harsh male r&b line introduced by 'Louie Louie' and extended by English arrivals.

The Beatles and Beach Boys, more than any other male groups of the mid-sixties, owed the girl groups. Brian and Carl Wilson, and Al Jardine, could be mistaken for women, on vinyl, when the occasion called for it. But while they nurtured and developed the style, the Beatles rather exploited it. The UK scene was instead geared to provide bulk, redone r&b from the many hundreds of groups scattered from Liverpool to London; its studios were technically capable of little else. As major production outfits only Motown (and later Atlantic) had the impetus to take on the British Invasion. Three teenagers from the Brewster Projects on the east side of Detroit, showing signs of life after four years, would suffer a further nine months before living up to their name in commercial success.

B RIAN WILSON, AT TIMES IMMERSED IN THE GIRL group sound, was pursuing a girl project. Wary of the artistic pitfalls in producing a black girl group—he respected authentic r&b too much to attempt it second-hand—the group was, like Lesley Gore and the family-based Shangri-Las, Jewish, picked from his own circle.

The Honeys were Marilyn Rovell, sister Diane—schoolmates of Carl—and cousin Ginger Blake. Like Elvis and Jerry Lee, Brian 'mentored' a young teenager: Marilyn, soon his fiancée. Four singles were produced by Brian and Nick Venet at Capitol, but no career took off past professional recognition around Southern California—but for one curious exception: Their first release, 'Surfin' Down the Swanee River', in April 1963 was a no.1 in Denmark. They are best remembered as the spirited cheerleaders on 'Be True to Your School'. A decade and a half later a simmering Brian infatuation for Diane would culminate in divorce.

Brian's other freelancing makes for dire reading: 'She Rides With Me' for Paul Peterson of tv's *Donna Reed Show*, teen idol material after 'My Dad'; 'Guess I'm Dumb' for Glen Campbell, another non-seller prized by collectors for its producer; and a melody for aspiring California girl Sharon Marie, speeded up to serve years later for 'Darlin''.

Highly independent, highly successful Phil Spector, 18 months older, was Wilson's idol in the making of records. A 'boy genius', at 17 a stereotypic, unprepossessing Jewish pipsqueak from The Bronx, Spector had relocated to Los Angeles and through sheer force of personality installed himself in a supergroup of star drummer Sandy Nelson, legendary rock pioneer Kim Fowley and future Beach Boy Bruce Johnston, 14. In his first year on the Coast his hit-making instinct had penned and recorded 'Donna', Richie Valens' biggest hit, and formulated a huge world seller with his own trio the Teddy Bears, 'To Know Him is to Love Him'. He collaborated too with Terry Melcher, a singer and then producer at LA's Columbia studio who would helm the Byrds' and Paul Revere & the Raiders' first records and join a select coterie in California pop with Lou Adler, Herb Alpert, Spector and Wilson.

At 20 Spector produced a revival of calypso-styled 'Corinna, Corinna' for teen idol Ray Peterson ('The Wonder of You', 'Tell Laura I Love Her') and, on joining Jerry Wexler and Ahmet Ertegun pushing Atlantic's move into Soul Music, co-wrote Ben E King's 'Spanish Harlem'. A New Yorker to his soul, he started his own game with fellow Bronxers the Crystals—in a pinch turning to Darlene

Love and Fanita James from LA's Blossoms. In quick time he had made his first million and set the dark glasses and art-on-the-run model for aspiring recording impresarios everywhere.

Brian was inspired by his omnipresence. Spector's first major hit on his own label, 'Pretty Little Angel Eyes' (Curtis Lee), accompanied the formation of the Beach Boys, quickly followed by the Paris Sisters' 'I Love How You Love Me', encapsulating a sweetness Brian would later liken to 'Surfer Girl'. Through 1963 his Crystals/Ronettes matched the Beach Boys hit for hit. 'Be My Baby' (see *Mean Streets*, 1973) especially would come to haunt Brian with its aggressive intertwining of the same elements he used from his own rainbow-hued pallet to paint his songs.

He was in awe not only because Spector co-wrote most of his hit recordings in a way that indicated he had full creative control but because he was a striking personality. Like Brian, Spector was intensely driven to perfection—but Brian's naïvete put Spector on a pedestal as someone scary: overtly cultured, flamboyantly cultivated, well out of his *milieu* in cultureless California—an anti-establishment, arrogant eccentric who wore his hair Dali-like, long and unkempt. He maintained close links with the New York-Jewish creative community, with Bob Dylan, Allen Ginsberg, Frank Zappa, Norman Mailer and Woody Allen in supporting stand-up comic Lenny Bruce's expensive legal battles over free speech and other common causes. It was a level of sophistication young Brian could only aspire to. But unlike him, in the creative realm Spector was the junior writing partner, involved just enough to ensure his ownership of the treatment of a song as it was to be recorded: The Wall of Sound.

Like Elvis Presley, and as Brian wanted to do, Phil Spector took universal elements of the best black popular music and formed a bridge not only from black to white audiences but from the Fifties to the Sixties. Inevitably something of the very 'blackness' was lost in the translation but all three proved themselves among the best white interpreters of r&b. And all three, by the late Sixties, would be in self-imposed retreat traumatized by an eclipse hastened by the Beatles, who were by the consensus of the day in the UK and US no better at interpreting r&b than most Britons.

S O, AS HAS BEEN AGONIZED OVER OFTEN, WHEN DID
Fifties music end and The Sixties really begin? Official
histories tell us that Rock music was *dead* and America was left
somewhere between slumber and coma until the Beatles breathed new
life into it in '64. But evolution was all around and had never stopped,
in innovative recordings by Elvis Presley and Buddy Holly, then the
Leiber-Stoller productions for the Drifters—'There Goes My Baby'
and its orchestration of r&b—and the coming of Chubby Checker,
Roy Orbison, girl groups…. This was known by, was obvious to,
those who rejected the Beatles as well as the Liverpudlians
themselves, who tried at every stage to emulate—copy— *current*
music and recorded sounds coming out of America. It was quite
apparent to many people around the world, who kept buying
American records in preference to any others. The Beach Boys, Phil
Spector, Motown and the Four Seasons brought new forces to bear in
1962-63, and were picked up on and absorbed by the English
groups—the Beatles no less than anyone else, long *before* their arrival
in America. And the Beatles found at least as much kinship with pure
pop from Bert Kaempfert, Burt Bacharach and Don Kirshner as with
its progressive creatives.

There were still divisions in radio between stations along race lines
or, more accurately, according to how black/white the music. Black
acts had been crossing over the racial barrier into broad popularity
since blues/jazz artists Ma Rainey, Mamie Smith, Bessie Smith and
Louis Armstrong in the Roaring Twenties, when 'lude' delivery
wasn't a problem. In the hung-up Fifties when interracial sex was
more of a possibility and therefore more threatening, only balladeers
engendering genteel romance were accepted: the Platters, Harry
Belafonte, Johnny Mathis. The barometer of societal pressure was
measured by tv ratings counters, and that meant Ed Sullivan, since the
thirties the arbiter of what was okay on radio. Into the sixties he
barred black rock'n'roll groups from appearing on his tv show—
maybe fearing like other tv bosses it would appear to Southern
viewers as an on-screen race riot—while welcoming 'cultured' black
performers Lena Horne and Sammy Davis Jr. More cultured than
virtually anyone in the country had been Paul Robeson—opera star,

actor and all-star football player, but a one-time admitted ally of Russia and therefore reviled, blacklisted and exiled from home.

Black music was tougher. While the popularity of Nat Cole and Johnny Mathis—'Gina', 'What Will Mary Say?'—got old in '63 r&b's Sam Cooke continued to thrive. One of the great Gospel-Soul singers, he was a mainstay of r&b-pop through 'Wonderful World', 'Chain Gang', 'Cupid' and Grammy-winner 'Twisting the Night Away'. Cooke was the spearhead of Soul singers in the American mainstream and going strong into the mid-sixties—so needing no reviving by English acts. Still, they queued up to use his material: 'Bring It On Home to Me', 'Another Saturday Night', 'Little Red Rooster'. But the British imperative—the necessity of looking and sounding so 1964 through 1966—would stifle the emergence of new Soul stars, while those who didn't have a sufficiently 'African' element to claim a distinctive niche were swept away: Chubby Checker, Ben E King, the Drifters, the Shirelles....

Intended by RCA to be the black girls' Elvis, Cooke's subdued tone and laidback image—unlike some others he was not banned by BBC Radio—did almost fit a sweater-wearing pretty-boy image. Yet he got involved in civil rights and founded a record label, keeping pace with blues shouters James Brown, Wilson Pickett and Otis Redding who had more the image of what a black male singer should be in the mid-sixties. At his handgun murder late in 1964 the B-side of 'Shake', his classic Gospel-styled protest song 'A Change is Gonna Come', earned him joint ownership with Ray Charles of the title "Fathers of Soul". His vocal tone and timbre were reproduced through the rock career of Brit invader Rod Stewart, his number one fan.

Charles, blind behind dark glasses but a restless mover behind the piano, was taken as a model by highly energetic and sexually charged James Brown and Otis Redding. More popular with the white public than even Cooke—and through four numbers topping the Cash Box r&b chart twenty-one weeks '61-63—Charles' impact on white musicians came in 1959's 'What'd I Say', which might have started Sixties Music and that the Beatles and Beach Boys incorporated into their live repertoires. Both, understandably, declined to record it for fear of too obvious an authenticity gulf. Between huge Country standards 'Georgia On My Mind' and 'I Can't Stop Loving You' "The Genius" inspired the Soul explosion: 'Unchain My Heart', 'Hit the Road Jack', 1963's 'Busted'. His brittle, controlled voice can be heard in Bill Medley of the Righteous Bros, taught to sing by Charles, Eric Burdon (Animals) and Joe Cocker, who covered many of his standards.

James Brown and Jackie Wilson were double attractions, gifted dance stylists with potential to be universal rock showmen, only held back by dark-chocolate voices and visages—two 'handicaps' avoided by Michael Jackson, who was heavily influenced by both. Wilson was a perpetual-motion machine on stage, mixing spins, graceful leaps and splits all in one movement. So were the two responsible for Eighties Music? Jackie Wilson only captured world attention twice— with 1957's 'Reet Petite' (popularly revived ex-USA after four decades), then ten years later, '(Your Love Keeps Lifting Me) Higher and Higher', though in '63 he offered the hard driving r&b #1 'Baby Work Out'. Jackie's exquisitely controlled vocal gymnastics on his first hit—many claimed fellow Detroiter Aretha Franklin was his only equal—made it big also in the UK; Brown never did have a UK hit of any size, being just too black to taste. Mentored early on by Berry Gordy, had Jackie gone to Motown everlasting fame would have been his, but probably at the cost of stylistic castration.

Brown's first sizable pop hit, 'Prisoner of Love', didn't come until '63 and was accompanied by huge sales for *Live at the Apollo*—such a breakthrough for black popular culture that it was played in its entirety by black radio stations. He posed a viable, stark alternative to the white rock'n'roll of the Beach Boys and ultimately the Beatles with a no.1 album to prove it.

World fame was further delayed for two years and 'Papa's Got a Brand New Bag'—bringing further musical tumult to the summer of '65, followed at year's end by 'I Got You (I Feel Good)', his iconic chart-topper. With his accompanying dance he was the personification of funky as funk can be (avoid Robin Williams' tribute, *Good Morning Vietnam*). In advancing the cause of black music without the compromises of Motown's top artists, his multilayered rhythms and staccato horn backing pointed the way to Sly & the Family Stone.

Brown's explosion on to the scene as an alternative to the mainstream at the height of Brit Beat was propelled by listeners who had heard Motown's response to the Beatles—the Supremes and Four Tops—and wanted something more authentically black. James Brown was by the end of the decade "Soul Brother Number One", his ongoing dominance of African-derived r&b seeing him elevated to "Godfather of Soul".

MORE ACCESSIBLE TO WHITE LISTENERS, THE TOP black male group to late '64—until the Four Tops and the Temptations—was the Drifters. Evolving from Doo-Wop combos and produced by Leiber & Stoller, they posted 'Save the Last Dance For Me' as a massive hit in fall 1960 only for lead singer Ben E King to solo and take the brand with him in 'Spanish Harlem' and 'Stand By Me'. Anyway, they proved a pillar of Sixties music combining r&b and pop in innovative ways for Atlantic —though for a time overshadowed by the preponderance of girl groups. They came right in '63 with 'Up On the Roof' and 'On Broadway', followed up by 'Under the Boardwalk'. It was a startling success at the height of Beatlemania and British Invasion, which through the Searchers was regurgitating their 'Sweets for My Sweet' and 'I Count the Tears'. By 'Saturday Night at the Movies', a popular party number, they were sounding dated. Their new producer, Bert Berns (a.k.a. Russell, writer of 'Twist & Shout', etc), who had dragged out the *baion* rhythm past its welcome, went to the UK to be part of the Invasion.

The contemporary force compelling the Beatles and Beach Boys to pay *hommage* was a mainstream sound they could approximate without the vocal contortions of turning into a black man (though McCartney and Lennon strained to do that on occasion). Motown of Detroit was under its founder multiplying into the wealthiest independent record company by the mid-Sixties. First harnessed were the formidable talents of singer-songwriters Smokey Robinson ('Shop Around') and Barrett Strong (Beatle favorite 'Money—That's What I Want'), then prolific team Brian Holland, Lamont Dozier & Eddie

Holland and Stevie Wonder ('I Was Made to Love Her'). Robinson, admired for his fine, evocative lyrics—called by Dylan "America's greatest living poet"—would have been the envy of Dylan for mastering the musical side of the art too in composing-recording the emotive 'Tracks of My Tears' and 'Tears of a Clown', 'My Guy', 'I Second That Emotion' and 'Get Ready'.

Instead of enslaving mass instruments into a lump of sound as did the Spector-Nitzsche-Levine team at Gold Star, the Motown studio wizards featured individual talents and idiosyncracies of working Detroit jazz and r&b musicians, kept them upfront at the mikes, and left fully intact the live response of the snare drum, saxophone, etc, and avoided Spector's everpresent drum muffling, echo and other elaborations. Based on an intimate working pool known as the Funk Brothers, Motown broke the mold of pop production. Gordy's hands-on Svengali management with Holland-Dozier-Holland, Barrett Strong or Henry Stevenson producing, dwarfed the scale of Spector's one-man Philles operation.

Before striking a compromise 'black pop' formula exemplified by the Supremes (the Isley Bros' 'This Old Heart of Mine', sounded very much like the model for late-sixties Brit pop) that would bring it two dozen Billboard number ones, the early Motown records were raw and convincing, including those from its girl groups. To ensure inroads into the white market the appealing but recognizably black Mary Wells was introduced in 1962, two years later replaced by the breathlessly cooing Diana Ross, on every track sounding like Marilyn Monroe gasping 'I Wanna Be Loved By You' and squealing every now and again for effect, supposedly signalling the height of passion.

Holland-Dozier-Holland were now in '63 making their mark with 'Heat Wave' and Supremes protohit 'When the Lovelight Starts Shining Through His Eyes'. Smokey Robinson was more versatile. As the one highly talented string to Gordy's bow at the fledgling company he had become a co-director of the label and catered to his group the Miracles and the demanding vocal artistry of Marvin Gaye and the Temptations.

An array of talents was flourishing within the broad limits of Motown for three years before the Beatles hit America. While the

Beatles attempted to duplicate its sound on record they never came close, and afterwards the "Sound of Young America", displaying shrewd cross-racial marketing by Gordy, only expanded its popularity and influence through the so-called British Beat Boom.

Atlantic, as an artist-driven enterprise, avoided direct competition with Motown's factory of craftsmen. Led by closely cooperating Muslim and Jewish figures (God Bless America), it emerged as the definitive label of Soul Music, in '64 blowing off its rival the troubled Vee-Jay. Producer Jerry Wexler under Turkish-American brothers Ahmet & Nesuhi Ertegun was the preeminent creative force with, briefly, Leiber & Stoller, the Coasters—featuring "The Yakety Sax" of King Curtis—the Drifters and Ray Charles, Carla Thomas and father Rufus, Barbara Lewis, Wilson Pickett, Otis Redding, Aretha. The Mar-Keys, racially integrated—white Memphis guitarist Steve Cropper and bassist Donald "Duck" Dunn with drummer Al Jackson (see *The Blues Brothers,* 1980)—joined a local organist as Booker T & the MGs for 'Green Onions' and backed tracks for Atlantic-Stax.

It goes without saying both Beatles and Beach Boys owed much to black music. Lennon and McCartney nurtured an ability to simply regurgitate it rather than adapt it. But in trying to render it faithfully they can be seen to more often parody it. It is a rarity to find a cover that matched the original in quality of feeling; poor choice of material unsuited to their strengths was another failing early on that betrayed a stubbornly untrained, at times amateurish, approach.

IT IS INACCURATE TO SAY THE TEEN IDOL ERA BURNT itself out under these pressures. This would imply that it had been aflame, when passion didn't come into it. Newcomers the Beach Boys and Four Seasons had broken the industrial-strength mold set by industry bosses and came from a totally new direction: composer-and-group-driven recordings. The reactionary teen idol phase championed by parents, that killed the original rock'n'roll, finally gave way to authentic music made by youths who made music their lives, as Elvis had once done. By 1962 hits by tv and movie faces had become smaller ones, even in the diehard Hot 100 measured in part by airplay.

A hopeful survival tactic was to sing 'surf' songs. Chubby Checker, once a model for the Beach Boys, now returned the compliment. Cameo-Parkway of Philadelphia—no center of beach culture—issued a surfing anthology album with Chubby ('Surf Party'), Bobby Rydell and the Orlons. Shots of the artists in bathers looked odd—the clichéd African-American cultural anomaly on beaching. Sung on *The Flintstones* tv show, "James Darrock" almost got a hit with the catchy 'Everybody's Gone Crazy With the Surfin' Craze'. Most optimistic had to be Pat Boone, taken under Brian Wilson's wing in 1964. The sober 28-year-old's stab at the surf-hotrod teen scene via 'Beach Girl', written by the Melcher-Johnston team, backed with 'Little Honda', was no more effective than his early "rock and roll". Wilson's production participation did give the old-fashioned crooner his best chart showing in his last 13 outings, but couldn't prevent him going down in history as Elvis's milk-and-cookies alter ego.

The inspiration for all this, Brian Wilson's group was conflicted — guilty by association with the old guard while offering new, vital music struggling to be heard. Linking themselves with passé teen idols was tantamount to betraying their revered progenitors and the new rock'n'roll both. Aside from good-looking, moca-colored Chubby Checker and Sam Cooke, 'passing' marginally, black artists were barred from teen idoldom—its essence mass popularity with or without talent. It was this apparent alignment with the white worldview of pop that the Beach Boys would pay for in years to come. It was English writer Kingsley Abbott in *The Beach Boys' Pet Sounds: The Greatest Album of the 20th Century* who explained Wilson's total lack of political awareness as a result of being encapsuled in an isolating creative bubble, out of necessity through the group's Sixties career when he was expected to be "Mr Everything." Brian's peculiar stubborn naïvete was often counterproductive: in preferring an older-style name for his group; in staying loyal to the college-style uniform so long—making them squares unnecessarily when the 'counterculture' took over; withdrawing from the all-important Monterey Pop Festival. His strange business sense had them withdrawn from prints of the much-admired *TAMI Show*; later announcing the group's 'bankruptcy'. His reliance on astrology, numerology and any number of other 'disciplines' in guiding moves for the group qualified him as an eccentric anywhere but California.

The Beach Boys almost got caught by the outgoing riptide, lumped into the bleached-out beach movie scene of Frankie Avalon (a survivor after all) and his screen partner Annette Funicello. Their one feature film—aside from a number of cameo roles and an excellent performance in legendary rockumentary *The T.A.M.I. Show*—would be *Girls on the Beach*, a.k.a. *Summer of '64*, a teen-fodder flick not released until 1965 when even Frankie & Annette were tiring of beach movies. Disney's *The Monkey's Uncle* too was delayed from spring '64 for more than a year when Bob Dylan ruled and the supposed benefits of performing as Annette's backing band and vocal support in the opening sequence were long gone. Though a guarateed hit, the scene of an all-white Disney college dance, full of mechanically-gyrating greased-down jocks and 'flip' hair-styled coeds, was bound to retard the Beach Boys' image. The conservative All-American studio under Walt Disney propagated the mid-Sixties as something Monty Burns might imagine fondly from his youth. Maintaining a cautious lag time so as not to upset parents, by 1969 Kurt Russell, the studio's new top boy star taking over from Tommy Kirk, was allowed to wear his hair almost touching his ears, soon threatening to catch up with the Beatle cut of a pop generation earlier.

The Beach Boys' concession to popular Americana reinforced a superficial impression that here was a lightweight outfit—expensive stand-ins for the Disneyland house band, the not yet known Gary Lewis & the Playboys. The respect accorded them in the industry by the end of 1963 failed to translate to serious regard in the public eye—lightyears short of their place some two years later, the epitome of what was hip as discovered by flocking New York journos. It would take a miracle to bridge the gap to cross-generational icon status once the Beatles arrived. America took its time.

Perception wasn't helped by Brian, having attained teen celebrity status as group leader and creative director, reappearing in exploitation flicks *How to Stuff a Wild Bikini* and *Beach Blanket*

Bingo, a Frankie & Annette sequel (later dissed in *Good Morning Vietnam*). By 1965 25-year-old beachgirl—former Miss La Jolla and San Diego—Raquel Welch's 39-inch bust and flaring nostrils were enjoying their first starring roles: *A Swingin' Summer* with the Rip Chords, Righteous Bros, Gary Lewis & Playboys. Seen in beach movies were LA singer-songwriter Jackie De Shannon ('What the World Needs Now', 'Put a Little Love in Your Heart'), her career stalling under Searchers covers of 'Needles and Pins' and 'When You Walk in the Room'. At 19 she was a beached, bleached blonde in a flip hairdo and (like the Playboys) recording on LA's Liberty, soon to tour supporting the Beatles. Such unlikely beachgoers as "Polka Prince" Bobby Vinton, the Four Seasons and the Supremes were trying for on-screen tans too. Eerily out of his element, Godfather of Soul James Brown appeared in a skiing movie, for variety's sake, attired in Swedish pullover doing the father of the Moonwalk.

THIS LIGHT ENTERTAINMENT WAS PART OF SHOW business tradition but new for teens, especially in the UK where more polite screen vehicles were being produced for Cliff Richard, Billy Fury and others. Up to now with the takeover of the airwaves by creative musicians, stars had lined up for the chance to sell products for sponsors. Among the most prized spots were commercials for countless cigarette brands, each promising to be cooler, more refreshing and better for you than the last. Cuddling with capital was so ingrained in the American Way that even so staunch a leftist as Woody Guthrie signed in 1940 with a radio show owned by Model Tobacco, only to quit when the company tried to stop him writing his column for the communist Daily Worker. In the Sixties Pete Seeger had his career wrecked by demands from tv sponsors—Bob Dylan was big enough to tell Ed Sullivan where to go when the impresario insisted he change his act for television.

The new wave of English stars were mainly 'working class lads' or passed for such—and new to the high end of the capitalist hierarchy and eager to take advantage of it. Many lived for the Blues. Drawing inspiration from Angry-Young-Man literary circles of the late Fifties, now Albert Finney, Alan Bates, Richard Harris and

Michael Caine represented the type in British films: ambitious youth made cynical by the Class System, which America kidded itself it didn't have.

Having lived through real 'kitchen-sink' dramas growing up, personalities from upwardly-mobile British pop groups struck a chord of gritty reality with white audiences in America and Europe. Domestic labels Atlantic, Motown, Vee-Jay and a few other minors served young black record-buyers; now these English lads appealed directly to America's white working-class kids, the spirit of the original truck-driving Elvis, Gene Vincent and Eddie Cochran now making an impact, reflected back at them from across the Atlantic. This glaring but artificial contrast between 'real life' and Hollywood-slick product came to trivialize the Beach Boy image. Their recordings were seen by reverse class snobs as too smooth by far. Who ever heard of striving for aural perfection in rock'n'roll? —much better the Kingsmen's 'Louie Louie', consistent with the UK approach, made gritty and 'authentic' by amplifier feedback, fuzz tone, sizzle cymbal and extraneous tape noise. And far from the artistic, black-and-white *A Hard Day's Night* of the Beatles attracting serious critical attention, Beach Boy movie dross was seen for what it was, pitched at the same consumer level as that of the Dave Clark Five and Herman's Hermits: made into teen puppets, with the money-men pulling their strings to make a quick buck.

Groups like the Beatles and the Animals from working-class backgrounds—and the English working class was well below American blue collar, a grovel and a council house above trailer trash—were awed by the American scene: the luxury and conspicuous consumption that they lapped up in this parallel universe, economically so far above their own origins. John, Paul, George & Ringo believed in their showbiz-soaked souls that the roads leading to Radio City Music Hall, Broadway were paved with gold. At first the middlemen got most of the gold and the group had to settle for groupies and a revered place in pop culture; the world was theirs. While parents had hated the newly arrived Elvis, bringing everything that was black or uncouth into their living rooms, and gritted their teeth at the teen-oriented Beach Boys rebelling by cutting school and going off surfing, they loved the all-embracing Beatles with cuddly-toy appearance, their trite cooing love songs in the Music Hall tradition and veneer of European sophistication.

In 1965, bolstered by the sardonic wit of Bob Dylan and London-intellectual social commentary of the Stones and Kinks egging them on, the Beatles slipped into the eccentric custom of the English élite in appearing to tear down the idols of convention while actually stepping into the shoes of the Establishment: simply one more changing of the guard. It was soon easy for the Beatles to look down on money-grabbing commercialism and to exalt art for its own sake, and whatever treasure chests of loot that came with the deal. The Animals settled for a blues *cachet* (Eric Burdon), virtuoso reputation (Alan Price) and backstage influence (Chas Chandler).

The American parallel universe the English groups marvelled at — steeped in sunshine, blessed with open spaces for limitless playing in and around the ocean with surfboards and beach bunnies and a choice of big, powerful fast cars—was the environment, the domain, of the Beach Boys. Or so went the illusion they had created in everyone's minds, even those of worldly Yanks. English boys who were growing up at the time, Elvis Costello and Elton John to name two, swallowed it hook, line and surfboard: "Two girls for every boy!" Thus rests the fallacy of Brian Wilson's inarticulacy.

The Beach Boys could have chosen to reflect their own working class roots—and post a stronger image—by wearing biker outfits at shows, at least for automotive encores. No one but Murry would have quibbled and it would have made them a talking point. Denny Wilson, for one, always looked pointlessly confined by the button-down Kingston attire. Aside from the Beach Boys' and folk groups' casualness, it was the rule for Sixties acts, on the demise of the flamboyant fifties rock'n'rollers, to wear "Sunday best" for shows, including jackets and ties—until 1965, and then few but the Stones and Dylan got away with going casual, with the gimmicky Sonny & Cher and San Francisco blues fusion groups the first mainstream acts to go beyond that. The California group was pretty much unanimous: The music is all that matters.

The Southern California environment was no illusion to nature boy Dennis Wilson—It grew from his playground to a spiritual homeland. To the other Beach Boys it was secondary, to Brian Wilson something apart, a distraction at best, often scary. Later, the pristine beaches and romantic adventures were as inaccessible to ordinary Californians as the playgrounds of the English upper crust were to Cockneys and Geordies.

Contrast this seeming fantasyland with the dingy, cold, wet industrial north of England, still recovering from WWII bomb damage, poverty-stricken and not long over post-War food rationing. Anyone with 'nous' enough to salvage a vehicle from a scrapheap was automatically part of any aspiring group (*a la* Pete Best, the long-lost Beatle), the bulkier the better to carry the instruments. The Wilsons' father, indulgent as he was when it came to his boys' music, was a scrappy industrialist too, importing aviation parts from England—not far in spirit from English working class. He accordingly dealt out physical discipline, switching to verbal haranguing and a system of fines when they were older. He once threatened to fire Mike Love for backstage profanity, prevented only by the calm, calculating heads at Capitol. The pattern was ingrained in the next generation as Dennis, fifteen years later, reacted to Mike's needling by attacking him physically onstage— and was banished for two years.

The impression is of family dysfunction, in the jargon. Murry had anchored them in their sanitised image. Here they were, small-town Hawthorne boys of Midwest roots, venturing forth to conquer a rapidly expanding bohemian world with dark new corners. The Wilson brothers embraced sophisticated new acquaintances offering worldly experiences and ideas, while their father attempted to restrict them like Mormon noviciates. Mike rebuffed the invading drug culture for vegetarianism and stricter regimens. Al "wanted to retain the innocence".

Audree, self-confessed people-pleaser, was a moderator but maybe in denial, later unable to see long-lasting effects on Brian ("He was happy, though he might not admit it now") and Dennis. In 1964 the Wilson parents moved up to Richard Nixon's Whittier, an inland suburb of LA, but kept the family home—vacant, as a sort of touchstone. On Brian's first breakdown, Audree would take him there to ground him in safe surroundings. By then she and Murry couldn't live together, only co-habited on occasions.

Ten thousand kilometres away in Liverpool the Beatles had grown up the hard way, in real tear-jerkers. Paul McCartney lost his mother to cancer barely into his teens. John Lennon, comfortable compared to the others living in council housing, was forced to live without his father, and his mother deserted him to 'live in sin'; then she was run down by a car on a visit to his home—Aunt Mimi's—when he was 17. Ringo Starr, plain Richie Starkey as a child, suffered long stays in hospital from chronic ill health. He was once in a coma, near death, for two months. But these were ordinary, everyday hurdles of working class life in England's industrial north, where many working conditions and social expectations had not changed much since Dickens' time and life could still be 'brutish and short'. The prevailing culture was that traumatic events were meant to be taken in stride rather than endured, met with a stiff upper lip and a cheery "Chin up!" or "These things are sent to try us!" All this while a coalminer's family's life, to take a then common example, could be compared to the quality of that in West Virginia—the poorest state in the Union.

It has rarely if ever been mentioned that the Beach Boys' own optimistic philosophy had grassroots antecedents in American folk music—the egalitarian, leveling songs of Woody Guthrie ('This Land is Your Land') for the American everyman brought down by the Depression and World War II; and black folk-bluesman Leadbelly's descriptions of everyday life ('Turn Your Radio On', 'Driving Song') and relationships guided by emotions expressed directly ('You Don't Know My Mind', 'Keep Your Hands Off Her'). Pete Seeger, a friend and contemporary of Guthrie, in his *Incompleat Folksinger*: "Every folk song was a topical song at its birth, a comment upon the life and times of the singers and listeners". It is a definition that takes in almost every Beach Boy song recorded.

But a shallow pop media gave them a superficial reading. Four summers on, Murry Wilson's new protégés the Sunrays were singing about "sun, sun, sun" in 'I Live for the Sun'. In producing this best ever imitation of the Beach Boys he too hopped on the bandwagon. But, a first cousin of 'No-Go Showboat', it was still too good to be reproduced by Vanity Fare, a sub-bubblegum group who had a UK hit with it a further three years later. For now, the passing of surf music had been noted by the Trade Winds' mock tragic 'New York's a Lonely Town' ("when you're the only surfer boy around") on Leiber & Stoller's Red Bird label. Yet it has been an image that might stick to the Beach Boys for eternity.

TRANSPLANTED NEW YORKER PHIL SPECTOR NEVER contributed to California Music as it came to be known—though such a diverse range of sounds can hardly be categorised by geography. Spector kept his special brand of r&b alive, his girl groups sweetening it for the pop mainstream, creating an appealing teen image with a raunchy edge to the music and attitude in the delivery. His favorite female vocalist, Darlene Love, made the Supremes sound like tame choristers, on tour and on tv at the mercy of backing bands far from the funky rhythm section of Benny Benjamin and James Jamerson at Motown's Hitsville. TV clips show the distinctive sexiness of the streamline-model Ronettes with their slit skirts and exotic makeup, while the conservatively groomed Supremes looked like pleated high-school homecoming queens. How wedded Spector was to r&b was shown by wedding Veronica "Ronnie" Bennett, the Ronettes' Billie Holliday-cracked-voiced lead singer, having first fallen in love with her voice before meeting her, according to assistant Sonny Bono.

Brian Wilson used just hints of Spector's famous Wall of Sound monaural approach, being a monaural listener, "96 percent deaf" in one ear and not comprehending stereo. Spector used doubled-up instrumentalists in the studio, laying down a dense orchestration of three pianos and up to five guitars, recalled sound engineer Larry Levine—these two main traditional melody-carrying instruments used more on the main riff or for emphasis on key notes— as well as two or three basses, horns, strings, drums and myriad other percussion including bongos, castanets, bells, wood-blocks, tambourines, and sleigh bells, creating a clustered overlaying rhythm track, while the horns carried the chords. Brian chose his effects sparingly, using relatively sparse instrumentation—but layered voicings. Once when Spector requested Brian for a recording session at Gold Star to play piano the recording aces were un-simpatico; the Beach Boy was paid off at session scale and left.

All black sources absorbed by the Beach Boys have been forced to take a back seat to famous rockers Chuck Berry, Little Richard, Fats Domino. But when Al took his leave from the group early in '62 the band was playing "cute Chubby Checker tunes", apparently enough to drive a folk music devotee to study two thousand miles away. Dennis told of the Wilsons' bull sessions in the back of their father's pickup truck years before, immersed in the very roots of rock—singing 'Smoky Joe's Café' and the even earlier Robins hit 'Riot in Cell Block No.9' (that featured 'Louie Louie' writer Richard Berry as lead singer) revived in the late Sixties for Beach Boy shows and providing a blueprint for Mike Love's 'Student Demonstration Time'.

They had begun singing for the sheer joy of it, and sustained it into adulthood, music mainspringing in a natural stream of subconsciousness without any disrupting imposition of intellect on the creative flow. These songs were beyond obscure to the Beatles, rapt as they were in English tradition as it presented in the top twenty, the second-hand-American stylings of Lonnie Donegan and those of gentleman rockabilly Carl Perkins when they could get them. Inclinations to sing spontaneously were anathema. They would show an outright aversion to group singing, impromptu, for fun, as when asked simply to sing at their legendary first New York press conference—replying "We need money first." It was the inhibited response you would expect from aspiring schoolboy careerists, utterly disconnected from the well springs of what makes music the glorious, primal, participative act it is.

Brian twice sang, on his group's two Sixties live albums, the Rivingtons' big California r&b hit 'Papa-Oom-Mow-Mow'. He paid tribute to the Doo-Wop songs of his formative years, citing Otis Williams & the Charms' 'Ivory Tower'—and remade Frankie Lymon & the Teenagers' 'Why Do Fools Fall In Love?' and the Mystics'

'Hushabye', showcasing his sliding falsetto. Mike's influences were not only the two strong r&b stations in Fifties LA—his Dorsey High School buddies reinforced a naturally developing black r&b thang in his voice from the first, almost always employed effectively. He and Carl—whose favorite was the Johnny Otis show on KFOX—influenced Brian to listen to more r&b and as a result big brother changed his piano-playing style from Cool Jazz and started writing songs (Wikipedia). Long past the time when it was necessary to supplement their own material with others' the group saluted the Five Satins' 'In the Still of the Nite' and Little Willie John's 'Talk to Me'. The joy of simply vocalising was still there.

ALL THESE ELEMENTS HAD BEEN WELL AND TRULY integrated by the now famous Beach Boys when on 1st November 1963 they again played the prestigious 18,000-capacity Hollywood Bowl, closing a stellar show. Brian stood up for rock'n'roll to a reporter afterwards with hard words about the unsuitability of the venue's sound engineering. Despite the trauma of a presidential assassination soon overtaking them and their nation they could look forward to better. The world was theirs, as JFK had told young Americans in his inaugural speech a few short months before the group was formed. The Beach Boys showed they were attuned to Kennedy's thrust, inspired to compose 'The Warmth of the Sun', a song of loss and spiritual renewal akin to Sonny Til & the Orioles' 'Crying in the Chapel', on the evening of assassination, November 22nd, when Brian and Mike keyed off each other through a post-concert high back at the hotel in Sacramento, in the presence of Fred Vail and others of their entourage.

Barely audible exposure a quarter-century later (*Good Morning Vietnam*) took it to immortality, mocking all the 'progress' in rock since.

The world was suffering a spiritual crisis in 1963. Two more of its leading lights died just when they were most needed—Pope John and Pandit Nehru, heading India since independence and a world force for peace. US civil rights activist Medgar Evers was murdered, only partly eased by Martin Luther King's "I have a dream" speech, which averted a civil race war. The president of South Vietnam had been assassinated just three weeks before Kennedy. Ike Eisenhower, well aware of the danger a war machine posed to any democratic society, had warned of an uncontrolled "military-industrial complex" at home. And JFK's withdrawal of US support to the corrupt Diem regime had enraged gung-ho military leaders and hawks in Washington's bureaucracy entrenched in niches of power in the most powerful country in the world.

Coming years would see a perversion of the American Dream, fought at every step by protesters labelled radicals or traitors—for democratically questioning the direction of their country; blind patriots postponed their own crisis of conscience. On the evening of JFK's murder in Manchester, England the Shirelles were crying on stage, said Keith Richards of their supporting act the up-and-coming Rolling Stones. The black girl group was a strong favorite of the Beatles, but as far as real rock'n'roll in Britain went Stones lead singer Mick Jagger was quoted, "Can you imagine a British-composed r&b number—it just wouldn't make it" (Stanley Booth). Yet, for many teens only a new broom—or even better, a set of mops atop the Beatles—would sweep clean.

The Beach Boys had made their mark in recorded music and would lead the way for the rest of the decade, bringing the best mainstream America had to offer. And from now on they would bring their music to the world in person too. And so it seems doubly cruel that as President Kennedy told of the torch passing to a new generation of *Americans*, the public ignored the champions of their own culture to pick four showmen schooled second-hand in American idioms through the coarse filters of Hollywood movies, Tin Pan Alley songsmiths and Continental fashion designers. To a new generation Stateside these stand-ins singing and playing American music as a second language would, through the miracle of youth culture as sold by the mass media, pass as the real thing. The alternative to rock'n'roll the Establishment had searched for since the demise of Elvis and the other teen idols—and the unwelcome rise of Chubby Checker, Sam

Cooke, James Brown, Motown, Vee-Jay, Atlantic—was here. The two years of music the Beach Boys had produced to date—see Pop Culture Madness top 50 for 1962 and 1963—that would endure better to 2007 than any other, suddenly counted for zero.

4: "WE LOVE YOU BEATLES, OH YES WE DO!"

To be caught up in Beatlemania '64 was something as exciting as it was indescribable. Imagine Irish music, 'Riverdance' and leprechaun outfits taking over the world—held aloft for everyone else to aspire to: a crude but apt comparison. The Beatle phenomenon has been uncritically celebrated long past the point of drop-dead kicking-the-corpse boredom, so to this day no one has been able to say convincingly what their music had to do with it. But you had to be there—the pop culture 'happening' of the mid-Sixties. It was experienced so deeply by many youths it seemed all that was needed to fix the world was immersion in Beatledom so everything would turn "fab". Harrypottermania is the only phenomenon to compare with it today.

Tony Barrow, rock journalist and Beatle publicist: "The whole thing changed. The balance of power fell from an average age of 40 to 25 overnight."

Derek Taylor, Beatle and later Beach Boy publicist: "We saw them in that sense [of being saviors]. People saw them as being some sort of answer to the miseries of the world or in our own little lives. They were the four-headed Santa Claus."

Astrid Kirchherr, designer of the Beatlehair: "My heart just opens up with pride and joy to know I was so lucky to get to know these wonderful people who deserved all this fame and fortune."

Astrid Kirchherr: "You could tell Paul really hated [Stuart]" (Salewicz).

Murray Kaufman (Murray the 'K'), star DJ and self-proclaimed Fifth Beatle: "To this day when you hear [other superstars] you know it. With every album The Beatles gave us a 180-degree change. A completely different change, a different sound, a different attitude. They kept changing with us. The Beatles inspired a lot of the political and social revolution that took place, because from a subliminal standpoint The Beatles represented change. We saw the Beatles change right in front of our eyes." This habit of the Beatles being diverted every six months sounds alarmingly like a description of one of the Sixties' most charming and persuasive fakers, Andrew Loog Oldham, by his friend John Douglas: "... a dilettante: though he'd got natural ability, he didn't stick long with things, because there was always something new to have a crack at."

George Martin, who produced all the Beatle records: "In my book The Beatles were the greatest performers and writers ever... They were never satisfied with sticking to one style, one format, one sound... I think I was part of a five-piece group... My particular specialty in the beginning was introductions, endings and solos. The rest of the song was theirs. Later on it [was] the addition of things they hadn't thought of—all the backward guitar stuff and that kind of thing."—Excerpts from Pritchard & Lysaght's The Beatles: an Oral History *(1998).*

Note that Martin's "specialty" was composing beginnings, endings and middles of Beatle songs?! "The rest of the song was theirs", he adds amusingly. For Martin it all came down to how well crafted the song and the variety of ways they were presented. For Murray the K, how mutable the sound and attitude. Changeability was the common theme. So they might rate above Gilbert & Sullivan in adventurousness but below genuine artists in not having a recognisable style. Picasso changing his Blue Period and succeeding phases every four to six months?—the interval between Beatle albums. Novelty, and reading constantly changing trends— Murray the K: "They kept changing with us"—was their real stock in trade.

These four Liverpool lads of Irish descent had no small touch of the blarney in their blood: the pixieish wit; the crude, crying-into-your-beer sentiment and, encouraged by Dylan, self-pitying bitterness in layers; and Celtic "animal magnetism"—as ascribed by Brian Wilson to the Britons in general. If the Irish kissed the Blarney Stone for luck the Beatles and their minders must have ravished it full-frontal. Ritualistic mystique was all there staged in the Beatles—the Parisian styled hair, the Gallic cut suits, the Beatle bow in unison from the waist. Even Paul's intriguing German-made 'violin' bass guitar, like no other. Was he dead?—Only true initiates could read the signs. It all assumed titanic significance, like Lord of the Rings and Harry Potter overlapping into real life.

They had charm by the bucketful; presence—not the smarm or vacuous additood that passes for it today and is glibly called charisma. To immune observers they were interchangeable mop-tops, but fans knew better: John, the defiant leader with a loose chip on his shoulder, standing at the mike bowlegged gunslinger style; Paul, the smooth, fun-loving pretty boy and the most versatile musically, popping out melodies literally in his sleep—but called "the shrewdest and the toughest" by a teacher who knew them both; George, "the Dark Horse"—only fragments showing above surface, the most "vociferous" at the first meeting with George Martin and the most business minded, but passive-aggressive because dominated by his senior partners, overlooked until his death prompted a gushing media, when his palatial estate showed he had just as massive an ego; Ringo, contributing his personality on drums and off, the best actor in films—seemingly earthbound, living off a suitcase of baked beans on a spiritual exploration of India (the others ate theirs in the studio, scooped from silver service). Starting with no higher ambition than to open a hair salon once the Beatles had struck modest success, ironically he was probably the most spiritual one through his childhood illnesses. But he was painted goofy. Girls liked to mother him for his melancholy. Later, with his head shorn, on his unshaven days he bore an unfortunate resemblance to Yasser Arafat.

At the start they were so... fluffy—and so saleable. While little girls wanted them as cuddly toys who walked, talked, peed and sang, mature females too fantasized about cuddling up to one or other of them. It wasn't that the marketing strategy was inspired— just that everyone jumped on the bandwagon at once creating an unstoppable momentum, the more venal devotees grabbing fortunes hand over fist. The worldwide money-go-round was carved up continent by continent by seriously monied men, who made Elvis's Colonel Tom Parker look like a nickel-and-dime grifter. There were Beatle suits and ties, Beatle shoes, Beatle wigs, even Beatle guitars and drum kits. On their first trip to the US, from their tiny cut of the money generated by their own image the group made more from Beatle bubblegum than from performances.

Despite their "Luv, Luv, Luv" mantra, nasty personal politics emerged in breakup as all burst into song unflattering to all—tit for tat attacks in unbounded superstar self-indulgence, abusing their exalted position to demean their art form. Yet because the group died violently in its prime (and resisted all pleas for a rebirth) the Princess Diana Effect mummifies a far-fetched pristine image. There is no question of speaking ill of their legacy, and an objective reappraisal of their value will wait till all media contemporaries in their thrall have retired from the airwaves.

While the Beatles weren't responsible for every loopy gesture of fandom a finger points at them for hyping it: shaking their hair got their biggest audience reaction, not playing a favorite song—all of their songs were favored. The fans were screaming too loud to care how the music sounded, or if it sounded at all, so that the group at times stopped singing (or substituted bawdy rhymes) unnoticed. Their unbounded, unconditional success has a lot to answer for in foisting a travesty on the musical world, preventing a genuinely new course for modern popular music. They could be accused of corrupting rock in their own way as much as the tame Elvis-lookalikes they allegedly saved rock'n'roll from.

A S AMERICAN POPSTERS PROTESTED AT THE TIME, the Beatles—first called "the English Everly Bros" though Phil & Don weren't thrilled about it—were offering little that Stateside acts hadn't, musically; they had once even called themselves the Four Everlys. Their records were unsophisticated, producer George Martin having no experience in rock, coming from the show tradition of the Goons (Peter Sellers, Spike Milligan & Harry Secombe), forerunners of Monty Python. Sound engineer "Hurricane" Smith had to work with primitive UK studio equipment. So it is no wonder to the ears of American industry professionals 'Please Please Me' sounded like the Country Pop of the real Everlys. In fact it is *very* much like 'That's Old Fashioned' (1962)—so, an attractive recording but obviously nothing new.

English record producer and former rock journo Charlie Gillett: "For a while in the mid-Sixties, to be an American producer in Britain was to be in a distinct category, as Americans were recognized to have more adventurous production styles [and] played an important part in educating our engineers in American production techniques." Yanks in the UK included Jimmy Miller helming the Rolling Stones and Spencer Davis Group, Shel Talmy the Kinks and The Who, Bert Berns (a.k.a. Russell) of Don Kirshner/Brill Building pop producing recordings for Them and Lulu, Felix Pappalardi for Cream, and Phil Spector, eventually, for the Beatles themselves. Yet Gillett claims Beach Boy music, from the same mainsprings of rock, was outdated on the arrival of the Beatles— without offering any illustration of his point—and presumably came right on first hearing the Beatles in 1964 (?)! Maybe it is to fit this outlandish statement that Gillett postdates the commencement of Brian Wilson productions three years to '65.

While well-bred manager Brian Epstein put his twopenn'th in about what the Beatles should record, the group obviously knew better and were happy leaving to chance Capitol's doctoring of the master tapes in America—recognising virtually any Americans (and Capitol 'experts' fell into that category for rock'n'roll) would improve on Parlophone's work done with the Beatles' own input. No surprise that many Beatle records, especially releases outside the US, have a quirky feel of Tin Pan Alley uncomfortably mixed with rockabilly, or an English attempt at it.

Yes, they *were* different, in their Old World charm that urban Americans had long forgotten. If their charm and humor was Irish via Liverpool, the down-to-earth opportunism—and an awe of all that was flashy in American culture—was pure working-class England. An American equivalent might be experientially deprived hillbilly Jethro Beaudine coming to the big city and aping all he saw—in his fashion. Their presentation, via influences from Bert Kaempfert, Klaus & Astrid & Jurgen, Brian Epstein, came from Continental Europe. Not only appearance: Close your eyes and listen to early Beatle music, and picture everyman's Liverpool-via-Hamburg group putting out the same: an act that Rory Storm & the Hurricanes could call their equal. People who knew them and their music intimately at the time said it. It was on top of hundreds of years of European traditional music that they attempted to overlay rock'n'roll. Question: Was this rock'n'roll, an advance on rock'n'roll, or a diluted alternative more related to other Euro acts: Edith Piaf, Johnny Halliday, James Last, Kraftwerk?

Lennon & McCartney came up with a perfect combination of show tunes and ersatz rock'n'roll—not a blending of the two but a craft division as in two assembly streams in a song factory. Their rock'n'roll was as straight as they could make it, improving in the late Sixties with 'Revolution' and 'Back in the USSR'; and their Music Hall songs, which by *Sgt Peppers* they learned to give a rock veneer, were pure sentiment. Everyone could take something from it, and this catchall 'something for everyone' approach— that Elvis had turned to in 1960—brought unparalleled success.

It was all over after the music critic of *The Times* anointed Lennon & McCartney "the greatest composers since Beethoven"— not even Gilbert & Sullivan. Their habit of descending a third from minor to major, then another third back to major (as in 'Can't Buy Me Love'— personal communication from Celia Wood-Calvert)—brought comparisons with Schubert but was the sort of thing untutored musicians not hidebound by academic orthodoxies were likely to stumble upon in the normal course of exploring possibilities. It was their good fortune to be hailed for it.

A passage in Gerry Bloustein's *Musical Visions: Selected Conference Proceedings from 6th National Australian/New Zealand IASPM* compares Lennon-McCartney songwriting with Brian Wilson's. "The songwriters who most often utilised blues-based songforms were Brian Wilson and John Lennon-Paul McCartney. Wilson's surf and hot rod songs... often involve original and creative adaptations of the standard blues form, and in this sense Wilson should be accorded more credit as the songwriter who was best able to create a logical development of 1950s rock, and surf groups should be considered to be updated rock and roll bands.

"Wilson's use of the blues-based form is deserving of some detailed attention. He rarely used the form for a complete song... Most of Wilson's songs are verse-chorus forms, while in some songs (such as 'Little Deuce Coupe', 'Little Honda') the blues form is employed in the verse but not the chorus. In others (like 'Dance Dance Dance', 'Drag City' and 'Surf City') the reverse applies. The other technique employed by Wilson was to vary the standard chord progression over the last four bars of the form, thereby creating a striking hook effect, usually in combination with prominent multi-part vocals and a strong lyric hook. This technique is evident on 'Shut Down', 'Drag City', 'Surf City' and 'Three Window Coupe'.

"Lennon-McCartney also used (copied?) *[Bloustein's term]* this latter technique, most notably in 'Day Tripper' and they too created some idiosyncratic adaptations of the form... Like Wilson, Lennon-McCartney rarely employed the form for a complete song. Their normal procedure was to use the blues scheme for the A section of the typical AABA form and to create a strongly contrasting B section by using a progression totally unconnected with the blues idiom, as in songs such as 'I Feel Fine', 'Can't Buy Me Love' and 'She's a Woman'."

Bloustein goes on to point out that during 1963-66 no other successful writers but the Motown ones make significant use of the blues-based form. But Beatle use of it was strongly tempered by their AABA scheme, which "had been commonly used by popular songwriters for 'thousands of Tin Pan Alley tunes... a form totally predictable to mid-century listeners'."

The AABA songform is four 8-bar sections. Many Beatle songs were dependent on a quirky, not to say cute 'middle eight' (B) section that caused traditionalists to prick up their ears in gladness.

The myth of Beatle omnipotence—almost a religious belief in which faith triumphs over facts—was reinforced by the likes of Gillett when he misinformed his readers (1975) that "the Beatles brought the idea of the organic songwriting, singing and instrument-playing unit to the American record business"—a myth perpetuated by Murray Kaufman as late as 1998. It was there in germ form in Johnny Cash & the Tennessee Three; even, mostly, Elvis Presley, Scotty Moore, Bill Black & D J Fontana; and Buddy Holly & the Crickets. The Beach Boys took it to the ultimate before the Beatles, as such, were ever recorded.

ACCORDING TO THE ROCK HISTORIAN'S BOOK OF Genesis one summer 15-year-old Paul McCartney saw John Lennon, twenty months older, singing with his band for the local Woolton village fete in their home city of Liverpool, the chief north-of-England port that serviced Lancashire's coal mines and had cargoed cotton from the Confederacy during the American Civil War in defiance of Abraham Lincoln. Equivalent to New York City's East River dockland but without the prosperity—Great Britain had won the war but "lost the peace"—Liverpool working people were clannish and proud of their scrappy cum entrepreneurial Irish roots. For the Dead End Kids, in the Hollywood B-movies that had informed so many British Empire kids, read John, Paul, George & Ringo. Who can imagine latter-day serene guru George Harrison as the head-butting kid he was, as described by Paul, when he joined the Quarry Men? Lennon, better at lyrics, and McCartney took quirky Scouse humor and added clever wordplay for their songs. Once they started mixing with the fashionable-arty London crowd in 1963 literary pretentions crept in.

It was early 1958 that the three-man core of the Beatles consolidated. This was three years after Lonnie Donegan hit with skiffle, and Bill Haley & His Comets impacted rock'n'roll on Britain with devastating results via 'Shake, Rattle and Roll' and 'Rock Around the Clock', the theme from gang/rebellion movie *Blackboard Jungle*. English youths—egged on by violent Teddy Boy subculture—reacted accordingly when Haley & the Comets toured just a few months before, rioting and tearing up seats with flick knives. More than the Teddy Boy image and attire rubbed off on the Quarry Men. Reportedly, the lads themselves were not above a bit of opportunistic rough-housing to get what they wanted from the mean streets of Liverpool or Hamburg.

And it was two years after Elvis Presley. The younger and better looking Elvis had burst from the Tupelo, Mississippi backwoods into throbbing blues center Memphis, Tennessee to mix r&b and country music and take over Teen America. His scintillating, melodramatised performances of 'Heartbreak Hotel' and 'Hound Dog' were frenetic and frailly breathless, and held to be extraordinary, coming as they did from a white man's vocal cords. His 'Jailhouse Rock' broke a year later at the time Lennon and McCartney were meeting, with Buddy Holly's 'That'll Be the Day' and 'Peggy Sue', and Jerry Lee Lewis's 'Whole Lotta Shakin' Goin' On' and 'Great Balls of Fire' just as popular.

Though less authentic than Elvis's earlier Sun recordings of 'That's Alright Mama', 'Mystery Train', 'Baby Let's Play House' and 'Good Rockin' Tonight', white rock'n'roll was, after a breach birth, coming out of incubation. Always just a heartbeat and last gasp away from crib death by misadventure, it would soon be rolled on in its slumber by hefty corporate America, rock'n'roll's domineering stepmother.

Little Richard, Chuck Berry, Bo Diddley and Fats Domino had already scored their first hits on the (white) pop charts—'Tutti Frutti', 'Maybelline', 'Bo Diddley'/'I'm a Man', 'Ain't That a Shame'. All were remorseless rock'n'rollers, until Richard repented, and were black—so couldn't be teen icons in the eyes of the music industry of the time. The substitutes who were allowed to make white girls go all gooey were pale-complected, fussily groomed Italo-American boys—Bobby Darin, Frankie Avalon, Fabian, Freddy Cannon, Bobby Rydell, James Darren, Lou Christie. Ethnics like Tony Orlando, Teddy Randazzo and Steve Alaimo who didn't 'regularize' their names had viable recording careers but were obviously less stellar. The teen idols were promoted by *Bandstand* and Pat Boone's series from the 1957-58 tv season, Billboard magazine and its new Hot 100, and a host of other mass media outlets.

The absence of Elvis Presley in the army for two years cleared the way for these ballroom imitations to replace real rock'n'roll. By the time of Elvis's release in April 1960, Little Richard, Chuck Berry, Bo Diddley, rock'n'roll's doomed integrationist DJ Alan Freed, Buddy Holly, Richie Valens, the Big Bopper, Jerry Lee Lewis—and two early, genuine Elvis rivals, Eddie Cochran and Gene Vincent—had been killed, maimed, incarcerated, scandalised, called to religion, or otherwise incapacitated. Bland cyphers posed limply in their places.

Worst of all was the seeming deathwish by Elvis himself as a driving force in rock'n'roll. The all-new model stopped playing live and wiggled his pelvis exclusively on cue for a stream of everworsening fan flicks, now a danger only to the sheltered coeds who populated them. His abdication didn't escape the Beatles and Beach Boys, who each retained loyalty to rock'n'roll in their manner in the face of stolid opposition from their elders and impotence from rock'n'roll's founders.

A PARALLEL UNIVERSE AWAY IN LIVERPOOL, LONG before Elvis was a disappointment, Paul came across John & the Quarry Men singing 'Come Go With Me', a current hit that would feature more in the career of the Beach Boys than the Beatles. John stepped down to chat and sang Gene Vincent's 'Be-Bop-A-Lula', and in the language of young rock'n'rollers Paul replied with Eddie Cochran's 'Twenty Flight Rock': a mating call and on-the-spot audition, with Paul trying to avoid his new 17-year-old partner's beer breath. They had barely begun rehearsing together—Buddy Holly and Everly Bros—when seven months later Paul brought George Harrison, just turning 14, in as the sixth of a fluid group. Though much closer in age (eight months younger than Paul) than Paul was to John, George was a callow observer caught in no-man's-land with a battle of dominating egos constantly raging around him. Later, despite the enmity between the co-leaders, John confirmed that he chose Paul as his partner and George tagged along. George, despite early on being overshadowed by Paul on guitar, would claim Paul ruined his guitar playing by telling him what or how to play.

Grinding attrition blew off two less aggressive Quarry Men (from John's Quarry Bank School)—John and Paul's mutual friend Ivan Vaughn and Len Garry. John, after he'd left school, reserved a ritual assassination by washboard of best schoolmate Pete Shotton, who was now deemed outdated. He, like other friends, was used as a toadie-employee—much like Elvis's "Memphis Mafia"—to do dirty work right into the Yoko Ono era. George clung on, ingratiating himself and showing impressive self-preservation skills until the two leaders said he was in; incumbent guitarist Eric Griffiths was cold-shouldered by the three one rehearsal day and had to be told by drummer Colin Hanton. Hanton was useful as long as he had his drum kit. It was a mock-macho, essentially cowardly strategy John, Paul &

George would pull at least once more in their determined climb to the top.

Ivan Vaughan, who wasn't serious about music, was probably the biggest loss. He became a successful academic, and many have testified he was the source of Lennon's outlandish sense of humor. The three remaining played through incarnations as the Everly Trio, Silver Beetles, ridiculous Silver Beats (after the vegetable) and many more with a succession of co-opted drummers—usually jazz-trained 25-year-old Tommy Moore, when he was available. Late August '59 they got a regular gig at a basement coffee club owned by the Best family. After a year's residency they needed a permanent drummer to be considered professional—an overseas tour was imminent. Pete Best, at loose ends just finishing school, was the only applicant. He had a drum kit, so he was in. George had left school with no qualifications, heading towards a life as a street tough with John, saved only by art school. Paul, easily the most successful at school, let his grades slide in favor of devotion to his guitar and image as a Teddy Boy rock'n'roller. Summing up reviews of the group at the end of the year—when John's art school friend Stu Sutcliffe had informally joined the group—other Liverpool groups judged them way less than good. The four hung out at the art school or nearby at the Jacaranda Club, where among the intellectually curious they got to know Gerry Marsden and Rory Storm & the Hurricanes.

In 1960 through their agent, Jacaranda owner Allan Williams, self-styled Svengali-stuck–in-backwater-Liverpool, the boys auditioned as backing band to Billy Fury, one of the stars, with Cliff Richard, of *Oh Boy!,* a ground-breaking, highly popular pop show produced by Jack Good—hailed as the savior of tv pop and soon to go on to great success in America sponsoring a lot of other Britons on tv. Fury, like Richie Starkey raised from the Dingle slums of central Liverpool, was the most authentic of a stable of ersatz rebels handled (rumor had it in more ways than one) by Larry Parnes, London's leading pop impresario. Parnes put the Beatles with Johnny Gentle instead, for 18 pounds (about $44) each for an eight-day tour of Scotland. When they were coopted on the spot to back a stripper they knew any other pasture must be greener. Williams had contacts in Hamburg....

Just graduated from a not-very-good (to put it kindly) garage band, the Beat Brothers imagined they had reached the big time though still playing sleazy, small-time provincial UK venues. They raised themselves to compete with "artistes", Parnes' pool of pruriently named teen idols, Tommy Steele, Billy Fury, Marty Wilde, Johnny Gentle, Vince Eager, Duffy Power. The one-time Johnny & the Moondogs chose what they considered stylish—that is, flamboyant— stage names in the tradition of overblown amateur dramatics: Johnny Silver, Paul Ramon, Stuart de Stael, Carl (Perkins) Harrison... The guitarist of Rory Storm & the Hurricanes, Liverpool's top group, was Johnny Guitar, from the Western movie; and another fan of cowboy mythology in the group had recently elevated himself too, after two legendary gunslingers: Ringo Starr.

They continued to learn to replicate, in their way, the playing on r&b records brought to Liverpool by seamen who had visited the States—inspiring the city's youths to make it a rock'n'roll center. Over two Hamburg tours they fulfilled their first contracts playing Bruno Koschmider's Indra and Kaiserkeller clubs, and Peter Eckhorn's Top Ten, where Liverpool vocalist Tony Sheridan was playing. Germany's main port and an entrepreneurial hub quickly recovered from the war through the German "economic miracle", money flowed there more freely than the trickle in Liverpool, though as a group they received about 15 pounds a week according to Paul, instead of the 100 they'd been promised (Chris Salewicz, 1986).

In early 1960 John, at art school (where he found wife-to-be Cynthia, from a better-off family), had cajoled best friend Stu Sutcliffe into buying a bass guitar so he could join the band on stage. Stu learnt—or rather didn't learn—to play standing with his back to the audience to hide his bumbling fingering. According to Pete Best, Stu's cultivated James Dean charisma by itself was a prime attraction. His sole vocal, 'Love Me Tender', hardly made up for his inept playing. But, an accomplished artist, his less than two years with the Beatles was only ever a second-best infatuation. The clincher was an on-stage fight with Paul, supposedly having insulted his Hamburger girlfriend Astrid Kirchherr. The real Beatles, xenophobic as any other post-war working-class Briton, didn't dream of wooing a foreign girlfriend—prostitutes were different. Like more than one of the Beach Boys, on return from their first tour John and George were treated for venereal disease.

John had a nasty, destructive streak—especially when drunk or high, which was often in the Hamburg days—admitting later he fantasized at being a Teddy Boy, a cutesie name (based on their Edwardian era coats) for gang thugs infesting the UK: a nightmare world of *West Side Story* meets *A Clockwork Orange*. At one of the Beatles' Liverpool gigs gangs of a hundred a side confronted each other. At another Paul was threatened with imminent death by a blademan, and the group once watched from the stage as a 16-year-old boy was kicked to death. It was from such a kickfest to the head when the group was ambushed after a gig that Stu succumbed to brain haemhorrhage, his death delayed for a year by John jumping to his defence (Ross Benson, 1992). John suffered a broken wrist punching Stu's attacker.

The Beatle look morphed from Teddy Boys in full, black leathers with add-ons and substitutions from Beatniks Astrid and former boyfriend Klaus Voormann, later a Beatle session musician in the UK and sometime member of Manfred Mann. Existentialist was the look, now the Beatles had to look up what it meant. Liverpool was rough enough, but Hamburg ingrained a toughness necessary to win over the harshest audiences—playing eight hours a night relieved by sleeping in an excrement-littered dosshouse, rubbing shoulders with pimps and slashers daily. Despite all the internal ructions—and George and Paul's humiliation at being deported from Germany—a group bond was formed. The advantage was that the Germans at this time had no conception of rock'n'roll, so there were no critics. All Koschmider wanted was a good show, enabling the Beatles to develop their showmanship and formulate a repertoire combining old standards with r&b, which improved remarkably according to the visiting Rory Storm & the Hurricanes. Although he didn't know it at the time, Pete Best wasn't really in the club at all—he hadn't taken the secret trials of initiation: He wasn't a drug-taker or much of a boozer, and when the time came he didn't switch to Beatlehair either.

Back in Liverpool they took advantage of a return residency at Pete's family's club the Casbah, and in a show two days after Xmas 1960, wowed a Liverpool crowd for the first time at a Merseyside town hall, though many of the kids thought they were German. From March 1961 for two and half years they would play nearly three hundred lunchtime shows for token pay at the Cavern, a jazz club remodelling itself to the Liverpool beat that had taken over in popularity. But an offer from the Top Ten's Peter Eckhorn of forty pounds a week, alternating with Tony Sheridan, still playing eight hours a night, was too 'good' to turn down (Salewicz).

It was on this second trip to Hamburg that they met local bandleader and record producer Bert Kaempfert, who took them under contract starting 1st July 1961 to record them behind Tony Sheridan (from *Oh Boy!)* on hoary 'My Bonnie', 'When the Saints Go Marching In' and crassly sentimental 'Nobody's Child'. George's instrumental 'Cry for a Shadow', intended as a parody of clean-cut Shadows music, was recorded, plus an r&b version of the old standard 'Ain't She Sweet' sung by John. For now, only the first was released. Kaempfert had his world breakthrough that year in 'Wonderland By Night', a kitsch classic that went to number one US—showing a remarkable insight into conquering the Easy Listening market of what was after all a foreign culture. He is a strangely neglected influence on the Beatles' career, possibly because he listened to the best compositions Lennon & McCartney had to offer and rejected them all—though according to *Mersey Beat* editor Bill Harry "by 1960 they'd done between eighty and one hundred songs: a lot of the songs that became the hits in the sixties they'd already written long before. Initially they were unsure of introducing them to local audiences, because I don't think they believed their material was all that good" (Salewicz). When the Beatles got big in America Kaempfert licensed the recordings out to MGM and Atco and made a profit off them.

They returned home hoping to lift the Liverpool crown from all contenders—not a very majestic crown where the highest aspiration of a band was just to be recorded: only one had achieved it. For now they were third in box-office pull, visibly behind Cass & the

Casanovas and Rory Storm & the Hurricanes, according to Bill Harry (in Salewicz), who set about redressing the order by featuring his favorites at every available opportunity.

Kaempfert had no interest in the Beatles as a group, and their wayward gigging continued until late autumn '61 when the crowd reaction at Liverpool's Cavern Club was seen by spiffy young chainstore heir Brian Epstein. This nice legend of instantaneous zapping by lightning strike is refuted by Terry McCann, the assistant at Sam Leach's Iron Door Club, who said Epstein was there in July watching the Beatles—implying he'd waited four months before signing them (Salewicz). His terms were an astronomical 25% cut of the gross take, all expenses—his too—to come from their 75%, and would ultimately cut Lennon & McCartney out of majority rights to their songs, but in the nicest, well-bred way, choosing loyalty to such other members of the born-to-rule class as Dick James (that same acquaintance of George Martin and of 'Robin Hood' fame), Epstein's partner in Northern Songs publishers. Martin rejected offers of shares from James on ethical grounds (Barry Miles), deliberately excluding himself from this windfall being enjoyed at the Beatles' expense. It is estimated by McCartney biographer Miles that their manager's share of the income all up came to well over double that of each Beatle, even though Lennon and McCartney were nominal partners in Northern Songs.

For all Epstein's smooth etiquette, his approach was reminiscent of the hand-over-fist grab Tom Parker made in preempting rights to Elvis Presley's income. Epstein afforded his four green clients no legal advice, keeping them in pitch dark—if not callously duping them, and was otherwise ineffectual in getting them top dollar (his romantic devotion was another matter). This contrasted with the Beach Boys, advised by Capitol producer Nick Venet—who had no business responsibility to the group—to set up their own publishing company and so capitalise on songwriting. But there would come to be some basis for comparison, fiscally if not in manners, between managers Brian Epstein and Murry Wilson.

Don Arden, English promoter and part-owner of the Star-Club where the Beatles played their last Hamburg tour, 1962: "It was discovered after [Epstein's] death that the deals he arranged for the boys, such as recording contracts, were very small deals... He understood that he was on to something big, he was becoming a personality, and he'd wallow in that glory, but he wouldn't let anyone talk to The Beatles. When it came to actually negotiating or renegotiating a recording contract, he never had the slightest idea. And when he died I firmly believe The Beatles were on something like a ridiculous royalty of five percent on a worldwide basis."

WHILE THE OTHERS WERE AS INFUSED AS ANY Englishman with the familiar clang and patter of show tunes from the local Tivoli or Strand, Paul sucked up Music Hall tradition almost with his mother's milk: "[Liverpool had] lots of musical history combined with all the old music hall stuff, which my dad played in a band.... He certainly influenced me." Paul's father bought him a trumpet and he learnt 'The Saints' and jammed it with neighbor boy George, 14. John too, whose cousin Julia claimed that their whole family knew her mother, John's Aunt Mimi who raised him, "had far more talent than John because he only inherited a slight spot of it." Mimi taught John banjo and "later, in the studios... they had to cut, cut, cut, cut because John was back on banjo chords" (Pritchard & Lysaght, 1998).

Paul penned 'When I'm Sixty-Four' at 15 and then 'I'll Follow the Sun'—both of which might as well have come from Paul's father's father; neither were considered worth recording when presented in turn to Dick Rowe of Decca, George Martin and the BBC. Who could guess they would end up among the admired songs of the most admired group of the Sixties? In developing his stagecraft as a lead singer and ambitious professional Paul had the group play slow romantic standards: 'Till There Was You' from *The Music Man*, done by Anita Bryant, whose biggest hits were the 'Paper Roses' prototype for Marie Osmond and fittingly, Kaempfert's 'Wonderland By Night'; 'Over the Rainbow', Judy Garland's theme from *The Wizard of Oz;* and torch song 'Falling in Love Again' "never vonted to, Vot am I to do—can't help it" popularised by Marlene Dietrich thirty years before. Paul's was a real showbiz brain, full of it. By sheer luck all but one of these mercifully disappeared into the ether before the Beatles became famous. Even so the visage of leather-jacketed toughs cooing all these live is too much to conjure.

Pete Best was the heartthrob of the quartet for the growing number of girl fans thronging to hear the Liverpool Beat in gestation at the Morgue, Blue Angel (also owned by Allan Williams), Grosvenor Ballroom and Jive Five. John had summarily got rid of Pete Shotton; Paul had needled Stu Sutcliffe and other members out; and now all Liverpool but drummer Pete must have known he was living on borrowed time.

Likely too much a rock'n'roll drummer and not versatile enough for what they wanted to encompass, Pete was dumped after two years in August '62 on the eve of their first Beatle recording, Paul's 'Love Me Do'—George and Paul were the prime movers. Epstein, as manager, broke the news to him, days after assuring him his place was permanent. George Martin, given the lion's share of blame/credit since, was unimpressed with Best compared with the personality boys but had hardly heard his drumming. And Martin was unsure of the adequacy of Best's replacement, George's mate Ringo Starr. If the reason for Best's dumping was his shyness, coming across as "moodiness"—this was ideal, one would have thought, for a rock star (photos show the virility of a Brando and confusion of Dean) but at odds with the other Beatles' showbiz chirpiness and dedication to practicality in showing pleasing personalities to get to the top. As retrospective justification, the long depression Best's ousting plunged him into was proof of incompatibility of temperament. Pete was left to local stardom back in Liverpool—with Lee Curtis & the All-Stars, then the Pete Best Four. Or rather, local notoriety and shiploads of pity. Later he released several solo singles in America (including one on Capitol) and an album entitled hopefully *Best of the Beatles*.

MARTIN AND EPSTEIN HAVE BEEN UNDERCREDITED as 'fifth Beatles'. Martin deserved at least third ranking in their recorded output, and any detailed assessment must credit recording engineer Norman Smith as an associate Beatle for his constant efforts to present the group as American rock stars. Martin was very often the telling element of this creative-genius-by-committee, as with 'Please Please Me', first presented to him by John as a gooey ballad with a Roy Orbison treatment. In "doubling" its speed, Martin was responsible for the Beatles' best early recording and went a considerable way to defining their sound.

Martin: "I told them they needed to speed the whole thing up, make it much more vibrant. So they played it to me again in the studio and I modified a little bit of an ending and so on. At the end of the session I was knocked out because it really was a great record."

Epstein was the one critical factor—equally pivotal in their career—in presenting the new Beatles tidied up in their first conventional suits and ties on stage and for the audition for Martin and Parlophone. Their leather jackets and dungarees, the 'threatening' theatrical mode of Brando, Dean and Gene Vincent, had to go. The title of his autobiography—*A Cellar Full of Noise*—describing the circumstances in which he found the Beatles at the Cavern Club—tells what he thought of his protégés' music. But he was a natural showbiz salesman eager to sell what the majority of the public wanted. What did it matter whether it was personality or music that sold the Beatles?

Yet, in Guinness's *Rock Day by Day* his obituary remembered him solely for "taking the Beatles from their black leather roots into the collarless suits that they became famous for"—actually attributable to Astrid Kirchherr and famed designer Pierre Cardin, who created the collarless look. Given their Liverpool popularity someone would have picked them up sooner or later. But without Epstein's unique infatuation for them (or rather, John) and devoted vision they might never have been bigger than the Four Pennies or Fourmost. Chances are they would have become ancient Teddy Boys ageing disgracefully on the oldies circuit—a lot like nascent septuagenarians the Rolling Stones.

Chapple & Garofalo: "The Beatles had more going for them than their light-hearted sexuality and wit, although both were new images for rock singers in America. Their manager, Brian Epstein, was extremely astute in promoting them.... The clean, suited image that Epstein built for the Beatles greased their way into the hearts of parents, as well as teenyboppers. Most significantly, Epstein promoted his act with coordinated press campaigns that emphasized the personalities of the Beatles as much as their music."

Cynthia Lennon: "I don't think they really felt it would happen. They dreamed of it.... If they hadn't met Brian, who was a conservative, well-dressed, well-spoken man with a quest, I'm sure they wouldn't have gone anywhere. I don't think Brian has had the acclaim he should have" (Pritchard & Lysaght).

Multitudes of sixth, seventh and eighth Beatles have had champions over the years, most peripheral to the music but all essential to the legend: Stu Sutcliffe; Sutcliffe's girlfriend Astrid Kirchherr and her friend Jurgen Vollmer; Mal Evans, Alistair Taylor and Neil Aspinall, essentially gofers but two of whom claimed to have co-written hit songs. After the power of Martin and Epstein had gone, Yoko Ono would be third Beatle, contributing nothing but wielding the power of life and death over the group.

The best American claimant was WINS-New York DJ "Murray the K" Kaufman, who played a critical role in plugging them in the key market place when no one else was interested. Picking up on 'She Loves You', he stuck with it despite rejection by the public for the station playlist. When the Beatle carnie cranked up for America in December he was already on the bandwagon.

George Martin too bought into Beatle destiny—obviously a self-fulfilling prophecy when so many people in key positions can tweak destiny. He imagined his group had made inroads in the American scene: "The Beatles records issued on the Swan and Vee Jay labels were getting more and more prominent. So, by the time 'I Want to Hold Your Hand' came along, Capitol realized they had to get behind it before the dam burst" (Pritchard & Lysaght). But insiders from Capitol say that its execs practically had to have a gun put to their heads to have anything to do with Beatle records— precisely why they were leased out to Vee Jay and Swan and would have been dumped elsewhere if EMI-London hadn't muscled its subsidiary label.

Martin continues: "The pressure was too great, and that's really what contributed to the enormous success of The Beatles in America." True, but it was not pressure from the public. According to the UKMIX Beatles website the best a Beatle single did in the US in 1963 was 'From Me to You' in selling barely 21,000 copies—triple that of 'Please Please Me' before it; after it 'She Loves You' sold, quote "hardly any". Vee Jay's *Introducing the Beatles* too sold fifteen times as many copies on relaunch February 10th 1964, when the Beatles were famous: from literally nowhere on the charts to number one.

THERE IS LITTLE EVIDENCE IN THEIR RECORDINGS— the early ones especially—that the Beatles absorbed the essence of r&b. In England any band with electrified guitars and a permanent drummer was called a "rhythm & blues combo" if only to distinguish it from the skiffle groups who got by with a washboard and biscuit tin for percussion, a stringed broomstick handle and tea chest as stand-up bass. The Beatles, especially John, held up as their hero tame showman Lonnie Donegan, whose latest American hit (fall '61) was embarrassing novelty 'Does Your Chewing Gum Lose Its Flavor on the Bedpost Overnight?'. John's later assertion "Before Elvis, there was no one" reveals more about his pitch for superstardom than any search for authenticity.

His group would repeatedly recall unrecorded Hamburg and Cavern shows as their best playing, recollecting through a nostalgic speed-induced haze great memories that maybe never were. Their rock'n'roll tracks as recorded, starting in '63, have more mechanical reproduction to them than instinctual feel, including Paul's talent-quest imitations of Little Richard, even John's impressive throat-screech on 'Twist & Shout'. Ditto their remakes from contemporary girl groups whom they much admired. New versions of the Marvelettes' 'Please Mr Postman' and the Shirelles' 'Boys' were attractive alternatives but others were simply inadequate; but hardly anyone in the UK had heard the originals because the BBC, which severely rationed public exposure to rock'n'roll, especially the black variety, was the only game in town until the first "pirate" radio station got underway in March '64.

While the Beatles resuscitated interest in early rock'n'rollers, unearthing Chuck Berry's and Richard's careers, no one asked the black artists who started it all if they wanted their music co-opted note for note, lick for lick, by white men with flowing locks whom they had no chance of emulating in white (therefore world) public favor. The Beatles and Beach Boys both paid frank tribute to their progenitors by reviving rock'n'roll standards, and any assessment of relative success is obviously subjective. The Beatles' remakes of the three songs mentioned above maybe have improved energy levels because fresher: the hits they were taken from were recent. Having performed many others for five years before recording, they seem all out of spontaneity, their delivery stale. This was the view of the English industry including Dick Rowe, head of Decca, who had heard hundreds of English rock'n'roll covers in his time and heard nothing special at all in the Beatles'.

The Beach Boys at times fell short *reinterpreting*—'Louie Louie', 'Rock and Roll Music'; the Beatles, generally, didn't attempt it. For the most part copying instead of remodeling, they put themselves up for direct comparison with the originals—and too often fall on their face. Beatle takes on Berry standards 'Rock and Roll Music', 'Roll Over Beethoven', Little Richard's 'Kansas City', 'Lucille', 'Long Tall Sally', Larry Williams' 'Dizzy Miss Lizzy', 'Bad Boy' are the real thing to fans and those who haven't heard the Fifties 45s. With the odd exception, nothing is added to the originals by the Beatles but a sense of contrived melodrama—and something essential is taken away: that rawness of performance and feeling of wild abandon, actually precisely controlled, conveyed by the best Fifties rock'n'roll/r&b—its reason for being.

The Beatles' performance of black Soul Music seems distinctly lacking in soul in favor of replicating the technique: 'You've Really Got a Hold on Me', which compared with Smokey Robinson & the Miracles' is bereft of any saving individuality; even the dynamic 'Money (That's what I want)'—in which John Lennon's screech technique is again employed. So unnatural was Lennon's performance on 'Twist and Shout' that it was always saved for the end of their Cavern concerts because his voice was useless after it.

While their rendition of gentle 'Words of Love' is without the poignancy of Buddy Holly's, still other re-recordings sound something like amateur-night tributes to their heroes, much in the vein of the Stones' 'Under the Boardwalk', light-years behind the Drifters'. Note: Mick Jagger's tone and phrasing, which made the Stones' career, can be traced back to one performance—Ben E King's delivery on the Drifters' 'There Goes My Baby'. In this category must be placed 'Chains', 'Anna (Go With Him)', 'Baby, It's You', 'Honey Don't'.

The Beach Boys through 'Surfin' USA' *improved* on Berry's 'Sweet Little Sixteen'. With an all-new production for an updated sound, they don't pretend to be serving up the original rock'n'roll: they've moved on, shifted the music forward by a quantum leap—a gargantuan contribution to Sixties music that has gone all but ignored until recently. *Q* magazine nearly forty years later judged 'Barbara Ann' too to be among the best ever remakes.

IT WAS '65-66 BEFORE MAINSTREAM BRITISH GROUPS showed any signs of funk in their playing or singing— the Yardbirds and Cream, the Beatles as late as mid-'67 on parts of *Sgt Pepper* and '68 with 'Lady Madonna' after being exposed to Jimi Hendrix in Britain and in direct association with keyboard-player Billy Preston, formerly with Little Richard in Hamburg and Sam Cooke.

Since it is claimed that the Beatles rejuvenated a stagnant rock scene on their arrival in the American consciousness, this cries out for some depth perception. Informed by contemporary American music for years—that which was already forming the basis of Sixties Music—they learned to create music with that imagination and variety inherent to the Sixties, whose standards have been admired ever since, in time infusing their own efforts with distinction. Purely objectively, in 2003 a complex computer program designed to analyze all aspects of a musical piece found that Beatle music was most like that of Elvis Presley—and geared to maximum hit-making potential. That journo at their first New York press conference who questioned whether they were "four Elvis Presleys", struck on something since overlooked. Ringo made a joke of it. But likewise, film producer Walter Shenson, who believed they were "copycats" of

Elvis and the Beach Boys, and music expert Gerry Bloustein who suspected the Beatles might have copied Brian Wilson's songwriting, just might have got it right.

Apart from their imaginative wordplay there *was* something distinctive about Beatle and other English styling as performed. Playing rock'n'roll over many years, their sound also took on the stamina with which the Merseyside groups played all night on their Hamburg gigs, inspired by their steady diet of speed. They had "more electricity" as admitted by Brian Wilson, coming down especially hard on the accented beats, George on lead, John on rhythm, and Paul's bass all striking in unison, reinforced by Ringo's heavy Ludwig snare-bass and tom-tom variations.

It was later, perhaps influenced by the Beatles in one way, that Brian told Dennis to keep a two-handed backbeat—on snare or snare/tom-tom so as to concentrate the attack on the beat rather than diffuse it with cymbal work: If at times the Beach Boys' live playing has been criticised it was for a perceived lack of body. Though the likes of 'She Loves You' played live on the Sullivan show bears no comparison to the Beach Boys live on the *TAMI Show*, on vinyl Ringo's Chicago-made Ludwig not only gave out a thumping beat, he filled in Liverpool's version of a rock'n'roll sound with a constant noise (you couldn't call it a rhythm) by riding his ever-present sizzle cymbal—*the* easily recognisable Beatle background signature, making for imprecise music noisy enough to cover a multitude of sins through numerous rockers. Dennis couldn't match Ringo's ballroom-slick technique but was more adventurous, by 1964 teaching himself piano and guitar—and developing real expression in his singing.

The motives of Beatle pushers in the USA have to be questioned simply because they had heard the original music and knew the Beatles (mostly) weren't clued up to it. But in a homeland fundamentally ignorant of rock'n'roll the four Liverpool lads were at Christmas time 1963 the toast of Great Britain after a year of hitmaking: 'Please Please Me', 'From Me to You', 'Twist and Shout', 'She Loves You', a British record 1,890,000, and 'I Want to Hold Your Hand' 1,640,000—the two biggest they would ever have at home. Albums made a total for the year of some six million discs UK.

In truth at this stage there was little separating their music from Liverpool mates Gerry & the Pacemakers, who with the Searchers, Rory Storm & the Hurricanes, the Swinging Blue Jeans and the Merseybeats (and the unsung Derry & the Seniors—the first Liverpool group to be recorded, the Big Three, r&b specialists King Size Taylor & the Dominoes, Cass & the Cassanovas and Bob Evans & His Five Shillings), defined the Mersey Beat. The Pacemakers set a home record of three debut number ones, 'How Do You Do It?', 'I Like It', 'You'll Never Walk Alone', each four weeks on top. The last, a remake from an American musical, with its stirring "Walk on, Walk on..." refrain became an enduring anthem tugging wiry Liverpudlian heartstrings harder than any Beatle song. But there were few domestic records left to break as "Beatlemania" came to full flourish in October; now there was even a professional girl band, the Liverbirds, trimmed in Beatle cuts, who played all Beatle songs (Stanley Booth). Within two years they would break *world* records and be awarded MBEs as a major British export industry in themselves.

They had performed before royalty and produced sales figures that would have impressed in the US with over triple the population. But they seemed to have blown their chance at American fame, as merely a twinkle in the eye of a few Yanks and expatriates who had pushed their records for the past nine months to no visible response. Yet, two weeks after Christmas their first stateside hit was racing up the charts, number one in another two to eventually sell an estimated 12 million-plus worldwide. Six weeks after they were nobodies they were greeted at New York City's JFK Airport by 10,000 screaming fans (so the legend went—it has since been revised down to 5,000 then 4,000 by most sources), and the cheeky jokesters proceeded to charm and entertain the hardened newshounds at that first press conference that has ever since been a favorite clip in retrospective rockumentaries.

They would conquer America via radio, tv and movies and by June 1964 so dominated the pop world that they attracted a quarter-million souls gathered to pay homage in sparsely populated Australia. In the mid-Sixties their music and lyrics were synonymous with the spirit of the times. By the end of the decade their 'philosophy' and, mostly, their hair had been adopted as *entre-nous* not only by dedicated followers of fashion but by society at large.

How did it happen? It wasn't as if they hadn't already had as much of a chance as anyone else. They had scored articles as well as paid publicity in nationally distributed US trade papers and appeared in influential top forties from New York through Chicago to Los Angeles—and went no further. Who's to say this first verdict wasn't the *right* one? Could so many people have missed something so supposedly transcendent, or was it just not there? Even the experts who came to know them best said they could hear nothing special in them *until they met them*—then they were *very* special. Did it all come down to a personality cult in the end? They were backed by a powerful corporation that could ensure them as many bites at the cherry as it took. And big corporations and the money that went with them could make the sky look green and the grass sky blue to a willing public.

T HE STORMING OF THE FORBIDDING SHOW BUSINESS pantheon of the USA by a group of self-taught musos from a chronically depressed corner of England has taken on the aura and awe of mystic Arthurian legend, heralding the return of the Britons to a place of honor and power in the world after the morale-sapping Second World War and its aftermath. It was alleged too to have replicated the creative power and genius of a Beethoven, somehow aggregated among five or six people. At the time, to most adults, the event was about as important as the Spice Girls in the nineties—providing good press space in the tabloids on those deemed to be A-list celebs.

Abba, too, have been deified by fanatical nostalgia trips dredging up everything from their fashions to their sexuality—and eventually lauding the music unquestioningly in a lump sum as part of the mystique. But listening to Beatle fans and those who have since swallowed the myth it was as if a light was turned on, the dawning of a new renaissance. The world was turned on its head to a new reality and was now the way it should, must, be—the bible goes. There was no—never had been—girl groups, Beach Boys, Phil Spector,

Motown; nor, most tragically, a core of *authentic* r&b that the Beatles displaced in the public consciousness. All bad things were washed away as the Beatles, after a musically uneventful five-year labor, gave rebirth to a superior form of rock'n'roll— it was devoutly believed.

Cynthia Lennon's depiction of the Beatles' never-never success as a fluke gifted by Brian Epstein probably comes close to the truth. At least he, then Martin, and then the whole of EMI, made the difference between their chances and others' starting out with at least equal talent. Once discovered and groomed by Epstein, and second, fortuitously taken up personally by multifaceted Parlophone boss George Martin, who liked *them* much more than their talent, and third, backed by the overwhelming corporate weight of the EMI power structure—What intelligent and ambitious young men wouldn't assume the confidence to develop as good songwriters and proficient musicians?

Granting this, the group's born-to-rule air must have been no small bluff or sheer naiveté—until their abilities could catch up with the super-hyped publicity. Performers more gifted than the Beatles relate how decades into their career they are still plagued by the fear of being "found out"—a living nightmare of someone in the crowd standing up, shouting down all the applause and listing in pointed detail each of the performer's deficiencies: an excrutiating stripping off of the 'emperor's new clothes' bit by bit to reveal a thickly candied ham putting it on. Pop culture heroes are rarely subjected to the same scrutiny or held to the same standards as disciplined artists, but are much more at the mercy of the majority's unreasoning likes and dislikes of the moment. The Beatles having leap-frogged from a five-year career as a club band straight to a supposedly top recording act, bridging the gulf took a heap of the power of suggestion by one of the slickest publicity machines ever. If this is far-fetched then maybe incompetent, inflated presidents have never been elected by majorities of voters thanks to hype and 180-degree spin.

The Beatles themselves, with all their public bravado, obviously felt they had lucked out at all three major advances in their career. Why else were they happy just to be taken up by a manager and be blindly led by him despite the attendant grooming out of their self-image as rebels, and no matter how disadvantageous the terms? Then happy just to become a recording act, no matter how penny-pinching their cut of proceeds? And acquiescing in their conversion into products, the merchandising of imposed images—not their music— being their main source of income through their entire touring career to come.

The picture is painted of a group of pliable, not very serious young men—if not quite dilettants—used and abused by the system, and lapping it up for the instant gratification and spill-over power landing in their lap. The usual counter argument, of artists oblivious to business matters and other power relativities, doesn't do it. Their looking-out-for-number-one mindset as the toughest Quarry Men whittled themselves down to a rock hard core of three, and then ongoing elbowing for position within the Beatles, speaks for precisely the opposite. These were four tough lads raised to be go-getters in a carnivores' environment—and so more experienced and 'older' in the ways of self-preservation than most contemporaries they would meet along the stardom trail.

Once at the top they were extremely protective of that status— usually via Epstein until his death but then shown by Lennon and the rest on occasions, displaying a sense of entitlement not seen in an entertainer since Al Jolson and only replicated today by the most self-absorbed divas. There is an account of Lennon going for an outsider inadvertently wandering onto "a Beatle stage". By the end they all took an exclusive stance. Their vaunted sense of humor was taken in by osmosis from their hard-nosed environment growing up, then was partly derivative from the Goons and English variety. Their hero Peter Sellers—maybe even their model in regurgitating, parroting others—maintained an image of devotion to his art while taking on trophy girlfriends and on a movie set physically measuring co-star Alec Guinness's dressing trailer to assure himself of his own validity. And just like the question was asked of Sellers, It's remarkable but is it acting?, the question asked of the Beatles is It's highly entertaining but is it real?

Commentators have ever since sought a rational or even an irrational explanation for the Beatles' easy conquest of America, or rather its wholesale surrender. The generally accepted theory is that, a month after the traumatic destruction of President JFK and his idealised image, American youth needed something new to believe in—an article of faith. To which it must be said, it's lucky they didn't pick Herman's Hermits or Freddie & the Dreamers as the new messiahs to step into the psychic vacuum, though Freddie's manic high-pitched laugh and Herman's dopey "I'm 'enery the eighth, I am, 'enery the eighth I am, I am!" have about as much profundity as "I wanna hold your ha-a-aa-a-a-a-aand!"

The Beatles, best of all, recognized that Beatlemania had taken on a life of its own that had nothing to do with them as real, flawed people, and particularly as musicians. But finding the throne vacant, given an unprecedented media platform and handed the golden sceptre on a velvet cushion, it was easy to step into the roles of teen gurus. For the first year after it hit America the music was virtually irrelevant—as can be seen looking back at several songs that ended up hits beyond magnitude. No matter how big their egos inevitably at some point their Scouse scepticism kicked in, and sensing the insanity of their situation the Beatles to varying degrees would come to detest their own biggest fans, the ones who bought every record, went to and screamed through every concert and lived by every word from the Fab Four's lips, every arch of an eyebrow. Despite their over-healthy self-belief, devotees' indifference to quality came to erode their pride as musicians. So they courted intellectuals like Bob Dylan as peers to get meaningful feedback—and guidance for direction. Their swerve to 'folk' in his wake came at the expense of quickly dissipated rock energy.

But in the nature of mania, the love affair continued one-sided, which might help to explain how in the year 2000 an Oldies DJ, his obsessive belief unabated, can perpetuate the age-old propaganda by spinning the Isley Brothers' 'Twist and Shout' then announce: "The guys who *wrote* that song, the Beatles, the Fab Four—up next!" The rewriting of history to exalt the whole British Invasion hardly bears thinking about. As a great media man once said, "When the legend becomes fact print the legend."

Finally, published in the June 2001 issue of *Reason* magazine, came a chink in the Beatles' pervasive aura over the media. In a lengthy article *Still Fab: Why we keep listening to the Beatles* senior editor Charles Paul Freund reasoned that their lasting appeal was based on ingrained showbiz cues centered on Music Hall sentimentality and frequent resort to tried and true pop, citing 'Till Their Was You' and 'Red Sails in the Sunset'. Lyrical influence came from Dylan and Paul Simon but, he says, they drew more and more on British pop: "The corny, melodic sentimentalism of the Music Hall repertoire was a rich vein for the group and they were never to abandon it…. Indeed, the influences that shaped their major, later output—most of the music for which they are best known—emerges from an antique pop style."

Freund proffers "It is [narrative and Music Hall] that are able to claim the attention of an audience that was born long after the group broke up. But what do either of these elements have to do with the mythology that the rock establishment embraces? Precious little. In the end, the rock world's head was turned by music that was sweet, corny, artificial, and intensely sentimental. Rock has yet to come to grips with this." He concludes that their reputation has been sustained "through mythmaking and obscuring."

Further, according to Freund, just as Easy Listening stations had allowed American exposure to Frank Ifield, Cliff Richard, Helen Shapiro, they initiated interest in the Beatles' 'I Want to Hold Your Hand'. One copy brought into the country weeks before its US release by the girlfriend of an MOR Washington DJ started it, travelling hand to hand to St Louis and Chicago. Radio station policies assured the Beatles' success. From WINS, new program director Rick Sklar at WABC—New York's clear-channel powerhouse that broadcast across the landscape to Philadelphia and to the Catskills in the north—unequivocally favored the group above all others. *All* their product was added to the playlist without having to demonstrate sales—a promotional coup for the Beatles and station stars Radio Hall of Famer "Cousin Brucie" Morrow and sportscaster Howard Cosell but a betrayal of obligation to objectivity. And the #1 song was now played almost every hour, allowing the Beatles to stay there.

On release, with its pushing by EMI and incessant plugging by New York stations, it sold 200,000 or so in its first week ending January 1st and an estimated 500,000 or more nationwide by the 5th— for a time selling at the rate of 10,000 an hour around New York alone. The Big Apple's directive sank in across the country. It wasn't necessary in Washington, where WPGC had long championed Petula Clark, Shapiro and other MOR English sounds. It adopted the Beatles as station policy and littered its top ten with innumerable album cuts, unlike other acts who had to issue a single and wait for it to sell before just one side might register.

THE BEATLES HAD KNOCKED FELLOW WHITE MAN Elvis Presley off Rock's throne—as the well-clued-up Brian Epstein had predicted two years before—but it was not for a year and a half that they would be granted an audience with "The King" (it was Colonel Parker's PR brainchild). After the initial euphoria of expectancy had worn off the opinion of one Beatle hanger-on present was that their one-time idol was now something of a boring old fart—related by Peter Guralnick in his book on Presley. Other sources indicate that Lennon and McCartney, whom Elvis knew were the important ones, being the writers, were picked out for a separate conflab, and they were accordingly flattered and enthralled—despite John expressing reservations to the King about his recent music. Paul "really liked him... He was a really cool, casual guy." They played bass together. The Beatles were also said to have been mightily impressed with Elvis's prototype tv remote. And there was that later Lennon summation, "Elvis died when he went into the army." It might equally be said that John 'died'—as a creative force—when he met Yoko.

So, barred from the King for now, on first touchdown in New York their first priority was an introduction to Lennon & McCartney's songwriting heroes Carole King & Gerry Goffin, probably the American songwriters most like them, of 'Crying in the Rain', 'The Loco-Motion', 'One Fine Day', 'Chains'—to name the better ones, and much teen idol mush for Bobby Vee, James Darren, Tony Orlando; adapting quickly to the British Invasion in spades, providing for Herman's Hermits, Manfred Mann, the Animals and Monkees. And they asked to meet Hollywood's former blonde bombshell Jayne Mansfield, in decline even before the death of Fox stablemate Marilyn Monroe and reduced to soft porn. Presumably the mammary-obsessed Liverpool lads, touted as sophisticated minds, assessed Jayne as the equal of Marilyn in essentials, or even superior: 40-18-36. Jayne too, notwithstanding her reputed 163-point IQ, was reportedly dismissed, at 32, as an "old bag" by a Beatle spokesman. On their trip to France they had reserved the same treatment for Brigitte Bardot ("She seems so old"), the nymphet who at barely 30 had been her country's most famous export for seven years. John had years before been so enamoured that he requested in his chauvinist way that girlfriend Cynthia model herself on the "sex kitten". Dark horse George, a junior partner in the band but showing conspicuous maturity, was on his own nominating Margaret Rutherford as favorite film star. He would stay aloof, too, on the visit to Elvis's place. George only tipped his hand in public when drunk, accidentally (he was aiming for someone else) throwing a drink in third-ranked buxom blonde Mamie Van Doren's face at the Whiskey-A-Go-Go, LA's swankiest rock club.

Undoubtedly, at 29 in 1964, after eight years at the top, the "Tupelo Mississippi Flash" had lost some of his dash, not the inspiration he had been at the start of it all. For all his pink Cadillacs, he was an army veteran after all, a stalwart of the Establishment, pillar of the American Dream. He hadn't died, but was it terminal? Out of the public eye three years, preoccupied with his movie career and precisely aware of how bad they were, his own idol James Dean, certifiably cool by dying in a high-speed car accident at 24, must have been sulking more than ever, in spirit, at the gutless star vehicles Elvis's people were pumping out: *Kissin' Cousins* (in March), *Viva Las Vegas* (May), *Roustabout* (November).

Musically, Elvis seemed spent, relinquishing his crown to drop to fourth male vocalist at the end of 1963 in the Gilbert poll after Johnny Mathis, Frank Sinatra and Bobby Rydell. What he summoned to challenge the new upstarts was weak. Of four A-sides 'Kissin' Cousins', the most successful, just broke the half-million in US sales;

'Viva Las Vegas' almost as many but barely made Billboard's top 30; 'Such a Night', 'Ain't That Loving You Baby' less (figures from Guralnick). Probably his best, 'Suspicion', by Doc Pomus & Mort Shuman, was consigned to a B and only reflected glory was left him when an inferior cover by Elvis-imitator Terry Stafford sold the million that was eluding the King lately.

Apart from issuing ever-weaker movie tracks as 45s, Elvis was a champ of album filler, his three soundtracks containing such unalluring titles as 'El Toro', 'The Bullfighter Was a Lady', 'No Room to Rhumba in a Sports Car', 'Carny Town'. Late in the year *Roustabout* was his first number one album for three years, accumulating the Gold 500,000—his last of the Sixties. Faithful UK fans—never to see Elvis but for a glimpse at a remote Scottish airport in transit from Germany—were beginning to revolt too; at his best, 'Kissin' Cousins' only equalled its stateside placing, no.10.

The Fab Four, new rulers of Rock, were interpreted in extremes from putting them down as zany mop-tops, mere objects of juvenile appeal, to comparing their songs to classical greats. On the receiving end of the invasion, conservative intellectual William F Buckley, early on convinced of their malign influence, summarised the Beatles as "so unbelievably horrible, so appallingly unmusical, so dogmatically insensitive to the magic of the art, that they qualify as crowned heads of anti-music, even as the imposter popes went down in history as 'anti-popes'." On tv they were satirised by the Flintstones, the Simpsons of their day, singing "She says 'Yeah, yeah, yeah! He says yeah, yeah, yeah! We say yeah, yeah, yeah!'"— an obvious send-up of 'She Loves You'. For two years the Beatle phenomenon would be parodied with "The Bedbugs/Termites are coming!" But to the powerful, who made money out of them— and whose opinions counted—they were pushed to the heights. Though few might be as convinced as Buckley, the other extreme has deemed such patent lowlights as 'This Boy' and 'It's Only Love' playable and replayable by oldies stations the world over promoting themselves as "The Home of the Beatles!"

The intellectual level of the original infatuation is shown by a tribute song that charmed the world—conceived, composed, arranged, recorded, distributed and a hit within a month of the Beatles' touchdown. It went: "We love you Bea-ee-dles, oh yes we do-oo. Da-da-da-da-da-da, and nighttime too-oo. When you don't sing to us, we're blue. Oh Beadles, we love you!" The Carefrees sang in carefree girly voices to capture the vacant sound of unconditional fan worship. And a long dormant fellow 'animal' act came out of hibernation with a tribute of sorts, *Chipmunks Sing the Beatles Hits*—popular enough to help promote the Beatles—and issued a cover hit of 'All My Loving'. The second "America's answer to the Beatles" was surf band the Pyramids, who shaved their heads.

Critics from respected publications such as The London Times who found "Aeolian cadences" in Beatle music must have dealt a massive psychic blow to the creative leader of the Beach Boys, searing Brian Wilson's susceptible ego. Here he had mastered the intricacies of composition, of vocal and instrumental arranging, and record production, only to have four amateurs swoop in to snatch the rewards with "not that great a song" as he called 'I Want to Hold Your Hand'. It must have grated every time a poor album cut from *Meet the Beatles* was played by bandwagon program directors. Unlike Wilson, who could complete his entire recording process solo, Lennon-McCartney often came into London's Abbey Road studio with sections of a song roughed out, tinkered with it, the others joining in, until one or the other 'completed' it that day—very often George Martin: Since his extensive revision of 'Please Please Me' he had written the beginning-and-end refrain of 'Can't Buy Me Love'. They depended on Martin to arrange parts and musicians for any additional instruments and to add required special effects, and on engineer Smith to approximate that American sound. On breakup all but McCartney called on Phil Spector to make their records sound like something.

Brian Wilson had defined a pinnacle of American pop music. From time to time he dwelt long and painfully on it all. His group's instant reaction was to feel "very jealous" and very threatened by their country's cathartic reaction to the Beatles, but facing this "big fad" spurred them on.

166

The Beach Boys had good reason to feel threatened. Through spring, summer and autumn '63 the three Beatle singles and album released in the US got nowhere, echoing their (non)impact in Canada. Del Shannon had taken 'From Me to You' to the charts but showed no telltale signs of being rock'n'roll's new messiah. Yet the Beatles were made of even less likely material: weedy English boys with collar-length hair and funny clothes, appealing in a land where the standard male—even rock fans—aspired to look like a US Marine? 'Murry the K', *the* Beatles' champion, played them to no one—when they were pulling over 15 million viewers on UK tv.

But then literally in weeks the entire landscape of American teen music changed. Girl groups, who had littered every level of the Hot 100 up to December 31st 1963, could now be counted on one hand. Slipping down were the Murmaids, Caravelles and Secrets, all to be one-offs. And nothing appeared in January from the Shirelles, Crystals, Chiffons, Marvelettes—premier acts. A new intake wouldn't appear for eight months: the Supremes and Shangri-Las. Lesley Gore, unstoppable for her nine months of superstardom, was on the slide. Gold idols Rick Nelson and Bobby Rydell were among the few soloists who had survived the new sounds of the Beach Boys and Four Seasons and (temporary) inroads made by black r&b artists. In the midst of top 20 hits when the Beatles arrived, who could have predicted they would be their last? And 'Louie Louie', the first from the Kingsmen, was almost their last: British groups took over their white r&b niche in a swoop.

BETTING ON A SURE THING—THE FIX WAS IN FROM EMI, Capitol finally rolled with the arm twisting and went all out promoting their English charges to New York City, the gateway to the heart (purse strings) of the American entertainment industry and rubber-stamp passport to the rest of the continent. Capitol bosses initiated a "The Beatles Are Coming!" media blitz and New York radio stations bolstered by Capitol's promotional budget gave away dollar bills—then enough for dinner at McDonald's and a movie—to those who would turn up to greet the Beatles at the airport.

Capitol lavished $50,000 on promoting its London boss's spoilt pets—exactly ten times more than on any previous PR project. Persons of influence whose palms had been greased in the past with services and merchandise worth maybe $100 in hopes of extra airtime—two weeks' pay for most people—could now expect $1,000. One small, malleable station in the Big Apple threw out all the program schedules and any thought of fairness and played *nothing but Beatles*, 24-7. Instantly on release date, December 26th, New Yorkers, who had been slipped the Beatles with their breakfast, lunch and dinner for two weeks, bought up the new single as if a subliminal addiction had set in, amounting to a million nationwide by January 10th.

The company execs who had barely roused themselves from their easy chairs for the automatic, self-driving success of the Beach Boys, gave away free lapel buttons and bumper stickers— five million of each were manufactured—and cavorted in Beatle wigs to have their photos taken and circulated to press outlets. A million copies of a four-page Capitol 'newspaper' on the Beatles were distributed, presumably to explain what a Beatle was and how it should be used. In further contrast to their work for the Beach Boys—always relying on Murry's perpetual motion—they made special efforts to see every radio DJ in America had a copy of 'I Want to Hold Your Hand'.

"There was a lot of hype," Capitol VP Voyle Gilmore admitted later (in Stanley Booth). The crass commercial strategy by these masterminds set the tone for America's greeting of this new business opportunity, from the start more a get-rich-quick scheme than a musical experience. It worked, though better for Capitol, Brian Epstein, music publishers and a score of merchandisers than for the Beatles.

Promoter Sid Bernstein, a seer who had booked them long before for Carnegie Hall: "By the time the end of 1963 rolled around, The Beatles were a household word in America, and my long-shot guess turned out to be a very important one for me. We sold out in one day." The Beatles were nationally famous via saturation media campaign before hardly anyone had heard their records. Those who had, March to October, mostly dissed them.

Murray the K, buying into the rapidly-improving-Beatle-music theory: "There was something in the air. We had lost President Kennedy, and the kids seemed to sense we were missing something in America, something The Beatles were ready to give us.... A change in attitude... I was impressed, as were a lot of people. Not so much with their music, because how the heck can you compare the music from *Sgt Pepper* to 'She Loves You' and 'I Want to Hold Your Hand'?"

Brian Epstein, after examining American tastes on a highly successful promotional trip, had been sure they had the disc to finally crack it. "Plus the fact that a lot of information had filtered through from the British press from the Royal Command and Palladium shows and the scenes in London and Beatlemania in general. There was great interest, and it was just the right moment for the issue of 'I Want to Hold Your Hand'."

Dave Dexter too: "I called them to see if they liked the sound of the Capitol issue—we changed some of the sound characteristics from the British Parlophone record—and they assured me the sound was even better, a hotter sound and a little more volume" (Pritchard & Lysaght).

Despite the abject failure of their previous releases, and regardless of the new one, as Sid Bernstein said, instant fame was the Beatles' simply through promotion *before* the release of 'I Want to Hold Your Hand'. Gilbert's nationwide US poll of 3,184 teenagers in the closing days of 1963 placed folk singers Peter, Paul & Mary, Kingston Trio, New Christy Minstrels and Chad Mitchell Trio ahead. The Beach Boys were consigned to runners-up in a "most promising vocal group category" in which the first rock'n'roll placer was the Ronettes, famous in magazine culture for La Ronette hairdo—and in sixth place came "an English group, the Beatles" (Eugene Gilbert).

At the unrolling of the red carpet and implied invitation "Come get our children!" the entire domestic music industry was up for grabs, and its teen clients sacrificed. Through the simple dynamics of power marketing, concentrating on pushing one item and neglecting your other 'lines', anything the Beatles touched was odds on for top spot including the three utter flops on re-release. 'Please Please Me', which had made a lone appearance in Chicago last March hovering for three weeks on the lowest rungs of the WLS top 40—only that high because it was Vee-Jay's home city—now unnervingly returned a year later driving almost to top.

The Beatles had been just one—the most *un*successful—of an array of British acts released by Capitol of Canada through 1963 including Helen Shapiro, Frank Ifield, Cliff Richard, the Hollies, Gerry & the Pacemakers and Freddie & the Dreamers. It was the second half of the year before the Beatles began to chart at all, in Vancouver, Winnipeg and smaller Ontario centers—Hamilton, London, Kingston—then seeped into Toronto in November (*Encyclopedia of Music in Canada*). This presence in a key hub in the North American radio and record distribution networks helped them be heard in the USA. Capitol of Canada continued to happily pick up more UK groups as they came on stream: the Dave Clark Five, Swinging Blue Jeans, Manfred Mann, Animals, Hermans Hermits, Yardbirds.... Leakage over the border of any number was inevitable. In months most of these and others would be among America's biggest stars. The Hollies and The Who would dip their toes in the vast, trans-Atlantic waters only to be sent back. Their time to swim or drown was three years later.

Writer Stanley Booth: "Steady publicity in the British press had been picked up by the London offices of the US news media; *Time*, *Newsweek*, and the *New York Times*, as well as NBC and CBS television, did stories about the Beatles." The media machine working on the Beatles' behalf was unstoppable—so how could the Beach Boys with only disdained rock'n'roll to work with, combat it? From 'Surfin' Safari' and '409' through 'Surfin' USA', 'Shut Down' 'Little Deuce Coupe' and 'Be True to Your School' they had shown a commitment to the genre that was refreshingly hard-driving compared with any other white act (and many a black one) on the teen scene. This would bring out of them even higher quality, opening eyes and winning hearts over. They had to be that much better to shine through, for soon after Capitol's enforced 'discovery' of the Beatles the Beach Boys were a distant second billing on the label's nationwide print advertising.

It was before their first overseas tour in the New Year of '64, of their stronghold 'Down Under'—Australia and New Zealand—that the Beach Boys heard of the Beatles. Company scuttlebutt about how much Capitol was spending on the Beatles surfaced. Sharp eyes noticed on the Xmas week chart of CHUM-Toronto—the unofficial Canadian national chart—the discarded 'She Loves You' leapfrogging over 'Be True to Your School'. On January 3rd a video clip of the Beatles performing at seaside resort Bournemouth was telecast by Jack Paar, famous as founder host of *The Tonight Show*—the original Johnny Carson, but witty. On this occasion he was wittily dismissive of the English group. The highly popular Huntley-Brinkley news hour featured shots of UK Beatlemania.

NEWLY FAMOUS IN THE US, THE BEATLES HAD BEEN huge for ten months in parts of the British Commonwealth, where their Parlophone recordings were distributed—now maybe bigger than the Beach Boys. For a week or two the Beatles must have been mere curiosity value to their American counterparts: It was unheard of for unreformed, unassimilated English popsters to make it big in America. During World War II patriotic Englishwomen Gracie Fields and Vera Lynn were hugged to Yank bosoms but more in a spirit of wartime solidarity. Lonnie Donegan and oleaginous movie crooners Anthony Newley and Frankie Vaughan left fading impressions in the Fifties, and bosomy sexpots Joan Collins and Diana Dors were deflated in Hollywood. The biggest current pop stars, Cliff Richard, the Shadows, Petula Clark, Shirley Bassey—and recently the Beatles and the Pacemakers—made not a ripple.

Across the scope of show business, though, the British were established worldwide by virtue of their native language. For a century such illustrious names in entertainment as Charles Dickens, Oscar Wilde, George Bernard Shaw and D H Lawrence had made tours of America. And for nearly sixty years film had drawn many British Isles personnel, translating on to screen what America stood for. Audiences had integrated as their own the best that England had to offer, from early comics Charles Chaplin and Stan Laurel, matinée idol Ronald Colman and director Alfred Hitchcock to child stars Freddie Bartholomew, Roddy McDowall, Elizabeth Taylor. They were tacit recognition that the United States was the dominant cultural power, though many including the English would continue to claim that it was best noted for its lack of 'culture'—i.e. European restraint and historical sense. The Beatles would show both, in their somewhat inhibited, careful rock'n'roll, and their adherence to historical precedent in music, shown mostly (but not solely) by their devotion to the ancient British tradition of the Music Hall.

To this day, despite having fought a traumatic war to escape English social and political control, American aristocracy sees Britain as a mother country and cultural touchstone and, in the way of snob value, attributes class and sophistication to anything done by 'Britishers'—as if a part of Shakespeare and Dickens lives in every Benny Hill. English muffins and tea have been adopted as mandatory by the American upper crust and gutter English swear words "bugger" and "bloody" are used casually and publicly by US authority figures like baubles of status.

In popular music there had been two smash hits from England in the past two years, Acker Bilk's 'Stranger on the Shore' and the Tornadoes' 'Telstar' under independent producer-manager Joe Meek, one of the few sources of distinction in the UK industry. Neither act had the corporate push to make a career in America but broke the ice for independent thinkers. Success for a London girl duo, the Caravelles—actually office workmates who enter-tained their friends at parties—said more for the possibilities of the Beatle approach: The Beatles were cajoled to write their own songs as an added gimmick, but they were as manipulable and amenable as any girl group in Producer Pop and actually a good deal less professional: untrained and batch-picking various skills and styles. Facing the professional orientation of American girl groups, who normally underwent training in voice and made careers in music, the English girl pair took their folk-pop hit (a cross between the Breakaways and Springfields) to no.3 in Billboard December 21st when the Beatle push was full on. Epstein and the boys were encouraged, given the gargantuan backing they were armed with.

Throughout show business it was already the age of the British. Elizabeth Taylor and Richard Burton in still-running megahit *Cleopatra*, Sean Connery in the British-made James Bond series, along with the wildly successful Disney adventures of Hayley Mills (her films grossed higher in the USA than Elvis's) and comedians David Niven, Alec Guinness, Peter Sellers and Terry-Thomas had made Englishness a highly desirable image in pop culture. The most unlikely success had to be Margaret Rutherford, an MGM superstar for the past two years on the strength of her role as Miss Marple in a series of murder-mystery black comedies somewhat distanced from Agatha Christie's intentions.

And if a 72-year-old turkey-jowled matron could command a world market, why not a trendy group of young men hyped to the maximum? All who went before them, as well as emergent young stars Peter O'Toole as *Lawrence of Arabia*, Albert Finney as *Tom Jones* (1963's biggest US screen hit), Julie Andrews (to star in the biggest hits of 1964 and 1965), Julie Christie and Michael Caine, carved the way for automatic acceptance of the Beatles once they'd captured the media limelight: one more in a flood of broadly appealing acts, a curiosity piece made into a showbiz phenomenon. Serenading America, all played the English card like Stradivarii.

So, no shooting stars out of a dark sky, the Beatles stood on their compatriots' shoulders to peek over at an untapped well of world adulation. Always considering themselves something special —a group set apart from the others, if only by their personalities— the Beatles as individuals expected it as their due, and growing fully conscious of their 'destiny', behaved their way to success. A deliberate, populist tactic, as admitted by Paul McCartney to personalize their songs, was constant use of the personal pronoun in titles and themes—"I", "Me", "You"—so self-involved teenagers could put themselves into the song. A trademark device to capture public sentiment, a transparent ploy from a trite showbiz tradition, was to croon about "luv"—the hackneyed songsmith's cliché, not the genuine emotion. Many songs had both key insertions in the title: 'Love Me Do', 'She Loves You', 'PS I Love You', 'All My Lovin", 'Can't Buy Me…', 'And I … Her', 'All You Need is…'— to the extent that they became known overnight affectionately in radio vernacular as "those ever-lovin' Beadles".

A scene is conjured of John and Paul and George Martin tacking together with a craftsman's pride a song, like ornate furniture-makers with standard fittings and adding whatever curlikew elements would appeal to most consumers. This while the creative flow oozed organically from Brian Wilson's piano….

B RIAN MOVED WHEN THE SIGNS WERE PROPITIOUS. On New Year's Day—one of few public holidays in America and one that symbolized a new start—the Beach Boys recorded 'The Warmth of the Sun' and 'Fun Fun Fun' and were twelve days from their first foreign tour, to the brave new world of Australasia. There too they had started the surfin' music craze— though hidebound by obvious typecasting: most of the derivative Australian bands were real surfers. 'Pipeline' was 3rd biggest hit for 1963, 'Wipe Out' 6th. Vocals were less popular—'Surf City' 10th, maybe reflecting that Aussie blokes preferred their musicians like their women, close-mouthed. The Denvermen ('Surfside'), Atlantics ('Bombora') and Delltones ('Hangin' Five') listed in the ten biggest-selling Australian-made hits and in the two months leading up to the visit no fewer than ten surf hits by Aussie acts entered the national top thirty.

The Beach Boys had inspired two about a surfer and his surfer girl by Little Pattie, vocalist at Sydney's Maroubra Surf Club. When they arrived, in a publicity event for the 14-year-old arranged by EMI, the boys held a blown-up photo of her aloft for the gathered media. Her bigger hit was 'He's My Blonde Headed Stompie Wompie Real Gone Surfer Boy', making it to no.2, blocked by an English quartet the Beach Boys were hearing more of.

Australasia, with its wide-open spaces and car-dependent, marine-obsessed lifestyle—as large as the contiguous US, 90% of its fourteen millions lived within fifty miles of a beach—was rich soil for the outdoors approach to stardom. Bee Gee Maurice Gibb— raised in Australia with his brothers—testified Beach Boy music was the "national music of Sydney and Surfers Paradise". Two thousand kilometres southeast along the Pacific Rim the elongated islands of New Zealand/Aotearoa, two thirds the size of California (spanning latitudes equivalent to Santa Barbara to Seattle) but dotted with two and a half million people among sixty million sheep, took the group as their own. Australia and New Zealand were used to picking music from America and Britain and this mix reflected in their own acts, who aped trends in Anglo cultural capitals.

Surfside '64, as the tour was tagged—after tv series *Surfside Six* — was a roaring success. 'Hodad' Roy Orbison and the Beach Boys were billed over the Surfaris and Paul & Paula, fresh from a Dick Clark Caravan of Stars tour with Gene Pitney and Philly's Tymes and Dovells. Package shows, which teen-rave concerts typically were, went at a whirlwind pace, each act having twenty minutes or so to make its impact. The support acts might have been struggling at that, having already reached their career peaks with just one big hit each to their names. The Surfaris were hardly the most original band—they had covered 'Little Deuce Coupe' and 'Be True to Your School' on their New Year '64 album, and like Jan & Dean and other LA bands after the surf flattened would switch to folk music—but could whip up a *tsunami* with their live performances. Fans hailed these Californian invaders, carrying uncovered pearls to the top of the charts. *Surfer Girl*'s 'Hawaii' track was released as a single (in New Zealand covered by the Four Fours) to become a huge hit, inevitably by year's end slipping to Australia's 11th best-seller of 1964, overtaken by a flood of six Fab Four songs as the full extent of Beatlemania gripped the South Pacific. Of fifty-two weeks of the Australian singles chart the Beatles would score 27 at no.1; Beach Boys none.

January 21st the tourists were greeted by 5,000 screaming fans at Melbourne's Essendon Airport, foreshadowing a more famous touchdown in New York seventeen days later. Five days earlier, in anticipation, New Zealanders had sent 'Be True to Your School'/ 'In My Room' up to no.3 on the national Lever hit parade, where 'I Want to Hold Your Hand' was already perched at top. They were captured in color performing 'Monster Mash' with the usual bilious lights on "Boris" Love's face, culled for promo stills. In an intriguing shift the Beach Boys added to their setlist 'What'd I Say?', the Ray Charles &

the Raelettes r&b standard, as the Beatles had jammed in their early days at the Cavern and in Hamburg. It was still another dare taken on by this supposedly milk-white act, featuring Mike's yakety-sax. The subject of a romance via media while on tour, back home Mike would father a child out of wedlock and be sued for maintenance.

The Beatle tour in June would attract a quarter million-strong reception committee in Melbourne—a body count not seen since Mary Pickford and Douglas Fairbanks' welcome in Moscow two generations before and not again until the Seekers' homecoming. They took over the world while their Yank confreres were working their asses off just to stay in the slipstream. Over the first three years of Beatlemania the Beach Boys would regularly outdo them musically just to gain something approaching the same effect. With Roy Orbison claiming first billing due to seniority he might have shared with his juniors his eye-opening experience of touring England just months before: Having started the road show as the superstar supported by the Beatles, the Merseysiders' star burst pyrotechnically so that "The Big O" finished out that tour opening for them.

Ben E King, famous former lead singer of the Drifters, had also met the Beatles touring Britain, and gave *them* career advice. He was one of many who suffered through the Fabs' ascendance, personal disappointment still showing in interviews three decades later. Phil Spector, too, befriended them as they crossed paths during the Ronettes' tour of Europe. He accompanied the Beatles on their maiden Pan-Am flight to the US, but more out of suspicion than friendship: Ronnie Bennett, lead singer of the Ronettes and the future Mrs Spector, much later alluded to a 'relationship' with John Lennon. Spector arranged for his girl(s) to travel back on a different flight, avoiding all temptations of the Mile High Club.

The Beach Boys arrived back in Los Angeles on February 3rd in time to find *Little Deuce Coupe* climbing to a new Billboard peak after four months in release—to retail over a million US by the end of summer—as if their fans had risen in loyalty against the imminently arriving Beatles.

January 11th 'I Want to Hold Your Hand' by this 'new' band had appeared at #80 in the Cash Box chart, running two weeks behind actual sales and a week ahead of Billboard. The next week it was joined by 'I Only Want to Be With You', Dusty Springfield's solo debut. The Beatles had shot straight on to WABC-New York's survey; Dusty's number had been its hit-pick three weeks before. In another three weeks UK archrivals the Dave Clark Five material-ised with Carl Perkins' 'Glad All Over' and it was official: *anything* English is Fab!, Gear!, Wizard!—worth listening to over and over and buying in quantity. It seems the stars were aligned for some new contagion from Britain, no matter who the carrier.

On the 25th in two huge leaps the Beatles were at number one with two million sold. Ten days into a three-week stint at the Paris Olympia, they were aware of what was happening in America, having been interviewed on the peculiarity of their phenomenon as it took off by network tv reporters based in France. They had effortlessly overtaken girl groups the Ronettes ('Baby I Love You'), the Chiffons ('I Have a Boyfriend'), the Secrets ('The Boy Next Door'), the emerging Supremes ('When the Lovelight Shines Through His Eyes'), the Murmaids ('Popsicles and Icicles') and admired female solo numbers 'You Don't Own Me' and 'Anyone Who Had a Heart'. Women would hardly be seen near the top of the chart for the next three years, losing out to a conservative male-dominated music regimen. It would be more than three months before the no.1 position was wrested back by an American act— Louis Armstrong, one more fact that spoke volumes about the new direction in music, i.e. backwards.

TO THE BEACH BOYS IT HIT LIKE A SUCKER PUNCH to the pit of the stomach that there was a new world order —especially as it seemed so much like the reactionary old, pre-rock'n'roll one. The next three years would plumb lows in the rock'n'roll era for the number of best-selling black singles and albums (Chapple & Garofalo). And where had all the girls gone? Chart-toppers from "the good old British Isles," as Mike Love called them, there had been, but the saturation play the first Beatlehit was getting and—more frightening—others of theirs dug up from obscurity, hailed something monumental, a showbiz first: It was not just instant world fame but worldwide *mania*, Beatlemania as Britain had coined it.

Reissues of the previous flops under Swan and Vee Jay, and others under its subsidiary Tollie, flooded the stores—all assumed by record-buyers to be new recordings. The storm tide of flotsam and jetsam washed up only abated in October '64 when Capitol won back the rights to all Beatle product; Calvin Carter, of Vee Jay's ruling family and its promotions man, claimed 2.6 million Beatle 45s sold on the label in one month, and a million-selling e.p. It also meant non-stop 'Sie Liebt Dich' (#97), 'Why?' (#88), 'My Bonnie' (#26), 'Ain't She Sweet' (#13) and 'Sweet Georgia Brown'/'Take Out Some Insurance On Me', a rare miss, from their German career, among those they later wished had never seen the light of day. At first they didn't mind—they knew the vast majority of it was rubbish anyway, as they acknowledged most of their own material to be. How long could the siege go on?

The Beatles and Brian Epstein landed 7th February so white-hot that many US mediamen and businessmen had to reverse their attitudes, if not their opinions, about these decadent, subversive, luxuriant longhairs: The mop-tops seemed to be sneering at everything a good American crewcut stood for. The Capitol bosses could make fun of the phenomenon—playing in Beatle wigs—at the same time as exploiting it. According to Chris Salewicz, on the flight, Paul, always with his feet on the ground, grilled Spector: "They've got their own groups. What are we going to give them that they don't already have?" But if anyone did shrewd Paul knew when to 'keep shtum'; on the rapturous welcome on landing he knew it was safe to go through with the bluff. Two days later the group broke all ratings records on *The Ed Sullivan Show*: 73 million US viewers, nearly 40% of the entire population, a greater proportion than any *Superbowl*: so compelling to watch it was as if they were visitors from outer space rather than staid England.

The Beatles were greeted with regalia flying at the British Embassy to officially bless their visit and their show at 9000-capacity Washington Coliseum on February 11th was filmed for theaters across America and shown a month later. There was one important alteration: Brian Epstein cannily agreed to distributor CBS's suggestion that Beach Boys concert clips (and Lesley Gore) be inserted to broaden its appeal—and ease the way into whichever American hearts were still holding out on the Beatles. It was good exposure for both groups to be seen with the other, each recognising joint primacy and so sharing the biggest slice of the fan-cake.

Oakland Tribune's Bob MacKenzie at the local Paramount: "The screaming for Miss Gore was comparatively mild, sounding something like the cry of a wounded elephant. The Beach Boys—antic purveyors of surfin' music—prompted screams in the higher registers, something like a dozen pigs with their tails tied together. But when the Beatles finally hopped on stage, with abundant mops bouncing over their eyes, their pocketless pants tight as skin and lapels trimmed in velvet, young Oakland screamed in earnest.... Their eyes shone with the vacant, transported glow of hero worship.... And when it was over, they filed dazedly out, their foreheads dripping, their hair in damp strings and their eyes aglaze with exhausted satisfaction." It was predicted that four screenings at 143 theaters across the country on Saturday 14th March and Sunday 15th would draw 1.5 million paying viewers.

Next day the Beatles went one better with the Sid Bernstein gig at New York's hallowed Carnegie Hall. On all three of their first major American dates this rock'n'roll band trotted out their crowd-winner, a faithful rendition of 'Till There Was You', the Broadway show tune. Humorously, Paul overpronounces "saw" as "sore" in straining for an American accent. A week after their first they made another appearance on Sullivan, broadcast while on vacation in Miami. In six weeks an unknown act had been invited with open arms into the élite of American show business—the inner circle it had taken genuine artists Sarah Bernhardt, Igor Stravinsky, Enrico Caruso, Charles Chaplin, Greta Garbo, Maria Callas years to pry open. Most daren't attempt it. Gracie Fields, plying the same down-to-earth Lancashire charm and never-say-die chirpiness, had failed in America with the personal favoritism of Hollywood mogul Darryl F Zanuck and all the resources of 20th Century-Fox behind her. She came in cold into an isolationist prewar environment often hostile to or uncomprehending of England, unlike the paved road laid out for the Beatles.

The Beach Boys, being hooked at the hip on film with the Beatles, were confirmed as America's finest; yet, constant reminders of the all-enveloping media attention greeting the Beatles dogged them, and haunted the competitive psyche of Brian Wilson. Later in the year on their first tour of Europe, in the v.i.p. lounge at Ireland's Shannon airport, a discussion took place between Brians Epstein and Wilson. One asking the other when the next Fab visit to America was due and being told not for almost a year, Brian Wilson is said to have exhaled visibly with relief. On that tour Mike Love and Carl Wilson would visit them backstage—to congratulate them, and maybe reconnoitre tactically for their secret. Carl, one more fan with posters festooning his walls, was close to awe, and already by summer '64 had his own Rickenbacker 12-string emulating George Harrison, one of four dozen in the world.

February saw born an alternative, macho 20th Century icon. Cassius Clay, reigning Olympic Gold Medallist, defeated Sonny Liston to be world heavyweight boxing champion. The Beatles, visiting him at his training camp, further ingratiated themselves to broad American society by having their photos taken taking a 'knock-out' punch; and obviously compared gimmicks, the Mouth vs the Mops. As Muhammed Ali his empowering of black people around the world would dwarf that of Martin Luther King or any political figure: a truism of the Sixties. Celebrated on the new Beach Boy album, 'Cassius Love vs Sonny Wilson' had Mike and Brian poking fun at each other's voices, and provided good evidence they could perform their recorded music impromptu: 'Fun Fun Fun', 'Surfin' Safari', 'Farmer's *Mother*', etc. In their crisp-hot guitar lines, solid beat and confident harmonies they were reminiscent of the Beatles on their recent BBC studio recordings, but with more intricate and precise vocal interplay.

THERE WOULD ALWAYS BE ROOM FOR GOOD, HARD-driving rock'n'roll!? 'Fun Fun Fun'/'Why Do Fools Fall in Love?' was released without a designated A-side, allowing station programmers to decide their favorite. To Capitol's credit, it is notable how many other Beach Boy B-sides were promoted just as prominently as the A on picture sleeves in recognition of prolific quality. As it happened, Miami was the only major city to plump for 'Fools', stalling top 20. Brian took boy-soprano lead and bumped up the echo at Gold Star studio for this good, rocked-up Sixties reworking of Frankie Lymon & the Teenagers' 1956 hit.

So, facing the acid test was 'Fun Fun Fun' by Brian & Mike. Though full of now recognisable classic Beach Boy elements— remodeled Chuck Berry guitar intro, driving Little Richard rhythm, insistent beat, well-honed evocative lyrics, soaring harmonies and propelled by Mike's confident nasal drone—an insecure Brian delayed release till February 3rd, just as the Beatles were celebrating their second week at number one. One of their best enduring creations, since universally acknowledged as a rock'n'roll classic, on March 21st it landed at #5—a higher Billboard placing than their last two outings, and edging the Dave Clark Five's 'Glad All Over' — some feat since the London group had maximum exposure via the Sullivan show. Inevitably, amid Beatlemania, it was shut out by 'She Loves You', 'I Want to Hold Your Hand', 'Please Please Me' with the Four Seasons' 'Dawn'. Then it was jumped by 'Twist & Shout' and forced down a spot.

The Gilbert Youth Research nationwide survey had 'Fun Fun Fun' no.4 the same date. It excelled in the Midwest, rising to one or two places shy in Chicago, the Twin Cities, Milwaukee and across Ohio to Pittsburgh and Baltimore-Washington—where it was 25th for the year, as high as most toppers. It did top in Boston (WRKO ranked it 11th for the year) and Buffalo, and bounced up and down #4-5 at KFWB-Los Angeles. New York—"Home of the Beatles"—had it scraping top ten, better than recent efforts but no indicator of its huge long-term sales in and around Gotham. It was 11th for 1964 in Montreal, made par in Vancouver and Toronto, and over the Great Lakes in normally Beach Boy-immune Detroit.

The unparalleled sales rate of Beatle singles in March—their all-time career peak—drove the US total for the year up to $862 million

(Chapple & Garofalo). So the Beatles can be credited with bursting the 1959-63 ceiling and the annual total would continue to rise through the Sixties, contrasting with the UK's steady slide. Beach Boy sales followed them upward. 'Fun Fun Fun' was reputedly their bestselling side yet—a million in a few months—though their three 1963 *doubles* averaged between a million and a quarter and a million and a half over their chart runs. Given its success across the biggest US markets, and particularly long term, no wonder it went on to sell over four million (Tim Allen, *Home Improvement,* 1996).

On reflection, the Beach Boys saw that even an 'also ran' won kudos up against the Beatles, estimated to have captured a gut-churning 60% of the US singles market for three weeks in March — monopolising the Billboard and Cash Box top five at the end of the month and placing ten more songs in the charts one week. Long-term, in a 1976 survey of sales and votes taking in a large part of the Eastern Seaboard, New York's powerful NBC network station would rank 'Fun Fun Fun' 3rd of 1964 hits after 'Hello Dolly' and 'I Want to Hold Your Hand'. It would garner over two million plays on US radio, ranking with 'I Want to Hold Your Hand' and 'Twist and Shout'; above 'She Loves You', 'Love Me Do', 'Can't Buy Me Love'.

As one car song faded another rose: Jan & Dean, no.8 nationally with the dramatically produced 'Dead Man's Curve', prefiguring the more famous death ride of 'Leader of the Pack' later in the year. Brian's contribution was acknowledged, and on 'New Girl in School' (#26), the B.

A SLAP IN THE FACE AWAKING THE BEACH BOYS TO the fact that they were being dished up as a distinct second best against the Beatles was the disrespect shown by Capitol and the media to their latest offering, *Shut Down Vol 2*, containing 'Fun Fun Fun', its well-executed B-side, and two Brian Wilson classic ballads, 'Don't Worry Baby' and 'Warmth of the Sun'. Their distinctive new version of 'Louie Louie' was copied for the *Coffee & Cigarettes* movie theme (2003). Packaged with a cover showing the group in racing-jacketed tough-guy poses around two of the guys' muscle cars, Japan made it one of their best ever sellers. In the States, hardly promoted by an appearance on the now late night, low budget *Steve Allen Show* almost four weeks after release date March 2nd, it took six weeks to chart and once on stayed a shorter duration than usual, nine months. It stalled short of top ten in all three major charts including Record World, a new major trade publication derived from Music Vendor.

Yet, when Cash Box sized it up near year's end, of rock albums *Shut Down Vol 2* had sold 4th in the USA in 1964. It had been #1 in Miami, in Salt Lake City's top 5 for six months, among many regional triumphs. Nationally, it placed after Capitol's *Meet the Beatles*, *The Kingsmen In Person* and narrowly behind Vee Jay's revived *Introducing the Beatles*. Fifth came *The Beatles Second Album* (Capitol), then Dave Clark Five's *Glad All Over*, *Little Deuce Coupe* 8th, and *A Hard Day's Night* 10th and *All Summer Long* 12th because only in release a few months. The first *Shut Down* and *Surfer Girl*, wilting after a year, made respectable showings, 19th and 32nd. Writer Lee Crane (in his article 'The History of Snowboarding: a Thirty Year Time Line', December 1st 1996) summed it up: "Nineteen sixty-four was a pretty big year.... By June The Beach Boys had sold 12 million albums, the Beatles had seduced the nation...."

In the face of repeated snubs by Capitol and the mass media the case for a timely bout of paranoia by the American group was looking justified. Still, appearances on the teen Mecca *Bandstand* and veteran comedian Red Skelton's broad-rating tv show kept them before the eye of the record-buying public in April and May. In May, polls by Radio Free Europe covering much of Central Europe including some countries behind the Iron Curtain such as Hungary, reported Elvis Presley, Paul Anka, the Trashmen, Beach Boys, Beatles and Rick Nelson as most popular rock and roll acts (Gilbert Youth Service). The Beach Boys were dismayed by the Beatle phenomenon, but resolved on their own path.

To further this they dared what other parent-dominated groups — the Jacksons, Osmonds, Cowsills, Beatles (parented by Epstein and Martin), Monkees (Columbia-Screen Gems), Partridges (ABC network), Carpenters—dared not. Recurrent ructions on their Pacific tour were enough to decide Murry's fate. Public rebukes and humiliations were temporarily avenged on behalf of the band while getting off the tour coach in Sydney: Brian turned on Murry and floored him with a punch in an ugly scene witnessed by the tour promoter, New Zealander Harry M Miller. It was on the day of their *Bandstand* screening, 2nd April, that the last straw dropped—at the 'I Get Around'-'Little Honda' recording session. The Honda song would be the group's last real hotrodder, celebrating the new Japanese 250cc road and racing model motorbikes just out and quickly sucked up into the American lifestyle. Some time after Dennis did the honors for 'Little Honda', yelling the frenetic "Go!" that starts off the driving bass and bass-drum intro, Murry bawled him out so severely that the drummer got up from his kit, put his fist through a wall and stormed out. Brian and Mike, concerned over the stability of their group, fired Murry on the spot.

A month in bed with depression brought Murry back with a vengeance, still occasionally appearing at recording sessions. The group must have revelled in his absence at first, but gone were the overseas promo trips on their behalf, shipping home bulk gifts intended as trinkets for radio staff, record distributors and store managers in a multitude of cities across the USA (Timothy White)— backslapping with his free hand: the schmoozing, personal payola that had become a pleasantry of the American music industry. He took up, briefly, Dave Marks' new group, then the Sunrays, having hits with Beach Boy sounds he wrote himself.

Left on their own the group tended to run wild, notably Dennis and Mike's womanising on the upcoming European tour. Later they grossly overspent on recording projects. A more lenient punishment for Murry might have been considered—suspension or banning from recording sessions. The loss of Murry, no longer in their corner with, as Timothy White said, "constant (though warranted) questionings of Capitol's accounting practices" meant there was no one to harry their career enemies with a father's zeal for the family cause. Brian and Dennis took their ambivalent relationship with Murry hard, didn't attend his funeral (in 1973), and at the end of the millennium Brian couldn't talk about the sacking without stammering.

Amid all this personal/professional turmoil, far from the defenseless angel conjured up by Brian freaks or the paranoid head case sent crazy over relentless, obsessive competition with the Beatles—the scenario much loved by media dramatists—days later in a transcontinental on-air phone conversation over a New York radio station, Brian took good-natured ribbing from the Beatles over the Beach Boys' vocal style, and gave it back. The eight-minute banter bout was recorded, lost for many years, then issued as a special edition disc in 2001.

R ELEASED MAY 11th AND AIRED ON RED SKELTON'S show the day after, the double 'I Get Around'/'Don't Worry Baby' made up for their first nose-bloodying, after Beatlemania had cooled a tad. For Italian critic Piero Scaruffi (1999): "Ballads such as 'Don't Worry Baby' were both a synthesis of Phil Spector's 'Wall of Sound', Chuck Berry's teenage vignettes, Doo-Wop's stately four-part harmonies, and the cornerstone of a new form of pop music. That form was born with 'I Get Around'…."

From its startling fuzzed-guitar opening and refraining riff to closing reverb effects, Brian introduced as the A-side a deceptively simple collage of brilliantly integrated sounds making an impact that left all far behind including the Beatles. The song carved its way through the mass of hits by acts now strong contenders just by being British, making up a rotating phalanx of four or five of the top ten every week. The million sale was recognised fast, before that of 'Fun Fun Fun'. In Mike Love's intro at the Sacramento Municipal Coliseum on 1st August he claims it—six weeks after entering the Cash Box top ten, still six weeks to go in the twenty. And that month Capitol vice president Voyle Gilmore confirmed it in an interview with American Melody Maker correspondent Ren Gravett. In both Los Angeles (KFWB) and San Francisco (KYA) it was top for five weeks, and in Chicago, Boston-New England, Detroit, Washington DC, Dallas-Ft Worth, Seattle, the Twin Cities, Milwaukee, Denver, Pittsburgh, Louisville, Buffalo; Montreal ranked it 2nd for 1964 and in Miami and Cincinnati where it didn't top it was one of the half-dozen biggies. It went high too at WQXI, Atlanta's r&b station. Blocked by the Four Seasons' rags-to-riches American Dream 'Rag Doll' in New York (WABC, WMCA), it was runner-up for a month and their only *big* hit for more than a year past and almost a year to come there, the center of American radio.

The long-awaited Billboard chart-topper* was in the national top three for seven weeks against career-toughest competition from their two rivals' most famous songs, 'A Hard Day's Night' and 'Rag Doll'. Each spent two weeks at top. Assessed a decade later by Record World, 'I Get Around' was top for the month of June, runner-up for July—borne out by the UPI nationwide survey, which from the week ending June 8th to August 3rd had it 5-1-2-1-1-1-2-2-6. 'I Get Around' would rate over two million radio plays in the US, with 'A Hard Day's Night', and ahead of the Seasons.

(*Not to overstate the value of number ones: Despite their sacred status bestowed by the radio industry—eager to maintain its hold over the public week by week—it is a puerile, attention-grabbing status symbol. A no.2-3 from a high-selling time would place top put in a poorer-selling one. Through 1962-65 there were eight to ten number ones annually that weren't listed by Billboard among the twenty top sellers for their year, while in two of those years ten of the year's top stopped short of top in Billboard's own weekly chart. Through 1969-71 Creedence Clearwater Revival was America's top group without a no.1 45 in Billboard or Cash Box— but scored eight consecutive Gold Discs with mostly double-sided releases. Many songs have sold a million worldwide and become classics without entering the weekly top forty or even hundred.)

The Cash Box sales chart for 4th July 1964:

1. I Get Around — the Beach Boys
2. Memphis — Johnny Rivers
3. Rag Doll — the Four Seasons
4. My Boy Lollipop — Millie Small
5. A World Without Love — Peter & Gordon
6. Don't Let the Sun Catch You Crying — Gerry & Pacemakers
7. Chapel of Love — the Dixie Cups
8. Can't You See That She's Mine? — the Dave Clark Five

9.   No Particular Place to Go — Chuck Berry
10. The Girl From Ipanema — Stan Getz & Astrud Gilberto

Sales must have promptly approached two million in the US, counted 5th in the top sellers of 1964 by Billboard and Cash Box. The lists were led by 'I Want to Hold Your Hand' and 'She Loves You' audited at two and a half million, jostling places with 'Hello Dolly' 3rd. Roy Orbison's 'Oh Pretty Woman' was 4th, the Supremes' 'Where Did Our Love Go?' 10th, 'A Hard Day's Night' 13th; other confirmed US million-sellers, 'Love Me Do' and 'Please Please Me', were lower in the twenty top discs. It topped too in Canada on the new official RPM chart.

This time the B only enhanced the success, under its own steam mounting #1 in Washington DC (WPGC), Montreal (CKMG), Boston, the Twin Cities, New York capital tri-cities—five weeks; top 5 Detroit, Miami, Vancouver, the 10 Seattle, St Louis. Both were nominally car songs but there any similarity ended, each complementing the other in the strident rocker b/w emotional ballad format that had become a trademark: one of Rock's best-ever doubles, if not *the*.... Maybe uniquely for a B-side, it entered an all-time élite 240 songs played more than three million times on US radio. New York's NBC network had it 9th in long-term regional sales over the next decade with 'I Get Around' 6th and 'Fun Fun Fun' 2nd, giving the group three Eastern Seaboard high-fliers for the year though just one had ranked high in the weekly charts.

'A Hard Day's Night' was awarded a Gold Disc by the RIAA on 25th August, and one came that year too for 'Rag Doll'. One materialised for 'I Get Around'—18 years later, under new Capitol/EMI management.

The Beatles having—after 'Can't Buy Me Love' (1,590,000 UK sales)—settled down to normal proportions of superstardom at home, 'A Hard Day's Night' sold just half what they were used to — 720,000—and apart from double-siders 'I Feel Fine'/'She's a Woman' and 'We Can Work It Out'/'Day Tripper' Beatle 45s would never again touch a domestic million.

For ALL HIS CREATIVE GENIUS, THE ELDEST WILSON brother was bedevilled by a retarded social IQ. Evidence of his ambivalence in public situations was surfacing in Brian. On Dick Clark's *Bandstand*, as Brian lip-synchs to 'Don't Worry Baby' he stands awkwardly in the middle, hands clasped in front; Denny and Carl flank him, looking self-conscious, arms folded; Al and Mike loose-limbed, outside. As Clark approaches and searches for a spokesman, Brian, still in the middle some distance away, seems distracted by something (or nothing) off-stage. The others, embarrassed, try to defer to Brian. When the host asks, "You know it's an amazing thing 'cos you have hit after hit. Who, Brian [striving for his attention], determines what will be done next?" Brian, a blank mask in passive-aggressive mode, answers detachedly, "Well, I guess I do, I don't know—I write the songs and produce them... so I have a lot to say about it." As his brothers giggle nervously, Mike smiling wryly (or gritting his teeth?), Brian breaks into an untimely smile. The grinning, pixieish stage patter of the Fab Four, always on, is absent in spades.

The Beatles took the dictates of showbiz in their stride; the Beach Boys were too aware of the unreality of stardom, and showed it. Never happy with phony staging for tv shows, least of all lip-synching (miming to the record/tape), performances for British tv later in the year and most US ones thereafter would be live or live vocal/playing backed by instrumental tape. More and more, tv appearances would be personal communications to their fans without regard to commercial potential.

Carping about Brian's vocal timbre continued, as if a light tone indicated lightweight music. No critic ever wrote off Frankie Lymon or Clyde McPhatter ('Lover Please'), Smokey Robinson, or Eddie Kendricks of the Temptations, nor Sam Cooke, for their undeniably light tones. High-tenor Bobby Hatfield ('Unchained Melody', 'Ebb Tide') of the Righteous Bros and Aaron Neville ('Tell It Like It Is'), light as a feather, were hailed as artists for their caressing touch of a song. Some vocalising was becoming too mannered to be anything but irritating—the falsetto lead of the Stylistics. But however misunderstood the Beach Boys' music, they would soon pass through a phase, rejecting the surf'n'hotrod scene, where it might all turn out academic.

Beatlemania had not only toppled all on the music scene, when the movie *A Hard Day's Night* was released in August it matched Elvis's *Viva Las Vegas*, his biggest-ever—though two more kept Elvis fans on life-sustaining drip-feed. The Liverpool lads would earn the suspicion of America's first pop icon, who later volunteered his services to President Richard Nixon as a junior G-man fighting the drug culture popularised by the likes of Bob Dylan, the Stones and the Beatles.

The Beach Boys' lame reply was the theme song for *Karen*, a tv sitcom about the trials of a dating teenager played by Debbie Walley, a former Disney starlet (*Bon Voyage*), an upcoming Elvis girl, to inherit the "Tammy" role from Sandra Dee. Old buddies the Surfaris put out a cover that made no.2 in Japan. Upcoming and long in gestation was the group's featured role in a teen movie named for a new album cut, *Girls on the Beach*, later a.k.a. *Summer of '64*. In a good-humored concession to Beatle box-office the plot has it that a girls' college sorority can't get the real thing for a fundraiser, try imitating them with Beatle wigs, then settle for the Boys lip-synching the sumptuous ballad of the title, 'Little Honda' and 'Lonely Sea'. Put out by Paramount as a quickie B-movie and trading closely on the "Beach Party" flicks, it did little for film critics though Ringo Starr later recognised 'Little Honda' as a "classic performance".

Despite co-star status with the popular Annette they didn't help themselves with a cameo as backing/harmony for the theme to *The Monkey's Uncle* from Disney, one of the stream of corny teen comedies in its Wacky-Townspeople-of-Zanyville formula that would almost sink the studio. During its run through summer '65 fellow LA-ers Paul Revere & the Raiders would star in a new tv show by Dick Clark, *Where the Action Is*, getting paid to promote themselves—a plum opportunity but not the Beach Boys' bag anyway: far too all-round-showbiz. They drew the line above the virulent strain of commercialism required to ingratiate oneself with the broadest possible audience. They could never have sustained the *schtick*.

Aside from the flurry of hits when they broke, when jostling Gold Records meant they couldn't logistically all reach the top, the Beatles would hardly miss top spot in Billboard. This is no real surprise. Sales taken into account for the charts were mainly factory shipments of 45s—with remainders returned by retailers later on nonsale. British EMI, putting its golden eggs in the Beatle basket, could keep the pressing factories busy 24-7 to ensure its pet clients got a quick no.1—as RCA had done on many occasions for Elvis Presley, whose true sales on specific 45s are uncertain to this day (see Peter Guralnick).

Detail seems superfluous, but the Beatle juggernaut its first year running amok: 'I Want to Hold Your Hand' (some estimate 15 million pressed worldwide), 'She Loves You', 'Can't Buy Me Love' (two million US orders, fewer actual sales), 'Love Me Do', 'A Hard Day's Night' and 'I Feel Fine' whose 1,400,000 sale in the home country was matched in the US. Exceptions included, from Capitol, 'I'll Cry Instead'/'I'm Happy Just to Dance With You' (#22), 'And I Love Her'/'If I Fell' (#12) and Carl Perkins/ Larry Williams' 'Matchbox'/'Slow Down' (#17), all released in the gap where a real follow-up to 'A Hard Day's Night' should have been. There were others a great deal less saleable from Vee-Jay, Atco, MGM. 'From Me to You' (#41) was their only '63 song not to pay off on re-release. Now as a B-side on Vee Jay it did much better than most of the Capitol Bs, heavily outweighed to just make the Hot 100 and no more, to prevent split sales and ensure the A got to no.1. If there was a guiding intelligence to Beatlemania, how to explain the comparative failure of so many better songs in light of the sensations made of 'Love Me Do' and 'She Loves You' the second time round?

The Beatles' best songs—'Please Please Me', 'I Saw Her Standing There', 'She's A Woman'—didn't quite made it to the top in America; nor according to Billboard did 'Twist and Shout', not written by them but just as good. Several Bs that are now seen to stand head and shoulders above their singalong number ones barely saw the bottom of the chart. Their equivalent of 'In My Room', 'There's A Place'— "where I can go, when I feel low, when I feel blue, And it's my mind"—slipped by as an e.p. track, #74. It was one of few heartfelt early Beatle songs, a rare case when the showbiz imperative of clever writing didn't intrude on the creative process. The dynamic Little Richard-styled 'I'm Down', the B-side of 'Help!', would stall at the uncoveted 101st spot bubbling under the Hot 100.

THE BEACH BOYS HADN'T RECIPROCATED MANIA IN the Beatles' homeland, but provoked informed comment beyond their cultural relevance or exposure. A video clip of 'Fun Fun Fun' was probably their first tv outing and the recording was admired by those in the know; from afar by potential buyers. A surf episode of *Ready Steady Go* later in autumn featured them playing 'I Get Around' live. And little short of miraculously at the end of the year the Brits would vote the Beach Boys world's 5th top vocal group in the annual New Musical Express Readers Poll—just short of the inner circle of Beatles, Stones, Shadows and Kinks and above Manfred Mann, the Animals, Hollies, Dave Clark Five, Herman's Hermits, Peter & Gordon, Gerry & the Pacemakers, Searchers, Brian Poole & the Tremeloes, Bachelors, Billy J Kramer & the Dakotas, Freddie & the Dreamers, Swinging Blue Jeans, Honeycombs, Zombies, Nashville Teens, Barron Knights, Pretty Things and many lesser who had bigger hits.

London was centre of the mod universe. International hit tv series *Thunderbirds* (British ITC), its call sign "F-A-B", made it obvious: futuristic American action figures and London-based spies in mod attire and using James Bond gadgets—best of both worlds. Americans were highly curious about their long-lost British relatives. Top teen sitcom was *The Patty Duke Show*, the star playing identical trans-Atlantic cousins, and the British one was the cool, fashionable one; the Brooklyn Heights one a gum-chewing vivacious airhead. Another, *Fair Exchange*, featured cultural misunderstandings between two sets of parents of teens who'd swapped places to opposite sides of the Atlantic.

British youth took the rock scene deadly serious. Through spring '64 gangs of Mods took on hordes of motorbike-powered Rockers in running battles through the countryside of Essex to the Brighton seaside. Where once the Beatles had been leather-laden Rockers, they were now via Brian Epstein effete Mods, if not as frilly as career mods P J Proby, the Kinks, the Beau Brummels.... By early '65 the split was so bitter that The Who, mod challengers to the Kinks, making their tv debut on *Ready, Steady, Go!,* had to play to a carefully selected audience to ensure rockers wouldn't literally bring the house down. Such star rockers remaining in Britain—Gene Vincent, Billy Fury—were becoming so rare that the Beach Boys might have squeezed into this niche in UK culture, as they had into the hotrodders' Stateside.

On release in London early July 'I Get Around' was effusively pushed by Mick Jagger guesting on tv's celebrity song-judging show *Jukebox Jury.* And Jagger personally circulated copies to the new pirate radio stations. Eric Clapton, then a young guitarist with the Yardbirds, recalled on hearing it thinking "It's all over. Where do we go from here?" One dissenter was West Indian ska singer Millie Small, who through the previous three months had sold bouncy, innocuous 'My Boy Lollipop' to over 600,000 Britons, following with formlaic 'Sweet William' and 'Oh Henry'. World famous for her exaggerated sweet-little-girl vocals, she nixed 'I Get Around', declaring it sounded childish.

'I Get Around''s biggest impact on pop culture was here—penetrating on 8th August what had been months earlier an all-Brit chart down to no.14. It was the bumper year for UK sales, though easing since New Year rush, and it matched Cliff Richard's topical 'On the Beach' week by week at something around 300,000. Twelve years later the New Musical Express would name 'I Get Around'/'Don't Worry Baby' fourth greatest single of the Rock Era—best of 1964, heading Martha & the Vandellas' 'Dancing in the Street' and Righteous Bros' 'You've Lost That Lovin' Feelin''.

The 29th August BBC/Record Retailer chart, jockeying so fierce that Dave Clark Five's 'Can't You See That She's Mine?', Peter & Gordon's 'Nobody I Know', Searchers' 'Someday We're Gonna Love Again', Lulu's 'Shout', Marianne Faithfull's 'As Tears Go By', Zombies' 'She's Not There', Animals' 'I'm Cryin'' and Elvis's 'Kissin' Cousins' and 'Such a Night' couldn't pass the Beach Boys. Memorable 'Tobacco Road' anchored no.6 for four weeks.

1. Have I the Right? — the Honeycombs
2. Do Wah Diddy Diddy — Manfred Mann
3. I Won't Forget You — Jim Reeves
4. You Really Got Me — the Kinks
5. A Hard Day's Night — the Beatles
6. Tobacco Road — the Nashville Teens
7. I Get Around — the Beach Boys
8. It's For You — Cilla Black
9. It's All Over Now — the Rolling Stones
10. Call Up the Groups — the Barron Knights

The exclusivity during the wildest throes of the Brit Era put the Beach Boys on a plateau as world greats. But the new self-belief of the English, though still for the most part covering American songs, was now such that the number one Yanks wouldn't quite crack top 20 again for a year and a half. In France the song bettered their previous best, 'Little Deuce Coupe'. Germany's reception showed cautious progress, going one flight better than 'Fun Fun Fun' into top 40.

The popular worldview in 1964, contrasted to the now-accepted myth of a Beatle monolith, posed the Beach Boys as a countering force of virtually equal weight. They were recognizable trans-Atlantic equivalents, the English group often called the Beatle Boys in America as a nod to their precursors. Featuring the same four-piece instrumental lineup—lead, rhythm and bass guitars, plus drums, in a move almost unique in Rock all five Beach Boys and all four Beatles sang lead vocals when suited, set off by backing harmony. Both ascended to premier status in their home countries early spring 1963 after a warm-up hit. Both wrote their own material, supplemented by rock'n'roll tributes to their (usually black) heroes' hits. Both, in their early recordings, show a similar undoctored raucousness in their playing—of Little Richard rhythms and Chuck Berry riffs. Both attained overwhelming popularity with the key qualities of longevity and musical quality. And they are the two groups of the Rock Era whose music shows the clearest signs of transcending not only the context of Pop but their own time. This was all self-evident in the

Sixties but is now lost under decades of journalistic expediency that has settled for the simplistic angle of Beatle divinity.

While the Beatles dominated the Beach Boys in popularity according to the venerated, century-old Billboard, in Record World's retrospective assessment of monthly sales published 1976 fortunes wavered. 'I Get Around' narrowly beat 'A Hard Day's Night', both at or near top for two months, but #1 & #2 versus #1 & #4. There was a long break ruled by the Beatles. When the Beach Boys returned in May '65 'Help Me Rhonda' beat 'Ticket to Ride' into second place. 'Help!' nudged 'California Girls' into second for August. January '66—'We Can Work It Out' (#3) beat 'Barbara Ann' (#5); 'Nowhere Man' and 'Sloop John B' tied fourth March /April; 'Wouldn't It Be Nice' (#4) beat 'Yellow Submarine' (#5) in September; and 'Good Vibrations' was top single of all, not a Beatle in sight, over November-December of '66.

THE BEACH BOYS WERE THE ONLY YANKS WITH A competitively distinctive image, bringing a topping 45 and album in the USA just at the time English power was at its zenith, under the noses of new household names the Animals, Rolling Stones, Dave Clark Five, Kinks, Peter & Gordon, Manfred Mann, Dusty Springfield—and fashion icon Marianne Faithfull, pushed by American tv and radio but never catching on. More importantly to youth culture, they were the only Americans to compete with Beatle audience reaction, drawing thousands of screaming fans to their headliner concerts. Package tours to bolster box-office power were now a memory, and for the next decade the Beach Boys would call the shots—holding absolute seniority in any multi-act show they appeared in.

They celebrated Independence Day weekend as 'I Get Around' /'Don't Worry Baby' topped out, by headlining "A Million Dollar Party" in Hawaii over Peter & Gordon, England's top duo whose 'A World Without Love' they had displaced; the Kingsmen— 'Louie Louie' continuing as their claim to fame across generations —and Jan & Dean, their 'Little Old Lady From Pasadena' joining the Beach Boys in the top three later that month. Also arriving were Ronny &

the Daytonas' 'GTO' and, resurfacing, the Ventures with a Space Age 'Walk Don't Run '64'. The Beach Boys were still "the no.1 surfing group in the country" a year after their last surf song was released, without ever asking for the dubious accolade. In a world dominated by Mods, and then Afros, the tag was becoming a ball and chain.

World politics were taking a violent turn. August 2nd the US Navy enters North Vietnamese waters to draw fire and provoke the start of War. Two more wars follow that month, sparked by Turkey bombing Greek-owned Cyprus in the Mediterranean, and Indonesia invading Malaysian territory. For now Vietnam isn't news, and anyway through three weeks of October attention is grabbed by the Olympic Games in Tokyo—Japan's chance to shine as a new major player in the Western Hemisphere. Four days into the Games on October 14th USSR premier Nikita Kruschchev goes on vacation, maybe to watch them on tv: the Union of Soviet Socialist Republics, dominated by Russia, is the main challenger to the United States in medals. He never returns, deposed by Leonid Brezhnev and Alexei Kosygin.

The Beatles, in July returning from their tour of Australia & New Zealand (with a substitute drummer for most of it—Ringo was ill), are greeted by street-lining throngs of 150,000 on a homecoming to Liverpool. After another fleeting trip to Sweden, August saw them back in North America for the first of three highly lucrative summer tours: twenty-six dates covering 15,000 miles. On the 12th New York's daily bible of entertainment, Variety, totted 80 million discs worldwide for them, something under a quarter in the USA given they were topping charts in most countries. Venues included the Cow Palace, San Francisco with former stars the Exciters in support, the Hollywood Bowl and tennis's Forest Hills, New York. It was here that Bob Dylan got them on to marijuana as an alternative to their constant diet of booze and amphetamines.

The craving for the group meant they, or rather, Brian Epstein, could call the shots. Epstein charged reporters $1,000 each to accompany the tour, quite a nerve since any publicity from these imbedded showbiz columnists had to be good. The group fee for a Kansas City concert was raised from $100,000 to $150,000 (figures from Pritchard & Lysaght)—far more than anyone but Elvis could have commanded for a single live appearance. Up-and-coming California duo the Righteous Bros were cannon fodder singing before Beatle-befuddled kids for half an hour. Other support acts weren't even billed, and Bill and Bobby quit with several dates left. A consortium of US businessmen offered Epstein $10 million to buy his contract. He would not even have been tempted, devoted as he was; plus, as far as anyone could tell, there were uncounted tens of millions still to be made from his clients.

At the end of summer, with LA abuzz over the Beatles' visit—three days in Bel Air—the Beach Boys were glad to vacate on an extended tour starting in far-away Cleveland and Pittsburgh, taking in Oklahoma City, Buffalo, Seattle, Boston; breaking back home to remake the Ronettes' 'So Young'; resuming at Hartford, back west to Salt Lake City the next day, to Boise, Idaho the day after that. September they went on to a Miami Beach concert and the racial hotspots of Alabama—Montgomery and Birmingham—before Atlanta, Knoxville, Washington and New England (itinerary from Keith Badman).

The Beach Boys were more than holding their own pitted against Limey-come-latelys who could do no wrong in teen approval, combing their hair forward to cash in on the Beatle look. Many did much better Stateside than on home turf. In early September, marking seven months' Beatle rule, came the van of a second wave. The Animals, 'House of the Rising Sun' on the rise, began a ten-day booking at Brooklyn, New York's Paramount Theater with Jan & Dean, Chuck Berry and Del Shannon. At the rival Fox Theater the Searchers, arriving almost with the Beatles and now hosted by Merseybeat aficionado Murray the K, opened as the main attraction over the best of Motown—Smokey Robinson & the Miracles, the Temptations and Marvin Gaye, with the Ronettes and Jay & the Americans thrown in. The Searchers had appeared on Ed Sullivan's tv show as early as April 5th.

In a strange case of cultural cringe by the overwhelmingly dominant world culture—and Americans had never been shy about shouting it—the Beach Boys, who had screened on network tv for 18 months, had never cracked the big one: *The Ed Sullivan Show* —the royal seal of approval from American society at large. It finally happened September 27th, slotted in eight months after the Beatles—appearing the third time the week before—and a long line of other Englishmen. Obviously confused over their Minnesota-Swedish ancestry via Audree, Sullivan introduced them as Swedes.

Eleven days before, a new hour-long pop show, *Shindig*, produced by British pop impresario Jack Good, had aired. Devoted wall-to-wall to the latest music unlike Sullivan's family format, it shaded the somewhat dated *Bandstand*. Good, the innovative producer of *Oh Boy!* in the UK, showed his loyalty often, showcasing his countrymen whenever possible in whatever numbers available. The Beach Boys would guest on NBC's *Shindig* just once more over its 16-month run. When British acts weren't in the country, *Shindig*, and Good's upcoming *Hullabaloo* on the rival ABC network—to premiere in January with its mini-skirted go-go girls— featured promo clips from the UK often introduced by the Beatles or Brian Epstein, ensuring coverage for the Liverpudlians. Just as the *Bandstand* that aired 'Don't Worry Baby' was all-Brit apart from the exception made for the Beach Boys it was no surprise when a *Shindig* in the New Year was devoted entirely to English acts: the Rolling Stones, Kinks, the Dave Clark Five, Gerry & the Pacemakers—and Petula Clark, a 20-year international show business veteran just breaking in America as the latest thing from swinging London.

THOUGH THEY HAD BEEN A WORLD NAME FOR TWO years the prestigious Sullivan show helped stamp the Beach Boys' permanence as *the* icon of American youth culture overseas. More immediately, their lip-synching to the rousing 'Wendy' brought it great popularity for an e.p. song—similarly 'Little Honda', to make a belated appearance on *The Andy Williams Show* and partner it on *Four By the Beach Boys*, charting at #44 and #65 respectively in Billboard; #57 together in Cash Box. The two Beatle e.p.s on Capitol, *Four By the Beatles* (#86) and *4 By the Beatles* (#68), only combined matched the Beach Boy e.p.'s seven weeks in the chart. Beatle standards that peaked mid-chart in Billboard included 'Roll Over Beethoven' (#68), 'All My Loving' (#45), 'I Should Have Known Better', 'If I Fell' both no.53.

'Surf City'/'Lonely Sea', 'Catch a Wave'/'Hawaii' and now 'Little Honda'/'Wendy' were great doubles that got away from the Beach Boys. Brian apparently received no encouragement for 'Honda' in or out of the group. Sung by Mike, Brian introduced faintly fuzzed guitar—an effect Carl thought sounded "like shit" until his own playing was played back to him. In a few years a guitar sound wouldn't be acceptably cool unless it was over-fuzzed beyond recognition. Not for the last time, they had arrived without fanfare, too early and too subtly for the rock world. 'Honda' was best appreciated in LA, Minneapolis-St Paul, Richmond, Virginia and Sweden—all #2—Vancouver #3, Norway #8, Washington DC #12, Canada and Miami both #15. The cover by the Hondells, rumored sung by a speeded-up Brian (that is, his tape)—or squeezing his nose to sound like a California-cool nasal tenor?— made no.7 in the USA and is said to have sold a million.

Despite the old 'Day By Day' Four Freshmen harmonies there was something enormously daring about 'Wendy' in its sparse, evocative introduction heavy with pauses and anticipation and offbeat guitar strokes throughout. A #2 in Denver, top five through the rest of the Rockies and in Washington DC, Louisville and Tucson, it was top ten San Jose, Twin Cities and Vancouver, fell just short in Toronto, Miami, San Diego, Ohio. On the Beach Boys' recent tour 'Little Honda' was added to the live setlist to go with 'I Get Around', 'Shut Down', 'Be True to Your School', 'Don't Worry Baby'—at the expense of long-time regulars the Freshmen's 'Graduation Day', 'Papa-Oom-Mow-Mow', 'Long Tall Texan'. 'Johnny B Goode', their tribute to Chuck Berry, was a keeper.

A third e.p. track, 'Hushabye', a widely admired update of doo-wop, also got international play. The fourth was 'Don't Back Down'—their last song with surf lyrics but symbolising what not to do in life when faced with a 20-foot wave. All came from *All Summer Long*, according to myth their first album to foot it song for song with the Beatles, boasting also, with 'I Get Around', 'Little Honda' and

'Wendy', the title track—a regional airplay hit around California stations and later chosen by Steven Spielberg as the *American Graffiti* closing theme; movie theme 'Girls on the Beach'; the driving Little Richard-like 'Drive-In'; 'Do You Remember?', a rocking tribute to "all the guys that gave us rock and roll" when "The critics kept a-knockin' but the stars kept a-rockin'". There were only two real fillers, a fly-on-the-wall 'Our Favorite Recording Sessions' and 'Carl's Big Chance', a 12-bar blues instrumental going nowhere. For once there was an unworthy, by-the-numbers soap-opera ballad, 'We'll Run Away' "and get married" complete with the tinny, mournful *As the World Turns* organ backing that wouldn't have been out of place on the soundtrack of *A Summer Place*, or for that matter a Beatle album of the period.

The twelve months from now, as Elvis failed and the Four Seasons eased, was one of improving Beach Boy album sales and recognition—peaking higher: *All Summer Long* #3, *Beach Boys Concert* #1, *Beach Boys Today* #3, *Summer Days (and Summer Nights!)* #2. But after solid groundwork laid down through spring and summer, in their first concerted thrust away from car songs they bore the brunt of a backlash from 45-buyers attached to the genre. It was a big move. Chuck Berry was 38 years old and still mining car culture: 'No Particular Place to Go', 'Nadine'. As a result it was common in regional markets to see the Beach Boys outshone by the Hondells' 'Little Honda', Jan & Dean's recordings of Brian Wilson surf-and-drag 'Ride the Wild Surf' and 'Sidewalk Surfin'' and challenged for a place on the local top forty by Ronny & the Daytonas' 'Bucket T' (covered by The Who).

In September came self-examining double 'When I Grow Up (to Be a Man)'—heard in talking-baby comedy *Look Who's Talking* a quarter-century later—and 'She Knows Me Too Well', their turn to 'peak' at #101 in Billboard; as an A its best showing was Vancouver, #7. Both marked creative advances, the hit featuring harpsichord sounding like Bach on speed and closing with a cyclical three-part harmony, becoming a signature of the group's style. It ripped to the top of Canada's new national RPM chart (two weeks); top three San

Francisco, San Diego, Honolulu, Salt Lake City, Dallas, Montreal, Pittsburgh, across Virginia and many Northeastern towns; Washington DC #4, #5 St Louis, #6 Miami.

Just two months later speedster 'Dance Dance Dance' closed in. It looked like a big hit—the highest-debuting Beach Boy 45 so far nationally (#57), the best first-weeker in the Cash Box 100 in three months. But in the end it stuck just as fast—scuttled by a combination of British firepower, America's own all-round-showbiz favorites, the Supremes, and novelty songs. A rocker with imaginative sound effects, the lead guitar has the ringing tone of a Rickenbacker 12-string. It sounded cool but its lack of variation in pace made it somehow less interesting than their other hits. Its B-side 'The Warmth of the Sun' ranks as one of Brian Wilson's, and pop music's, all-time great emotional ballads, finding belated fame again a quarter-century late, via *Good Morning Vietnam*. 'Dance Dance Dance' rose #1 San Jose and Providence, above par in California's Central Valley, Oregon, South Dakota, Dallas, Washington DC, Montreal, Vancouver and Albany and Scranton tri-city areas.

'When I Grow Up' was 7/8/9 in the three big national charts, its follow-up 8/9/10. Each was assailed by deserving, rotating number ones: 'Pretty Woman', 'Do Wah Diddy Diddy', 'We'll Sing in the Sunshine', 'Last Kiss'—and under-appreciated classics 'Dancing in the Street' and 'Remember (Walking in the Sand)', 'Time is On My Side', the Zombies' 'She's Not There'; also Lorne Greene's (Paw in tv's *Bonanza*) shrewdly named 'Ringo', and Bobby Vinton's 'Mr Lonely', made ridiculous by a 2005 remake. Beach Boy strongholds Chicago and the Twin Cities punished 'When I Grow Up' for straying from the narrow surf-car format; New York, Detroit and St Louis, 'Dance Dance Dance'; Toronto both.

Drummer Denny devised a distinctive, punctuating rhythm for the verses of 'When I Grow Up', repeating a busy snare, hi-hat and floor tom-tom combination similar to 'She's Not There' that would show up in simpler form on Ringo's treatment of 'Ticket to Ride' and 'In My Life'. For 'Dance Dance Dance' Hal Blaine played on the record—Dennis showing himself fully capable of replicating his playing on tv. And, as Blaine said later in his book, the two knew each other's playing so well that he made a point of playing like Dennis on Beach Boy recordings anyway.

T HE BEACH BOYS' THREE 45s FALL '64 TO SPRING '65 —'Do You Wanna Dance?' to come—must have eventually sold a North American million. Given Murry Wilson's continuing sales oomph they would not fall short through out-of-stocks. Like the Beatles, they were top sellers too through the Capitol record club, second only to Columbia's—figures not recorded by the charts. By 1965 roughly one in seven of all records pressed went out through three big record clubs (Chapple & Garofalo)—so that a Beach Boy single moving retail sales through stores of three quarters of a million nationwide might expect to pass the million through club sales.

Associated Press reporter Doris Klein quoted Beatle sales in the US on Capitol alone in 1964 as nearly 19 million singles and "a like number of albums"—contributing to the increase in total Capitol sales over 1963 of 65%.

Motown captured 10% of 1964's pop market—including some 20 million singles—three quarters of its hits written and/or produced by ace team Holland-Dozier-Holland. In late summer the breakthrough by the Supremes and Four Tops threatened the Beach Boys' American-Rock territory. The Temptations had enjoyed their first big hit in May, as Mary Wells had her last, "No muscle-bound man can take my hand from" 'My Guy'. For the Supremes, headed by 20-year-old Diana Ross, 'Where Did Our Love Go?' was followed by 'Baby Love' and 'Come See About Me'—three no.1s. Four Tops' 'Baby I Need Your Lovin'' was top 20 through October, but under 'When I Grow Up', and still sold a million, and in the next two years they would post more classics, 'I Can't Help Myself', 'It's the Same Old Song', 'Reach Out' and soundalike 'Standing in the Shadows of Love', no less stirring.

The Supremes were, like the Shirelles before them and the Chantels before them, square. Conservatively groomed with not a wig out of place, they were welcomed by the Establishment. Their appeal to the white audience—judged by boss Berry Gordy to be at least

70% of their constituency—took an audience sector from the Beach Boys, who had developed the best girl group sound of '64 without aid of actual girls. Pushed by the white PR and sales teams at Motown, the Supremes eased into a niche as the one superstar girl group and as Americans created a lurch against the Beach Boys in a way the Beatles, purveying foreign appeal, hadn't. Facing the Supremes' dominance of the singles chart and sensing no whiff of a national chart-topper, the Beach Boys saturated charts further down. 'Warmth of the Sun', recorded a year before, made it on to Billboard's R&B chart—thanks to Brian's soulful falsetto sounding like a black gospel singer, just as emotionally affecting. There were two Xmas singles, and Jan & Dean, with their two Wilson hits, sounded as much like their young gold diviners as they could; ditto the Surfaris with 'Karen'. That made ten "Beach Boy" hits in three months.

In December they pulled off their six-albums-charting-at-once coup, to boot. A poll of America's radio DJs across all station formats returned 1964's most played acts as: Bobby Vinton, Frank Sinatra, then Elvis Presley male vocalists; Connie Francis, Brenda Lee, Lesley Gore; groups the Beach Boys, then Four Seasons, followed by the Beatles, Four Freshmen, the Kingston Trio seventh. Only hitch: The rock champions were again headed by folk favorites Peter, Paul & Mary crossing over from pop and played also on Easy Listening stations.

By taking on the Beatles head first they had risen in status to where, in one of those rare gestures from the Establishment of mature musicians to the coming generation, the Hollywood Strings put out a bestselling *Beach Boys Song Book* just as the Johnny Mann Singers would of *Beatle Ballads*. It was as close as they would get to official recognition, and they notched another victory when *Beach Boys Concert* rode through the four weeks to Christmas at the top—the first live performance ever to head Billboard, reckoned to have gone on to sell in the multi-millions. It was no mean breakthrough, Easy Listening soundtracks *South Pacific*, *West Side Story*, *My Fair Lady*, *The Sound of Music* having dominated the charts for years, now *Hello Dolly!*, *Fiddler on the Roof* and *Goldfinger* joining them. Comedy was the other genre to sell quickly by the million. *Concert* was 4th biggest seller of the rock year according to Billboard, after three Beatles'. *All Summer Long* too placed in the ten biggest with just four months on the charts counted—after *five* Beatles, *Concert* and *Shut Down Vol 2*, one Elvis and a Supremes.

Beach Boys Christmas, blanded out with schmaltzy backing, was another matter—a conundrum over creative direction. In an era of increasingly hard rock it sounded like an Osmond-Lettermen teetotal Xmas in serious need of a Harvey Wallbanger jumpstart: still like the Four Freshmen but without the usual energizing rock. Brian's consolation was its orchestration by Dick Reynolds, coming from the Freshmen's records, but it compared woefully with Phil Spector's rockin'-good Xmas celebration of '63. *A Christmas Gift for You* had featured some of the best work of the Crystals and the Ronettes, backed by the Philles house band in top form, with no little credit due arranger Jack Nitzsche and sound engineer Larry Levine for its enduring rarefied classic status.

Too late to affect the fortunes of the Xmas turkey, the group appeared Xmas week on their first *Shindig* and on a Bob Hope special—*the* place to be on tv this time of year. The middle-of-the-road Beach Boy holiday stiffed and they contented themselves with sixth on the special Xmas chart; a place lower next Xmas. A backhanded distinction accrued as one of the few albums ever to miss the Billboard top 200 chart entirely and still go Gold (awarded 17 years later); their other albums were taking two to six months to be so audited. But it too has in recent years been greeted as a classic, probably for its undeniably pristine harmonies and maybe in the spirit of greeting anything from the Sixties as superior.

The pleasant, uptempo track chosen as Christmas single, 'The Man With All the Toys', reached isolated Top 40 playlists—third on Billboard's Xmas list—and according to an internet site places three-quarters down the top 100 of all-time seasonal sellers. 'Little St Nick' from last year reappeared sixth. 'Merry Christmas, Baby', the only other almost-rock track, was revived for Australasia in '67. To this day selections—'Christmas Day' (Al's first lead vocal), 'We Three Kings of Orient Are', 'Blue Christmas'—can be heard over public address systems by Christmas pudding shoppers in the finest malls, elevators and supermarkets everywhere.

D UE TO MANY OF THEIR VIDEO-RECORDED SHOWS being misplaced the early Beach Boys were for decades largely unknown quantities as live performers—a great pity, since it has resulted in the patently phoney, lip-synched tv appearances, neatly lined up in their pinstripe sport-shirts and slacks, being held up as what the group was in the flesh. *The TAMI Show*, the renowned doco-style feature film, once and for all dispels their image in some minds as guitar-wielding Osmonds. The Beach Boys were showcased in a sparkling setting with Phil Spector, the world's most respected record producer, acting as musical director.

Shot late October 1964 at Santa Monica Civic Auditorium—a few miles and a world away from the group's origins three years before— it was a two-day package that boasted bigger names and a wider array of pop styles than any other Sixties gathering: new superstars the Supremes, fellow Motowners Smokey Robinson & the Miracles and Marvin Gaye, radical leader of black music James Brown, epitome of rock'n'roll Chuck Berry, white teen queen Lesley Gore. Beach Boy shadows Jan & Dean acted as comperes, and top Brit invaders the Rolling Stones, Gerry & the Pacemakers and Billy J Kramer & the Dakotas came. Jack Nitzsche, best known for his work as Spector's arranger and solo hit 'The Lonely Surfer', conducted the house orchestra.

All accounts have it that the Stones were, justifiably as it turned out, nerve-wracked at having to follow James Brown's dynamic authenticity. Brown, as he promised beforehand, made them wish they'd never left England (Stanley Booth). The Beach Boys' own frenzied run through 'Surfin' USA' for the occasion—a highlight clipped for retrospective documentaries—has to stand with any other of the era as a hard-rocking live rendition for the sheer kinetic energy given off. Their knockout rendition of 'Surfer Girl', also recovered from early unavailability, has been shown and reshown on tv over recent years.

Screened at a thousand theatres worldwide over the Xmas holidays, producers Electronovision had to place the largest order for prints "since the founding of the film industry 57 years ago" (Times Recorder, Zanesville, Ohio, 20th December '64) for simultaneity. It was only later recognised as a cult classic containing the best mid-Sixties Rock footage. When it went into general release in the UK in April '65 the Beach Boys' huge contribution kept the group in the public eye, heralding the long-awaited British breakthrough. Not long after, their top-billed segment was excised at Brian's insistence, fearing it would date them—while he kept the Kingston Trio outfits stamping 'oldies' on his band.

Three days after filming, November 1st, they touched down at London Heathrow Airport for a promo trip to tape clips for Independent Television's *Ready Steady Go* and *Discs A-Go-Go*, BBC's *Top of the Pops*, *Thank Your Lucky Stars*, the *Open House* current affairs program and a documentary on *The Beat Boom*. On the flight Brian had experienced a panic attack—a small taste of worse to come. The welcome from a smallish crowd braving the autumn elements, mainly girl fans waving copies of outdated *Shut Down Vol 2*—the only Beach Boy album released in Britain for 15 months—could only look forlorn compared to the overdone carnivals the Beatles whipped up, and that the Beach Boys were used to at home.

There was a feature magazine article by Vicki Wickham, London's hostess with the mostest, and a memorable meeting with her publicist brother Andy. Andy and Andrew Loog Oldham had represented Murry Wilson on publicity trips to the UK. Andy Wickham misguidedly expressed a liking for Murry on meeting Denny Wilson, who, still smarting from numerous bouts of fatherly 'discipline', punched Andy on reflex (Wickham in *Stoned*, Oldham).

The timely career fillip—the important occasion of their first peek-in at the shrine to Mod-dom—pushed 'When I Grow Up' back into the UK chart. But their music was better appreciated on the Continent, and after the British Isles leg including a Dublin concert at the national boxing stadium they followed up their very recent French triumph in 'I Get Around' (#3 in Paris) by performing rave shows at the Paris Olympia and in Milan, also attending a reception in Rome.

French tv featured them on *Age Tendre Et Tete De Bois* and *Au Dela De I Ecran*. Their live set included their well-liked version of 'Louie Louie'.

A Stockholm show to thank their early and loyal Swedish fans also helped to lay foundations for superstar longevity in Europe— despite repeated attempts across the Continent by imitator bands to usurp the Beach Boys' place. And there were concerts in Frankfurt, Hamburg, Copenhagen—where Brian wrote new classic 'Kiss Me Baby'—and Oslo. On a sightseeing tour of Berlin, Al was the only one curious enough to breach The Wall, for a daring walkabout of the communist police-state territory of East Germany.

In France, traditionally the bastion of the artistic *avant garde* but now in partial eclipse with its *je ne c'est quoi* overshadowed by crass Anglo-Saxon mass-produced moddery, virtually every Beach Boy hit had been covered. While surf music *per se* and its California-counter-cultural accoutrements had met with curiosity, their work was treated with extra regard by a broad range of musicians eager to reflect its freshness and vibrance. Paris-based Petula Clark, probably Europe's biggest star of the day, had adapted *Little Deuce Coupe*'s complex hotrod song 'No-Go Showboat' to something less strenuous, 'J'ai pas le temps', and Brian Wilson would prove an important influence on Clark's producer-arranger, Tony Hatch. The French language's premier Beach Boy covers group was Les Excentriques—'In My Room', 'Fun Fun Fun', 'Dance Dance Dance', with 'Help Me Rhonda' still to come. Tending more to beach specialists were Les Bretelles: 'Lulu d'Honolulu' and 'Les filles du soleil' ('Girls on the Beach'). Multilingual versions of 'Fun Fun Fun', its Gallic interpretation necessarily substituting cigarette-smoking as the teenage girl's crime rather than resorting to a hamburger stand, came from squarish quartet Les Missiles, still popular enough in 2000 to warrant a compilation reissue in France. Popular rocker Michel Page co-opted 'I Get Around' ('Elle aime tout sauf moi') and 'When I Grow Up' ('La ronde des heures'). And there were renderings of 'Dans te Yeux' ('In My Room') by Bruno Marchal, 'J'ai peur de l'ete' ('Don't Worry Baby') by Jean-Pierre Fall, and from Orfino, 'Aide

Moi Cherie' ('Help Me Rhonda') following a Francophone 'Man With All the Toys' (details from Beachboysmax website).

Dennis, almost 20 and still single, and Mike, between marriages, felt sufficiently amorous in Paris to take on more indiscretions. Unlike the Beatles, who now ordered women for delivery to their hotel rooms, the two Beach Boys ventured out on a riskier *modus operandi*. Tom Nolan (1972) reported a story of Mike being confronted by a pimp with a gun for sampling some high-class Paris goodies *gratis*—feeling up a hooker who'd paused too long within arm's reach.

A FTER THE FIRST MONTHS OF BEATLE BALLYHOO their earth-shattering impact with retro sounds encouraged back into the charts old showbiz favorites, often lowering themselves in the process: legendary Louis Armstrong and his first-ever million-seller in a glittering 40-year jazz career—'Hello Dolly', from a musical; Dean Martin and Perry Como striving to rejuvenate themselves; and Tony Bennett out of his element replicating the Beatles' cooing of 'A Taste of Honey'. Early in 1965 dormant "Old Blue Eyes"—Frank Sinatra, long wilting under the onslaught of rock'n'roll, would come back enlivened by the Beatles' direction and covering such tunes as 'Anytime At All'. Doris Day, five years without a hit in America, made her comeback ('Move Over Darling'), but in the UK. All that remained was to welcome back the fullblown British patriotism of Vera Lynn and the sweet pre-rock lullabyes of Patti Page…. That too would come.

A burgeoning Soul scene, the Beach Boys, Four Seasons, Motown and girl groups had turned the tide by the end of 1962— eliminating from the game the old timers and their heirs the teen idols who had carried on the crooning tradition. Now, far from making the airwaves safe for rock'n'roll once and for all, the Beatles had made trite, old-time sentimental tunes respectable again —a recipe made to order for over-the-hill troupers. It made it easy for Sinatra, long on record loudly hating rock'n'roll, to help further weaken it, hoping to obliterate its memory altogether. British showbiz institutions Matt Monro and Shirley Bassey took heart from the Beatles' success, riding their coattails and enjoying their biggest US hits in the wake of the Fab Four.

The Establishment marveled at Lennon & McCartney's versatility as they popularised so many old forms of music simultaneously. This widening appreciation through the older generations made possible a huge assault also by new Adult Contemporary musicians and armies of orchestras well short of the unique jazz stylings of Henry Mancini (*Peter Gunn* and *Pink Panther* themes) and Nelson Riddle (tv themes *The Untouchables, Route 66*). Hard on the heels of soppy Beatle ballads 'If I Fell' and 'And I Love Her' came the MOR Latin-American pace of Herb Alpert & the Tijuana Brass—though he did improve 'A Taste of Honey'. Fittingly, the Beatles' Hamburg producer Bert Kaempfert made a comeback as, briefly, the king of Easy Listening with his million-selling 'Red Roses for a Blue Lady'. And a whole new slew of soggy harmony groups, the Association ('Cherish'), the Sandpipers ('Guantanamera'), the Arbors ('Symphony for Susan'), brought back the somnambulent days of the Lettermen that the Beach Boys must have hoped they had superseded.

Deftly navigating around the powers-that-be's earlier dismissal of rock'n'roll, the Beatles wrote so many placid old-fashioned 'adult' songs that they couldn't miss. Their claim to critical kudos was that their l.p.s had little or no filler, supposedly all the songs being of roughly equal quality—if that's what you wanted in a listen, no standouts. Capitol chopped and changed Beatle albums to ration hungry US fans to ten tracks per l.p.—a round figure Brian Wilson intuited to conserve his creative energy, and solved by including two throwaway tracks per album to make up his group's standard twelve.

From their first, *Meet the Beatles*, through *A Hard Day's Night* and *Beatles For Sale*, the Fabs sold albums in unheard-of quantities in 'rock' music—If Elvis Presley's *Blue Hawaii* could be called rock, so could Beatle albums. In the Fifties when long-playing records were first introduced, even the biggest stars, Elvis and Frank Sinatra (and l.p. specialists Harry Belafonte and Johnny Mathis), might wait years to be awarded Gold. From 1963, the biggest l.p.-selling groups, Peter, Paul & Mary and the Beach Boys, cut the lag time down to months. Now the question was would the Beatles pre-sell a million of their long-play vinyl merchandise, sight unseen and sound unheard? *Meet the Beatles*, issued only in the US, sold 750,000 in its first week and continued at almost that rate to 3,650,-000 by mid-March, five weeks after their arrival. July, *A Hard Day's Night* was first to register advance orders of over a million (statistics from Joseph Murrells, 1978).

For a few years yet individual songs—hit 45s—would be the instant sign of popularity. But a nonstop stream of number ones was undreamt of until the Beatles, almost duplicated by the Supremes. For a time it seemed all over, the Beatles occupying Billboard's top spot twenty weeks their first year and other UK acts ten. After the first frenzied half-year of Beatlemania, Mary Wells, Dixie Cups, Beach Boys, Four Seasons, Roy Orbison, Supremes (times three), Shangri-Las and Righteous Bros all joined in the fight-back taking turns at the top.

Detroit, with a swollen mid-Sixties metro population of five million, was the only large US market that resisted Beatlemania. Like Chicago, it attracted many Gospel and Blues-singing migrants from the Mississippi Delta and its record-buying preferences intriguingly hint at what the States' reception might have looked like had it kept its head over the Beatles. A peek into what was happening music in the last weeks of pre-Beatledom on the new WKNR chart shows that after a top ten entry for the Secrets, by the first week of December girl vocalists were piling up at the top: the Marvelettes and 'As Long As I Know He's Mine'; 'Nitty Gritty' (Shirley Ellis), 'When the Lovelight Shines' (the Supremes), 'Popsicles & Icicles' (Murmaids) clustered in the top 5, Martha & the Vandellas' 'Quicksand' just below, and the Orlons, slowly fading from their career peak a year before.

After the Beatles hit, Detroit made regional hits of the Exciters' 'Do Wah Diddy Diddy', former Cookies lead Earl-Jean's 'I'm Into Something Good' and 'Oh No, Not My Baby' by Maxine Brown. All would be homogenised in the British fashion to make readily digestible for international consumption. Motortown's young and heavily black record-buying and radio-listening public would stay loyal to modern blues, championing more female vocalists in Aretha Franklin and Barbara Lewis. It led the nation in r&b and as a radio market matched Philadelphia, fourth largest. Via Motown it influenced Chicago to convert to Soul without the same success, and outdid Los Angeles in homegrown talent. Home also of Dinah Washington, Jackie Wilson, Mitch Ryder and Freda Payne—with Aretha, another childhood acquaintance of the Supremes—it couldn't help but be a world focus of, and a world authority on, great Sixties music.

For once the Beatles had no *carte blanche*. Detroit rewarded them but treated them as mere mortals—a novel idea at the time. Curiosity ensured thin no.1 welcome mats for 'I Want to Hold Your Hand' and 'She Loves You'—ranked for the year just ahead of 'I Get Around', with *Meet the Beatles* heading *Beach Boys Concert* and *All Summer Long*. The Beach Boys, dissed just as often when the city was in a mood to, won some head-to-head duels: 'I Get Around' eight weeks in the top five over 'A Hard Day's Night' (#5). 'When I Grow Up' leapt twenty places to overtake 'Matchbox'/'Slow Down'. 'I Feel Fine' was the Beatles' last local chart-topper until 'Hey Jude' four years later. 'Ticket to Ride' stalled at #6, leap-frogged by 'Help Me Rhonda'. 'Help!', #5, stayed three places clear of 'California Girls'. 'Good Vibrations' ranked 3rd for 1966, after no Beatles'.

B UT ON THE WORLD STAGE, HOW DID CAPITOL RATE the Beach Boys vs the Beatles—the world's two most popular, most lucrative groups? Far from encouraging quality, as it did with the Beatles' leisurely two albums a year, the label demanded bulk product from the Beach Boys—their first eleven albums were delivered in just over three years. It knew a good milch cow when it saw one, and it is painfully obvious that the moment the windfall of the Beatles landed in its lap the Beach Boys were on their own.

After Capitol was force-fed 'I Want to Hold Your Hand' by EMI—and converted from bulimic to glutton in a week—the Beatles were willing corporate prey as multiple business partners caught up on their back catalogue. No fewer than five other labels with claws in the Beatles joined the feeding frenzy: Chicago's Vee-Jay, its subsidiary Tollie, Swan of Philadelphia, movie major MGM and Atco, an arm of Atlantic that handled Bobby Darin and the Ikettes among others, and would take on Sonny & Cher and the Bee Gees. Real dogs only a mother or the most rabid Beatles fan could love were dumped on the public to make a buck. Vee-Jay, with rights to the potentially lucrative pool of 'Love Me Do', 'PS I Love You', 'Please Please Me', 'From Me to You', 'Do You Want to Know a Secret?' and 'Twist and Shout', contrived the Fabs' Stateside competitors to be fellow clients the Four Seasons via an exploitative Beatles-Seasons compilation l.p. Pitched as a Yank-vs-Limey grudge match, record-buyers weren't fooled and didn't buy it—Four Seasons fans didn't want the Beatles, and vice versa. From minor labels only two—'She Loves You' (Swan) and 'Love Me Do' (Tollie)—had the push to reach Billboard's number one spot, totalling three weeks compared with Capitol issues' 17 weeks that first year. Capitol threw all the rules about release schedules out the window and added to the clutter, averaging just two months between singles over the first year and a half.

For sure, "The Beatles" was a freak and no one could hope to equal its selling power at peak. But Capitol had improvised with the Beach Boys before and would again. Aficionados have ever since fantasized what might have been. Why did Beach Boy songs— unique among all acts—have to be surefire top ten to warrant release? Vee Jay had issued Beatle and some Four Seasons sides in hopes of beefing up overall sales. Spector's records, too, often surfaced in the bottom fifty while accruing respect. Just 25,000 copies needed to be sold for a label to break even. 'Catch A Wave' was left to the mercy of Jan & Dean, who turned it into merely a catchy pop song with skateboard effects and blaring trumpets. The powerhouse 'Little Honda' was snapped up by Gary Usher for the Hondells, who would also have designs, thwarted in time, on 'Help Me Rhonda'. The answer must be simply that EMI, putting its promotional muscle behind the Beatles, rationalised that it couldn't have *two* top groups. Both could not grab the lion's share of attention and exposure, and the Beatles were the boss's pets. *And any special notice given the Beach Boys might easily detract from the Beatles' singular success.*

In the long run the Beach Boys' deserved reputation for perfectionism served them well. Mastery of rock styling and of the recording booth were complete by the time the Beatles arrived, pushing beyond rock music before their later acknowledged triumphs, leaving the Liverpudlians lagging though enhanced by George Martin.

A comparison of the groups' two dozen best to the end of '64:

Surfin' Safari * 409 * Lonely Sea * Surfin' USA * Shut Down * Surfer Girl * Little Deuce Coupe * Catch a Wave * Hawaii * No-Go Showboat * Be True to Your School * In My Room * Little Saint Nick * Fun Fun Fun * Warmth of the Sun * Don't Worry Baby * I Get Around Girls on the Beach * All Summer Long * Little Honda * Wendy When I Grow Up * She Knows Me Too Well * Dance Dance Dance

Please Please Me * From Me to You * Money * Twist and Shout There's a Place * I Want to Hold Your Hand * I Saw Her Standing There * All My Loving * Hold Me Tight * Roll Over Beethoven Boys * Can't Buy Me Love * You Can't Do That * Please Mr Postman A Hard Day's Night * Tell Me Why * Things We Said Today * Anytime At All * When I Get Home * Eight Days a Week * What You're Doing * Every Little Thing * No Reply * She's a Woman

Imagine Oldies Radio without these indispensable Beach Boy recordings (all but three or four), then those from the Beatle list: 'Please Please Me', 'Twist and Shout', 'I Want to Hold Your Hand' for breakthrough impact, 'I Saw Her Standing There', 'Tell Me Why', 'A Hard Day's Night' (*or* soundalike 'Eight Days a Week'), 'She's a Woman'…. Then it's a bit of a struggle. Good as they are, due to the Beatle habit of writing similar songs several are interchangeable, a case of either/or inclusion: 'Anytime At All', or 'When I Get Home' will do just as well; 'Every Little Thing' or 'What You're Doing'….

For the non-fan, the listenable standard of most Beatle material doesn't redeem weak A-sides 'Love Me Do', 'She Loves You', 'Do You Want to Know a Secret?', 'I Feel Fine'. Worse, their B-sides and e.p. tracks often descended from mediocre to banal: 'PS I Love You', 'Ask Me Why', 'This Boy', 'A Taste of Honey', 'Till There Was

You', 'I Wanna Be Your Man'. The "no filler" myth dies a quick death considering not only their covers/tributes but such originals as 'Thank You Girl'—a song that goes nowhere with its trite lyrics. Its repeated "Ow... Ow... Ow... Ow" prompts the memorable quote from *The Simpsons'* Monty Burns: "I seem to recall their off-key caterwauling on the old Sullivan show."

Some better songs from the Beatle catalogue were saved by not much more than a single striking feature—John's strong performances on 'No Reply' or 'Every Little Thing'. But because they are Beatle songs, every last one is deemed worth playing—as Oldies stations did on the death of George Harrison, for days, non-stop.

To Martin, who referred to the Beatles' "arrogance", "They always had enormous self-confidence that the world was theirs for the taking." It was this quality of silly, unquestioning self-belief that Brian Wilson—and a large dollop of the rest of America— picked up and fell for without discerning this essential ingredient in their makeup. America perceives it in Oprah 'I don't believe in luck' Winfrey and Dr Phil 'There are no accidents, everything is as it should be' McGraw, and saw it in Kennedy—an overconfidence, labeled charisma, that makes joiners join a self-ordained spiritual leader. John Lennon personified it for most devout Beatle fans, an aura made untouchable by a martyr's violent death. The posture of an ultimately confident person can convince some people of anything. The power of suggestion, plus faith, equals divinity.

Begging to be laughed off as braggadocio by rational thinkers, such icon building was anathema to the Beach Boy ethos. They were too impulsively naïve, too spiritually humble—even, especially, Murry at bedrock—to ever stop questioning themselves: the opposite of the calculated 'good form' of those English people who apologise in advance when they're about to be 'frank'. In a debriefing interview fresh from their first European tour, a filler track on *Beach Boys Today*, Dennis offers as his highlight the triumphant Paris concert where "I only made three mistakes." Without pause, Brian chips in outlandishly, "I've never made a mistake in my whole career." Mike, going along with the quirky bravado of oneupmanship, answers indulgently, "Brian, we keep waiting for you to make a mistake."

Within a few short weeks the implied perfectionism on top of an edgy insecurity leads to Brian Wilson's first serious breakdown.

5. ENGLAND SWINGS

"Eng-a-land swings like a pendulum do/ bobbies on bicycles two by two/ Westminster Abbey, the Tower, Big Ben/ the rosy red cheeks of the little chil-dren."—Country Music's Oklahoma stump philosopher of the mid-Sixties, Roger Miller, observing the myth of Merry England. By the time of Miller's paean—what, in any other era, would have been a giant pain—England had ruled pop music for two years and was conquering the rest of pop culture. The miniskirt, fashion designer Mary Quant, supermodel Jean Shrimpton (Twiggy to come), and Carnaby Street were all household names around the world. In London they took their fashion so seriously that anyone walking down Carnaby Street or Chelsea's King's Road out of fashion might have been ritually stoned, in both senses of the word.

The coolest tv program was The Avengers—karate-kicking Emma Peel and immaculately Savile Row-attired John Steed. The chic actresses were Julie Christie on the big screen, by acclaim, and by definition Paul McCartney's girlfriend Jane Asher, and Mick Jagger's, Marianne Faithfull—by her own account blessed by an accident of birth with "The Look" and so doubling effortlessly as a chic rock star.

The Beatles came in 12th at American box-offices for 1965, 6th UK. America's two no.1 movie stars through 1965-66 were Brits Sean Connery (James Bond) and saccharine songstress Julie Andrews, displacing all-American team Doris Day and Rock Hudson — suddenly hopelessly outdated 40-year-old born-again virgins, plopped down from Planet Quaint into The Swinging Sixties. The British had cornered the movie market (apart from westerns, fading fast): Bond and Michael Caine the nattiest dressed screen spies; Peter Sellers superseded Jerry Lewis as America's most popular comic; Hayley Mills still the world's no.1 child star, turning 20; Margaret Rutherford was the screen's adored septuagenarian. An entire generation of British actors—Peter O'Toole, Albert Finney, Alan Bates, Tom Courtenay, Julie Christie, Terence Stamp, Glenda Jackson, Oliver Reed, Susannah York, Sarah Miles—were said to be the most interesting on screen. The swingingest middle-aged affair involved fifth-time-around Liz Taylor/Cleopatra and her consort Richard Burton/Marc Antony. And more UK actors—Richard Harris ('MacArthur Park'), Noel Harrison ('Windmills of Your Mind')— were held to be the most expressive vocalists in recording.

For the first time in centuries England defined cool. Three months after the Beatles arrived in America, Chuck Berry and Bob Dylan were trying their luck with extended tours in England, previously a whistle-stop. Those who could fake being English to Stateside audiences were flavor of the month, often literally. New LA groups the Byrds—first goofily calling themselves the Beefeaters— and the Turtles, false-advertising themselves as from England, strained mightily for Beatle accents in the frenzied quest for fame before stumbling on to Dylan and folk rock. Others hoping to fool the public were the Buckinghams and Golliwogs (later Creedence Clearwater Revival). For more than two years Americans were mindlessly Anglophile, and it took an English songwriter, Ray Davies of the Kinks, to debunk it all in the spring of 1966 with the flaying derision of 'Dedicated Follower of Fashion'. Still, only slowly was the spell broken: Britons had nine number ones in America that year.

While it lasted the edict—more powerful than if a law had been passed—shut out the all-too-American Beach Boys for their obvious aural and visible handicaps: being so un-English as to commit a heresy against revealed wisdom. The Four Seasons, older and more brittle, broke—no longer superstars in '65 due to media neglect. Wide-ranging surveys in the mid-seventies by WNBC-New York, WFIL-Philadelphia and WRKO-Boston to discover the most popular hits long term showed that the Seasons were done in by someone: 'Dawn', 'Ronnie', 'Rag Doll', 'Bye Bye Baby', 'Let's Hang On', 'I've Got You Under My Skin', 'Opus 17', 'Can't Take My Eyes Off You', 'C'mon Marianne', mostly greeted without fanfare on release, ended up like most Beach Boys hits among the top dozen or so Eastern Seaboard sellers from their respective years— rated higher than Beatle number ones 'Ticket to Ride', 'Day Tripper', 'Yellow Submarine'.

Frankie Valli: "A lot of American groups got lost... Everybody has to have their own identity—it's very important. That's what we

*did. We said, 'Sink or swim, but we're going to stay with what we do'
and it's the only chance that anyone could have."*

*The towering, enduring irony was that the best to come out of
Britain in the Sixties by its best—The Who, the Kinks, the Stones,
Cream—was created on vinyl by American record producers,
resettling in Britain because anxious to get in on the scene. Foremost
among an array of dominating American producers was Shel Talmy,
who described Dick Rowe, "the man who turned down the Beatles",
as "one of the few people in England who was pro-American". The
anti-Americanism was a pathetically hypocritical defensive screen
erected by a domestic industry built on a framework of American
music as its direct inspiration, and now heavily reliant on imported
American talent to make it work.*

*The Beach Boys would have to overcome the dictates of fashion —
a feat unheard of in the pop scene—generated in London and
pervading America via New York, always susceptible to trends
crossing the Atlantic. In choosing artistic integrity they chose values
that held no currency in the prevailing showbiz climate. And if they
won they presented a danger that show business might never recover
from, a threat to the whole basis of marketing: "Go with the
bestselling commodity of the moment. Undersell, then dump,
yesterday's goods."*

*For Capitol/EMI, the Beach Boys' primary business connection —
the multinational that manufactured and distributed their recordings
but was now dependent on the quick-sale Beatles—the course was
clear.*

WHEN SIXTIES HISTORIES RECORD THE BEATLES
saved pop music from dreary, saccharine crooners of
no originality it is partly true—*in the UK*, not the multifaceted, everchanging American scene. The Cliff Richards, Shadows and Joe
Meek acts including the Tornadoes had already made strides in
Britain. For all their individual qualities their passing would not be
mourned by the Beatles who, pre-fame, derided them as smoothies in
suits. While rock'n'roll had cooled from its original white heat, the
American mainstream had the vital three-pronged thrust of the Beach

Boys, Motown and Atlantic primed to explode, a mainspring integrating black and white performers now put on hold by the Beatle-led aberration.

The year the Beatles had their first hit—1962—the UK top 20 was full of inferior covers of American records, as bemoaned by Britain's own industry spokespersons: 'Moon River', 'Tower of Strength', 'The Lion Sleeps Tonight', 'When My Little Girl is Smiling', 'Roses Are Red', 'Spanish Harlem', 'Bobby's Girl', 'Up On the Roof'.... These remakes and their performers—Danny Williams, Frankie Vaughan, Karl Denver, Johnny Spence, Craig Douglas, Jimmy Justice, Shane Fenton, Ronnie Carroll, Mark Wynter, Susan Maughan, Maureen Evans, Kenny Lynch—weren't heard overseas except in dutiful British Commonwealth markets loyal to the mother country. Orchestra leaders left over from the big band era purveyed restful ballroom numbers: Acker Bilk, Joe Loss, John Barry. If Kenny Ball—popular in America with 'Midnight in Moscow'—hadn't introduced post-War-styled 'Sukiyaki' it is unlikely Americans would ever have let the original out of the bottle to contribute to the apparent malaise of 1963.

While rare knowledgeable British fans have been praised by American rock'n'rollers for recognising quality, the UK had an all-powerful clobbering machine keeping rock'n'roll down—"Auntie BBC", which in its duty to young and old ears alike efficiently suppressed black music under the guise of preserving the country's cultural heritage: akin to the White Australia Policy elsewhere in the Empire. It was the brief liberalisation of the airwaves, 1964-67, when they finally got some exposure as private 'pirate' radio stations flourished around the British Isles, that the rock'n'rollers were thankful for.

So it was that the run of new UK groups formed by 1963 left much to be desired in originality and style, but what did America's fashion-conscious youths, white middle-class teenyboppers who hadn't heard real rock'n'roll, care? Most British rock'n'roll in the invasion was about as convincing as Italian westerns or Japanese Elvises. The Beatles and other UK r&b groups always preferred the original US recordings, if they could get them—then spoilt the effect by performing inferior covers themselves, true to the English spirit of anyone-can-put-their-hand-to-it-rock'n'roll, one level removed from the makeshift skiffle groups. Obviously, like the Rolling Stones, the more up-close exposure the Beatles had to American practitioners the better they got.

Still, Music Hall style and sensibility were deeply ingrained in the Brit psyche. David Jones, a struggling singer with several bands, as late as 1967 put out novelty parodies of rock'n'roll: 'Love You Till Tuesday' and 'The Laughing Gnome' in the style of early-sixties comics Mike Sarne ('Come Outside'), Bernard Cribbins ('A Bird Up On My Bike'), Tommy Steele ('Little White Bull') and Anthony Newley ('That Noise'). It was a breakthrough tactic that caused immense embarrassment later. With a leap towards cool and a hefty push by Yank producer Shel Talmy he released 'Space Oddity' to be one of the great English figures of the early Seventies. By that time he had changed his name to David Bowie.

A persuasive view contra to Beatle omniscience comes from the British documentary tv series *Dancing in the Street*: American music was progressing very well, thank you, on diverse fronts most broadly represented by an r&b/soul barrage, only to be stifled by a cheapened homogenised product from UK groups with fashionable hair as their claim to popularity, a qualification unmatchable by the black originators of the music.

The coup was resented in some circles to the lengths that a "Stamp Out the Beatles" campaign was organised by Detroit student activists, fans of Motown and devotees of the grassroots r&b and blues of their city. When Paul McCartney heard of it he sensitively riposted that the Beatles would stamp out Detroit. British musicians were by and large clueless to the nuances of Blues, Gospel, Soul and any number of other American idioms of expression. And entrepreneurs of Epstein's ilk would never have understood the dedication to quality and authenticity of Jerry Leiber & Mike Stoller, Phil Spector, Doc Pomus & Mort Shuman, Jerry Wexler of Atlantic, Barry Mann & Cynthia Weil of Brill Building 'pop' and many others in the American recording industry of that time: Jewish aficionados of black music.

Fans of Motown invaded the broadcast of the Beatles' second Sullivan show in Miami, in vain. By the end of that year, 1964, a Leiber-Stoller produced, blues-tinged 'Go Now' was commandeered by new English group the Moody Blues for their US debut; and the Shirelles' 'Sha La La' overwhelmed by a Manfred Mann cover following up 'Do Wah Diddy Diddy', yet another song (by Mann-Weil) with girl group written all over it. As *Dancing in the Street* concluded, if the English acts had saved American music, what had they "saved" it from?

THE BEATLES WERE WORKING-CLASS LADS RAISED as pets of the aristocracy and enthroned by America, having freed itself from the British Empire two centuries before only to now don the chains wholeheartedly. Homebred musicians withered from unrequited wooing, shunned by their own media. Who would challenge the invaders?

Not a few bluecoats turned redcoat, going mod in a half-assed process totally out of cultural context. Peroxide-blond 'surfers' had carried surfboards through fashion-governed Chelsea in 1963, just for the look, and now the tables were turned with a vengeance. To make the switch was to be "fab", "smashing", "gear". But instead of carrying it off with aplomb as the Beatles and Kinks did, Yanks started looking and acting like Austin Powers: aping foreign fashions, and parroting music alien to them. Just as the English did, to American music. In some twisted sense of karma the Byrds and Righteous Bros latched on to British wartime heroine Vera Lynn, suspecting that her flagwavers of a generation before might be just the ticket, and produced hideous remakes of 'We'll Meet Again' and 'The White Cliffs of Dover'. The Beau Brummels ('Laugh Laugh', see John Candy comedy *Uncle Buck*) posed English enough to appear on *The Munsters* as Beatle standins. Their Revolutionary War period costumes were outdone by the bluecoat uniforms of Paul Revere & the Raiders, cashing in on lace and frills but sticking for a while to a tough LA r&b produced by surf music alumnus Terry Melcher.

Ponytailed and knee-breached on the same theme, P J Proby from Texas was befriended by the Beatles, annointed by them on UK tv and had his career made—in England, joined by Righteous Bros-soundalikes the Walker Brothers. Proby blew his chance of continuing superstardom (or more important, widening it to his homeland) when in early '65 he was banned by UK theatre chains and BBC-TV for deliberately splitting his tight britches to get a reaction. Tom Jones, on the same tour, took over as the star. Jones and Dusty Springfield squeaked in by the back door—welcomed by American audiences who thought they were black. The favored groups in both Britain and America now typically offered a maximum of volume and minimum of finesse, or hummable singalong melodies set amid this mishmash of so-called "rock and roll".

Precipitating all this, the shock of the Beatles hitting America was all the more so when it was realised they were only the tip of an ever-broadening iceberg. England was soon so central to the pop culture of the Western World that within two months of the Beatles landing her two feeblest rock and roll pretenders, Brian Poole & the Tremeloes and Freddie & the Dreamers, were greeted with screaming fits in Australia on a package tour with Gerry & the Pacemakers, Dusty Springfield and adopted Yank Gene Pitney. That May the Dave Clark Five were mobbed by 5,000 fans in Washington DC, helped by well-placed pre-publicity; Fred Vail recalls being told that only two of their tour dates made money. In June the Stones dropped in to Chicago's Chess studio to jam as equals (in fame) with their teachers Chuck Berry, Muddy Waters and Willie Dixon; but in Sacramento the Stones managed an audience of only a thousand, not helped by the exorbitant $6 price (personal communication, Fred Vail). Yet by the end of the year top US acts Bob Dylan, the Beach Boys, the Supremes and almost the entire Motown star roster on a package tour—aside from the Shangri-Las and many less stellar—were obliged to pay return visits to England for sheer commercial reasons, if not to bow to the new Mecca of reconstituted rock and roll.

English teen idols with swished-back hair—but otherwise hardly differing from the Beatles—were not welcome in the US and chief among them, Cliff Richard, had suffered more initial rebuffs than the Beatles. 'Livin' Doll' (1959) had made top thirty, prompting an invite from *The Pat Boone Show* in the New Year. But his only apparent advance was to lead Elvis Presley's move from rock'n'roll. A huge seller in Europe, especially Germany where Elvis was still stationed in the army, it is hard to believe the song's sedate shuffle beat didn't lead directly to 'Stuck On You', 'Good Luck Charm' and more sounding a lot like Cliff's pace.

'Lucky Lips', another massive world seller, made a reentry and then late 1963 Cliff's remake of 'It's All in the Game'. Unfortunately the Beatles arrived in America just as Cliff was entering the thirty again and his pompadour went stone-cold-dead out of fashion. Songs like 'Don't Talk to Him' and others written by a combination of Shadows/Cliff were better than Beatle music of the time except maybe 'Please Please Me'. But he was disqualified from serious consideration Stateside for another twelve years, continuing a household name almost everywhere else. His biggest English teen rivals, Adam Faith and Billy Fury, each had a dozen (shrinking) hits into Beatletime at home. Though Faith was pushed by the influential Jack Good, resulting in a solitary US top forty hit backed by the Roulettes, and Fury too had contacts, neither got within a bargepole of American acceptance.

The Shadows too—backing Cliff but having a spectacular career of their own ex-USA—were surplus to requirements. They'd been blocked in 1960 by one-hit-wonder Danish guitarist Jorgen Ingmann's cover of their world multi-million seller 'Apache'; after that, well America already had the Ventures, thanks for askin'.

For UK audiences local teen raves Helen Shapiro, hitting at 14, and Kathy Kirby, specialising in speeded-up Doris Day retreads, vied with Brenda Lee and Connie Francis. Shapiro even went to Nashville to record in 1963 but remained unknown to the rest of the States but for minor Easy Listening hit 'Tell Me What He Said'. Anyway, Lesley Gore already had the teen girl franchise in America, Connie Stevens runner-up, and sultry Connie Francis and wholesome Annette Funicello between them cornering beach movies. In January of that year the Beatles, with just 'Love Me Do' under their belts, were ranked fifth on the Helen Shapiro show touring the UK, behind secondary American teen idols Tommy Roe ('Sheila') and Chris

Montez ('Let's Dance'). By the end of the year they were at the top and she was nowhere, her demise highlighting the useless waste and anti-female bias at the onset of the Beatle era. The Beach Boys would choose her as the main support act on their spring 1967 UK tour and she later made a go of a jazz career.

There were legitimate, barely decipherable routes to American hearts other than on the lacy cuffs and billowing shirttails of the Brit Invasion. The husky 'black' voices of Dusty Springfield ('Wishin' and Hopin'', 'You Don't Have to Say You Love Me') and Tom Jones ('It's Not Unusual', 'What's New Pussycat?') saw them embraced as Blue-Eyed Soul, as coined by the Righteous Bros. Neither was quite as successful in the blue-eyed genre as Bill Medley & Bobby Hatfield under Phil Spector, though they lasted longer. And each was courteously credited by black artists with opening ears to black tones, though Britain remained immune for some years yet. In reality, Dusty was an acceptable torch singer, her forté the intimate whisper that Cilla Black did badly. There was a whole vocal ladder between her and Nancy Wilson or Dinah Washington, and a good few rungs up to Betty Everett or compatriot Shirley Bassey. In the UK real soul singers of the day like Madeleine Bell and the Flirtations were hardly appreciated compared with the acclaim showered (mainly justly) on Macy Gray, Joss Stone and Amy Whitehouse two generations later.

Touring America early on with the Springfields, Dusty settled as a solo in New York City and remolded herself from a wholesome Irish-styled colleen belting out country-folk to the first Brit girl replicating Soul. To highlight the new image she took up a bleached-blonde variation of the big backcombed beehive hairdo and black eye makeup of the Ronettes. She cited the Exciters' 'Tell Him' as her style model, and her backing vocalists the Breakaways had done a UK cover of 'He's a Rebel' though Phil Spector and the Crystals' original became the hit. Thank goodness for small mercies because the Brits had accepted everyone from Tommy Steele to Max Bygraves as stand-ins for the real thing—and continued to, as the French did their own in a *rock toujour* spirit.

Dusty rivalled Dionne Warwick as top songstress in the States through '64, but then with the second big wave of invasion a songbird reminiscent of a French-styled Vera Lynn won over sentimental (white) hearts. 'Pet' Clark was over thirty and well established in middle-aged French cabaret when she introduced 'Downtown'. A parallel movie career and accomplished stagecraft assured her place as long as the Invasion lasted and an American career as long as there were musicals on Broadway. In 1967, when Aretha Franklin discovered Soul, Pet's days on Top 40 radio were numbered though two of her biggest hits came the first half of that year: movie director Charlie Chaplin's 'This is My Song' and 'Don't Sleep in the Subway' by her writer/producer Tony Hatch, by his account modeling it after the Beach Boys' *Pet Sounds*.

It wasn't until this point, when the thrust of the Invasion was blunted, that Lulu made her biggest impact in the US, 'To Sir With Love', helped by the movie starring Sidney Poitier, America's new no.1 box-office star. Resembling a Scottish Brenda Lee, Lulu went on from her ersatz stab at the Isley Bros' r&b classic 'Shout'— faked well enough for the British Commonwealth—to develop an individual delivery on her classics including 'Oh Me, Oh My'. Some years later the Brits would again show their weakness for little girls in their early teens with big, put-on gravel voices by making Lena Zavaroni a star for her talent-quest renditions on tv of 'Ma, He's Making Eyes at Me' and 'Personality'.

But at the height of the Invasion America was impervious to Britain's two best-liked girl vocalists, Cilla Black and Sandie Shaw, both tressed in Brit bobs, enjoying one Top 40 hit each, 'You're My World' and 'Girl Don't Come'. Cilla, a Liverpool/Cavern mate of the Beatles, was *the* US flop for manager Brian Epstein—but a British institution, moving effortlessly to television hosting. Model-like Sandie, discovered by Adam Faith, scored a small consolation in '(There's) Always Something There to Remind Me' outselling Dionne Warwick's version. But she reached her peak in Eurovision Song Quest winner 'Puppet on a String'—not the Elvis ballad but a horrendous Bavarian-style oompah song beloved of Brits and other Euros that sold four million-plus.

Gawky Cilla, overflowing with English working-class "If she can make it I can make it" appeal, made pseudo-operatic versions of

Bacharach-Warwick's 'Anyone Who Had a Heart' and 'Alfie'. English aping led to such disasters as a cover of 'You've Lost That Lovin' Feelin'', just pipped to UK no.1 by the original. Cilla, with Manfred Mann, the Hollies, Tremeloes and Dave Dee, Dozy, Beaky, Mick & Titch, participated in the decline of British pop in the late Sixties, now reliant on homegrown writers and producers, laid to rest by styleless Marmalades and Love Affairs.

But with all this—1964 being above all a novelty year—the biggest American impact by UK-based females was made by one-off novelty takes. Overshadowing Dusty and Dionne for three months, "Millie", Small by name and frame, promoted her native Jamaican *ska* beat with 'My Boy Lollipop' performed at the World Fair in New York with a bevy of dancers sponsored by the newly independent Jamaica's tourist board. It was a bouncy ditty that went to #2 in Billboard, attracting as much airplay but not sales as the Beach Boys and Four Seasons through early July. The same beat, same everything, was trotted out for lesser hits. Julie Rodgers in early fall trod her footnote in history with 'The Wedding', moving seven million in the next eight years—seemingly played at every second wedding in the Western World in that time. The key line "You by my side—that's how I see us" rang out the death knell of a romantic era.

IN AMERICA PRODUCERS AND SIMPATICO ENGINEERS had wholly realized advances in the studio. Hailed above them all was Phil Spector as creator *extraordinaire*—now coming to be rivalled by George"Shadow" Morton and Motown's team Brian Holland, Lamont Dozier and Eddie Holland. All were widely acknowledged for weaving spells at the control panel—a bewildering press-button device looming large in the lives of girl artists as a metaphor for a loss of control over self expression and their own careers. Spector in particular was widely modelled by aspiring Svengalis around the world but living up to the substance was something else. In Britain the dark shades and bodyguard-henchman clearing the rabble for the royal procession were embellishments adopted by Andrew Loog Oldham, the echo chamber effects overdone by independent producer Joe Meek.

Along with the scene came girl group songwriters admired by the Beatles, Rolling Stones and others. Goffin & King, writing for Little Eva, the Chiffons and Cookies ('Chains'), wrote 'Don't Bring Me Down' for the Animals and later Aretha Franklin's breakthrough 'Natural Woman'. Other major New York spousal teams were Mann & Weil—now with 'Walking in the Rain' (Ronettes), 'We Gotta Get Out of This Place' (Animals), 'You've Lost That Lovin' Feelin'' and 'Soul and Inspiration' (Righteous Bros); and Barry & Greenwich—an array including 'Leader of the Pack' and 'River Deep, Mountain High'.

Spector, the model of the go-getter entrepreneur, reveled in the *chutzpah* it took to make a hit out of nothing in a make-or-break showbiz world as the rock'n'roll era wound down in 1959 and businessmen who made their livings from teen music looked for certainty in trends—a predictability that the best, most vibrant rock'n'roll abhorred, by definition. Three of the Beatles turned to Spector above anyone to produce their starting projects and reignite their solo careers. But as rock moved on, the spontaneity of the original rock'n'roll would only be recaptured in moments, and by the most talented artists.

It is doubtful whether the Kingsmen, from the Pacific Northwest, qualified for this category. But they were current enough to set a trend. On the spot two months before the Beatles, through the New Year of '64 their garage remake of Richard Berry's 'Louie Louie' spent a month as runner-up in national sales, went to number one for two weeks in mid-January and then hung in the top three below the Beatles, selling over two million. Their sound was tougher than the Beatles', as heavy as the Stones and Kinks (to record their own version) would be. With the Kingsmen, two other groups from the Seattle-Portland circuit, the well-established Ventures and the upcoming Paul Revere & the Raiders would be distant runners-up to the Beach Boys as album sellers among US male groups of the mid-Sixties.

The trend was clear—confirmed in a rush by the oncoming dominance by English r&b groups performing along similar lines. Girls needn't apply, playing just a subordinate, supportive role in

English working-class culture, unless the girl was as glamorous as Shirley Bassey, Dusty Springfield or Sandie Shaw—or could belt 'em out at a party like Cilla or Lulu. For the Ronettes, 'Baby I Love You', another peak in girl-group music, was climbing the US chart ten places at a time until it hit the Beatle-wall in February. From then on, even with classics 'The Best Part of Breaking Up' and 'Walking in the Rain', their place was down the Top 40. The shimmering, haunting 'You Baby' wasn't released as a 45, and by the end of the year, seeing the girls' epitaph writ large, Spector had switched to the virile Righteous Bros—a well known r&b duo around California who gave the Wall of Sound another year at top.

Poised for a brief turn in the spotlight midyear was 'It's In His Kiss', much later remade by Cher. Betty Everett's soulful original sent Dusty back to her seductive Claudine Longet whisper. Leiber & Stoller's Red Bird label, hosting the most successful new girl groups, sounded more like a candy store, far removed from the tough girl-group r&b as it had been four months before: the Dixie Cups with 'Chapel of Love' and 'Iko Iko'; emoting Jelly Beans, 'I Wanna Love Him So Bad'.

Epitome of the new unthreatening approach were the Supremes, on a fast track to all-round entertainers. Their modest peekover at fame the previous Xmas—'When the Lovelight Shines Through His Eyes', covered by Dusty—was more exciting than their subsequent formula hits, that however well crafted seemed fabricated up against the primal spontaneity of pre-Beatle girl groups. Neither could they match the drama and scope of Martha & the Vandellas and the Shangri-Las, the best current 'girl' recordings. But the doorway to network television did widen for this particular black group, because they presented as a cabaret act, not rock'n'roll. The Toys made a thorough copy of their sound: 'A Lover's Concerto' hit number one on the sales chart, certified a Gold Disc, but stumbled in Billboard unable to win the guaranteed mass exposure of the Supremes, made-to-measure by a hands-on boss of a mainstream corporation.

The Shangri-Las—'Remember (Walking in the Sand)', hitting six weeks after the Supremes' first no.1, and the iconic 'Leader of the Pack' a bare six weeks later over October-December—made a cult from a nasal foursome of two sisters and two twins from New York's Queens borough, cajoled to tears—and to perfection—in the studio by self-styled B-movie tough "Shadow" Morton. They followed up through '65, still producing records on the cutting edge in the supposedly outmoded girl-group genre—'Give Him a Great Big Kiss', 'I Can Never Go Home Anymore'. Of similar cult status but without the same success were the racially integrated Reparata & the Delrons, 'Whenever a Teenager Cries', and later ex-US 'Captain of Your Ship'.

While the Shangri-Las were actually white, the Supremes did their best merchandising Supremes White Bread with their photo on the packet. In contrast, the Shangri-Las appealed as hard-boiled and street-wise. 'Leader of the Pack' was menacing enough to British authorities to be banned by Independent Television's *Ready Steady Go*. The Beatles conquered the known world that year by wanting to hold your hand. Red-blooded American boys in motorcycle gangs hailed by this new girl group threatened more. In the UK an acceptably polite equivalent was sung by pretty, elfin Twinkle, urging her biker boyfriend 'Terry' to "Please wait at the gates of Heaven for me."

As a follow-up to 'Baby I Love You', girl group producer Brian Wilson had offered his best new love ballad 'Don't Worry Baby' to the Ronettes, the sexy threesome who had sung his all-time favorite record. It was rejected by Phil Spector, who seems to have taken a defensively condescending attitude to Brian's efforts from the start ("Brian is a very sweet guy… but"): luckily as it turned out. Brian took the 'feminine' lead vocal to make it into a Beach Boy classic. Spector apparently found the unremarkable 'Don't Hurt My Little Sister' usable after reworking and assigning new lyrics, but Brian kept it to appear as one of the also-rans on *The Beach Boys Today*.

IN THE *DANCING IN THE STREET* EPISODE BRIAN WAS interviewed for in 1997 he was obviously still sorely confused and frustrated thirty years after at how the Beatles could sweep all before them. He had naïvely searched all that time for a *musical* explanation, on the assumption that the throngs of pubescent girls who fainted or peed themselves at Beatles/Stones/Monkees/ David Cassidy/Bay City Rollers shows were music lovers. And groupies are patronesses of the arts? Yet his ongoing insecurities in no way matched the rivalry within the Beatles that would end after six years in the limelight with their vituperative breakup.

Brian was renowned for his effusive, often overboard praise for anything he liked. By 2007 he was indoctrinated enough in Beatle mythology to concede songwriting honours to them and only matching them in "group sound". Attending a recording session of the Rolling Stones in LA at the time he had just completed 'Good Vibrations', he called *them* "remarkable". The Stones quickly outdid the Beach Boys as media fodder—a goal only one of them was racing for. It is not known by this writer what Muddy Waters and other bluesmen thought of the Stones. Undoubtedly they learnt quickly but in the UK there was a fair bit of disdain from serious musicians and others, especially when they started out. On being called in 1963 to help with a recording session by producer-manager Andrew Oldham, one of the Shadows, Tony Meehan (at the time manager to Gene Vincent), who could read and write music, remarked horrified that the Stones' instruments weren't tuned and so they weren't playing in tune for the recording. Oldham, basing his boys' success on the "We don't give a shit" image he created and spun throughout, replied, "Yeah, great isn't it!" (*Stoned*, ed. Andrew Loog Oldham, 2001). It was a scene that would be replayed at other sessions, Oldham calling in another producer when frustrated at not being able to get anything coherent out of them.

In fact the Stones' first big hit, after a warm-up from Chuck Berry, was personally gifted to them by Lennon & McCartney. This was late autumn '63—the Beatles' execrable 'I Wanna Be Your Man'—and as played by the Fab Four a frantic, mop-shaking excuse for a song going for a maximum of rauc and minimum of finesse—that must have set culture vulture William F Buckley's teeth a-grinding and which might just be the very quintessence of the British Invasion. It would be tempting to think the two main Fabs wrote it that London evening they bumped into the Stones as a Liverpool-lad joke to sabotage their upcoming rivals—had they not included it on *With the*

Beatles. Music like this is responsible for the now widespread 'taste' of rock fans for decibels above all. It made the Stones image—if not their commercial success—big enough in Britain to graduate from supporting Gerry & the Pacemakers to the Ronettes, to end up supported by them and dating them, on a UK tour.

For 'Not Fade Away' they were well enough connected to have Phil Spector and Gene Pitney at the session, manager-'producer' Andrew Oldham being UK publicist for both—though Pitney was the facilitator here in the standoff between Jagger-Richards and Brian Jones (Stanley Booth). It was a Bo Diddley riff via Buddy Holly, and for a while "We didn't like anything we wrote, and we couldn't seem to get anyone else in the band to play it" (Keith Richards). For now their UK earning peak was a one-day shoot for a tv ad for Rice Krispies.

They still made only faltering progress in the US. Their June '64 tour was only successful on the Coasts—though 'Its All Over Now' gifted them by Murray the K, hired to be a sixth Stone, became their first UK no.1 and made top 30 US. Oldham got them publicity on national tv by having the group misbehave and get arrested in Chicago. Yet they died in the backblocks where short hair was an unspoken but enforcible law: "We were just entertainment-business freaks, with long hair, just like a circus show" (Richards). It might have been shock reaction to their cultivated wildness that drew complaints from the Stones that Chuck Berry and the Beach Boys "wouldn't speak to us" when they first ran into the American stars (all quotes from Booth).

It was November that they made it big with 'Time Is On My Side' via two dates on *The Ed Sullivan Show*, then to superstardom when their image kicked in with a vengeance on '(I Can't Get No) Satisfaction' and 'Get Off of My Cloud' from mid-'65. Just prior their first self-penned hit, 'The Last Time', remained their biggest-ever seller in Britain. A proportion of record-buyers realised the group had already progressed as far as it could in its particular groove, yet they inevitably won narrower appeal as the obvious flipside of the Beatles, the official Bad Boys of Rock. Real fans were attracted by Jones-Jagger-Richards' drive to be evermore outlandish, others alienated by the pose of five rich men pretending to be outsiders. They would switch to reggae or disco at will—hardly rivalling the Beatles or any other creative group in scope or originality. But as the decades went by they were catering for less demanding fans anyway.

John Lennon complained long and hard that the Stones had stolen the early Beatles' image and envied that they had got away with it—even thrived. The thought must have eaten him up that had the Beatles stumbled on to Oldham first, instead of Epstein, his group would never have had to clean themselves up. Yet, that was without factoring in Paul McCartney's proactive ambition to be adopted by the Establishment. And John too always wanted an undivided world audience, not an alternative one. From the Stones side, offered a picture deal by Decca and asked by a reporter if they would be like the Beatle films, Jagger retorted angrily, "We're not comedians!" (Booth).

It rings true that the deciding factor between the Stones and many other English acts was the well-known needle-sharp business acumen of Mick Jagger—never letting his London School of Economics education and aspirations show lest he let the cat out of the bag—and brilliant management through their first three years by whizzkid Oldham, one of the leading personalities of the Swinging Sixties. According to Bill Wyman, image, publicity, and "putting on a good show" rather than recording great music was most of what counted with the group. Ever conscious of star image and who was in and who was out, they kept almost-Stone Ian Stewart out of the group from 1963 and retained him as a sideman for 22 years until his death while Jones, repeatedly missing dates, and to a lesser extent Richards played up but remained stars—enhancing their appeal to fans. The entry on the band by Peter Shapiro in the intelligent *Rock: the Rough Guide* (1996) asserts convincingly: "Of course, without Robert Johnson, Chuck Berry, Bo Diddley and Buddy Holly, Keith Richards (guitar) and Bill Wyman (bass) would probably be lowlifes propping up the bar at their local pub...."

Lying about their ages to be in step with rebellious teens—Wyman was born in 1937, the same age as the oldest Four Seasons; Jagger as old as Ringo and John but understating his age by three or four years—they made good on Oldham's image as men "raised by a toothless bearded hag". Reverse Dorian Grays, they morphed into craggy gargoyles ludicrously pretending rebellion as they near seventy and continue to rake in hundreds of millions of dollars every tour, taking great pains to live between homes internationally and shift their tax rate down to 1.6% (from their 2006 income of 84 million pounds)—so low it hardly covers the cost of what must be a labyrinthine collection process.

In the face of the group's less than inspiring survival story, a myth was conjured by rock journalists of a great rivalry between the Beatles and the Rolling Stones. There was never any competition in it, both groups obviously recognising that the Stones' success was dependent on playing off the Beatles. Though creating some of the unforgettable moments in rock history with their sound—'(I Can't Get No) Satisfaction', probably because of its borrowed Robert Johnson riff, is today often held up as the greatest song of the rock era—at no time has Jagger or Richards given an inkling that they are capable of the wild flights of creativity produced by the Beatles and Beach Boys at their frequent best as they pushed the boundaries of popular music repeatedly through the Sixties.

"Ironically, the real contender [for the Beatles] was always Brian Wilson, the composer and arranger of the Beach Boys..." (Barry Miles). Jagger had demurred to the Beach Boys, pushed 'I Get Around' in the UK and on the Stones' '65 tour of America used 'California Girls' and *The Beach Boys Today* album to jump-start his day.

Through the Sixties wannabe unwashed rebels lined up for their dose of anti-sociability with each new release of Stones merchandise. Quickly, the group realized that the most striking doom-laden titles—*Out of Our Heads, Aftermath*—had the best chance of going all the way. Before long they came to parody their own creation, to the point of overkill just to sustain the hype and kick for their fans: *Their Satanic Majesties Request, Beggar's Banquet, Let It Bleed, Get Yer Ya-Yas Out, Goat's Head Soup...* Anything revolting would do.

By mid-'67 virtuoso musicians in supergroups like Cream and Jimi Hendrix Experience were taking over Britain. The Stones, trying to keep step with the Beatles—deliberately cribbing on their music as claimed by Lennon, and timing their single releases so they wouldn't be steamrollered by Beatle sales—had started seven months behind in their recording career and assiduously stayed there, through Oldham and/or Jagger apparently watching every move the Fabs made. Stamping their secondary status as long as the Beatles lasted, they were lost on what to model themselves against after their photo negatives' breakup, finally following 'Honky Tonk Women' two years later with a soundalike, 'Brown Sugar'. In between, ever anxious to retain their market share by an anti-Establishment slant, they participated in the Altamont debacle (see final chapter).

Brian Jones, original leader and a multi-instrumentalist who had lent them another dimension (e.g. the sitar on 'Paint It Black'), was pushed to the background by Oldham and the Jagger-Richards writing partnership long before his sacking and murder by drowning in 1969. Reportedly Marianne Faithfull, a confidante to all three key Stones at one time or another, witnessed Jones on his own roughing out almost the complete melody of 'Ruby Tuesday' —a song attributed to Jagger & Richards.

Of the arty in-crowd, Marianne enjoyed four songs in the top ten at home, all just reaching Billboard's top thirty but not US sales charts. She featured in films too. Described at that time by acquaintances as "spoilt and affected", she performed in a persona "coy and sweet", which she attributed to nervousness. Her vogue lasted less than a year—best known for her version of 'As Tears Go By' that tied her to the Stones, backed by the venerable 'Greensleeves', which would have been fine had she not been posing as part of the rock *avant garde*.

When the Stones and Marianne Faithfull made it, such was the crush of English acts America had to choose from that the Pretty Things ('Don't Bring Me Down', #10 UK) got lost in the rush—as their name ironically suggests, too close to the Stones' image to carve a distinctive niche as antisocial scruffs—though they outdid their rivals in hard-out playing and hard living. A founding Stone, Dick Taylor, had pulled out early on and formed the Pretty Things, but by the time they got into the swing *two* like groups had been selected by the media. A hilarious just-off-the-plane interview by a young network newsman of Mick Jagger during the Stones' second US tour showed just how little distinction was made between English groups. Jagger, fielding a remark about the Stones' image, jokingly replies "Yeah, the Animal Five", to which the confused interviewer enquires "You don't like them—the Animal Five?" Jagger, barely restraining from breaking up, explains patiently there is no group the Animal Five, but he likes *the Animals* very much. Groups jockeyed for lucrative positions Stateside. Confusion reigned, and with time the indifference to the early UK scene only grew: In 1976 the editors of the authoritative *Rolling Stone Illustrated History of Rock&Roll* captioned a photo of Gene Vincent and Eddie Cochran with English teen idols Billy Fury and Joe Brown as "...with Tommy Steele and a fan."

The Stones survived though many of their best singles relied on a single fortuitously introduced gimmick. Young surf music writer/producer P F Sloan, one half of the Fantastic Baggys group, claims to have produced the 'Paint It Black' session and to be responsible for improvising with the sitar—found in a corner of the studio— because the track needed something more. Typically, another American, Jimmy Miller, was responsible for what many Stones experts consider their best recording period, 1968-73, directing them back to their roots after two years of inaction and vague psychedlia to produce four of their best albums and tracks including 'Jumpin' Jack Flash', 'Street Fighting Man', 'Honky Tonk Women' and 'Brown Sugar'. Guiding them hands on, he played drums too on many tracks. Not incidentally, Miller also produced the most admired and progressive Brit groups of the late Sixties including the Spencer Davis Group, Traffic and Blind Faith (Wikipedia.com).

L IKE HERMAN'S HERMITS, THEIR CANDYASS BED-fellows, the Animals were recorded on Columbia by Britain's most prolific producer, Mickie Most. And both were released in North America by MGM, which shrewdly pitted them against each other for prime sales.

From Newcastle in the depression-ridden industrial Northeast, the Animals were the next English band with a number one after the Beatles' six-month rush on America. With the Stones, only more so, they were the first English blues act to be taken seriously by black commentators in the States—who hadn't heard Long John Baldry, Chris Farlowe, John Mayall, etc. Having toured for two years in support of John Lee Hooker, Sonny Boy Williams and other Blues artists, in rotgut authenticity their 'House of the Rising Sun'—Alan Price arranger and keyboards, Eric Burdon vocals, Hilton Valentine guitar, Chas Chandler bass, John Steel drums— stood head and shoulders above any other English contribution that year. They plied the blues with competent renditions of Sam Cooke's 'Bring It On Home to Me', Leadbelly's 'See See Rider' and John Lee Hooker's 'Boom Boom', and after returning from their first US gigs in October '64 they toured at home supported by rock'n'roll veterans Carl Perkins and Gene Vincent. But they were most consistent with definitive versions of new material in 'Don't Let Me Be Misunderstood', 'We Gotta Get Out of This Place', 'It's My Life', 'Don't Bring Me Down'—without ever quite reaching top ten again, as if American youth understood the new "blues"—i.e. hyped antisocial image—was primarily the Stones' turf.

The Who, from London, eventually greeted as the fourth great Sixties group, barely stuck their toe in the Atlantic. Their broad-vistaed leader-songwriter Pete Townshend and bass-playing multi-instrumentalist John Entwistle were obviously influenced by Beach Boy harmonies, just as drummer Keith Moon, an early surf music importer, recognizably borrowed from Denny Wilson. 'I Can't Explain' starting '65, 'My Generation' ("hope I die before I get old")—their enduring theme song, 'Substitute' ("for another guy") and 'I'm a Boy' ("but my Ma won't admit it") defined their theme of alienation. Introduced in New Year '66 with the Kinks on the last *Shindig* show, America was not ready for any radical creativity coming from England.

Helming the first few hits for The Who—'I Can't Explain', which had impressed Detroit and Ohio, 'Anyway, Anyhow, Anywhere', 'My Generation'—was a Los Angeles recording engineer, Shel

Talmy. Two years before he had bluffed his way into Britain as a rock producer—Who was there in the UK to say he wasn't?— by presenting himself to Dick Rowe, head of Decca, and claiming to be the producer of 'Surfin' Safari', on the strength of which Rowe was glad to snap him up. Talmy guided the Kinks too into their recording career, saving them from being just another Stones by taking them from blues covers expertly done to power chords and writing their own songs. His work with the Kinks through the mid-Sixties— including introducing the sitar sound to British rock in 'See My Friends' months before 'Norwegian Wood' and 'Paint It Black'—and The Who—introducing deliberate feedback for the first time on record through 'Anyway, Anywhere, Anyhow' and radically rearranging 'My Generation' into the aural storm it was —virtually defined a generation. Talmy, a Yank through and through, is therefore arguably the greatest record producer of the British Beat Boom, perhaps only challenged by compatriot Jimmy Miller and the strongly US-influenced pioneer Joe Meek. In making great records Talmy introduced American production methods, a key one using the best session musicians. In the studio for both the Kinks and The Who that meant, repeatedly, Jimmy Page (guitar) and Nicky Hopkins (keyboards). Simultaneously, Talmy worked with the Nashville Teens, the Fortunes and others before guiding David Bowie and jazz-rock group Pentangle ('Light Flight') to stardom (Wikipedia.com).

Just as Shel Talmy broke the Kinks and then The Who in the States, in his pre-Stones career Jimmy Miller did the same for the Spencer Davis Group, going top ten for the first time with 'Gimme Some Lovin'' and 'I'm a Man', which he co-wrote with Steve Winwood. As Winwood departed to form Traffic, Miller went with him, producing 'A Paper Sun', 'Hole in My Shoe' and 'Feelin' Alright'—and then on to the highly influential *Blind Faith* involving Winwood and former Cream members Eric Clapton and Ginger Baker. It was from there that Clapton, at a loss and in an apparent reversal of fortunes, joined the Plastic Ono Band led by John Lennon and Yoko Ono.

Townshend among many others admired Ray Davies, the Kinks' singer-songwriter. Davies' wittily sceptical and incisive social comment came before and came on stronger than John Lennon's. England's equivalent of the Lovin' Spoonful—each commenting knowingly on the intimacies of their own society—his group were leaders of the Mod look, getting in before The Who. Alternately in frilly Regency or stately Edwardian attire, Byronic coiffed hair tumbling imitation-casually, they quickly dated the Beatle look as merely cutely fab. They were maybe the Invasion's best-looking group, in an androgynous kind of way.

Scoring big just two weeks before the Stones, October '64, with 'You Really Got Me', the Kinks had two quick follow-ups also edging top five and no.1 UK—its sister song 'All Day and All of the Night' (both featured Dave Davies' much admired fuzzed riffs) and disillusioned ballad 'Tired of Waiting for You'. Though Ray Davies wrote much of his music in the English Music Hall vein as did the Beatles, he was genuinely affecting and didn't pull punches, employing bitter sarcasm. So his best songs were too realistic for America, e.g. 'Dead End Street'; and his most personal songs— 'Waterloo Sunset' (1967)—too alien: Their best-loved, most enduring song in England, and #2, it scored #146 US where their career was cut off from mid-'65 by a musicians' union dispute. As a result 'Dedicated Follower of Fashion' was under-appreciated; 'Sunny Afternoon' (#1 UK) fell short of a richly deserved top ten spot. They only returned post-Invasion, with 'Lola'.

Hitting also that fall with the Stones and Kinks were the Zombies, no.1 with 'She's Not There', then 'Tell Her No', but barely known at home. Registering high too occasionally were the Moody Blues and Them ('Here Comes the Night') featuring Van Morrison. The Spencer Davis Group had Steve Winwood as vocalist but like The Who didn't make it in the States until '67.

The Yardbirds—'For Your Love', 'Heart Full of Soul'—were popular as the Animals, rated high as musicians and at their peak one of a handful of truly innovative Sixties bands, seen in 'Evil Hearted You'/'Still I'm Sad'. They had followed the Stones as resident band at the Crawdaddy Club at the height of London's blues boom, each member having studied and grilled them until they knew their entire act (Stanley Booth) and eventually came to challenge the Stones in international following through 1965. Original guitarist Eric Clapton had given way to Jeff Beck then Jimmy Page, joining multi-instrumentalists Ian Samwell-Smith and Chris Drea, vocalist Keith Relf and drummer Jim McCarty. There were more American hits in 'I'm a Man', 'Shapes of Things' and 'Over Under Sideways Down' but the classic lineup was breaking up by '67. Last straws for Beck must have been a cover for the US of Manfred Mann's UK hit 'Ha Ha Said the Clown' and a revival of 'Ten Little Indians' for a desperately small hit—as the Beach Boys were moving on to 'Wild Honey'. A New Yardbirds under Jimmy Page were renamed Led Zeppelin.

Coming in '65 to join the rush of Americans to the UK was Nick Venet, official producer of that first 'Ten Little Indians' and justly styling himself as discoverer of the Beach Boys—and reaping tremendous kudos for it. He took over the Walker Brothers, re-imaging them as Britain's answer to Spector's Righteous Bros. The borrowed classic Spector sound translated as one of the true triumphs of the British Invasion in a magnificent restatement of Four Seasons original 'The Sun Ain't Gonna Shine Anymore'.

Liverpool and Manchester groups, sharply distinct from London blues, plied their trade in a popped-up rock and roll. And Beatle music, measured against other examples, can be seen to be well within this style. Working alongside the Beatles in '63, the Swinging Blue Jeans had an almost-big US hit with an obvious ripoff of Little Richard, 'Hippy Hippy Shake', then blew their scam with the original, identical 'Good Golly Miss Molly'. As more faces fronted on '64's beat scene the Merseybeats were just as popular at home, with the Fourmost (Parlophone/Epstein stablemates of the Beatles) and Four Pennies—the Applejacks, Mojos and Rocking Berries less so. None made it nationally in the States.

Of course, Epstein's total devotion to the Beatles spelt slow death for his other clients. Cilla Black left Epstein's management because of the inordinate time he was spending with his favorites. It could be argued Paul McCartney, in writing songs for them and mentoring to some degree—giving them hints in the studio—had more of a hand in the British success of the Fourmost ('Hello Little Girl', 'I'm in Love') and Cilla ('Love of the Loved', It's For You'). Epstein acts much less successful than the Fourmost were solo singers Tommy Quickly and Mike Haslam and a group called the Rustics: just one British top 50 hit between them. They were left hoping some magic from the Epstein name would rub off.

Gerry & the Pacemakers and Billy J Kramer & the Dakotas were both under Epstein's management and impacted America late spring '64, three and four months after the Beatles. Why hadn't Epstein struck with them while the iron was white-hot? Was it so they wouldn't spoil the Fabs' grand entrance, even delaying long enough so not to stand on their bridal train? The Pacemakers' 'How Do You Do It?' and 'I Like It' weren't as successful as most of the Beatles' comparable material. And after 'Little Children', his biggest US hit, Billy's repertoire was restricted to Paul McCartney tunes: 'Bad to Me' also top ten, 'Do You Want to Know a Secret' —his crack backing band doing a better job than the Beatles (the Dakotas had played on the same show at the Star-Club, Hamburg). It has to be said Epstein failed with Billy: a hunk of a modernised teen idol, and just two top-tenners. It didn't help that Billy turned down McCartney's offers of 'World Without Love' and 'Yesterday'—both of which would have been huge hits for anyone in the prevailing climate.

Gerry Marsden scored best with thoughtful, self-penned 'Don't Let the Sun Catch You Crying', matched by equally contemplative 'Ferry Cross the Mersey'—in retrospect both better than 80% of what was released in America under the Beatles through 1964. But Gerry and his mates were not in the race for enduring stardom, unable to look or act remotely like rock stars. Their piano-player sat stiff-backed like a schoolmarm, a thin, upright Liberace; of Sixties Brits, Alan Price, Manfred Mann and few others managed to make keyboards look remotely sexy, and only on organ. They did reach a point when their singles did better in the US than at home but were a qualified success; they had just two top 20 albums each side of the Atlantic. Yet, practised showmen Freddie & the Dreamers, who had worked along with the Beatles at Hamburg's Top Ten club, were even more unprepossessing than the Pacemakers, and a two-year delay didn't hurt their hits—even topping in the US, outdoing all Epstein acts who weren't Beatles.

CHAMPIONS OF FORGETTABLE INVASION EPHEMERA were the Dave Clark Five and Herman's Hermits. The Five scored 15 top twenty hits in their three years in America, the Hermits one more, all but seven in total reaching the ten. Most sounded fairly catchy at the time, yet only a handful are at all memorable. The Five were hailed for the "Tottenham Sound" of North London—the greatest local stars since the Tottenham Hotspur Football Club (the original "Spurs") and the media's hopeful successor to the Beatles. Arriving hot on the heels of John, Paul, George and Ringo, and undertaking a full American tour even before them, they at one time outdid everyone but them for big hits —eight their first year—including the Beach Boys '64 and '65. Despite this, they are really only remembered for their breakthrough 'Glad All Over' and 'Catch Us If You Can', best of a limited style. In England they managed just four top five hits.

Through 'Over and Over', their sole US chart-topper, and 'Bits & Pieces', their formula treatment fast grew monotonous but their almost effortless stay near the top only ended when even their fans realised the upbeat "chunka-chunka…" rhythm was most of what they had. Typical of English groups, they couldn't leave American classics alone and six rehashes were big: 'Do You Love Me?', 'Can't You See That She's Mine?', 'Reelin' and Rockin'', '(The Name of the Place is) I Like It Like That', '(Baby) You Got What It Takes' and 'You Must Have Been a Beautiful Baby'. Sounding something like Kenny Ball & His Jazzmen would if ordered to play rock'n'roll with a gun to their heads, they looked the part too, with pasted stage smiles. Dave played like a wind-up drummer-boy doll, centre-stage of a semi-circle lineup for tv spots, lead singer-keyboardist Mike Smith off to the side.

Despite poor tour receipts the Five set a record dozen appearances on *The Ed Sullivan Show*, the ultimate gauge of Establishment acceptability. They were most impressive in their film *Catch Us if You Can*, showing that with the right director (John Boorman, later of American classic *Deliverance*) they could look as cool as the Beatles on screen. Musically, even in their claim to fame they were outdone by the Honeycombs, who featured the same boomba-boomba beat by their girl-drummer leader, "Honey" Lantree—on the attractive 'Have

I the Right?' (#4), their debut produced by Joe Meek of 'Johnny Remember Me' and 'Telstar' fame.

From the end of Invasion Year One Herman's Hermits were the darlings of the second wave over the Rolling Stones, Kinks, Manfred Mann, even Petula Clark, with three number ones to boot. The Stones didn't achieve that volume of hits, nor as big. They were signed in the States by the faltering MGM, who seized on these English lads as a deliverance, to take up the slack left by fading Connie Francis. Their biggest achievement was to wrest most of the Beatles' pre-pubescent audience from them.

The Beatles had struck on a secret formula through the sequence of influences they'd been exposed to: from Tin Pan Alley and all-round showbiz to Lonnie Donegan, through Tony Sheridan, Easy Listening's Bert Kaempfert and other beat groups gigging in Hamburg. Paul McCartney, adding to his music hall father's tutoring, had fashioned a vocal veneer of Little Richard, whom they'd supported on tour just as they started recording seriously and distilling their own musical image. All was superimposed on a cardboard cutout of Elvis Presley and a template of his music as they were manoeuvred to be the new Great White Hope.

If Herman's Hermits took any inspiration from American music it was from the businesslike atmosphere of New York's 'Brill Building' pop, led by Don Kirshner's Aldon Music and designed to milk every exploitable emotion via teenagers' purses. To the end of 1964 the Beach Boy franchise had scored 26 hits in the US top 100 including the Brian Wilson songs performed by Jan & Dean in such an unmistakable style that most people couldn't tell them from the real deal: an average of one a month. Kirshner, supplied by teams of battery-housed writers, had produced more than that in one year: Not a great deal of soul-searching entered, or delayed, the creative process.

At their best the Hermits' style of delivery could be likened to that of the Cascades, the Southern California group who had recorded the sweet 'Rhythm of the Rain' almost two years before—a gentle, pretty melody. But unlike the Cascades, for the Hermits sincerity of delivery didn't come into the equation. The key to their sustained success was that frontman Peter Noone, just turned 17 and an actor from soap opera television, was cuter than anyone on the scene—until Davy Jones became a Monkee. Courtesy of Jack Good, Davy was currently performing a Music Hall soft-shoe shuffle with boater hat and cane on *Shindig*, an up-to-date teen pop show except when catering for English proclivities. Herman/Peter had cheeks as rosy and smooth— and Davy had eyes as big and round—as Hayley Mills', all the better for androgynous appeal to the pre-puberty market.

The Hermits' first hit, 'I'm Into Something Good' written by Kirschner's Goffin-King partnership, sold over 250,000 in ten days, contending with the Stones' 'Time is on My Side', the Beach Boys' 'Dance Dance Dance'/'Warmth of the Sun', Beatle double 'I Feel Fine'/'She's a Woman' head on, and the Kinks, Zombies, Supremes and Shangri-Las. It was catchy—better than nine tenths of what followed. Their next, the thickly candied 'Can't You Hear My Heartbeat?', was their first US million seller and made no.1.

If that wasn't puerile enough, their two biggest of all, 'I'm Henry VIII, I Am' and 'Mrs Brown (You've Got a Lovely Daughter)', cutely sung by Herman/Peter on tv, posing sub-Shirley Temple with a finger babyishly stuck in his mouth, could be charitably called children's songs. The novelty had worn off—but no one, anyway under 13, noticed. They swooped on the subteen niche as the Fab Four progressed to more serious songs though returning to children's Panto with 'Yellow Submarine' and many more. Their advance orders were higher than anyone but the Beatles, oblivious that 'Silhouettes' and 'Wonderful World' were r&b standards mercilessly and thoroughly hashed, among the very worst recordings of the entire British repertoire—and the Hermits' punishment was that they only got to no.4 while selling their million.

In March '65 the Hermits' fellow Mancunians Freddie & the Dreamers, styled more frankly as clowns than musicians, moved in on their territory. Retreading like the Hermits the same bouncy Brit-beat sounds the Beatles and Gerry & the Pacemakers had done two years before, they were another "biggest thing since the Beatles". Through promotion on Jack Good's *Shindig-Hullabaloo* monopoly they presold a Mercury label record of their album and drove 'I'm Telling You Now' to no.1 for two weeks. Their gimmick was to bend ludicrously from side to side at the hips in unison in a way that was thought mod (or simply ridiculing real rock'n'roll?—they thought of themselves primarily as comedians), in time as they played, looking like Rock was totally foreign to them and so following instructions second-hand from a rock'n'roll training manual; or misprogrammed robots performing calisthenics for a freak circus. Freddie, out front performing rope tricks with the microphone cord, would leap frantically in the air, waving his limbs uncoordinatedly but apparently according to some plan known only to himself and the group (see *The Ed Sullivan Show*, April 1965). This caught on well enough with the least discerning fans for it to become a dance—a feat of bad taste duly called "The Freddie". A new generation of mods a year on would be left wondering, as ever, What were they thinking?

On the Hermits' May tour of the US, though held from no.1 by the Beach Boys' 'Help Me Rhonda', they collected six golden discs from their record company for world sales over their first six months. And they received two of the most elusive prizes of all: official Gold Discs from the RIAA in a year that saw ten awarded in total—and when even the Beatles' latest single was slow getting one. The Hermits were big album sellers too, a "Best of" conglomeration reaching 900,000 its first year in the States—not as high as the Beatles because most Hermits fans only had a nickel allowance.

But as with the Dave Clark Five only their debut song got to the top at home, their four biggest American hits and other big sellers not released in the UK, presumably superfluous effort. They continued into '66, their records using more sophisticated pop arrangements and sounding a lot like Kirschner's Monkees would on arrival in September: 'A Must to Avoid', 'Listen People'. They reverted to oozing Music Hall impishness through 'Leaning on a Lamp Post' and 'Dandy', losing its bite in translation from the Kinks, and in '67 sold cloying Victoriana worthy of a West End *Oliver* production: 'There's a Kind of Hush', their last Gold Disc.

PETER/HERMAN CAME FROM THE ENGLISH VARIETY
stage—"panto"—a route also shuffled to American
superstardom by Davy Jones of the Monkees. Both Peter and Davy
had apprenticed as juveniles in the cast of perennial tv soap
Coronation Street based in Manchester. Afterwards, Herman/Peter
returned home for another eight big hits extending his career in the
same sticky-sentimental Music Hall rut....

It was a wide-scatter buckshot, lowest-common-denominator
entertainment whose shallow depths the Beatles themselves would
continually plumb for their singalong tunes that proved them all-
round entertainers appealing to the broadest possible cross-section of
the public: 'I'll Get You', 'Baby's in Black', 'Sergeant Pepper's
Lonely Hearts Club Band', 'Good Day Sunshine', 'Magical Mystery
Tour', 'Ob La Di, Ob La Da', 'Maxwell's Silver Hammer', 'Octopus's
Garden' and on and on.... None would have been out of place on
London's variety stage circa 1890—hardly what might have been
expected from musicians held up as the *avant garde* of the Sixties and
the mark to reach for two generations to come. 1964-66 inclusive it
all but ruined rock'n'roll and tainted much of what came in '67. From
then on the English went back to their Brit Pop, allowing a few
genuine converts to American music (the Who, Cream) to escape.

The cherished place in the English psyche reserved for all-round
entertainment can't be overstated. Teen idol Adam Faith, Paul Jones,
the lead vocalist of Manfred Mann, and Jeremy Clyde (Chad &
Jeremy) were equally well known as straight actors, while the
importance of films in the careers of the Beatles—Ringo Starr and
John Lennon separately—Mick Jagger, David Bowie, et al, is
obvious. Ringo and Freddie Garrity were later better known on
children's tv. Gerry Marsden, who later took to pantomime, was
called by John Lennon "a showman in the best sense of the word,"
whatever species of beast that be. Cilla Black, top songstress bar none
on the home front through the Sixties, later hosted tv game shows.
Tommy Steele, who passed as an early English 'rocker', found
fleeting fame in Broadway musicals and on film in *Half a Sixpence*.
Rod Stewart has found his real home in cabaret, reviving *very* oldies,

dressed in glittering Las Vegas lounge suits. It was as if all were reverting to their true *metier* after years posing as rock stars.

Maybe what is most frightening in retrospect is the reaction of the media to this avalanche of new faces with old sounds. Each one in turn was hailed as a new *avatar* with cynical endorsements. After Dave Clark failed to knock the Beatles off their throne the Hermits and Dreamers thrust to the center of preteen consciousness. The Hermits' impact was such that their fourth big hit—proof they would see their fans through puberty—'Mrs Brown', debuted on Billboard's chart at an all-time high of no.12 (no entries at no.1 in those simple days). To have outdone the Beatles—These must surely be no ordinary musicians, but super-Mods. With the Invasion's second wave came its flip side. Posing as villains opposite the children's heroes on a pantomime level of creativity, contributing to what was obviously the same carnival production, were the Rolling Stones—Punch in the Punch & Judy show. The media on both sides of the Atlantic, recognizing they were in the same game—not journallism but entertainment—collaborated and lapped up the stylized moustache twirling. It was all good for business.

But factually, this Invasion led by the Beatles was no revolution in rock at all—rather the opposite, a watering down of real rock music as much as 'Rock and Roll Waltz' and the Elvis imitators were. Aside from The Who, the Kinks and few others, were they even originals, playing music along their own intuitive tracks? The Beatles claimed to be rock'n'roll revivalists, while putting forward such obvious Tin Pan Alley material as 'Ain't She Sweet', 'A Taste of Honey' and 'All My Lovin''. Their signature refrains of "Oh yeah" and "Yeah, yeah, yeah" were the antithesis of the spontaneous rock-rebel yell heard from Little Richard or Jerry Lee, becoming as comforting to listeners as a pair of old slippers, keying automatic responses as the introduction or tag to a song, serving the same purpose as the catch-phrases worn out in the patter of their Music Hall heroes from Arthur Askey to Tommy Trinder to Bruce Forsyth: to reassure the audience that here were their old friends again with a familiar, staged act—here just to share a cosy evening's singalong. The veneer of rock'n'roll rebellion was overwhelmed by an arty new look and strategic mop-shaking—another signal to the audience to elicit applause. Herman's Hermits, less imaginative in working the crowd and with no song catalogue to fall back on, merely cemented in the retro-trend to Music Hall.

Freddie and his Dreamers 'perfected' the approach, their whole act being a novelty turn; the difference was that whatever appeal it had palled overnight, as novelties are meant to. They were big while "The Freddie" dance lasted, but luckily the US audience that had soaked the whole Brit experience up as a temporary diversion was satiated with this brand of entertainment and the Dreamers quickly wilted. Chubby Checker, please come home!

After his disheartening foray 'Let's Do the Freddie!' not only Chubby, but Elvis was nowhere to be seen, The New York Times in December '64 reporting him to have gone into seclusion at the trauma of it all, coinciding with Beach Boy leader Brian Wilson's nervous breakdown.

A T HOME, FOR THE TIME BEING, THE BRITISH LOVED themselves to distraction, to the near-exclusion of everyone else, even more than America loved them. A pop-cultural revival—in fashion, films, television, music—had begun. Through the entire length of 1963, '64, to the summer of '65, Roy Orbison and Elvis Presley (twice each), the Supremes and Roger Miller were the only Americans to top UK charts. With the rider that two Jim Reeves' hits sold slightly more, Orbison's 'Oh Pretty Woman' was the biggest American rock recording reported in that peak period of sales at 680,000-plus copies: moderate popularity indeed compared with the adoration the British reserved for their own, several selling a million and many more approaching that figure.

Conversely, there is ample evidence that English musicians who troubled to polish their sound were penalised by the US market for sounding American, i.e. 'slick'. P J Proby ('Mission Bell') and Dusty Springfield ('Stay Awhile') had astonishingly good recordings that suffered. One act consistently punished was the Ivy League, so called for modeling their harmonies on an updated collegiate sound; another the Searchers, who, the further they strayed from the Mersey Beat the further down the charts they slipped in America and at home.

Ivy League vocalists John Carter and Ken Lewis had been on the BBC's *Pop Go the Beatles* radio series and went on to record high harmonies on The Who's 'I Can't Explain'. At that time (early '65) 'Funny How Love Can Be' hit, followed by 'Tossing and Turning' (not the Bobby Lewis hit). Both were exquisitely arranged vocally and instrumentally, prefiguring 'A Groovy Kind of Love'—and didn't register an anthill in the US. The same happened to their Beach Boys/Four Seasons-sounding 'Round and Round in Circles' and 'Run Baby Run'. In loyalty to a cause whose time hadn't yet come they did a version of 'Don't Worry Baby'. After the heavy-handed prejudice eased in the next year another group going somewhat soulful, the Fortunes, but without the Ivy League's handicap of an American name brand, sold in much better numbers Stateside ('You've Got Your Troubles', 'Here It Comes Again') and then the Mindbenders' 'Groovy Kind of Love' made no.1 trans-Atlantic.

Merry England was what sold, unless you were the musically enterprising, truly nonconformist Beach Boys or Four Seasons or an exponent of the Motown Sound—i.e. so American as to be "alternative". Nothing was more English than music designed for an English country garden. The pleasantly soporific interchangeable duos Peter & Gordon and Chad & Jeremy didn't exactly hit— they sighed longingly from late spring '64 between the decline of the Everly Bros and the rise of Simon & Garfunkel. David & Jonathan were another—a cover of the Beatles' 'Michelle'; and still another, the Overlanders, had a UK number one with it.

Peter's sister was actress Jane Asher, Paul McCartney's then world famous steady girlfriend. As *the* trendy young couple through the mid-Sixties, Jane and Paul (with Mick and Marianne) were teen icons. Paul, Peter, Marianne Faithfull's then husband John Dunbar and writer Barry Miles formed a coterie and business partnership in an art gallery. According to Miles, later McCartney biographer, "Peter and Gordon spent two years circulating tapes to record companies, trying to make a name for themselves, but to no avail— until Paul began going out with Jane. Then record companies suddenly became very interested indeed." Now all were in the inner sanctum, boosted into the royal strata of swinging London, the barometer of social importance. Paul was elevated as a member of the monied, cultured Asher household in London's Mayfair for three years, ensconced in the room next to Peter (where he and Millie Small made out) where the most ambitious Beatle wrote his group's biggest hits with or without John Lennon.

One he wrote was Peter & Gordon debut 'A World Without Love', taking top spot in the US from 'Chapel of Love'; also their second and third hits, 'Nobody I Know' and 'I Don't Want to See You Again', and their best of 1966, 'Woman' "do you love me?". As a test of whether Lennon-McCartney on the label was what would sell it, Paul created an identity called Bernard Webb, supposedly the composer of 'Woman'. As English as the song was, as a result it was Peter & Gordon's first release to miss UK top 20 though it made a respectable showing at no.14 in Billboard.

Aside from the Beatles and the Beach Boys, Peter & Gordon were the only other major new act signed to Capitol through the mid-Sixties. Essentially what Jan & Dean were to the Beach Boys— at worst leeches, at best benign limpets promoting the same genre — Peter & Gordon were to the Beatles. As with most trans-Atlantians adopted with open arms and checkbooks by Uncle Sam their first hit was their only Blighty #1, after which, on a career path wearing a deep trench, they moved on to greener pastures: the USA. Such was the anathema to Americana in the UK at this time, though, for a year Peter & Gordon were bigger sellers at home too than any US act including the Beach Boys.

If Peter & Gordon might be called soothing, Chad & Jeremy were downright sedating. Their sole native hit, 'Yesterday's Gone', barely was and in America was slowed down by a competing version from the Overlanders. Their biggest, 'Summer Song' and 'Willow, Weep for Me', were delivered with the wan spirit of Marianne Faithfull's 'Greensleeves', far better suited to that country garden than a rock movement, even an English one. But, with the *cachet* of the Asher and Faithfull circles, genteel breeding was their trademark—an upper-class chic that was obviously supposed to be admired for its own sake.

Fortunately for the future of all music that stirred the soul, Chad & Jeremy lasted only to the summer of '65. Peter & Gordon prolonged the agony for another year after their last McCartney hit with, once again, novelty songs dripping with Music Hall cliché —'Lady Godiva' and 'Knight in Rusty Armor', tributes to opportunism that, with much other tripe put out in the mid-Sixties, worked to hammer more nails into the coffin of rock music. Only after decades had passed would it be apparent how many pop acts had attempted a premature burial for this most energetic and energizing form of music. If in doubt stick with *schtick*, and so it was that Peter & Gordon finished in spring '67 with 'Sunday for Tea', extolling the virtues of "lettuce and ham" and "crumpets and jam" among the thrills of the parlor—to a US audience now *formerly* besotted with all things teddibly English.

They had sounded and looked like refined Oxbridge-accented Beatles, so far removed from rock as to be baroque. It had been as much a class takeover as when the wealthy socialites at New York's Peppermint Lounge coopted The Twist under the nose of Chubby Checker—and far more dangerous to rock'n'roll because taken more seriously than Zsa Zsa Gabor and Marlene Dietrich twisting. Rock'n'roll in these hands was a casualty in need of critical care. None showed anything like the musical authenticity of their American cousins: the vocal imagination and upbeat propulsion of the Everlys, or self-penned poetry of Simon & Garfunkel.

As Peter & Gordon left the stage, cue a comeback by the Everly Bros, sublime rock harmonisers coming from deep country roots with their first hit in three years, 'Bowling Green'—thankfully not about the English pastime. They had influenced everyone from the Beatles to the Beach Boys, not least Simon & Garfunkel, who finally succeeded with folk rock. But the exquisite ballad was an isolated success for them.

OBVIOUSLY THE BEATLES LED UK HARMONY ACTS. The Hollies, Searchers, Tremeloes, Fortunes and Ivy

League—all probably better harmonisers than the Fabs on the whole—made attractive recordings for the most part. Irish MOR balladeers the Bachelors ('Diane', 'Marie'), another group under American émigré Shel Talmy, were energized enough to compete — more than American counterparts the Lettermen and Sandpipers, until the Vogues more than matched them ('You're the One', 'Five O'Clock World').

No English harmony group would threaten the primacy of the Beatles until the Bee Gees in '67: boasting a maudlin tear-jerking facility just as tuneful and even more brazen than Paul McCartney's, but the rock was missing. Missing the same broad sweep, they proved to be a singles group—and a wealthy one, especially after switching to disco. Their opening gambit—a highly successful one with the Invasion badly waning—was to still sing in Beatle tones but namedrop for the American market, as in 'New York Mining Disaster 1941' and 'Massachusetts'—this selling five million around the world, one of seven trips to the USA top twenty in eighteen months.

The Tremeloes—now without Brian Poole—made a good attempt at being English Four Seasons, covering 'Silence is Golden'. And the Hollies encroached on Beach Boy territory in 'I Can't Let Go' and its three-part counterpoint harmony, with Graham Nash on this occasion an adequate falsetto stand-in for Brian Wilson. The Who made forays into harmony too towards the end of the Invasion on 'Substitute', 'I'm a Boy', 'Happy Jack', 'Pictures of Lily'; the Kinks to good effect on 'Sunny Afternoon', 'Waterloo Sunset', 'Days'. But it was the Searchers who made harmony their forté from launch time on Uncle Sam's shores and were probably best at it of the UK groups until the arrival of the Hollies. The only major Liverpool act not under Brian Epstein's management, they further dared the fates in not paying obeisance to the Mersey Beat and so fought an uphill battle putting across a defining image, coming from Tony Hatch's rather select stable which included Petula Clark. They were one English group who did better at home —seven top three hits. In America, after a first year full of hits starting two months after the Beatles, but only one top ten, they branched out from the Mersey sound and were soon treated as something of a background hum to the main event.

Carving a niche with Jackie De Shannon's 'Needles and Pins', and 'Don't Throw Your Love Away', both were UK number ones and more thoughtful than ninety percent of what came out of England in 1964. A routine remake of Leiber & Stoller's 'Love Potion No.9' was easily their American summit, a disputed number one, while a subtle, affecting 'Goodbye My Love' slid by. Today their brightly performed 'Sweets for My Sweet', 'Sugar and Spice', 'Someday We're Gonna Love Again' and 'When You Walk in the Room' are a respite from the usual dross played on oldies stations. Rewarded by posterity as precursors of folk rock, electrifying a jangling 12-string 'What Have They Done to the Rain?' from Joan Baez, their rocking version of 'Have You Ever Loved Somebody?' in late '66 almost defied its source—Tommy Boyce & Bobby Hart, composers for the Monkees. By then they had given way to yet another wave of mainly light British fare.

Named in tribute to their hero of rock'n'roll, the Hollies spent their career avoiding it for straight commercial pop—after opening with remakes of American r&b ('Just Like Me', 'Searchin'', 'Stay') so average they haven't been heard since. Ranked up with the Dakotas among Mancunian pop musicians, they moved into their own groove and should have gone in with the first wave with 'Just One Look' and 'Here I Go Again'—both upbeat and sporting excellent harmonies but ignored in America. They made a mistake sounding like Gene Pitney if they wanted to catch US attention in 1965—'I'm Alive'. More going to or near top in the UK, 'Look Through Any Window' and 'I Can't Let Go', the latter edging out 'Barbara Ann', just made top 40 US. At home they were consistent until 'If I Needed Someone': Releasing a Beatle song as a 45 only emphasized subordinate status to their Parlophone labelmates.

In a burst from the following autumn—'Bus Stop', 'Stop Stop Stop', 'On a Carousel', 'Carrie Anne'—they finally broke through as harmony contenders in the US, each presented a gold disc by their record company not the RIAA. Despite their attractiveness all but the first were as cutesie and thumbing-your-nose-trivial as Herman's Hermits could have wished for in their heyday two years before. Hampered from the start by a lack of adventurousness and originality

251

innate in the derivative British movement, a clear lack of creative nerve resulted in the defection in early '68 of writer-vocalist Graham Nash, who went on to Crosby, Stills & Nash to provide the only real bright spot for harmony singing on the discarding of the Beach Boys at decade's end.

Today, just as the Beach Boys and Beatles can be linked conceptually across the Atlantic, the Hollies can be seen clearly as accordingly toned down, English Four Seasons, their staple recordings catchy harmony-pop ditties ('Jennifer Eccles', 'Sorry Suzanne') even further from rock'n'roll. A critic could be forgiven for imagining the resemblance extends to snare drum breaks heard on Seasons records in 1962-63 being reproduced by Bobby Elliott.

The remaining Hollies were left with Manfred Mann ('Just Like a Woman', 'Mighty Quinn') to cover Dylan, a surefire fashion icon. Ultimately, they must be lumped in with the Manfreds and Tremeloes in the chase for the next UK top tenner—a field for chart habitués including Beatle protégés Marmalade and Grapefruit, both about as exciting as their names would indicate. The Grapefruit, conceived by Yoko Ono, had as their high point a poor, year-late 45 of the Four Seasons' 'C'mon Marianne'; Marmalade, an inferior version of the irredeemable 'Ob-la-di, Ob-la-da'.

Simultaneous with the Seasons' rare rocker in early summer 1967 the Tremeloes in the UK were basing their career on another Four Seasons B-side, 'Silence is Golden', the flip of 'Rag Doll' three years before—to be the biggest hit the revived English group ever had. The gulf between original American pop—the Seasons/ Bob Crewe combine—and the imitative from the UK in the mid-Sixties was unbridgeable. The fealty of Brit musicians to an American idiom is all the more striking in the face of UK pride in trumpeting a false independence, even superiority.

MANFRED MANN TOO EPITOMISED THE APPROACH of making it by whatever means. Some of their lineup starting as players of pure jazz and the rest of hard r&b, they were shown up as artistically compromised from their first UK hit as the Beatles were touching down in New York: '5-4-3-2-1', commissioned as the theme of tv's *Ready Steady Go*. Through 'Do Wah Diddy Diddy' and 'Sha La La', both written as girl group songs, and a dozen far less memorable they clung to a narrow pop format on record (while performing live more to their roots) that showed considerably less guts than Bubble Gum. With the Brit Pop 'Fox on the Run' and 'Ragamuffin Man', nearing the end of the Sixties they were finally sick enough of themselves—by their own admission—to implode. Shel Talmy dallied with them before going on to the better Brit pop of Amen Corner and the (Australian) Easybeats, then to direct David Bowie into rock.

The mindset was of the showbiz trouper—supposedly linking rock rebellion with acting and game-show hosting, treating careers in entertainment as all interchangeable and of equal value—and by implication superficial enough to be acted or posed: "The show must go on," in whatever form. The Brit Invasion had hijacked the mantle of Rock's originators in mid-flight, sapped the initiative of its heirs-apparent and, rather than revitalising it, cheapened it. No pre-Beatle American teen idol had ever released the torrent of trivia gushing from each of a dozen English groups. The Beach Boys, inevitably lightening the shade of Rock with their harmonies and given their mix of talents, sustained the momentum of rock as a movement through emulating the rhythm-drive of Little Richard and socio-realist lyrics of Leiber & Stoller and Chuck Berry. And, far beyond traditional song structures, they introduced layered, complex elaborations through deceptively simple, primal music mosaics, daring to play Russian roulette with commerciality.

What was produced by the Brits and their American converts was more an effect of parody—not art expressing a subculture of youth rebellion (Britain did not even have a word for "teenager" until adopted reluctantly from America in the late Fifties, and then even the concept of youths having their own subculture continued to be mocked by this staid society at large—Salewicz), nor any true emotion but mostly an expedient and artificially reproduced, faded print of the original that turned out an enormous moneymaker and a happy hunting ground for songwriting hacks, pluggers, *artistes*, and producers with more cynicism or pick-and-hope than artistry. Norman

Smith tells the story (Salewicz) of the Beatles turning up to their audition pristine in suits but with pathetic equipment, a very ordinary performance, no visible originality—and of George Martin picking the group on the basis that they kept him and Smith doubled over with laughter for twenty minutes afterward with their Scouse humor. Gimmickry, not inspiration or improving one's craft, would be the common currency of rock—anything to improve business. In diverting rock music onto a false trail (*Dancing in the Street* doco) the Brit phenomenon unjustly ended the productive, innovative careers of many. Pure voices were drowned out by the din of musical chameleons on Top 40 radio who endlessly compromised themselves to be cool.

Of all English groups noticed in America those reaching above and beyond trivia—The Who, Kinks, Animals, Yardbirds, Spencer Davis Group—were among the less appreciated, even the Stones at first until they stamped a strong image opposing the Beatles. It was cuddly Beatles-64 and the other ingratiating Merseybeat groups, the Dave Clark Five and Herman's Hermits that America warmed to in its desperation for sentimental ownership—the prototype Fabs most of all. It was not until two years after they staked their claim on Uncle Sam, when they were ensured a huge fan base to fall back on, that the Beatles dared to break out of teenybopper mode lyrically and musically. Only after they loosened the sentimental straight-jackets they had tethered themselves in, and that America, Brian Epstein and other middle-men had padlocked, were the Monkees (even their name was based on the Beatle concept, a cutely misspelled animal) invented and introduced for public consumption—and the Muzik Biz again had its ideal: purpose-designed entertainers focused on wooing audience sympathy.

Bogusly billed as "America's Answer", this time it turned out to be literally true. The Monkees were groomed and trained into as close a copy of the Beatles as could be made. And the tv series format of non-stop action closely resembled *A Hard Day's Night*. Each was selected specifically to fill an individual Beatle role but inevitably ended up a caricature, American disciples of the British imperative straining to be Mod and ended up merely 'zany'. Even the early fluffed-up Beatles would never be caught trying quite so hard to please.

The full flourish of UK acts saturating the American scene lasted a little under eighteen months and waned before most noticed. Names that were almost household in that time just stopped having hits— Manfred Mann, after a brief top twenty span of four months (two hits), and Billy J Kramer after a year. The Searchers and Gerry & the Pacemakers too had a year. Freddie & the Dreamers beat all for a disappearing act after a span of ten weeks (three hits) ending May '65 also. Marianne Faithfull left top forty at the end of summer with Chad & Jeremy; Peter & Gordon returned only fitfully thereafter. At the end of 1965 such worthies as The Who, Small Faces, Cliff Richard, P J Proby and the Walker Bros hadn't made a real American impact, while against the odds Herman's Hermits and the Dave Clark Five were still going strong.

By whatever formula of stickability, the DC-5 and Herman's Hermits survived most by two years, going home in summer '67 to enjoy a string of hits more than ever in Music Hall mode. It was as if all had spent their careers to date gearing down to nostalgia acts, now ideally placed: There would always be a warm welcome at British pubs and soccer matches for boozed-up singalongs led by names like the Swinging Blue Jeans, the Merseymen, the Manfreds —and later, the US oldies tour.

In spite of the mediocrity glazed over by transparent hype, to this day program directors the world over deem perky Englishmen to have nostalgia value, dominating the airwaves over committed American practitioners of the real r&b. This travesty hits home when Brian Poole & the Tremeloes' cover of 'Do You Love Me?' is preferred to the Contours' raunchy authenticity; Sam Cooke's 'Wonderful World' is cooed with a bubbly nothingness by Herman; and classic Spector productions 'You've Lost That Lovin' Feelin'' and 'River Deep, Mountain High' are substituted by local covers that would never have exposure in an ideal world.

THE BRITISH 'INFUSION', AS SYMPATHIZERS CALL IT (I can see no net gain) traumatized African-American performers—thankfully deficient in English Music Hall technique. In Britain blacked-face white performers continued playing Al Jolson-style 'nigger minstrels' on BBC television from 1958 to 1978 in the highly popular *Black and White Minstrel Show*—despite ongoing complaints that embarrassed tv authorities even in farflung, relatively unsophisticated corners of the British Empire. But it was the just claims of genuine black performers that were more likely to irk the BBC. And when a government department acted this way with impunity, how likely was it that the general population would be any more sensitive to Black American music idioms? When black groups finally emerged in the UK they stuck to Brit pop with barely two exceptions, 'Baby Come Back' (the Equals) and 'Build Me Up Buttercup' (the Foundations); it took Jamaica's Desmond Dekker & the Aces ('The Israelites', 'It Mek') to import reggae as an authentic 'native' musical form.

The inroads of the whole British effect showed year by year in drastically reduced exposure for black rock Stateside. The USA's 50 biggest hits of 1963 show near the top such raw, vital discs as Little Stevie Wonder's 'Fingertips' and the Chiffons' 'He's So Fine', then the rollicking good 'Be My Baby' and 'My Boyfriend's Back'; Ray Charles' 'Busted' and the Impressions' 'It's All Right' just below with exquisite *a capella* 'So Much in Love' and ground-breaking 'Sally Go Round the Roses'. Undisputed classics 'Heat Wave', 'Up On the Roof' and 'You've Really Got a Hold On Me' make the big fifty, with 'Baby Work Out', 'Hello Stranger', 'Then He Kissed Me', 'One Fine Day', 'Mockingbird' and 'Just One Look' just missing: every one an r&b gem.

In '64, on the British Invasion, a complete turnaround: The two best-selling black recordings are Louis Armstrong's show tune 'Hello Dolly' and a lullaby treatment of 'Chapel of Love' (which Brian Wilson would revamp out of sight twelve years later); then cooing Mary Wells' 'My Guy' and gooey Supremes' 'Where Did Our Love Go?' and 'Baby Love'. 'Leader of the Pack', the first real stunner—with a black sound—comes halfway down the list. The ultra-pop 'My Boy Lollipop', and better 'Come See About Me', 'Under the Boardwalk' and Martha & the Vandellas' 'Dancing in the Street', the last two the only other classic performances, follow toward bottom. Below the 50 top: 'It's in His Kiss', 'Anyone Who Had a Heart' and well out, more real r&b, 'Nitty Gritty', 'No Particular Place to Go', the Tams' 'What Kind of Fool Do You Think I Am?' and Sam Cooke's 'Good News'. Out of even the 100 most popular discs are such neglected events in pop history as Jerry Butler & Betty Everett's 'Let It Be Me', Nancy Wilson's '(You Don't Know) How Glad I Am', r&b great Bobby Bland's 'Ain't Nothing You Can Do', and the Ronettes' 'Baby I Love You' and 'Walking in the Rain'—disregarded as much as anything for lack of Brit credentials and mop of fluffy hair.

1965 brought even fewer rewards, for 'I Can't Help Myself', the only big black recording, 'A Lover's Concerto', 'Stop in the Name of Love' and 'I Hear a Symphony' all edging the twenty top discs—two thoroughly infused with Music Hall and recorded as if all sense of spontaneity had been banned. Scattered on the fringes of the fifty are the real thing: 'I Got You' a.k.a. 'I Feel Good', 'Rescue Me', 'Yes I'm Ready', Motown's cookin' 'Back in My Arms Again' and 'It's the Same Old Song', Shirley Ellis's 'The Name Game', 'Hold What You've Got' (Joe Tex) and the rhythmically infectious 'Shake' (Sam Cooke). Losers: 'Papa's Got a Brand New Bag', 'In the Midnight Hour', 'Mustang Sally', 'Tracks of My Tears'—maybe Smokey Robinson's all-time greatest, 'Nowhere to Run'. Next year: Otis Redding's 'Try a Little Tenderness', Carla Thomas's 'B-A-B-Y' and Ike & Tina Turner's rivetting performance of 'River Deep Mountain High' virtually banned from the airwaves.

It was not until mid-'67 that authentic 'Soul' (r&b was something British now) had won back enough ground through James Brown and the artists at the Atlantic/Stax studios—Aretha Franklin, Otis Redding, Wilson Pickett, Sam & Dave, Booker T & the MGs— to launch a multi-pronged offensive against a new English front: The Who, Cream, the Spencer Davis and Jeff Beck Groups, and Jimi Hendrix rebounding irresistibly back to the USA. Justice delayed was justice denied, and to what purpose? Paradoxically, responsible for their sidelining, the Beatles Machine was lent some street cred: the universally hummable Lennon-McCartney tunes adapted to Soul, injecting the vital juices into rock that the Beatles hadn't. With Hendrix's return and Otis Redding's surge—both in the Monterey Pop Festival, June '67—the wheel was turning full circle. Amid the reclaiming of territory came Soul takes on 'Yesterday' by Ray Charles, 'Day Tripper' and 'Satisfaction' by Redding, 'Revolution' and 'Here Comes the Sun' by Nina Simone, as well as unlikely 'Hey Jude' (Wilson Pickett) and 'Eleanor Rigby' (Aretha Franklin). Taking the process to assimilation, and pointing up an exquisite irony, Black activist Simone embraced Beatle soundalikes the Bee Gees' catchy melodies 'To Love Somebody'/ 'I Can't See Nobody' and crushed the ponderous Englishness out of them.

Of the Invaders today mostly their conventional cores remain, little or nothing of rock'n'roll: Paul McCartney, now looking as well as sounding like his father and taken to writing conventional symphonies; Eric Clapton and Van Morrison unplugged and unguardedly sickly-sentimental; Rod Stewart smarming show tunes; Joe Cocker and The Who—raucous by nature, but somehow lacking the original spirit... and the Rolling Stones. The Stones have prolonged their commercial value by switching to... whatever, as expediency warranted. Variations on the 'Jumpin' Jack Flash'/ 'Street Fighting Man'/'Honky Tonk Women'/'Brown Sugar'/ 'Start Me Up' riffing could only last them so many years, thirteen to be exact.

If the legacy of the Beatles—that is, Lennon & McCartney—is compared to that of the other world famous pair of clever English song-crafters, Gilbert & Sullivan—and it is difficult not t—then this mid-Sixties phenomenon can be seen as a momentary throw- back to English tradition (except authentic blues-based The Who, Cream, etc) which grew into a hydra-headed roadshow saturating the world for three years... the Beatles, Gerry & the Pacemakers, Dave Clark Five, Manfred Mann, Herman's Hermits, Freddie & the Dreamers, Peter & Gordon all inescapable via radio, television, film. Trans-Atlantic businessmen creamed it in an unprecedented bonanza while it lasted. But just as Monty Python might lampoon "The punishment fit the crime", Peter Sellers poked pointed fun at 'She Loves You' and 'A Hard Day's Night'. Just as school children perform Gilbert & Sullivan today to learn their A-B-Cs of music, so might they Lennon & McCartney a hundred years on.

The Fabs would create such a body of infantile songs that they were memorialised (again) in *The Simpsons*, as Bart explains to Milhous who they were: "The Beatles... They wrote the songs on Maggie's baby records."

6. SURFIN' US/K

In 1965 the world was looking scary—and not only because the most inane warblings of the British Invasion looked like they were here to stay. Twenty years after the end of WWII it turned out that old tensions and seething enmities between cultures had only been swapped for new ones. The USSR, China, and satellites Eastern Europe, Cuba, North Korea and North Vietnam lined up against The West. In January, Britain's Winston Churchill, savior of western democracy and hawk of the Cold War, died. Khruschev of the USSR had been deposed for not bringing the West to heel though his USA opposite number John F Kennedy was dead a year. In little more than twelve months the three potent figures of the post-War world were gone.

In February and March two events denied all the brief Kennedy Era stood for. Malcolm X, Black Muslim and leader in the civil rights movement, was murdered, spurring race riots in the Watts district of LA. And President Lyndon B Johnson ("Hey, hey, LBJ, how many kids did you kill today?") committed the first combat troops to Vietnam, an undeclared war plaguing the American psyche long past its ten-year duration.

The Beach Boys, victims of their idealism, were about to be trapped in a time warp, objects to be vivisected by the fashion police. For a year pop commentators had questioned the reason for being of these stubborn squares who seemed naïvely unaware of all Beatledom had to offer. The Byrds, switching to folk rock and Dylan, still made the effort to look and sound like Beatles; everyone knew they were "America's answer" to them. It was "in" and "far out" to conform to the new 'Counterculture'.

Dennis had gone some way toward beatlesque, hair-wise, in summer '64; a year later the others were looking fluffier too, if not longer, yet. Mike grew a neatly trimmed beard to distract from his thinning hair, lending a 'Peter, Paul & Mary' professorial look to the frontman of a group already up against it with ever younger record-buyers. Touring the UK the eldest Beach Boy—months younger than Ringo Starr and John Lennon—went the whole hog for the Oxford don look, posing for group publicity stills dressed eccentrically in British tweed, country gentleman's cap and holding a pipe. Brian (replaced by the lean and handsome, if bland, Bruce Johnston on tour) and Carl were unfashionably chubby— and still clean-shaven unlike the bulky turned-on musos of San Francisco psychedelia just emerging, who knew where it was at and let it all hang out: Jerry Garcia of the Grateful Dead, Bob Hite of Canned Heat.... It was all a clear snub to populism: the Beach Boys would go their own way, in their own time.

THE MOST TAXING WORK FALLING TO BRIAN OVER their three-year career so far, he not surprisingly had his first nervous breakdown, on 23rd December 1964—the day the group was broadcast spreading merry yuletide greetings on tv. It was aboard the plane to start yet another tour, barely into the air from LA International Airport *en route* to Houston. He would have two more mental crises in the next seventeen months, miraculously as he created his most admired work. The legend goes, Brian somehow got through the performance that first night and session man Glen Campbell, the Beach Boy/Phil Spector associate and later expert interpreter of Jimmy Webb's music, was called in by Carl and Mike to fill in on the next tour stop, Dallas. Brian returned to the comforting arms of mother Audree—not new bride Marilyn, whom in his paranoia he suspected of having an affair with Mike.

Three months later Bruce Johnston was appointed Brian's permanent touring replacement, though Brian would reappear for tv and album sleeves—Bruce receiving no media recognition as a full-fledged Beach Boy for another three years so not to break his contract with Columbia. Only in 1970 would he take a creative role as singer-composer (later Grammy winner, 'I Write the Songs'). He seems to have been seen as something of a 'temp' and when his solo inclinations became obvious the others tried to replace him with Carl's brother-in-law, Billy Hinsche of Dino, Desi & Billy. But at 20 Bruce was a worn-in veteran of many groups and moreover sang a Brian-sounding falsetto for concerts—but no leads.

The Gilbert Youth Research Survey over Xmas '64-New Year '65 told that "rock and roll", a catchall term if ever there was, had overtaken folk as America's favorite music and 26% of youths favored the Beatles over any other vocal group, "the Beach Boys, the Four Seasons, the Supremes and the Dave Clark Five distant trailers." Brian Wilson received the BMI prize for composing seven Billboard top ten hits that tumultuous year—'Drag City', 'Fun Fun Fun', 'Dead Man's Curve', 'I Get Around', 'Little Honda', 'When I Grow Up', 'Dance Dance Dance'—but still came well behind Lennon-McCartney. How long could he fight the uphill battle against mania?

On the group's return from the Southwest tour, Brian broke the news that he would stay home to concentrate on studio work and do justice to their business interests so they might continue to rival the Beatles. He was already laying down tracks for *Beach Boys Today*, one of their most admired albums, presaging *Pet Sounds* in its alternately rocking/melancholy spirit. There was also the periodic deterioration of his one good ear, forced to take the burden of ever-loudening amplification systems at concerts. They had come this far and conquered worlds together. Mike wailed there was no reason to go on; Al broke out in stomach cramps, ministered to by Audree; Dennis threatened outsiders in the room with imminent injury by jumbo ashtray if they didn't leave this intense family scene. Baby Carl, just turned 18, calmed them; henceforth he would lead the touring band as spokesman-musical director.

But it was the start of ongoing dissension. No sooner were they rid of Murry as the thorn in their side than they contrived to create internal tensions. The album currently recording included the beautifully plaintive 'Please Let Me Wonder', which lyric writer Mike Love deemed "not a real Beach Boy song." As if to spite his claim it registered as an A-side in many markets including overhyped Los Angeles. But a point was made.

Brian asserted his independence for the future of the band and the survival of his mental health. A sensitive introvert who liked performing for the most part but not mixing with strangers, being forced into a role might have provoked untold damage—may have already. The new group democracy via a clumsy voting system was unlikely to lessen the stress. And there was his growing drug habit.

All of this was aggravated by his father's festering frustration and the group piggy-backing on Brian's huge talent—His brothers would emerge as self-sustaining creative talents but not for another three years. Marilyn, Brian's 16-year-old bride, could hardly be expected to understand let alone cope with the situation her husband was in. She would show a maturity beyond her years and it must be a tribute to her that the marriage lasted fourteen years. But it was Brian who had to deal with the users, hangers-on and wannabes that show business is notorious for.

THE SUPREMES, HOISTED TODAY AS PERVASIVE SIX-ties icons, were never in the race. Not only did they not compose, nor produce, nor play—their race was to superstardom, period. It is thanks to writer-producers Holland-Dozier-Holland and the Funk Bros as up-front backing musicians that any tracks endure as r&b.

Trying to cover all the bases, casting an image masterminded by Berry Gordy to not just cross the race line but launch his own Brownish Invasion on Whitey, their second album, *A Bit of Liverpool*, was obviously a deliberate piggyback on you-know-who, and they followed with albums dedicated to Country & Western, Sam Cooke, even Broadway's Rodgers & Hart. If artistic integrity is a total stranger to most performance artists, Diana Ross & the Supremes treated it as a sworn enemy. Neither did they meet the Motor City's gritty expectations, and after 1965 not one of their 45s performed as well locally as nationally. Despite thirteen nationwide chart-toppers they didn't register either as Uncle Sam icons overseas.

Almost in the same category were the Four Seasons, swinging to the cabaret and nightclub circuit, not rock venues, and all-round showbiz on long-players—a parody of folk/country, then lumping Burt Bacharach and Bob Dylan songs together. Gold was limited to two or three compilations. Though writing many songs and talented performers they were not a self-contained band and no way could they be called, by the most hopeful fan, a rock band—unless the

Tremeloes, Manfred Mann and Hollies could by some twist of the definition. And they were already on the slope. Trans-Atlantic signature tune 'Rag Doll' had passed, their three other undisputed chart-toppers at the very beginning, before 'Surfin' USA'.

Elvis showed some quality in 1965—but through ballads recorded years earlier, 'Crying in the Chapel', a rare US million-seller for him, and 'Puppet On a String'. This while to the end of the year seven Beatles singles on Capitol were certified. Elvis's Memphis good-ol'-buddy Roy Orbison had plateaued with 'Oh Pretty Woman' and dipped despite classics 'Too Soon to Know' and 'Communication Breakdown', though a major star overseas.

The Ronettes threatened to survive Beatlemania, but failed with some of the best recordings anywhere: 'Baby I Love You', 'Do I Love You?', 'The Best Part of Breaking Up'; only 'Walking in the Rain' clipped the edge of the Cash Box 20 late in '64. The last original girl group would record Jeff Barry's 'I Can Hear Music', better known as a classic Beach Boys remake. Spector, guiding the Righteous Bros into remakes of 'Unchained Melody' and 'Ebb Tide', would occupy himself with Tina Turner's 'River Deep, Mountain High', his last roaring, sumptuous masterpiece: a big UK hit but ignored in the US (#88) by radio programmers out for revenge at his arrogant independence and success. Spector from his side saw most of America as a cultural wasteland. Like Brian Wilson he had tread on too many toes with power to kick back harder for not playing their game. After a stuttering restart of the Spector career in 'Black Pearl' ('69) he would lend himself as the servant of the former Beatles: George Harrison's *All Things Must Pass* and *Concert for Bangla Desh* plus John Lennon's *Imagine* and two more for Lennon & the Plastic Ono Band.

Obtaining specifics on the Beach Boys' sales in their peak years has proved as elusive to this writer as a set of genuine accounts from Wall Street. Capitol's curious laxity in submitting figures for independent audit led in the seventies to ludicrous entries in rock encyclopedias: "Most of their singles sold in the hundreds of thousands but it wasn't till 'Good Vibrations' that they had their first million-seller." According to Chapple & Garofalo in low selling

1946-1952 there were 162 million sellers: almost one every two weeks. By 1969 there were seventy *certified* a year. This equated roughly to the number of singles annually that reached no.8 or higher in the Cash Box charts. So the Sixties cliché that a top ten record was a million seller wasn't far wrong.

On conquest of North America and Japan—the bulk of 'the known world' of the music industry—the Beach Boys had the now important British Isles in front of them. Theirs was a popularity that crept up on the world unlike Beatle razzmatazz. To millions it would be as if their music was infused through pores, not the power-injected media OD for Beatles, Herman's Hermits, Monkees. In fact, journalistic articles from 1965 remark on the group's lack of PR representation and having to track down Brian or Murry direct for interviews or information. Yet by the end of the 1980s, with one no.1 hit to show for the past twenty years, they were identified with America, so ingrained as an integral image of The West and freedom—as free spirits—that when the Berlin Wall came down it was said that East Berliners strode triumphantly across the crumbled political barrier singing Beach Boy songs.

FEBRUARY 15TH 1965 BROUGHT A REALISATION THAT irreplaceable figures had died in the past two months: Sam Cooke, murdered; Alan Freed of a failing spirit; now Nat King Cole of lung cancer. For the Beach Boys the year opened with their first ever shows in Canada—good for a dozen big hits so far, their second expedition into the foreign territory of the British Commonwealth. First came a date at Vancouver, the French city of Montreal, Ottawa and Toronto. Brian, hungry for new experiences, plays all but the last, replaced by Glen Campbell. They will take in the same round of cities again in September, this time with Bruce Johnston and supported by new stars Sonny & Cher.

On vinyl, from the completed *Beach Boys Today*, a new 45 is lifted that fatal February day. On top of a wall of sound but in a flourish of driving, modernized rock, is their rebirth of 'Do You Wanna Dance?' both spirited and lush—so maybe too American. Dennis's sole solo hit, it's the top debut in the Nashville top 40;

streaks fifteen places into the St Louis ten to quench a nine-month drought there (#6); L C Cooke, brother of Sam, rushes out an alternative version that hits the St Louis r&b chart. In Chicagoland, Dallas, Washington DC, New England, Twin Cities, the Rockies, Tulsa, Cincinnati it is top five with stray California districts—sales are taken by its B on the West Coast; top ten Toronto, Montreal, Vancouver. Taking off the gloss are slightly below par receptions in Detroit, Pittsburgh, Miami and New York, best at WINS, #12-13, its level in the major hit parades. Elevated to no.5 in Gilbert's nationwide youth survey for April 17th, mainstream it is no threat to Herman's Hermits and Freddie & the Dreamers with their red carpet treatment from the media and squatting pampered in the penthouse. The current WABC-New York sales survey lists Brit acts taking 11 of the top 16 tunes.

In the UK it wasn't released ('All Summer Long' was—a joke in terms of the hard tack Brits expected from groups at the time), maybe because EMI feared it could take long-term sales from its Cliff Richard & the Shadows' 45. Following as it did their recent European tour, 'Do You Wanna Dance?' should have reinstated them on the Continent, which had given the previous two singles the silent treatment. While it was bought in loyal Scandinavia and played in Italy, it was invisible in Germany, France, Holland and now Australia too, preoccupied with all things Fab.

'Please Let Me Wonder' was the chosen 'A' in San Jose, where it went to no.1; San Diego, Ohio, Idaho, upstate New York top ten; Los Angeles, Seattle, Vancouver, Denver and San Antonio the 20. It drove to no.9 on the Gilbert nationwide poll on April 10th but stalled halfway up the two big charts, to be a favorite on compilation albums and retrospective videos.

April 21st they played both sides on *Shindig*, 'Help Me Rhonda' just released and pocket jams of 'Fun Fun Fun' and 'Long Tall Texan', demolishing English guests Wayne Fontana & the Mindbenders and Cilla Black, producer Jack Good still plugging his countrymen and women though as many would come unstuck as stick; no.1 Italian songstress Rita Pavone also ran. They met up too on set with the Shangri-Las and the Ikettes—from that first bill over three years before.

Both hits were—happily—out of sync with prevailing (lack of) taste, which saw what was already a year-long lapse accelerate into a headlong dive. The public was forcefed the silliest pop ditties yet, Top 40 stations now programmed via remote control by bosses in other cities, even star DJs straightjacketed from injecting local content or personal favorites. Songs masticated into the new chew for a few weeks, losing what bland flavor they had. Previously this trend was signalled by the Beatles' superior 'And I Love Her' and 'If I Fell', lapped up by sentimental moviegoers. The Dave Clark Five succumbed to the Beatles' lead, and made them utterly sickening: 'Because', 'Everybody Knows'—two glutinous-syrupy ballads vying with Brian Poole & the Tremeloes' 'Someone, Someone' for most nauseating weepie of the era.

The Beach Boys sustained their fun-loving, exuberant image, seen in a stocktake-of-things-that-matter Carl wrote for *Tiger Beat*:

Brian: a Cadillac Eldorado and Mustang
Dennis: a Ferrari and Cobra
Mike, the real collector: a Pontiac MG, Jaguar and Classic MG
Carl: an Aston Martin (James Bond style), Triumph 500 motorbike
Al, ever sensible: a lone T-Bird, as featured in 'Fun Fun Fun'

By now the three Wilson brothers had bought their own homes on the outskirts of Hollywood. Mike and Al stayed close to home at Manhattan Beach. A roll call of Dennis's pets told much of the elemental Beach Boy: two (wild, freedom-loving) horses, an otter (at home in water), a parakeet named after mother Audree, a power-dog German Shepherd and ever-present underdog for Dennis to look after—a lost puppy run over outside his house, with a broken leg needing healing. Always a mass of contradictions, supposedly least talented when the group started, he was turning himself into a multi-instrumentalist. The most Beach Boy—runner-up in a Hawaiian surfing tourney, an accomplished danger-skier on hair-raising Rocky

Mountain slopes—he was also the most un-Beach Boy, developing a husky, cracked blues voice.

It was Dennis in full flight who pulled as much mob appeal as a Beatle. Fans would breach the carefully mounted barricades at concerts, and all of the boys had their clothes torn and were taught tactics to escape girls' clutches—rolling out of the tackle grid-iron style. Dennis, though, sometimes surrounded despite the best game strategies, had several times been literally k.o.'ed by love. In Louisville, Kentucky, coincidentally the home of Muhammed Ali, he required three stitches to his head. When audience reaction was deemed out of hand local police forces used their ultimate power of censorship, cutting the feed to amplifiers or yanking down the stage curtain mid-performance, much to the group's disgust. In l.p. liner notes Mike remarked on the Cincinnati fans as champion "cop-dodgers" and "Then there's the helpless feeling of seeing a girl, who maybe spent her last dollar to see us, crying or something, 'cause the cops wouldn't let her stay and get a Beach Boys autograph." Unlike the Beatles, the group never had sealed, womb-like limos to duck into to separate them from their public, and for less hysterical crowds would often stay behind for hours to sign autographs and chat.

U NLIKE THEIR HERMETICALLY PROTECTED RIVALS the Beach Boys no doubt felt themselves in the full swim of the Swinging Sixties. Carl named his favorite acts as the Beatles, Four Seasons, Supremes, Manfred Mann and the Animals — in preference over the Rolling Stones. The Stones, he said, showing considerable prescience, would be around as long as they made hits. Brian, in a 1996 interview, said that he and Carl "liked John [Lennon] a lot"—and that he wrote 'Girl Don't Tell Me' as "a kind of tribute to John." Said at one time to have been intended for the Beatles to record, it was one of Brian's favorite songs, written on vacation in Hawaii without a piano or guitar: "And it's the only song I wrote that way." He had penned 'Kiss Me Baby' months before in a Copenhagen hotel room, also without much in the way of composing aids.

Certain other revelations Brian has made about his lifestyle at this time have shed light on his creative processes: Put simply, take marijuana and sit down at the piano. For *The Beach Boys Today!* he was experimenting: "The whole second side had been written and arranged while I was high. Compared to previous Beach Boys albums the music was slower, more plaintive, and emotional. The chord patterns were more complex, the production denser, richer in sound, and my thinking in regard to making records was different. Able to break down songs to precise little increments, I began to deal with each instrument individually, stacking sounds one at a time" (BrianWilson.com).

Three months later in April he took a quantum leap into the drug world with his first experience of LSD. He at first justified this by the fact that it led instantly to the composing of 'California Girls'. Later, he noticed that it was the beginning of auditory hallucinations— voices talking to him, often threatening ones—and an everworsening fragility of mind. It was about this time too he wrote and recorded its flipside 'Let Him Run Wild' in *hommage* to Burt Bacharach's renowned chord progressions—and that's as far as any resemblance goes.

Brian was beginning to show an inevitable social isolation from the others, manifesting in their latest album's "slow side". In the face of the sickly dirges lately foisted on radio listeners by English groups, the emotionally direct 'Please Let Me Wonder' and particularly 'She Knows Me Too Well' and 'Kiss Me Baby' made fewer station listings and didn't attract the overwhelming commercial success of previous Bs. On stage it was difficult to reproduce their advanced level of production as recorded. The consensus, led by Mike, was that they slowed the show down too much when added to the obligatory 'Surfer Girl' and 'In My Room', later solved by a ballad medley including also 'Warmth of the Sun', 'Don't Worry Baby' and 'Please Let Me Wonder'. Their fast-paced show stayed intact, outdoing in rock'n'roll content the Beatles' hits package.

Capitol, in light of more complex, introspective music emerging on *Beach Boys Today*, disrespected what were being recognized as classic flipsides by cajoling Brian to restrict himself to what they saw as "good time" music. Others could hear the routine upbeat songs were weakest: 'Good to My Baby', 'Don't Hurt My Little Sister'. It is safe to say Capitol/EMI did not warn the Beatles about their music for the upcoming *Help!* and *Rubber Soul,* knowing it would be broadly acceptable—the more so with Parlophone/EMI rep George Martin on the spot.

Dennis, contributing a second, sinuous lead vocal—thoughtful, neglected 'In the Back of My Mind', in concerts exuding the Beach Boy spirit, in lifestyle personifying it, continued to be featured in a token way like Ringo. Lip-synching 'Do You Wanna Dance?' on a well-designed *Shindig* set, accompanying with two-fisted drumming on snare, he sent the teenage girls in the studio audience into wild, rapturous screams for him. Like the Beatle drummer, Dennis was likable and popular; unlike Ringo, girls wanted to do more than mother him.

Since his firing as manager a year before Murry Wilson had found new impetus with the Sunrays. And there was still some fatherly/financial satisfaction in promoting his boys' career—and his half share of Brian's song publishing interests—by personally ensuring music-department stores cross-country and overseas, and radio stations, were well stocked in back catalogue, bringing steadily mounting sales and airplays and payoff in royalties. The fatherly concern, however dysfunctionally it sometimes presented itself, would ease the group's reliance on megahits for a time latter decade, though given their profligate spending on musical projects later, contributed to a false sense of financial security.

B UT NOW HERMAN AND HIS HERMITS PUSHED THEIR double-sugar sweeties for the littlies—like Australia's kids' group the Wiggles, far from a rock'n'roll high: 'Can't You Hear My Heartbeat?', 'Mrs Brown', *old* Music Hall standard 'I'm Henry VIII I Am' at the rate of one fix a month through mid-'65 in a sustained market drive (mounting 45 weeks top twenty that year to the Supremes' 35 and Beatles' 34), all delivered in the follow-the-bouncing-ball audience singalong style that had gone out over fifty years before when Ragtime came in. The English had stuck quietly all these years to their Lambeth Walk, and millions of Americans appreciated the diversion from rock'n'roll. All six of these 'new' hits were Gold, commercially. The Hermits had divined the heart of the Beatle formula.

Alongside Freddie and his Dreamers' 'I'm Telling You Now' and 'You Were Made for Me'—equally derisory to rock'n'roll— and Searchers remake of 'Love Potion No.9' made pointless by extracting the Coasters' humor, American acts allied themselves: 'comedy' act the Detergents mocking the Shangri-Las, 'Leader of the Laundromat'; the Kingsmen's 'Jolly Green Giant'; Playboys' Music Hall 'Save Your Heart for Me'. The Four Seasons turned the clock back too, with the Al Jolson-style 'Bye Bye Baby'.

Oddities proliferated, proving this a phoney era of revived rock. Bland 'easy' listening continued to flourish through Petula Clark, Peter & Gordon, Chad & Jeremy, the Bachelors, Jack Jones, Trini Lopez, Johnny Rivers, Ronnie Dove, the Seekers. Three top-selling discs of ultra-retro 'Red Roses for a Blue Lady' vied for airtime. Early Fifties darling Patti Page—seven years in oblivion—came back with movie theme *Hush Hush Sweet Charlotte*. There was Gene Pitney-clichéd pining on 'Down in the Boondocks' by Billy Joe Royal; novelty-country songs 'The Birds and the Bees' and 'King of the Road', made a little ridiculous by answer song 'Queen of the House'. Of all the new *kitsch*, Wayne Fontana & the Mindbenders' 'Game of Love' and Sam the Sham & the Pharaohs' 'Wooly Bully' were probably best, at least showing spirit.

Classic black acts James Brown, Marvin Gaye, Stevie Wonder and others continued under-appreciated. Ray Charles would go through the first two years of Beatletime without a top twenty entry while the Beatles benefited from him. Their Latin-rhythmed 'I Feel Fine' was a poor refrain of Charles's 'What'd I Say?' Still, they were hailed for innovation: Feedback accidentally coming from George Harrison's speaker was reversed on tape by George Martin for the unmusical sound that forms the introduction. 'Eight Days a Week' sounded a lot like a shuffle-beat take on 'A Hard Day's Night'—probably why it was not issued as a 45 in Britain, where strapped punters were fussy about value for money. America was head over heels in love and couldn't help itself.

In the name of the Swinging Sixties sterile song craft was given a hefty push by Burt Bacharach's romances, many composers and producers settling for less than his quality or Dionne Warwick's. A Latin strand in train at least from summer '64 with 'The Girl from Ipanema' came to full flourish in Beatle ballads. The group's working-class Liverpool shackles had melted in the warm glow of America's media spotlight and they continued their upwardly mobile drive more confident and more pretentiously glamorous with Elizabethan 'Yesterday' and 'Michelle'—French wooing giving it that veneer of sophistication.

The cheap romanticism was a rich vein dug to the depths through the winter and spring of '65 via torch song 'Goin' Out of My Head', Petula Clark's 'Downtown' and 'I Know a Place', Shirley Bassey's sex-charged rendering of the *Goldfinger* theme. It would restart in Latin vein a summer later with the Sandpipers' 'Guantanamera'; then a sequence of chart-toppers processed by the Association, who lived up to their name by singing and playing as a committee might: 'Along Comes Mary', 'Cherish', 'Windy', 'Never My Love'.

Uncomfortable in this dire company are lightning flashes: the Kinks' 'All Day and All of the Night' and 'Tired Of Waiting For You', Beatle B-side 'She's A Woman', the Zombies' 'Tell Her No', Del Shannon's 'Keep Searchin'', Marvin Gaye & Kim Weston's 'How Sweet It Is', the Ad Libs' 'Boy From New York City', Martha & the Vandellas' 'Nowhere to Run'—none reaching the highest three nationally. And rare, deserving number ones: 'You've Lost That Lovin' Feelin'', with claims to being best rock recording of all—out on its own as the most played song in US history, eight million spins and counting—the Beatles' 'Ticket to Ride' and the Temptations' 'My Girl'.

The emergence of Roger Miller, the first C&W artist since the Fifties to consistently cross over to pop success, enabled a strong country undertow to develop underlying pop, through Nancy Sinatra & Lee Hazelwood, Sandy Posey and occasional welcome returns to the pop charts by Brenda Lee ('Coming on Strong'). Miller thrived in the face of Beatlemania with Grammy winner 'Dang Me', 'Chug-A-Lug', his theme song 'King of the Road' and 'Engine, Engine #9'. His upbeat strumming recalled Jimmie Rodgers, who spanned country and folk from a version of 'Wreck of the John B' to Rod McKuen's personal protest 'The World I Used to Know'. He had gently satirised the British phenomenon with 'An English Country Garden', ironically a big hit there.

While Roger Miller ruled genuine Country & Western, 'C&W' stars popped out from unlikely places. Again the Beatles were caught *following* trends in yet another move away from rock'n'roll for covering-all-the-bases mass marketing. There was Ringo on 'Honey Don't' and 'Act Naturally', and other Beatles went country in all but name on 'I'll Cry Instead' (John), 'I'm a Loser' and 'I Don't Want to Spoil the Party' (John/Paul), 'I'm Happy Just to Dance With You' and 'Everybody's Trying to Be My Baby' (both George).

Not only Miller but Dean Martin had scored the month of Jim Reeves' death: 'Everybody Loves Somebody', months before the Beatles came out with their C&W, his first big hit in six years—a miracle comeback heralding the return of Rat Pack buddy Frank Sinatra. Martin's image featured his brand of wry humor via Lee Hazelwood's 'Houston' and 'Little Ole Wine Drinker, Me' casting him as a lounge lizard on the skids. The Rat Pack was still scoring too in a movie series including *Ocean's Eleven*. And the Beatles had fully integrated themselves into the power stuctures of the music business.

Rat Pack power was not lost on Frank's daughter Nancy, a star through 1966-67 and the *You Only Live Twice* James Bond theme. Teamed with gravel-voiced record producer Lee Hazelwood on 'Jackson' and 'Some Velvet Morning', they were kinky with references to silver spurs she insisted he take off before sampling her 'Summer Wine'. Then she sank in pop's hierarchy to be Elvis Presley's latest squeeze in *Speedway*.

It was anything goes in Pop, welcoming such atrocities as media favorite Mrs (Elva) Miller's geriatric warbling. Eccentric Tiny Tim's 'Tip-Toe Through the Tulips', was a true novelty with the off-the-wall humor to send himself up. Damaging to Rock because taken seriously came megasellers the New Vaudeville Band's 'Winchester

Cathedral' and Esther & Abi Ofarim's 'Cinderella-Rockafella': British-based acts doing nonsense songs in 1920s style. The disease progressed virulently there into the late Sixties, throwing up passing fancies by the Scaffold, featuring Paul McCartney's brother—'Thank U Very Much', and 'Lily the Pink' selling almost a million UK—and Leapy Lee's 'Little Arrows', three million worldwide.

America's answer to Israeli comic European Song Contestants Esther & Abi, were Caesar & Cleo—a flop. The names didn't stick but the corniness did. Sonny & Cher, who approximated Esther's exotic Mediterranean look and Cleopatra-thick black eye-liner, camped up cute pop, becoming household names across all age groups and with the egos to pretend their music was significant. 'I Got You Babe', with Phil Spector's fingerprints all over it (they were session-backup for the Ronettes and Sonny was his sorcerer's apprentice), and less memorable follow-ups popularized Duet Melodrama into a genre all its own, joining Peter & Gordon.

The new duo carved their own niche via a wardrobe of stylised Native American buckskins and other 'statement-making' attire. If Dylan could make it as a singer then Sonny Bono could, and he and his influential friends in the record biz concocted a smokescreen strategy combining Cher's exoticism (part Cherokee), a folk-rock out-of-tune delivery, and Sonny's mind-numbing pretend-meaningful lyrics covered up by fixit tunesmiths and cluttered instrumentation—all made irrelevant by outlandish fashions and with-it patter that distracted attention from their songs, wisely in most cases. Cher, with or without Sonny, is (with or without body reshaping and collagen 'enhancements') such an attractive figure that her worst showbiz excesses over the course of 42 years have only enhanced her notoriety. What Mae West did with her body Cher did with her voice—identified herself as a blowsy sex machine. Her fans inflated into some of her biggest hits such drivel as quasi-ethnic 'Sing C'est la Vie' and 'Baby Don't Go'; and 'Bang Bang' ("My baby shot me down") about a sociopathic soulmate. 'The Beat Goes On', the duo's signature tune of 1967, has perhaps the worst lyric of any Sixties song purporting to be serious, never mind social commentary: "Men just keep on marchin' off to war" to get the profound bit of social change in, then to rhyme with it, "Electrically they keep a baseball score!"

The first week or so of July '65, sparking their gargantuan success, the duo supported "The Beach Boys' Summer Spectacular" around California with the Byrds, the Kinks on their first US trip, Righteous Bros, Sam the Sham & the Pharaohs, Sir Douglas Quintet and Dino, Desi & Billy. It was a lineup outgunning Dick Clark's famous Caravan of Stars, currently Peter & Gordon and a flotilla of Americans past their peak: the Drifters, Jackie De Shannon, Crystals, Brian Hyland—and hopeful Clark protégés. Billy Hinsche, guitarist/vocalist with Dean Martin's and Desi Arnaz-Lucille Ball's sons, eased into the Beach Boys camp: Carl married Billy's sister within months; and years later, Dino's sister.

Sonny & Cher found it a perfect springboard, catapulting their hit to the top. According to Murrells they grossed $3 million from all sources in 1965, or rather its last five months, going from session nobodies to superstars. Their first album, *Look At Us*, sold as much in its first two weeks as many top sellers did over a year.

L EADING ITS BEATLE NAMESAKE BY MONTHS, 'HELP Me Rhonda' was on first hearing a creepily lacklustre James Last soundalike on *Beach Boys Today*. But the redone track on 45 throbbed with heavy bass guitar momentum and exciting drum-tambourine play. The high-energy, repetitive chorus "Help me Rhonda, help help me Rhonda" sounded for all the world like an East African tribal chant: highly affecting on an intestinal level. As usual their ease of presentation made it deceptively simple and underrated. Their first 45 since the previous summer not to meet resistance, it was pushed live on the mass-appeal *Ed Sullivan Show* of Sunday, May 16th, a class lineup of all-time ballet greats Rudolf Nureyev and Margot Fonteyn, songstress of the year Petula Clark, comic Alan King. Rising top in the nation seven weeks after their previous hit peaked, it cut 'Ticket to Ride''s canter at top to one week, to be toppled after two by the Supremes' 'Back in My Arms Again'.

'Rhonda', propelled by a strong Al lead, was outstanding in Montreal (2nd for '65 to 'Satisfaction'), Washington DC-Baltimore,

Philadelphia, New England, Cincinnati, Cleveland, Pittsburgh, Richmond, Louisville, St Louis, Dallas, Miami, Salt Lake City, San Diego, Twin Cities—and their third Canadian no.1 in ten months; a solid #2 in New York, Chicago, Los Angeles, Toronto.

Top of Billboard's Hot 100, 29th May '65: Note favorites who wouldn't make it any higher, Elvis, Roger Miller, Tom Jones.

1. Help Me Rhonda — the Beach Boys (1st week)
2. Ticket to Ride — the Beatles
3. Crying in the Chapel — Elvis Presley
4. Wooly Bully — Sam the Sham & the Pharaohs
5. Back in My Arms Again — the Supremes
6. Mrs Brown… a Lovely Daughter — Herman's Hermits
7. Engine, Engine #9 — Roger Miller
8. I'll Never Find Another You — the Seekers
9. Silhouettes — Herman's Hermits
10. It's Not Unusual — Tom Jones

Billboard assessed ten songs ahead of it in the year's bestsellers but only 'I Can't Help Myself', 'Satisfaction', 'You've Lost That Lovin' Feelin'' (5th), 'Help!' (7th) and 'My Girl' (10th) had a right to be there. 'Wooly Bully' was top. As the 45 topped out, for the second time in six months they had top rock album, headed by Julie Andrews soundtracks *Mary Poppins* and *Sound of Music* on Cash Box's l.p. listing. Briefly overtaken by Herman's Hermits the week following, they stayed #4 overall for over a month and in that time were again top-selling rockers after the two soundtracks and Barbra Streisand.

The week before their no.1 they made the cover of *Time* magazine with the Supremes *et al* and the feature story on rock and roll. Each of the boys had a personal following and pitchmen weren't short on suggestions of how they could break the group into the status of a personality cult like the Beatles. Around this time one Beach Boy deemed a "cute little guy" by one promoter—so probably current lead singer Al—was pushed. His married status was kept secret, as customary for sex idols, to save putting off female fans. In the event, he didn't have what it took to be a Herman Hermit or Davy Jones—

trained professional actors oozing charm on demand. Paradoxically, if the power brokers had known how psychedelic Brian was by now he might have given Timothy Leary a run in drug cool.

Taken with parents' embrace of the so-far cuddly Beatles these were signs that a music industry increasingly focusing on youth was gaining commercial importance. The Beatles themselves constituted an industry significant in the USA and almost indispensable for the UK—97.5% of their (declared) income went straight into government coffers. In June, after eighteen months of sales Stateside, Capitol announced a total of 30 million discs sold by the Beatles there. Unique in matching Elvis in worldwide sales saturation, an August global tally was put at (a highly improbable) 150 million. Their sales rate would gradually slow—but with better-paying albums steadily increasing as a proportion.

Still on a derisory cut of their records' massive gross, touring is a necessity for the Beatles—and at venues as lucrative as possible. June 20th they kick off a European tour in Paris. Beach Boys summer dates might range from the county fairgrounds at Merced, California to the civic hall at Fargo, North Dakota to the college at Macon, Georgia— and any number of other towns and hamlets. Their more glamorous venues this time include The Lagoon at Salt Lake City (celebrated in song), the Hollywood Bowl, New York's Yankee Stadium—with Ray Charles, the Byrds—and Waikiki Beach with Dino, Desi & Billy and Detroit songstress Barbara Lewis.

It was near summer's end on August 22nd that Mike and Carl paid their visit backstage at the Beatle concert in Portland, Oregon. The meeting had reportedly been looked forward to by the Beatle camp; John and George were overheard expressing great curiosity about Brian in anticipation. Obviously disappointed by his no-show, on being told he stays home to compose and produce Paul hails it as a great idea. The Beach Boys have crossed paths this summer with support acts the Shangri-Las, Del Shannon, Skeeter Davis, Marty Robbins and Billy Joe Royal—most with current hits but all soon names from the past; and Brits the Kinks, Stones, Searchers, Zombies, and now the Beatles.

The new improved 'Help Me Rhonda''s album *Summer Days (and Summer Nights!)* made it to number two on 2nd September against *Beatles VI*—and *Help!* boosted by hit-movie exposure, the Fabs getting an uncatchable start on them again. Thirty years later Rolling Stone magazine would cite the Beach Boys l.p. in a non-ordered list of the thirty best albums of the Sixties. Authoritative UK paper The Guardian called on fifty experts in 1999 to name "The Top 100 *Alternative* Albums". The Beach Boys came first (*Today*) and second (*Summer Days*) for 1965.

Two tracks were well-executed answer songs to girl-group hits, 'The Girl from New York City' with Mike and the group giving a particularly tough account of themselves, and 'Then I Kissed Her' with Al wavering expertly between masculine strength and tenderness. The first was used as the theme of a contemporary documentary on an aspiring young female professional new to the big city. 'Salt Lake City' (Mike with inserts from Brian) was a tribute to their most enthusiastic fans, lording it over homeboy Osmonds, who as Mormons had local religio-political advantage. Introspective and generally more admired songs with Brian in the lead were 'Let Him Run Wild' and 'You're So Good to Me', uniquely in 4/4 time and with its distinctive riff sounding like it might have been inspired by the Stones' 'Satisfaction'; it was recorded in late May as the Stones 45 was circulated to radio stations, so barely possible.

It was almost a complete album of strong tracks, exhibiting the gamut of creative approaches the group had become known for but more confident than anything before. What would have been a hopeless conception in anyone else's hands, 'Amusement Parks USA', was made special by exuberant pacing and harmonies and evocative atmospheric effects. Carl performed his second lead vocal on 'Girl Don't Tell Me', and according to Brian's liner notes Dennis missed his chance by falling asleep in his camper van outside the studio—maybe on filler track 'I'm Bugged at My Old Man', applying best to his physicality: "Can't surf, can't drag, can't do a doggone thing!" Instead it was given a mock-operatic rendition by Brian in amateur recital style accompanying himself on piano—but going deep and melodramatic Elvis style: "But he took my phone right out of the wall!" Closing was *a capella* filler: "One more summer 'And Your Dream Comes True'" about a girl waiting for the age of consent.

Just as the Lettermen, with their six-years-late vocal of the *A Summer Place* theme, and others were jumping on another bandwagon created by the Beach Boys—'summer music', and inevitably bastardizing it into a species of Easy Listening, the originators delivered a *coup de grace* to define the genre and eliminate all contenders. In July 'California Girls' was taken from the new album, leapt from short of Billboard 20 to #9, then lodged high—4-3-3-5—holding out the now-revered (since *Ghost*) Spector production of 'Unchained Melody' and one of the Four Tops' greatest. A look at the top of Billboard's Hot 100 for 28th August '65 shows the thick logjam of enduring sounds that vied for a week at top spot mid-decade:

1. I Got You Babe — Sonny & Cher
2. Help! — the Beatles
3. California Girls — the Beach Boys
4. Unchained Melody — the Righteous Bros
5. It's the Same Old Song — the Four Tops
6. Like a Rolling Stone — Bob Dylan

In Record World it highjumped and was blocked at #3 for three weeks by the same two acts, though ten years later the trade paper would assess it as August's biggest seller after 'Help!'. To give credit to John Lennon, he admitted in his 1970 interviews with Rolling Stone magazine that 'Help!', with 'Strawberry Fields Forever', was one of his few genuine songs while writing for the Beatles, not just written to order (see Wikipedia.com).

'California Girls' has reaped true classic status. Brian coaxed out of Mike a performance—matching the swagger of any of the great jazz vocalists—he's never been able to match in concert. It is the group's most lucrative payer in royalties over the years— mainly from airplay (five million US) and cover versions. But from its time there are few traces of it topping Top 40s—Montreal (fifth most popular hit of the year), Dallas, Pittsburgh, Buffalo, Pensacola, secondary stations around LA, were some exceptions.

D IVISION OVER IT MIGHT STAND AS A METAPHOR for the Beach Boys enigma: impact blunted by the Beatles in America, underestimated in Britain by all but a few key DJs and a modest horde of keen buyers, missing the official chart entirely in Australia—while scoring number two in culturally comparable Canada and their biggest-ever hit in South Africa. After a decade of reflection the UK's New Musical Express would rate 'California Girls' 30th best single of "all time". Also in 1976 it was ranked second for its year (headed by 'Yesterday' and heading 'Satisfaction', 'Help!', 'Sounds of Silence') in a longitudinal survey of listener votes and regional sales by wide-ranging WNBC-New York. It was 1965's runner-up also in Philadelphia and the Delaware Valley (to 'Satisfaction') in a survey of long-term popularity conducted by station WFIL researchers.

Despite its shimmering magnificence, or maybe because of that, it was punished by the *fashionistas*—as being uncoolly slick in the new Era of Protest and designer fake-aged jeans when anything ragged, especially in music, was deemed "real".

Michael Gray, *Song & Dance Man; the Art of Bob Dylan* (1972): "[Control is] a thing that was missing altogether from rock when the British beat-group boom got going in 1964. One of the main things that marked out such groups... was that a loose, ramshackle sound was considered good enough and a rather erratic vocal technique came into vogue. Suddenly, singers weren't sure where they were throwing their voices and didn't care which notes, if any, they were going to catch... Little Richard was wild, but he was always in control. Presley always had this same sort of precision. So did the Everlys and Jackie Wilson."

But 'California Girls' has been retro-defined too as sickly white pop in an era black politicos now try to reclaim from the British. Thirty years later the song was abused by the Wayans brothers on tv's *In Living Color* as an example of ultra-white-preppy music and ten years later yet as a racial symbol in a family tv drama set in 1966 depicting friendship between black-white girls. When the black patriarch finds out his girl likes 'California Girls' and 'Wouldn't It Be Nice' his reaction is disdain, not to say disgust, at her betrayal of "our kind of music". Regardless of ignorant misunderstanding it still lives as one of the all-time Cool Jazz greats. The introduction alone miraculously combines languor—suitably suggestive of lounging in the sun "by a palm tree in the sand"— majesty, and subtle dexterity in arrangement. Brian Wilson claimed it as the best passage he's ever composed. To compare it with, say, the ultra-clichéd Marseillaise introduction to 'All You Need is Love' is revealing: one of George Martin's many tack-on jobs at Lennon/McCartney's request.

This was the Beach Boys' last romantic reference to beachgirls, for that matter the last gasp in the male rock world raising women on a pedestal. Women singer-songwriters in an increasingly feminist world would follow the philosophical bent of Dylan's bitter 'Positively 4th Street'. The next year Mama Cass of the Love Generation would belt out 'Words of Love' "so soft and tender won't win a girl's heart anymore." The folk poet's sales by themselves were no real threat to the Beach Boys—his singles were noted for their short shelf life, bought by his devoted coterie in a rush, and according to MGM who considered taking Dylan from Columbia and saw the figures, his album sales weren't all they were cracked up to be. But he was a vastly influential social force, more so than the Beatles among wannabe intellectuals right into lyrics but not particularly moved by music. Amateur musos, anxious to get by on flat, nasal voices and simple strumming, flocked to his banner.

Dylan was a fixture of London summers, settling in to protest in the first anti-Vietnam War march with Joan Baez, mixing business and pleasure. Influenced by his time amid the "Beat Boom", and reportedly, specifically by the Animals' version of 'House of the Rising Sun' and the Byrds' recordings of his songs, Dylan turned electric and was booed by a proportion of his American fans, folk purists, when he got home—first at the Newport Folk Festival in California, then at Forest Hills, New York.

From the point of his emergence to mass popularity and his industry-changing intellectualizing of rock the Beach Boys can be seen to start cringing at their own image as carefree *boys*, fresh-out-of-high-school jocks. The weedy unathletic male was in, and preferably dissolute—the better to emulate Bob's hero, drunken, objectionable Welsh poet Dylan Thomas. Even an act as square as the Four Seasons, who poked fun with a ridiculous falsetto version of 'Don't Think Twice', eventually came to pay tribute in some form—the folk-rock 'Tell It To the Rain'.

In a 2006 Rolling Stone article Dylan claimed with casual arrogance to "own the sixties"—speaking wryly so the interviewer thought he was joking—based on his songs being covered some 5,000 times and still being sung today, as compared with cited classics 'Tracks of My Tears' and 'What's Goin' On?'. Admitting that these two songs represented a legitimate sixties art form—that of recording—Dylan still rated writing his anyone-can-singalong songs as a higher achievement (Jonathan Lethem, 'The Genius of Bob Dylan', September 7th).

In measuring the Beach Boys long term against contemporaries I refer to Pop Culture Madness website with its ongoing tallies of plays/requests to rate current popularity of oldies. In 2007 the Beatles came well ahead of the Beach Boys in 1964 releases, listing five in the top 40 compared with the Boys' two, 'I Get Around' 6th and 'Fun Fun Fun' 13th. Come 1965's lineup and the Beach Boys placing 11th and 20th are ahead of the Beatles, who have only 'Yesterday' at 25th. The Stones have two in the lower half; Bob Dylan, one—notably outrated by Smokey Robinson's 'Tracks of My Tears'. Marvin Gaye, three in the top half, comes first; the Supremes rank with the Beach Boys, placing two songs in similar positions. In songs from '66 again the Beatles are outdone, placing two —but in higher positions—to the Beach Boys' four. Just seven Brit Invasion recordings remain popular from this year (c.f. eleven from '64, ten from '65). Conclusion: It is the early moptop songs for which the Beatles are still liked best: Beatlemania rules.

At the time, the top American group couldn't win either way. Their own media's preoccupation with Englishness hadn't let up—headliners of the opening *Shindig* of the season, mid-September '65: the Rolling Stones, Kinks and Beatle-lookalikes the Byrds. The

Supremes, more un-English-looking than anyone, had more success with 45s than anyone but the Beatles and even after an album of Liverpool music currying favor with the industry didn't crack the Sullivan show until October, after five number ones.

In pop impact the Beach Boys came off second best to Protest: Dylan, the Byrds—'Mr Tambourine Man' and 'Turn Turn Turn' both produced by Terry Melcher of former surf-music abode— ex-New Christy Minstrel Barry McGuire's 'Eve of Destruction' written by P F Sloan & Steve Barri of surf music heritage—and Stones. Yet, eschewing teenybopper mold, they were (happily) excluded from the designer preteen and young teen markets cornered by Herman's Hermits, Sonny & Cher and, learning quickly from the English Music Hall trade, Gary Lewis & the Playboys. These faces would be highly popular for just two years, but late summer brought major acts who could compete with the best of the English ones in new sounds they brought to rock: as well as Dylan and the Byrds, the Lovin' Spoonful, who even before their first hit were attracting Dylan and Phil Spector to their gigs in Greenwich Village; Simon & Garfunkel would join the eruption of talent early winter, weeks later the Mamas & the Papas. Between them by the end of the year they unveiled key hits and folk-oriented albums changing rock's emphasis. The Beatles joined them with *Rubber Soul*.

The American acts all benefited from the Beach Boys' sustained rearguard action in the face of overwhelming odds over the better part of two years through the British Invasion so far. The music industry had shifted under their feet twice, with seismic power, from their suburban landscape of woodies and surfboards, sun-tipped waves, hotrod dragstrips and hotdog stands they celebrated their first two years—to London-driven mod fashion, and now to Greenwich Village bohemianism. On their patch six days of race riots in mid-August centred on LA's Watts district left thirty-four dead and a thousand injured. They had always reflected the Southern California environment in recordings, but how to do justice to weighty racial sociology in a pop song? Instead, their art conveyed *personal* downers as the best art does.

Mass adulation came ready-made for the Beatles. In the media spotlight they were hailed for trends while actually swinging with them: reviving rock'n'roll, which the Beach Boys had accomplished on record before them; taking from the girl group sound and ending the genre simultaneously; striving to duplicate American state-of-the-art sounds at primitive Abbey Road; 1964 lounge music; now jumping on the Dylan-led Village Folk bandwagon; next, direct Beach Boy influence in harmonies; then, from the same source, psychedelia. Maybe in the future the Beatles will be remembered as originators of not much more than the John&Yoko sound.

T *HE MONKEY'S UNCLE* AND *GIRLS ON THE BEACH* still running this summer ended up a strong selling point, maintaining the Beach Boys' American status as primary drivers of the rock scene: the black and the cool James Brown, the Supremes and the Four Seasons lined up to be in beach movies. Plotless films such as *Beach Ball* (1965) had as their sole reason for being the music on show and were one of the few mainstream outlets open to black acts, and American rock'n'roll. Restamping the Beach Boy niche, it was one bound to sour on them. *Anything* British would win out. London retaliated with Jean Shrimpton, the first supermodel, introducing the miniskirt on an October tour of Australia. So the group's contribution to human endeavour was given less weight than this, probably the earth-shattering single event of the decade by the lights of pop culture. A group calling itself the Beach Nuts ('Out in the Sun') ensured they suffered something of the ridicule the Beatles had sustained, but without the mania to leaven it.

In earning power they still ranked with anyone, given the Beatles' poor contract terms. Promoter Irving Granz, handling both Beach Boys and Rolling Stones tours in the second half 1965, put the groups' average take equal at $22,500 per concert and the Beach Boys' net touring income at $750,000 for the calendar year (implying approximately $1,250,000 in concert grosses) and performers' royalties from record sales at least as much. Acts below this box-office level were stuck in package tours. One handled by the William Morris Agency included the Four Seasons, Yardbirds, Chuck Berry,

Mitch Ryder & the Detroit Wheels, Lou Christie and emerging Simon & Garfunkel: something for everyone?

Stuck with the deal Epstein had got them into—a tiny fraction of what the Beach Boys and the Four Seasons were on, 12-20% artists' royalties, plus publishing—their manager partly made up for it by insisting on thick under-the-counter bundles of tax-free cash for them from shows; witnesses of Paul's bedroom stash after their '65 American tour estimated close to a hundred thousand pounds—$240,000 (Salewicz). It was red carpet treatment all the way, with Ed Sullivan, the showbiz monarch who didn't know the Beach Boys were American, introducing the English group like old friends at their Shea Stadium concert, New York. A world record gross of $304,000 was achieved by promoter Sid Bernstein from a fairly steep admittance, averaging a little over $5. The Beatles got, officially, $160,000 of it— a record only beaten by next year's visit to Shea ($189,000). New York's élite, who wangled the best seats, could see them better, if not hear them. Beatles management congratulated themselves on keeping prices down in accord with the Fabs' image, boasting they could have got a million dollar gross if they wanted to—when at the Beach Boys Summer Spectacular kids could see eight top acts for $2 rising to $5. As it was, the Beatles improved on 1964's tour gross, at over a $million from 24 dates.

The August 1963 show at the Cavern Club would remain the Beatles' last performance ever for the home crowd—the people who had raised them to idols and given them self-belief. They justified this saying those who were complaining now about their absence were those who didn't go to see them before—avoiding the issue of making the effort to thank those uncomplaining masses who *had* supported them. Visits home to see relatives and friends were orchestrated with exaggerated Peter Sellers/Pink Panther cloak-and-dagger secrecy and loopy disguises as might be expected from superdooper-superstars cut off from ordinary humanity. Years later after the Beatles got over themselves, Paul, the most popular one, found himself able to stroll the streets of London from his home to Abbey Road studio unmolested. In Xmas 1964 the Fabs had played London, and a short

UK tour one Xmas later, but it was the deals offering most—Japan, the Philippines and most of all America—that grabbed their attention.

Over that Indian Summer the Beatles showed adaptable, going all out on 'Help!'/'I'm Down', but neutralized the effect with Paul's 'Yesterday'. This transparent (some would say pointless) reversion to a bygone age 400 years before is held aloft today by Beatle supporters as an advance pointing the way 'forward' to *Sgt Pepper*. *Help!* the movie wasn't the all-encompassing pop event that *A Hard Day's Night* was the previous summer—but plenty big enough to kick off the album in early August and tour on the 15th. Shea had been the opener, before 56,000 fans who didn't go there for the music—all that could be heard was their own screaming. When John Lennon ran into Sid Bernstein on the street a decade later he remembered the Shea din fondly, now obviously missing the uncritical adulation. On September 25th ABC tv debuted *The Beatles*, a weekly half-hour cartoon on the zany adventures of a pop group—a phenomenon still condescended to by industry leaders, except its money. The producers claimed the Beatles did the voices, leaving the group to deny it, much later. Over the next four years the Beatle myth was perpetuated via the tv series, and instantly led to the decision by Screen Gems to portray their image on tv via live personalities—the Monkees, for which auditions were already being held, a year in advance of screening.

Five days after receiving the Beach Boy delegation the Fabs had their audience with The King, Elvis Presley, at his mansion in Bel Air. Elvis wasn't that keen—It was his manager the Colonel who issued the invitation. The Beatles took the opportunity to enter some photo-aware 'play' as cowboys—with replica Western revolvers the Colonel sent them in remembrance afterward, in Elvis's name. Like the playing in the surf at Miami Beach for the second Sullivan show—when John gave instructions how he was to be filmed, when his hair was just right—this was no spontaneous instance of innocence. It is pleasant to think of the Beatles as manipulated or coerced into playing along with Big Business and mass media empires but they jumped at their roles like starving actors—or a band that had played dives for five years and saw a golden staircase magically appear before them.

While John complained the Stones stole the Beatles' erstwhile rebel image—Andrew Oldham switched from Beatle publicist to Stones manager, but in spring 1963, a year and a half after the Beatles had been thoroughly tamed by Epstein—he had no one to blame but himself for playing Epstein's game as what he believed was the price to ensure success: the same cleaned-up path Elvis took for the Sixties and that the Monkee Machine would make more millions from.

And in contrast to the Beach Boys' organic music-making— sounds germinating from seeds, nurturing, growing them over time into songs on tape, or wilting and dying a natural death—the Beatles' company approach permeated every facet of their lives. If the music wasn't working in the studio, in the time alotted, at the last minute George Martin or his assistants could always improvise something to join the dots.

Celebrity DJ Murray the K, their constant companion on their first US visit and groupie thereafter: "The Beatles didn't leave their rooms... What impressed me about them was that they were very disciplined, very together. They had to take care of business and to do what they had to do and try to enjoy as much of it as they could." And he discerned what their business was. At Shea Stadium he could decipher just two or three words over the space of as many songs, before retreating under the stands to see "over 300 or 400 girls carried out in dead faints" to ambulances.

On (not) getting to know them summer '65 Byrds leader Jim McGuinn asked George Harrison pointedly about his view of God and received the impersonal form reply, "'Well, we don't know about that.' That was the common mentality they all had. That was a protective device they had and that kept them together as long as it did." Back in Britain, John let his guard slip and revealed in an interview exactly what he thought of Jesus and his followers.

On whether the solo 'Yesterday' should be a Paul McCartney record, George Martin deferred to Brian Epstein in the company hierarchy, who ruled, "No, it's the Beatles." The product brand had been set in concrete. What was the point in having a commercially infallible name and not pushing it at every sale? And in that levelling English way of imposing false modesty—"Jack's as good as his master"—Martin too concluded, "It would have made him stick out too much otherwise" (quotes from Pritchard & Lysaght). Beach Boy Brian, and Brian & Mike, would release two independent singles over the next two years. But the Beatle brand couldn't grant increments of musical individuality that might lead to strides toward independence, jeopardising returns to increasingly wealthy stakeholders that the group was partners with. Unlike their on-show, bankable personalities they would remain largely unknown as musical individuals until The Breakup—when the dream was shattered, personally and musically.

At the same time John, who had been a visual artist more than a musical one in his art school days with Stu Sutcliffe, was broadening his *oeuvre* to literature. In that chronically punning manner, he had named his 1963 effort *In His Own Write*. Now he came up with *A Spaniard in the Works*—completely losing the American audience: "spanner" being English for monkey wrench, and a spanner in the works meaning gunked up. The odds against him being world class in even two of these three artistic disciplines were astronomical, but fans bought it in truckloads because it was so… beatleish.

THERE IS REASON TO THINK THE BEACH BOYS' failure to date in the UK owed something—in addition to the almost impassable hurdle of just being foreign—to an unimaginative, even defeatist approach by their marketers, British EMI. There was no rock'n'roll competition for them—American or homegrown — when EMI kicked them off in June 1962 and they theoretically had the resources of the giant corporate at their disposal. Instead, Elvis's 'Good Luck Charm', Cliff's 'I'm Looking Out the Window', Adam Faith's 'As You Like It', Billy Fury's 'Last Night Was Made for Love' and Brian Hyland's 'Ginny Come Lately'— that all somehow passed for rock and roll—were at or near top of the charts. Neither was there a viable schedule of albums. *Surfin' Safari* was released six months late, outdated in summer '63. On failure of a thin-looking Plan A, no album was issued for fifteen months—*Shut Down Vol 2*, again late, preventing them building a coherent Blighty fanbase. The uncool *Christmas* album, the least likely to make a breakthrough, was released on time; the classic *All Summer Long* a year late. By rights, after two years of sales failure the Beach Boys should have been a permanent wipeout in Britain. It was largely thanks to private 'pirate' radio stations sailing the high seas off the coast of the British Isles that they finally got a fair share of exposure. But somehow their fifth-in-the-world rating in UK polls by the end of 1964 still failed to translate into sales.

Vee-Jay, sitting remote in Chicago, marketed the Four Seasons 1962-63 to garner three UK hits out of three just in or out of top ten. How much better should have been expected from British-EMI, on the spot, for the Beach Boys? Brits didn't really take to the Seasons long term, nor the Supremes—apart from their first two hits that could pass for Betty Grable/Rosie O'Grady Music Hall numbers. It took real popularity to last. At 'I Get Around''s peak the e.p. *Fun Fun Fun* b/w 'Little Deuce Coupe'/'In My Room'/ 'Why Do Fools Fall in Love?' crept two places into the chart. Home confidence was at its height, the public devoted to its artists, yet Britons—the millions of listeners dissatisfied with the official service of BBC-Radio—dipped their toes into the wave again as winter '64 came on. *Four By the Beach Boys* with 'Little Honda' and 'Wendy' did a little better, edging top ten—as 'Dance Dance Dance' climbed just enough to gain familiarity. It was hardly the sales oomph expected of Britain's most popular foreign group. It was only from their personal popularity—working long-distance at that—that sales grew, eventually.

It was without fanfare that 'Help Me Rhonda' broke the spring ice at Radio London—frequently broadcast from the pirate radio station off Essex and rising to #4. In Germany it was the first big Beach Boy hit to go interstate, crossing cultures. In France Pathé/ Capitol had issued no singles in four years and few albums— *Surfin' USA* and *Concert*, and now an improvised *California Girls*. Their success came via a stream of e.p.s: *Surfer Party, Drivin' Cars, Louie, Louie*. A *California Girls* e.p. sleeve admirably advertised the French bikini of the song, picturing a pair of girls looking fetchingly at the camera, lying on a rocky shore that looked like Brittany, showing a maximum of cleavage ensuring an even suntan with undone bikini straps and succeeding in looking as Californian as any bleached-blonde French models had a right to. 'Mister John B' by the country's top songstress,

Sylvie Vartan—who had met the Beatles and Beach Boys in Paris—would be the next big cover version.

It was not until late summer '65 that a pan-European presence built to a critical mass. The last sighting of the group was the whistle-stop tour nine months before. *The TAMI Show* had enjoyed a limited European run from April, and maybe some of the video clips taken by Continental tv channels were still in circulation. The signs were that no American act could have real success in Britain at least without an intensive tour—just as Bob Dylan did in May, driving *Freewheelin'* to the top after floundering for a year, then *Bringing It All Back Home*. Inactive Elvis was almost a back number, buoyed by his most faithful, even masochistic fans, dogged British bulldogs having waited almost ten years, grateful for fanclub badges or other mementos the Colonel palmed them off with.

The Beach Boys' UK album breakthrough finally came in September, debuting (listed to twenty, like e.p.s) with *Surfin' USA*, two and a half years late. British DJs and public, to their credit, ignored label and media publicity and decided subject matter—'surf', passé in America and a cultural experience alien to Britain—was immaterial to the music. For five more autumns new albums, with one exception, would list in the UK's weekly top half-dozen.

B UT THE GROUP'S SUNNY DAYS WERE SPOILT BY oncoming dark clouds scudding over the horizon. As the interval to their next 45 lengthened to four and a half months the signs were that it would be a frigid winter: 'The Little Girl I Once Knew', an adventurous, energetic track combining elements of the previous two hits and more. Carl led a convincing rock vocal, growling in all the right places. Without benefit of album promotion, one more daring track that could not rely on the label's full backing, it did as well as could be expected. On November 11th two weeks before release influential WMCA-New York picked it as its 'sure shot'. Next it was seen more than thirty places up the chart, but then, one. It stalled too in LA. Barely a week into release it was being nudged by a new 45 from Capitol distributed early to radio stations. Still, December 13th it was biggest climber in WIBG-Philadelphia's top 50.

The 17th it rocketed to #5 in Orlando, Florida's top tunes only to drop as quickly when the new single, issued without the group's knowledge, appeared. In Vancouver too it had shot out of nowhere when cut down at #3—its destination too in the Twin Cities; Boston-New England, and Pittsburgh, Louisville, St Joseph of the Border States, Birmingham and Pensacola of the Deep South, top ten; the midteens mostly across the Midwest but limping into LA, Chicago, Toronto and New York twenties.

On Xmas Day, a surprise gift, it crawled into the national top twenty, five places higher in Cash Box and Record World than Billboard; top ten in Canada. Amazingly in light of no UK sales, on New Year's Day it faced the Radio Caroline ten; a day later, first runner-up at Radio London—their best recognition so far by the British audience.

The widespread shunning Stateside was attributed to twitchy radio programmers under the strictures of the Top 40 format— rejecting it for its silent pauses, a whole bar's worth of 'dead air' between verse and chorus. According to the myth this had never been tried before in Pop and had frantic listeners anxious for sound, any sound, switching stations. But there was a two-bar pause in 'Drive-in'—and a long one coming in 'Good Vibrations'; 'Good Lovin'' and 'I Had Too Much to Dream' by other groups. Again the Beach Boys were pioneers and paid for it.

They were left with the consolation of huge UK airplay and the United Press International (UPI) survey of the States, which had it at no.4 January 10th regardless of radio policies—challenging 'We Can Work It Out' and 'Sounds of Silence'. Again, in what was becoming a disturbing pattern, Beach Boy popularity won through *despite* the efforts of industry bosses.

Over New Year the group performs a Northwest double at Tacoma and Seattle. Support act Gary Lewis & the Playboys' 'This Diamond Ring' launches toward no.1. The Yardbirds are there with three big hits and a big reputation. And English-soundalikes the Beau Brummels, famous but fading, with the Mojo Men from San Francisco producer Sly Stone: both clients of songwriter Van Dyke

Parks, whom Brian Wilson meets at one of Terry Melcher's music producers' soirées.

The year had closed on a courageous but chastening note. By now disdainful of commercial dictates, Brian Wilson did not heed the warning. He had dared what has been called the strangest release by a big name in 1965, with its alternating organ arpeggios and galloping shuffle rhythm—scuttled by his label's issue of a retro sound. And 'California Girls'' flip, the pulsing jazz-toned 'Let Him Run Wild', was "the turning point" for Dennis Wilson, by most accounts the Beach Boy who best saw Brian's aim. Carl continues to be the biggest help to him in the studio, so the best translator of his music out on the road. But it was also the first B-side to miss any chart action, national or local, since 1962. Dennis, for four years seen as a makeweight—a Ringo—now has *two* songs to perform in the group concert setlist, 'Do You Wanna Dance?' and his faithful rendition of John Lennon's 'You've Got to Hide Your Love Away'.

The gulf in appreciation for Brian's new music to the overwhelming sales of wall-to-wall fun on *The Beach Boys Party* and its single caused a real crisis of direction. Mike's stance of "Don't fuck with the formula" left him to catch up incrementally with Brian's moves increasingly from left field. For now, January 1966, a tour of Japan—Tokyo, Nagoya, Osaka, Kyoto, Kobe, Fukuoka, Yokohama, all the biggies—and Hawaii, keeps them away from the studio. Brian plays his solo recordings for a new album over the phone to Dennis, Carl and Mike.

There was ample reason to worry over their commercial future. You might tweak the nose of the powers that be but only enough to infuriate them to kick ass back. The formula had done great commerce. In the past twelve months they saw six albums awarded the US Gold standard, the achievement belittled by Capitol's tardiness. Latest was *Summer Days (and Summer Nights!)* on February 7th, timed to extract maximum publicity as their latest 45 topped the chart. The Beach Boys might have noted wistfully that it was the second anniversary of Beatle touchdown. Their best-selling album of that time, *Little Deuce Coupe*, wasn't awarded Gold until 21st December 1966, two and a half years after estimated to have sold

Platinum, saved for a presentation with *Shut Down Vol 2* and their next no.1 single. Awards for all three 1963 l.p.s were treated as an afterthought—as if pre-Beatles history hardly counted anymore.

XMAS WEEK, SUPPOSEDLY TO PLUG A SALES GAP AND mercy-kill lingering 'Little Girl I Once Knew', Capitol had issued simple, exciting 'Barbara Ann'. An unplugged and reportedly well-lubricated party singalong of the five-year-old Regents r&b hit, it was recorded in summer '65 with the very vocal participation of the Honeys and other wives, relatives and friends with the rest of *Beach Boys Party*. Also recorded with acoustic guitars, bongos, bass and tambourine were knockoffs of better Beatle songs 'Tell Me Why', 'I Should Have Known Better' and 'You've Got to Hide Your Love Away'; Dylan's 'The Times They Are A-Changin'' (Al), novelty favorite 'Alley Oop', written by Bruce Johnston's old band mate Kim Fowley, 'Papa-Oom-Mow-Mow' (Brian giving a stronger rendering than on *Concert*) and 'Mountain Of Love'. Muffed lyrics and gaffes abounded in rushing the album out for the Xmas market—and by contract deadline. The world was treated to a big showbiz name taking itself anything but seriously—in Spike Jones style lending operatic treatment to 'I Get Around' and pretentiously earnest Latin touches to 'Little Deuce Coupe'—self-mocking all the way.

Having aired 'Barbara Ann' on tv's *Jack Benny Hour* November 3rd—appearing on personal appeal from the veteran comedian — Capitol shrewdly took advantage of its exposure as a surefire hit, reinforcing Beach Boy popularity if not musical reputation. On this outing of the popular weekly comedy-variety show, after the group does 'California Girls', guest Bob Hope and Benny come on carrying between them a Hawaiian-sized Big Kahuna surf board on their heads and joke about the Beach Boys "outranking us", confirming the group as an American institution. The boys oblige in the act with a wooden portrayal of surfer toughs staring down senior-citizen hodads. Walt Disney and Elke Sommer, Hollywood's German blonde, also guest. Shortly after came a "USO A-Go-Go" benefit at New York's Madison

Square Garden, hosted by Ed Sullivan—alongside the Supremes, Bobby Vinton, Jack Good's *Hullabaloo* singers & dancers and a smorgasbord of old showbiz greats.

Rubber Soul was released early December '65, the title conceived by Paul McCartney in reaction to American critics calling Beatle music "plastic" measured against homegrown rock; John Lennon admired the pun. But according to recording engineer Norman Smith, "With *Rubber Soul* the clash between John and Paul was becoming obvious. Also, George was having to put up with an awful lot from Paul... Paul would be saying, 'No, no, no!' And he'd start quoting American records, telling him to play exactly what he'd heard on such-and-such a song... Paul would take over and do it himself—he always had a left-handed guitar with him. Subsequently I discovered that George Harrison had been hating Paul's bloody guts for this, but it didn't show itself... Most of the ideas came from Paul [but] he couldn't write music. But he could certainly tell an arranger how to do it, just by singing a part —however, he didn't know, of course, whether the strings or brass could play what he wanted" (Salewicz).

The style, almost a folk music album, can be seen as brainchild of the 'joint' meeting of minds between Dylan and the Beatles in that smoke-filled room in New York. Out of this pot haze the perverse folk poet, just switched to rock, urged this 'rock' group to go folk. According to a Beatle website, Capitol excised 'Nowhere Man' and 'Drive My Car' from the US issue of *Rubber Soul* so it would be more in keeping with Dylan/Byrds albums. Certainly they did a good job of purging rock—what is left is a kind of folky pop, leaving just four outstanding tracks that stand on their own plus a similar number that are worth listening to.

The result was a much more laid back approach, without the excitement of the best *Help!* tracks or, come to that, anything like the spirit and drive of the best folk, e.g. Peter, Paul & Mary's 'If I Had a Hammer', the Kingstons' 'Greenback Dollar'. It sported much less energy too than Beach Boy albums. But the Beatles now concerned themselves with 'adult' themes. They pondered deep questions, and the ponderousness showed.

The early Beatle albums had each included six outside compositions (out of 14). *A Hard Day's Night* was the exception, and by the time of *Help!* the total not by Lennon-McCartney had reduced to four and two of those were George Harrison songs. From *Rubber Soul*, fully relying on their own material to increase royalty returns, began the tendency to compose cutesie, punning Beatle songs—tracks that meant the world to Beatle fans, and there were quadrillions of them to continue huge advance sales, but little to others who wanted rock.

Help! was more exciting—the title song, Paul's Little Richard-inspired 'I'm Down', Dylan-inspired 'You've Got to Hide Your Love Away', the 60/40-to-John collaborations 'Ticket to Ride' and 'You're Going to Lose That Girl', enough to carry a hit feature film. But *Rubber Soul* was their first really critically admired album, for its 'integrity': It was supposed to be listened to not song for song but right through, even the dull spots. Hearing *Rubber Soul* prompted Brian Wilson, who envied Dylan's lyrical ability almost as much as John Lennon did, to want to record an album of songs that "sound like they belong together."

Suspicion that this supposed integrity is hyped illusion comes from 'Wait', a track written for *Help!* but held over for *Rubber Soul* to simply even up the number of tracks—There was no great cosmic plan for the grandly named Concept Album. Because the new album contained most of the accessible Lennon-McCartney material written over the past year it rates top of their remaining albums, containing on the original edition 'Nowhere Man', 'In My Life'—one of their truly introspective songs, that can probably be totalled on one hand—'If I Needed Someone' (another) and 'Norwegian Wood'. It also had the benefit of better sound, from EMI-UK's newly acquired eight-track recording equipment. This prompted the Beatles to cajole Smith still harder to reproduce the sounds of current American records.

In maybe relying too much on others, some admired Beatle songs sound well-honed but less than inspired: the torturously crafted collaboration 'Drive My Car', Paul's 'I'm Looking Through You', his 'Michelle', John's similarly quasi-continental 'Girl'. In Barry Miles' biography Paul describes how, for 'Girl', the Beatles used the innocence of the "la-la-la-la" vocal background of the Beach Boys ('You're So Good to Me')—but couldn't resist making it a bit naughty in their schoolboyish way so sang "tit-tit-tit-tit" for their bridge. Miles goes on to state that the slightly later 'Paperback Writer' "has a nod to the Beach Boys' *Pet Sounds* in its complex vocal harmonies."

1966 STARTED WITH THE BEATLES DUELLING WITH Simon & Garfunkel. By its end a group of actor-singers formed by Brill Building magnate Don Kirshner to ape the Beatles, the Monkees, had sold two million 'Last Train to Clarksville's and more 'I'm a Believer's to young tv-watchers. At Columbia-Screen Gems auditions to select Monkee hopefuls John Sebastian, Stephen Stills, Van Dyke Parks and Charles Manson were weeded out.

In the UK the Seekers ('The Carnival is Over') and the Beatles ('Day Tripper'/'We Can Work It Out') did nicely, close to a million and a half. The Seekers' past year gave a foretaste of the Beach Boy phenomenon: out of nowhere—i.e. from overseas in the era of British Dominion. On a slow rise in the States was 'California Dreamin'', the new Mamas & Papas with producer Lou Adler moving over from Jan & Dean to a folk version of California Music. Nancy Sinatra was lightening the pockets of four million around the world with 'These Boots Are Made for Walking'. Biggest record of the USA year was Marine Sgt Barry Sadler's 'Ballad of the Green Berets', a one-hit surety. Its super-patriotism sold over five million Americans and almost no one else. Popular enough to inspire John Wayne to produce a movie on the subject, it was a sitting target for a group calling themselves the Beach Bums to sing in reply a ballad on the *yellow* beret that got away.

'(You're My) Soul and Inspiration' could have been addressed to 'You've Lost That Lovin' Feelin''—The Righteous Bros had broken with Phil Spector but were determined to sound like they hadn't: a perfect copy of his technique. The Walker Bros under Nick Venet took the same niche in the UK. The Rascals' 'Good Lovin'' topped in spring, Mamas & Papas' 'Monday Monday', then the Beatles and Frank Sinatra. With novelties like Peter Sellers' 'A Hard Day's Night',

Roger Miller's 'England Swings' and Barbra Streisand's 'Second Hand Rose' '66 started off as lightweight as '65. 'My Love' did for Pet Clark what 'Downtown' had a year before; and Herb Alpert did his thing with 'Spanish Flea'. The Overlanders topped the UK chart for three weeks with 'Michelle and there was a high-flying cover of 'Girl' to confirm Beatle Easy Listening as a trend. Death had only slowed Jim Reeves down to UK pace, and crooners Eddie Arnold, Ken Dodd, Val Doonican, Bob Lind and Andy Williams joined him in the top ten there. Luckily classic groups the Spencer Davis Group, Yardbirds and Kinks were at the height of their powers, joined by The Who, Small Faces, and soon the Troggs.

The new Beach Boy 45 was their first that was even bigger overseas. It topped too in the US (except Billboard), according to most sources their tenth single to sell above a million Stateside. In the Cash Box sales chart 'Barbara Ann' bumped 'Sounds of Silence', and lasted a second week in Record World, doing best across Middle America—Pennsylvania, Philadelphia to Pittsburgh; St Joe, Missoura and Dallas-Ft Worth 5th for the year, WNUR-Chicago and Minnesota Twins. Brian's falsetto co-led with Dean Torrance of Jan & Dean, whom Mike mic-ed louder, Brian thought. As familiar to partygoers of the Western World and beyond is Mike's monotone chant "Bar-bar-bar Bar-bar-bra Ann," answered by the chorus to start off each verse.

In newly hip LA circles—thanks almost solely to the Beach Boys—ironically the homeboys were already old hat, a trend that began after 'I Get Around', residing at no.1 for five weeks, almost as long as 'I Want to Hold Your Hand'. The Beatles had struck trouble too in LA, but while 'Nowhere Man' just made top ten 'Barbara Ann' was shunned, scraping top thirty.

Elsewhere across North America it was increasingly uncool to like them but evidently impossible to stop buying them in huge numbers. A Capitol spokesman at the millennium put the label's sales of Beach Boy singles at over 100 million—a total of 28 forty-fives averaging out to nearly four million each. In region after region, song by song, they endured. CFUN, in its twice-yearly listener vote (November '65) for the 300 most popular 'oldies' in the Vancouver area—attracting up to 225,000 voters a time—'Fun Fun Fun' made it to the ten most popular of all and 'Little Deuce Coupe' was top from 1963. Neither was anything like as popular on release according to the charts but where long-term surveys were done—New York, Buffalo, Boston, Philadelphia, Dallas-Ft Worth, Seattle—it was in ongoing sales they excelled, often over the Beatles. Eight years later WFIL-Philadelphia found 'Barbara Ann' to have sold more regionally than any other single from 1966 except 'Cherish', one of those "occasion songs" trotted out by sentimental Baby Boomers over the next few years on every half-suitable rite of passage: engagements, weddings, baptisms, bar mitzvahs, circumcisions....

Italy, as parochial as Japan, was after two thousand years as the centre of conservative christendom fundamentally resistant to primal American rock'n'roll. Sophia Loren's shimmy while singing "rock and roll" in *It Started in Naples* was about as heated as it got. The Italians took the same attitude to the Beach Boys as they had to the Four Seasons: local imposters. In a spirit of exorcising pagan rock'n'roll, under a firm impresario any choir of young men with electric guitars thrust into their hands, emasculated and sensitive to continental cultural imperatives would do nicely: *castrati bellissima*. There had been covers of 'Surfin' USA', 'Help Me Rhonda' and two of 'She Knows Me Too Well'. The country's most famous group, Equipe 84, had imitated 'Papa-Oom-Mow-Mow' and belatedly now went high in the charts covering 'I Get Around' and 'Don't Worry Baby', while the Jaguars from Rome replicated 'Spirit of America', 'Keep an Eye on Summer', an overlooked sweetie from *Shut Down Vol.2*, and 'Barbara Ann'. A bigger version came from I Pop Seven with celebrated vocalist Roberto Vecchioni. Another top group, I Nomadi, covered its flip 'Girl Don't Tell Me' (Aldo Pedron). Fighting uphill against operatic romantic ballads, the Beach Boys' 'Barbara Ann' was 10th most popular *foreign* recording of the year, peaking at no.4 with a sustained nine weeks in the national top ten and penetrating Italian consciousness through the millennium. 'We Can Work It Out', the only other foreign song prominent early that year, stalled five rungs lower.

But as they uniformly swept the world for the first time, persuading everyone from Europe via Africa and Asia to the South Pacific that Beach Boy music equals happy music and their lifestyle was a laid-back, sundrenched vacation, Brian Wilson was by Herculean creative effort (using six LA studios in seven months) laying down the first tapes for 'Good Vibrations', a piece of music far removed from 'Barbara Ann''s earthy simplicity. Inventing Symphonic Rock, Wilson breached all boundaries and crafted a pocket symphony, 'Good Vibrations', so evocative that even its silence was eloquent: the airy echo-pause following the *a capella* shout after the bridge.

And he was recording an l.p. to 'compete with' *Rubber Soul*. The creative-vs-commercial schism built to an emotional tension that alienated others and nearly destroyed him. What better scenario to give justification to latent drug-fed paranoia—the people one most relies on dragging the artist back from what he needs to do? To test the water, a month after 'Barbara Ann' set a commercial pinnacle he put out a solo single, 'Caroline No' (see next chapter).

Due to Brian's heavy involvement with new music, his group's next world-beater would again draw on the back catalogue, finished off in his 'spare' time. A song that for two generations had served as a popular sea shanty for folk singers under various names ('Wreck of the John B', 'John B Sails') was adapted in the early fifties by Lee Hays of the Weavers as 'I Wanna Go Home'— Lonnie Donegan had the UK hit in 1960. Urged by Al, Brian and he had in mid-'65 adapted lyrics from Twenties "city of broad shoulders" Chicago poet Carl Sandburg and arranged the calypso into transcendent new form, a radical production of stirring rock. It was self-evidently far beyond folk-rock performers Bob Dylan, Mamas & the Papas and Simon & Garfunkel—who performed straight folk treatments with drums tacked on. This was no less than the masterpiece of rock invention Jimi Hendrix would make out of Dylan's 'All Along the Watchtower'. It got a nod from television, inserted totally out of context by Will (Billy Mumy) of the Space Family Robinson singing it on *Lost in Space*.

'Sloop John B'/'You're So Good to Me' hit no.2 in Record World, reported (by Murrells) as their fastest-selling single to date in America: over half a million in less than two weeks—one more unofficial Gold Disc. In Boston, across New England, Pittsburgh to Cleveland to Cincinnati the Beach Boys' new release was a topper, and in the year's biggest hits of New York, Philadelphia, Washington DC, Toronto. It outshone the sedate, conventional harmonies of the Mamas & Papas blocking it—threatening to replace both Peter, Paul & Mary as Greenwich Village spokespersons and the Beach Boys as "California Music".

'You're So Good to Me' had directly influenced the Beatles as an album track and attracted cover versions around the world including, again, Italy—an American-styled group called Memphis. It featured near the top of playlists in Vancouver, Miami, Cleveland and New England, and in old England was a party favorite. Like its A-side it featured Brian singing lead in a much deeper register but sliding up to falsetto when required.

Esteemed writer Jules Siegel, who began visiting Brian, totalled to this point their US 45 sales on Capitol as 16 million—from 17 issued. Six fell short of gold, for now. The double thrust through the first half of the year rammed home the Beach Boys' world superstardom—some feat at a time of the "Yankee Go Home!" Cold War backlash when Western Europe, host to US bases for over twenty years, resented the cultural colonisation of its youth. In contrast, it was wooed by the Beatles' flattery in the likes of Europhile 'Michelle' and 'Girl'. Cultures then had their own strong tastes, largely broken down today with the world treated by the mass media as America's cultural backyard.

In Japan, since WWII a politico-cultural extension of the US, virtually a fifty-first state, *Beach Boys Party* was their eleventh consecutive entry in the top 12, a standard continuing unbroken for another twenty albums into the 1980s. Services newspaper *Pacific Stars & Stripes*, published out of Tokyo, printed the UPI American top twenty and the Beach Boys had become a household name in their four years of fame. Capitol used initiative in early '66 plucking 'Amusement Parks USA', just another overlooked album track in the

US, from *Summer Days (and Summer Nights!)* to release for the Japanese tour. It made runner-up, normally top spot open to foreign records, probably tallying in the neighborhood of a half-million when their touring support act the Spiders sold singles in the millions from months occupying number one.

Like the Brits—the most 'British' of them never heard of in America because not translatable—German popsters corrupted the completely strange experience that was rock'n'roll, and were all the more popular with the home audience for altering it to a local genre. Four Seasons cover group the Five Tops (?!) had scored the bigger local hit with 'Rag Doll' in '65. More successful than the Seasons, Supremes or Mamas & the Papas (the hit in Germany was an Italian version of 'California Dreamin''), the Beach Boys were still limited to isolated big hits. Even the Beatles, advantaged in having Germany as a spawning ground, had far fewer hits near top here than in English-speaking countries. Now 'Sloop John B' rested atop the national Hit Bilanz five weeks—the Beach Boys' longest reign in a major record-buying country to date. It rated 4th in sales in '66 above 'Yesterday Man', written and recorded by Sandie Shaw's collaborator Chris Andrews, that had set the record for a foreign recording at a German million in four months; and hits had an extraordinarily long sales life in Germany, years. 'Barbara Ann' too, 6th, finished higher than the Beatles' biggest, 'Yellow Submarine' (14th), 'We Can Work It Out' (16th)—Media Control website.

Particularly highly regarded in northern Europe, four years later far-reaching Dutch pirate station, Veronica, polled listeners to find 'Sloop' most popular disc from '66. 'Good Vibrations' and 'God Only Knows' too ranked high—the group's new music. But for now the group had to ease the public into this startling new knowledge....

ONCE EASED INTO IT 'WOULDN'T IT BE NICE?'/'GOD Only Knows' was their most admired double of all. During 2005-7 the A was commandeered to advertise Cadbury chocolate around the world; the B as the theme of a new American prime time drama. At the time, of major US markets, only in traditional r&b centers Detroit and St Louis did the A finish lower than #7—the level it found in Cash Box, Billboard a rung lower. It found #1 in Vancouver, top three Dallas & Houston, upstate New York, Boston-New England, Toronto; top five New York, Chicago, Ohio, Pittsburgh, Minnesota Twins.

Record World, September 4th '66, the Beach Boys down somewhat from their usual height, just overtaken by the Hollies—the competition so thick that Donovan and the Beatles had lasted a sole week at top, as would the Happenings and the Supremes:

1. See You in September — the Happenings
2. You Can't Hurry Love — the Supremes
3. Yellow Submarine — the Beatles
4. Bus Stop — the Hollies
5. Wouldn't It Be Nice? — the Beach Boys
6. Land of 1,000 Dances — Wilson Pickett
7. Cherish — the Association
8. Sunshine Superman — Donovan
9. Guantanamera — the Sandpipers
10. Working in a Coal Mine — Lee Dorsey

It should have been released by Capitol to promote their new album, but was delayed more than two months till late July—when it started well, debuting as high as ever. Long-term it emerged huge, across the Delaware Valley 4th for its year behind two other Beach Boys' in a 1974 sales and popularity survey by station WFIL-Philadelphia; 2nd in WNBC's decade-long roundup of the adjacent Greater New York catchment north into Massachusetts. But now it was up against *Best of the Beach Boys*, Capitol going all out to promote the 'old' hits of two or three years before.

Though maintaining their A-rocker/B-ballad schema there were few points of similarity to previous twin-packs. Arrangements were fully orchestrated, and the compositions used more chords in more complicated patterns. George Martin and Andrew Oldham were saying that 'God Only Knows' was melodically complex—and sublimely beautiful—by any standard. It had taken ten minutes to rough out its melody, no more than half an hour to complete the composing phase. But this was only the beginning. Arranging and production mix-down—the chores left by the Beatles to George Martin—were crucially important, and most of the fun, for the Beach Boys. 'Wouldn't It Be Nice?' was conceived the year before but took this long to bear fruit. As Brian would later say about this project, "It was the biggest production of our lives." The two tracks were the stars of the new album released in mid-May in the US—two months later in the UK; several others would qualify as key (see next chapter).

The B was the hit in Britain and Europe; in Canada it co-featured. British and North American sales must have nudged it on to a million. On the Continent reaction to 'God Only Knows' was favorable, almost making top ten in most major markets. Yet, the classics were not credited (by Murrells, writing twelve years later) even with a world million, qualifying both sides as the most downplayed of Beach Boy hits—a category expanding to ludicrous proportions by the year.

Although, with Brian piercing barriers again many US stations wouldn't play 'God', initially intended as A-side, because of the "blasphemous" title—the first ever such pop song—it featured as a top-tenner on its own on the West Coast: #6 in LA, Portland and Seattle alike, top three inland at Phoenix and Houston; topping in Louisville and elsewhere around the Ohio River Valley. It barely rated on national Top 40 shows. Carl, 19, came into his own as their most frequent lead voice for the rest of the decade.

The Beatles over the past eighteen months had widened their scope. 'She's a Woman' and 'Ticket to Ride' towered over everything they had done before and in mid-'65 John Lennon's 'Help!' emerged as one of the year's exciting hits. 'Yesterday' was the epitome of Paul McCartney's appeal-to-everyone melodies. 'We Can Work It Out' and 'Nowhere Man' continued the high mark, 'Day Tripper' and 'Paperback Writer' with its Beach Boy-sounding harmonies, not quite as good despite quickening pace.

Dragging them down now was novelty song 'Yellow Submarine' and the compulsion to include country songs and a mishmash of other types on each album. Their compositions hadn't eliminated filler, despite the hype. Flip side 'Eleanor Rigby' almost made up for the A: an imaginative McCartney composition, if too obvious in its melodramatic use of strings and containing obscure references: faces in jars, Father MacKenzie... adding up to a Georgian novelette. Shrewdly, Beatles.com judged the Music Hall song—not the supposedly daring one—to be the group's *metier*, and marketed it accordingly. And 'Eleanor' couldn't hold a candle to 'God Only Knows'/'Wouldn't It Be Nice' as advanced rock. During the six weeks recording it, ending June 6th, Paul took time off to go nightclubbing around London with Bob Dylan and the Rolling Stones, being seen in the right places and cementing their places as *the* A-list rock celebrities.

Still, no one else in rock, if they wanted to, was able to match the mass acceptability of the Beatles' *ennui*-inducing ballads— 'Yesterday', 'And I Love Her', 'Michelle', 'Girl'—which lent themselves to cover versions by A-list Easy Listening artists Frank Sinatra, Tony Bennett, Peggy Lee, Vikki Carr and new soft-samba harmony groups Sergio Mendes & Brasil '66, the Sandpipers, the Arbors, among many other acts around the world. Such was the group's bankability the early often-rejected McCartney songs 'When I'm Sixty-Four' and 'I'll Follow the Sun' were put on a pedestal as standards.

THE ADULT CONTEMPORARY SECTOR WAS TAKEN care of and now they went for intellectuals, per head the most powerful sector of the population but up to now the province of classical musicians and folk singers. They had just embarked on one flank with 'Yesterday' and 'Eleanor', and pre-*Rubber Soul* had already met Dylan for a dope session and taken direct advice from him—amounting to tactical business discussions on how to approach the other.

The biggest buyers of 45s—teens—were no longer quite as delirious over the Fab Four, in their mid-twenties now and steadily replacing their fanbase. Their rapidly widening catalogue of album tracks about adult concerns was soaking up a broad untapped audience: tired middle-agers who could afford albums and wanted art—i.e. sounds that oozed sophistication, like bloated orchestras and alternately gentle classical guitar, and maybe weird tangents that passed for originality. The smooth creativity and easy social climbing of Paul especially—and later Sinatra himself would declare George's 'Something' the greatest love song ever—resonated with a vast listener pool who had gritted their teeth through the rock'n'roll era and now were glad to foresee its passing altogether.

After *Rubber Soul* producer George Martin, midway through recording their next album sensing that the specialness had gone out of the Beatles, left EMI to form his own company though returned to Abbey Road to oversee each of their projects. But it wasn't like the old days when he was heeded closely, in due respect. The Beatles often left him or his assistants in the studio to finish off something they had grown tired of or considered beneath them. As they got very, very important with every new honor bestowed on them, obviously other people—even highly talented ones like Martin—got relatively less so. Norman Smith, who knew exactly the Beatles' strengths and weaknesses, stayed on as a full producer with EMI—but for his new, more rewarding find, Pink Floyd. A special effects whiz on deck just three months as tape operator to Smith, Geoff Emerick, was made the new Beatle engineer by Martin.

On picking up any Beatle album four to six tracks stand out as fairly compelling to play. Most of the rest have little more than curiosity value to the casual listener. Their next album, coinciding with ceasing touring in August '66, would struggle to sustain even this level of interest as they descended to a self-absorbed, self-defined arty plane where, no longer interested in communicating with an audience, they were best satisfied pleasing themselves: in other words, wanking. Losing interest in pleasing the public live, playing for them in any context lost its appeal. *Revolver* fully reflected this new "We're social commentators, not entertainers" attitude. Despite the turn towards maturity in their lyrics, in an early summer interview with the Disc trade paper Paul lamented their American image as "jovial mop tops"—still, after two and a half years of Beatlemania. With this album and developments arising from their last tour they were about to leap into fully-fledged adulthood with a vengeance and would barely survive the backlash as a partially functioning band.

With multiple releases registering each year in the top-selling rock l.p.s, the Beach Boys were America's most successful rock'n'roll act for 1963, '64, '65. In '66 they were selling more 45s than ever, especially overseas. With their senior status—their fifth year as stars in an unstable decade—their touring show was highly lucrative but only reflecting the work they were putting in, averaging two hundred shows a year. But competition in the l.p. stakes was fierce and—no surprise under Capitol's abdication from their new material—they couldn't sustain long US runs and were now overtaken by the Rolling Stones, Mamas & Papas, Monkees and Herb Alpert's MOR Tijuana Brass. The impetus of Alpert's combo on his own label, A&M, was such that they placed four albums in the top ten at once, three others in the chart, totalling 13.7 million l.p. sales in 1966, more than double that of the Beatles' six million (figures from Murrell). In their tv special one of the few vocals they ever attempted was a tribute to 'California Girls', knowing it couldn't be done justice otherwise.

For the first time youth music outsold movie soundtracks, and at an astounding rate. A new group broke the Beatle record for advance sales—a million and a half, second only to the Tijuana Brass. Hyped by their tv series from September and with merchandising grossing $20 million in Monkee toys and clothes in three months, the heirs in preteen fan worship (via Herman's Hermits) more than matched the Beatles in album sales: 16 million worldwide in a little over two years of fame (*Entertainment Tonight*, 2002). "America's answer to the Beatles"—a year after the Byrds had been sold with the same title— were recruited by New York's powerful Tin Pan Alley entrepreneur Don Kirshner on charm and nicknamed "The Prefab Four": actors Micky Dolenz (drums) and Davy Jones, alternating as lead singers; and musicians Mike Nesmith (chief songwriter, lead guitar and B-side vocals) and Peter Tork (bass/keyboards). Some of their popular numbers were virtually Beatles/Herman's Hermits refrains, 'Daydream Believer', 'Cuddly Toy', performed on their show by Davy dancing a soft-shoe shuffle with boater hat and cane just as he had solo on Jack Good's '65 *Shindig* segment called "Music Hall".

Despite Kirshner's best efforts the individual talents of Nesmith and Dolenz managed to peek out—showing well-crafted pop with some guts. Kirshner learnt better—after the Monkees passed fabricating genuine cartoon cutouts this time: the Archies, who couldn't answer back, nor teach him a lesson in good taste. At first vilified when it was found out they didn't play their instruments on records, the Monkees went on tour to show they could. Then, when it was too late and they'd been written off by more fans, it could be seen that they were on a steep improve—finally slipping the clutches of their image minders but losing their corporate backing and thereby their popularity in the painful process.

Taken purely for their musical contribution, disregarding their rivalry in popularity/hype with the Beatles as a pop phenomenon, the best the Monkees produced argues against definitive, overwhelming Fab superiority. 'Mary, Mary', 'You Just May Be the One', 'Different Drum' and other songs written and produced by Mike Nesmith, 'Alternate Title' (a.k.a. 'Randy Scouse Git') by Micky Dolenz, and 'Words', 'She', 'Steppin' Stone' among others contributed by journeymen writing team Tommy Boyce & Bobby Hart, can stand with any of the tracks on *A Hard Day's Night-Beatles for Sale-Help!* and several mid-Sixties Beatle 45s. The American answers were fulsomely welcomed into the Fab circle when they visited England, hanging out with the four themselves. The Beatles admired the music machine the Monkees were surrounded by, with Kirshner as overlord and commercial songwriters on tap—probably only regretting they hadn't stumbled onto this kind of sure thing a lot earlier in their own career. Few exalt the Monkees today as a creative force worth commemorating though many of their records are well crafted songs by any standard. The difference, say diehard last-stand Beatle boosters, is that the Beatles improved after *Help!*— But did they?

VIRTUALLY UNTOUCHED BY SHOWBIZ HYPE, BRIAN Wilson's group set a *musical* scene, a rather inspirational one. Their regular Summer Spectacular, the third, kicked off at San Francisco's Cow Palace: "One of the most impressive gatherings of pop music talent ever assembled in the Bay Area will be presented at the Beach Boys concert Friday at 8pm.... Headliners will be, of course, the Beach Boys, to appear with eight other recording groups, most of which have recently had records topping the charts. They are Chad & Jeremy, the Byrds, the Lovin' Spoonful, Percy Sledge (he's a single, not a group), the Leaves, the Outsiders, the Jefferson Airplane, Sir Douglas Quintet and the Sunrays" (Oakland Tribune article 'All This Talent in One Show', 18th June). A repeat performance due to high demand played the Hollywood Bowl.

Here the Beach Boys were mentoring the cream of new talent: the Byrds, winning credibility as more than Yank Beatles with 'Eight Miles High' and within eight months to have their career scuttled by radio executives for 'So You Want to Be a Rock'n'Roll Star' about showbiz and its fakery; Lovin' Spoonful, even more impressive, at pop pinnacle with 'Daydream', 'Did You Ever Have to Make Up Your Mind?', and 'Summer in the City' about to blow. Soul's Percy Sledge had headed Billboard days before with 'When a Man Loves a Woman'. The Sir Douglas Quintet were Tex-Mex forerunners of ZZ-Topp. California's Leaves were in the lineup on the strength of their minor hit 'Hey Joe'—to provide Jimi Hendrix with his UK breakthrough at the end of the year. New San Francisco band Jefferson Airplane, still a year away from classics 'Somebody to Love' and 'White Rabbit', were replaced by cult favorite Captain Beefheart for the Hollywood gig. The Outsiders were a successful r&b outfit on Capitol. The Sunrays were easy to arrange through Murry Wilson. Now well off the charts but still as Brits given top billing among the support acts by the reporter, Chad & Jeremy were those same English makeweights sighing over gentle summer breezes.

The personal-professional closeness of, collaboration among, and Beach Boys' leadership over the California groups is a fact lost to rock history, due to a specific event one summer later when the Boys would be labeled anachronistic misfits. Byrd leader Jim (later Roger) McGuinn credited 'Don't Worry Baby' with inspiring his group's studio treatment of 'Mr Tambourine Man', in their distinctive guitar-bass drum accented offbeat. Outside of California, Lamont Dozier, one third of Motown's classic writing-producing team Holland-

Dozier-Holland, has said that through this period his creative team was closely watching what Brian Wilson was doing as much as they were Paul McCartney.

These were simple matters of fact—that the Beach Boys were not only at the forefront of rock in America but treated with paramountcy by their new peers, *at least* on a par with the Beatles. But in the spotlight under the eagle eye of the fashion monitors the unwary Californians undid themselves with patent uncoolness, for tv's *Andy Williams Show* trotting out'Help Me Rhonda', a year old; 'Little Honda', two; *a capella* 'Their Hearts Were Full of Spring' — beautifully done but outdated by definition: the Beatles didn't (couldn't) do that. *A capella*/street-corner singing had peaked in the Doo-Wop era but went out with a thud on the British Invasion, which cared little for pristine voices and the humble self-revelation involved in putting oneself out there emotionally. It would be decades before it was cool again. What better opportunity—network tv seen internationally—to introduce *Pet Sounds* as a new signature to counteract the damage done by Capitol's retrograde policies? It wasn't done.

But across a globe that moved behind the trends, they rode a heaving swell of acclaim as they finally wrested the best musical artists' mantle from the Beatles—a safety net that would catch them on their fall from grace in America. Their touring schedule alone earned them $2 million in the year to August '66, say $100 million in this era of inflated concert prices. Apart from the all-important Anglo axis, impressive sales reports came from the Far East, Latin America and Europe/Scandinavia. Highly popular in some Iron Curtain countries of Eastern Europe, their records had to be smuggled in from Finland or Germany. The Beach Boys' universality, long before the days when a saturation worldwide market was assured by just being a celeb, carved them out a winner's place in rock history.

'BARBARA ANN', THE FIRST OF FOUR NO.1s IN A row at Radio Caroline—something the Beatles didn't achieve that year—shouted their UK arrival. 'Sloop John B' confirmed their indelible imprint on British society—5th in Record Mirror/BBC's year-end survey in chart points, 'God Only Knows' 8th, 'Good Vibrations' 6th in sales; not achieved by any American act before but Elvis. Unlike the Beatle triumph in the US it happened against all the odds at a time English pop stars were envied by all. Beyond that 1966 was a year the English were feeling fiercely patriotic. The Labour government was sponsoring "Buy British" campaigns to spur the economy. The Beatles and accompanying cultural revolution led by EMI around the world was a great export drive. 'I'm Backing Britain' was a public catchcry, made into a pop song. In June, England hosted and won soccer's World Cup, *the* premier international sporting championship, for a game they had invented and nurtured around the world. In autumn it commemorated the 900th anniversary of the Battle of Hastings, the founding event of the English kingdom. Yet, weeks later the Beach Boys, perceived as the most American of all pop groups, would prove England's most popular stars.

Their UK tour in November, supported by Lulu and other Brits, was their first presence in two years, led by a Bruce Johnston visit months before to promote *Pet Sounds*, assisted by The Who's Keith Moon. Most popular with British girls too was Denny Wilson, combining a "Hang ten today, for tomorrow we hangover" rock-drummer oath *a la* Keith Moon with the spectacular looks of Georgie Best, Manchester United's Irish soccer bad-boy who also sported a Beatlesque cut and would burn out his mercurial genius on addiction to booze and sex. Twins in temperament, in the late-Sixties Georgie and Denny were even bets as Britain's top groupie magnet.

Escaping the two-dimensional surfer dude image tagged on him, Dennis was the first Beach Boy to develop un-American *chic* with their rapidly broadening outlook as the well-travelled group came to look at home amid British and Continental surroundings. They took on an international hue at the same time as they entered a phase of experimental music that would last through the next six years. America, for the most part, stayed happy with Beatle mixing and matching: rock-and-rolling well enough for enough people, throwing in old singalongs and other stock styles.

August was also the month of the Chinese Cultural Revolution, starting with a mass Peking rally choreographed by self-ordained megalith Mao Zedong and resulting in the death or exile of millions. America struggles with race riots each summer and now anti-Vietnam War demonstrations, while the British armed forces finally abolish their color bar. Two years later polls still show three-quarters of the public support right-wing leader Enoch Powell's white-only immigration policy. Dearer to Britons' hearts, Mary Quant, fashion designer, is awarded an OBE by the Queen, a higher honour than the Beatles.

Bob Dylan, injured in a motorcycle accident near his home at Woodstock, releases *Blonde on Blonde*, with *Revolver* and *Pet Sounds* representing 1966's creative triumvirate. The Beatles and Rolling Stones are about to cease touring; Dylan will be out of the public eye three years. They know how to play the media, and their public. The Beach Boys, too unassuming and accessible, lack superstar mystique.

A last, ill-fated Beatle tour starts July 1st, Japan. There are threats from nationalists irked that the ancient, sacred Budokan Hall is used for a frivolous pop concert. Three days later in the Philippines there is the famous snub when Brian Epstein decides the group wouldn't attend the opening of a children's welfare home with Imelda Marcos. Vilified by the local press, deserted by Marcos strongmen as security, the Beatle entourage is lucky to flee the country unharmed apart from sundry kicks and punches.

America and its entertainment industry are still officially awed by the Beatles. But from some there is a feeling of love unrequited. In June the group hadn't had to show for the latest tribute by the Sullivan show—just phone it in via promo clips of new double 'Paperback Writer'/'Rain'. Competing for space is news of the OD death of legendary New York comedian Lenny Bruce, a genuine breaker of social taboos; and Sinatra's wedding to Hollywood starlet Mia Farrow, young enough to be his daughter's kid sister.

Early August when the USA leg of the tour is due to resume the essence of a John Lennon interview published months before in Britain leaks through to American christians—enraged at Lennon crowing that his group is more popular than Jesus Christ. An apology of sorts leaves a nasty taste in many mouths and among some former fans the air of happy-go-lucky chirpiness comprising the Beatle image is replaced by disillusionment, in others the certainty that this proves the Beatles' importance and it's only Northern honesty on Lennon's part to "call a spade a bloody shovel". Some radio stations in the South and Midwest boycott Beatle records, breaking vinyl for news cameras. Rage boils over at their Memphis concert, and they are pelted with garbage.

The Beatles leave the concert stage for the last time August 29th '66 at Candlestick Park, San Francisco—their individual feelings varying from ecstatic to overjoyed. It has been a whirlwind three years and they have had enough of their relationship with their public. Desire for fame was satisfied. On the other side millions cling to hope for years—generations—that they will reform. Five months after they quit, Sid Bernstein, the New Yorker who had backed a long shot, surmising that musicians couldn't just stop playing, offered them a cool million to replay Shea Stadium. He would have had to charge at least $20 a ticket ($1,000 today) just to recoup his outlay—but there were enough rich or desperate Beatle fans to make it viable. They weren't having any, content for the rest of the Sixties to rest on their laurels and make, for the most part, strange tracks that mostly Beatle fans, specially attuned to Beatleisms, fully comprehended and appreciated. There was still plenty of punning to be made and Music Hall routines to be got out of their systems, even a few rock gems— spitting from the cauldron almost incidentally as if they couldn't tell the difference.

7: PET SOUNDS *rebounds from* RUBBER SOUL — *gunned down by* REVOLVER

On hearing the Beatles' Rubber Soul Brian Wilson was spurred to create an album of songs that "sound like they belong together, like a collection of folk songs". The Beach Boys had done that with their first album, and each song distinctive. What the Beatles had really done was create an album of mood-related songs with an unvaryingly sombre tone. Wilson's group would try it, but he was temperamentally incapable of being monotonous.

By the US media and as the legend has gone ever since, Pet Sounds *was a flop album. The greatest masterwork of the Beach Boys, America's greatest-ever band, was said to have failed precisely in the terms that America appreciates best: dollars. Until the year 2000 it had never been awarded an RIAA Gold Disc to confirm a mere 500,000 sale. Then a three-month audit by Capitol, not counting "missing paperwork", tallied 670,000 copies over the previous 15 years and estimated a lifelong US tally of two million-plus—ranking it well up among their studio albums, all assuming naïvely they didn't have paperwork problems too. Lyricist Tony Asher's earnings from it were $60,000 by 1990—his cut of royalties at one quarter of 1%, implying world revenues by then of $24 million for known sales. Given that its price ranged under $5 in its heyday this might extrapolate to six million units by now. Even the boring 4-CD 'documentary'* Pet Sounds Sessions *(1996) quickly went gold in the US.*

It took the rock world by storm—the Beach Boy image unrecognisable under a sophisticated veneer—and softened the ground for Revolver *three months later. In this new millennium the album that has been most frequently voted the greatest of all, ever, is one that, according to the angle perpetuated by the press, came out of the blue, a fluke—the one (grudgingly) acknowledged work of genius supposedly by an idiot-savant cum schizophrenic. The same consensus of rock critics who hold his band up as America's most important ever belittles their other work in relation to the Beatles'.*

But Brian Wilson had been in direct competition with the cleverly crafted songs of Lennon-McCartney-Martin for more than two years. His highly developed sense of rivalry had finely wrought a style more distinctive and more celebrated than any other in modern pop, apparently without any reference to the Beatles or other contemporaries. Was it enough?

*R*UBBER SOUL, THAT 'PROVED' BEATLE PRIMACY, began recording on October 12th 1965, five days after The Moors Murders were reported to the police by a witness —a graphic shock to Britain with its unfathomably (to Americans) low murder rate: a series of sado-sexual snuffings-out of children on the bleak moorland above Manchester, committed (and recorded for their own enjoyment) by an ordinary young couple.

The day after the Beatles got underway the Beach Boys started work on 'The Little Girl I Once Knew', unattached to an album, and Brian was working solo on the first vocals for 'Don't Talk (Put Your Head on My Shoulder)'—for *Pet Sounds*, postponed by Capitol's insistence on new l.p. product by Xmas: hence the stop-gap *Party* released November 8th. For two days Brian holds court over a 40-piece orchestra led by Four Freshmen veteran Dick Reynolds. He goes home filled with ideas about how to apply orchestration to modern rock and starts sketching them out.

Rubber Soul accompanied 'We Can Work It Out'/'Day Tripper' in release the first week of December and set a US record of a million sold in a week. In Britain the 45 was their most popular post-1964, but album sales didn't approach their usual flood.

The double and upcoming single 'Nowhere Man' were by far the most commercial songs on the album but with all that—under the direct influence of Bob Dylan—the basis of the group's critical cred had shifted from their hit-making ability to a consistent general standard. So while 'If I Needed Someone' (by George), 'In My Life' and 'Norwegian Wood' were poignant and 'Drive My Car' and 'Run For Your Life' deserving as well, non-entities such as 'I'm Looking

Through You' and 'What Goes On?' were deemed quality because, given Beatle magnitude and their songs' huge exposure, every one found followers. Still, there are three tracks I can't recall hearing.

A vaunted innovation was the sitar on 'Norwegian Wood'— remembering that Shel Talmy had applied a sitar sound on Kinks single 'See My Friend'). What the Beatles did had to be successful — so the Stones used one on 'Paint It Black'. Used out of context of Indian music—also on Petula Clark's 'Color My World'—it lends a quirky trendiness rather than integrated musicality.

Since 'Yesterday' on *Help!* statisticians had been totting up cover versions of Beatle songs. That one reaped nearly 1,200 and now 'Michelle' from *Rubber Soul* scored half that—still a large tally. The similar 'Girl', this time from John, probably did well in the cover department too. They were all that kind of song—simple and memorable, of the kind that café and cabaret singers could take endless stabs at in the pre-karaoke era. Paul McCartney: "'Michelle' was a joke really. A French tune that you may hear at a party and you'd parody it to death" (Pritchard & Lysaght).

October 26th the Beatles, minus George Martin, had received their MBE medals from the Queen, recognizing their export value —the next bonanza, *Rubber Soul*, due for the Xmas market around the world. Interviews of George Martin in Pritchard & Lysaght's *The Beatles: an Oral History* show how integral he still was—three years on—to the whole process of creating Beatle music. "If there was a keyboard used it was generally me who played it... I was responsible, generally, for the solos. I don't mean that I would write George's solo necessarily, although sometimes that did happen, but I would say, "Right, we need a solo here." Or "We need a line here. How about this?" For example, in the song 'In My Life' I played the harpsichord solo. There was a gap in the song... They went away and had their tea... I wrote something like a Bach invention, and played it, then recorded it... They said, "That's fantastic. We don't need more. That's it." Later on, when we came to do the middle of 'Michelle', I actually wrote that."

In the works was a Beach Boy album to top the Beatles. Like other rare works of art that also qualify as creations of the soul, the impression looking in at Brian Wilson's soul is deep and enduring, a claim never really made for Beatle music, in contrast—and as admitted by John Lennon. The Beatles' recorded music was often exciting and sometimes even brightly toned, but always seemed infused, at its core, with the inhibitions of Englishmen. Their rivals' greatest album is generally not fully appreciated on first hearing but grows inexorably, immensely, on repeated listening.

ANYONE WITH A REASONABLE KNOWLEDGE OF Beach Boys music sees *Pet Sounds*, far from a one-off, as a natural development of a thematic tone obvious from the time of *Beach Boys Today* (its revered "slow side": 'Please Let Me Wonder', 'I'm So Young', 'Kiss Me Baby', 'She Knows Me Too Well', 'In the Back of My Mind')—and apparent in Brian Wilson's work from starting recording four years before in 'Surfer Girl', 'Lonely Sea','In My Room'.... Now in *Pet Sounds* he gave his music an orchestral setting—beautiful and moreover lending it a certain snob appeal that impressed culture vultures who wouldn't have bothered otherwise with such an obviously suburban figure.

In what the world construed as a sudden shift, Brian, left alone in the studio for once, was creating a personal masterpiece, honed to perfection without the pressure of others looking over his shoulder. But the legend that *Pet Sounds* is the one album on which the Beach Boys played not a single note is not quite right. After the band returned from their Japanese tour they got together on 'That's Not Me' with Carl, Dennis and Brian (organ) all playing. Brian as ever played bandleader and choir master on all tracks. Since summer 1963 he had employed the best musicians available, whether in the group or not. His second group still featured Hal Blaine on drums, Glen Campbell (guitar/banjo), Carol Kaye (bass) and other regulars from LA's "Wrecking Crew" as well as legendary black saxophonist Plas Johnson. Now symphonic players too were collected for their technical expertise and compliance to Brian's instructions, not for creativity. He cajoled all into a cohesive ensemble interpreting his most subtle nuances of tone, as the Beach Boys themselves had become used to.

No wonder the touring band was nonplussed. Said UK bible Melody Maker, "It was immediately obvious that Brian had travelled further than anyone in popular music, extended its scope beyond a fantasist's wildest dreams. *Pet Sounds* was a massive elaboration on the more interesting aspects of his earlier work; the harmonies were denser, structured in myriad layers, achingly lush, yet pure... It was the arrangements that blew minds. Brian had used a bewildering array of resources, more than Spector and the equally iconoclastic Burt Bacharach combined." To celebrate it, unselfishly, Rolling Stones manager Andrew Loog Oldham took out a full-page ad urging people to buy it.

Certainly, what stands the album above other 'pop' is not only the composition but its perfection particularly in arrangement. This is not the studio sanitisation of recent decades, interpreted as 'technical perfection' by today's critics: Brian's commands to instrumentalists ("Drums!") are audible in places. While the composition phase has an inevitability about its sequence of notes, as has been said about Beethoven—unlike the Beatles, renowned for their quirky twists—it still fills repeat listeners with surprise and delight. One gets a similar sense about The Who's sixties hits— maybe related to Pete Townshend's early affinity with recording technology. It has become a truism about Beach Boys music (and for different reasons the electronic tracks of the Beatles), that much of it is difficult if not impossible for other musicians, no matter how skilled, to reproduce never mind interpret.

The *piece de resistance* is that exactly the right instruments are chosen for each passage no matter how unconventional, e.g. the Japanese koto. What is played and how it is played is so right. As has been told so often, one can picture Brian going to each musician and showing him or her how to play to elicit just the right strain of emotion; and his vocalists—the Beach Boys—the same. Still, from the bewildering jumble that is the *Pet Sounds Sessions* it is impossible to see how a coherent work is finally delivered, never mind the unquestioned masterpiece it is. We can only stand back and marvel at the creative process of mind and heart that results in the finished work.

The supreme test of Wilson's achievement as a pure composer is that the two instrumentals, originally intended to have lyrics, stand as wholly finished works and lack for nothing—a testament to wordless poetry, pure music unadulterated by any other consideration like 'profundity' of lyrics. In *Q* magazine's September 2004 roundup 'Pet Sounds' was judged among the fifty greatest instrumentals of all ('God Only Knows' ditto in the ballad section).

As has been remarked on by many critics, perhaps coming new to Beach Boys music, the harmonies move in striking counterpoint as on the *a capella* break in the middle of 'Sloop John B', throughout 'Wouldn't It Be Nice?' and in the cyclical end of 'God Only Knows'. But what most appreciators of the new music have found most impressive had always been there—Brian's own transcendently expressive vocals for 'Caroline No', 'I Just Wasn't Made for These Times', 'You Still Believe in Me'…. In Europe it was fully appreciated for its startling emotional/artistic impact as an integrated whole which springs from every track.

RECORDING CONTINUED AT A SANITY-SAPPING PACE that had delivered five album-length projects in a 14-month span. *Party* was according to some sources their fastest-selling yet but was never awarded Gold. Over that winter the young advertising agency jingle-meister Tony Asher had observed Brian at home every day—the better to devise figure-fitting lyrics for his songs. Not least of Brian's abilities was in choosing a lyricist to work most perfectly toward his current aim: Gary Usher or Roger Christian for technical-teen appeal; Mike Love for the telling cultural image; on occasions his brothers, frequently *himself*.

The 'adult' lyrics Brian chose from Asher—which superficial observers have hailed as the big advance over Brian's previous songs—can be put down to the advertising profession wordsmith. Taking 'You Still Believe in Me' as typical, they are hardly passionate, more adult in a certain sense, meaning more of the 'grown-up', corporate world, but (mostly) they are non-intimate, even impersonal: They are not the kind of sentences a man would actually *say* to a lover, at least not one is close to; rather the politically corrected, gender-sanitised kind from a counselling session or *Oprah/Dr Phil* tv show.

Since when has passionless prose been a criterion to judge a work of art? Compare it with Brian's usual confessional, conversational style, say in 'Let Him Run Wild'. Statements on the world in general or personal expression? For this album, in this way he did emulate Bob Dylan, and the Beatles, who had recently switched from personal-pronouned—if not exactly personal—to pontificating lyrics ('We Can Work It Out', 'Nowhere Man'). It might be politics but is it art?

For four years so far, the last two in stiff competition with the Beatles, the street-savvy influence of Mike Love's lyrics in the Beach Boys' rock'n'roll had brought out the group's broad commercial appeal, while the emotional B-sides—'Don't Worry Baby', 'Wendy', 'She Knows Me Too Well', 'Let Him Run Wild'—had come direct from Brian's soul. Mike drove the group's hit status; Brian's overall creative command dictated that he push boundaries, whether the results were saleable to a mass public or not.

Capitol saw it differently. Having just had huge world hits with upbeat treatments of 'Barbara Ann' and 'Sloop John B'—still approaching its sales peak in Europe as *Pet Sounds* went to the presses—it wasn't about to go with a downer: an entire album exploring Brian Wilson's fragile soul, no matter how deep. Here was a man more capable than anyone else in pop music of expressing his emotions directly through music—and "They just didn't get it" (Bruce Johnston). Even many admirers including this writer had to take a couple of steps back on first hearing the album, such was its advance over *everything* else in pop. From the Beatles, Capitol had received a nonstop string of tunes everyone could sing along to, and now they were deemed to be important too. Why couldn't this boy genius produce the same? His avowed philosophy, "I've never written one note or one word of music simply because I think it will make money" was hardly in accord with the label's fiscal ambitions. Despite reported admiration from some at Capitol the blanket resistance can be judged from the fact that even the bands good 'insider' friend Karl Engemann is reputed to have pleaded, "Cant we have some more songs like 'I Get Around'?" Repeatedly summoned to Capitol Tower in Hollywood to please explain, at the last meeting Brian attended he refused to utter a word and instead played to the executives prepared tape loops of potted answers "Yes", "No", "No comment", "Can you repeat that?"

They initially flatly refused to release the album, and only relented when Brian threatened never to make another record for them. A compromise was reached—inclusion of the out-of-place 'Sloop John B', though its adventurous arrangement and sound meshes in with the original material.

Obviously, having zero confidence in the album—an attitude borne out by the execs' lacklustre promotion of it—Capitol sought to salvage a few sales through the hit at no extra expense. The label committed money to the first of the *Best of the Beach Boys* series. Capitol's denial of the new music—misleading the public by highlighting the hit—was a crisis for the group. The Beach Boys' business partner was effectively sidelining them by refusing to build a wider audience, so favoring the Beatles in their ongoing contest.

Brian acceded against his better judgment, only to be double-crossed by Capitol, pushing heavily the compilation mostly made up of songs from 1963—a planet light-years away from where the group was now. Five weeks after making Billboard, July 2nd, *Pet Sounds* hit #10. The label issued *Best of the Beach Boys* three days later and the masterpiece went no further, clinging on two more months top twenty. Five days after the compilation, in accord with its back-to-the-future mentality, Capitol reissued an anachronistic 'Help Me Rhonda'/'Do You Wanna Dance?' double *one week* ahead of the should-have-been showcased 'Wouldn't It Be Nice'/ 'God Only Knows' from the new album. Having put off the real double for so long, this left a yawning gap of two months with no Beach Boy single on the charts, and the favored *Best of...* inevitably overshadowing the new material left without a single to promote it (and vice versa).

In what would be a coincidence only to a blind optimist, Brian's third major nervous breakdown struck him soon after release of *Pet Sounds,* sensing what was in store. The question has to be asked, What was in their corporate mind, if anything? If the label was *compos mentis* the stakes must have been high to warrant pulling the rug out from such an important act—at potentially a substantial loss of profit. Was it a business write-off as far as Capitol was concerned—worth it to turn this group around? Better to stick to promoting the mod quirkiness of the Beatles, reissues of classic fifties Frank Sinatra and Dean Martin, *and early-sixties* Beach Boys, with their assured, predictable markets?

Mike Love, in retrospect (1975): *"Pet Sounds* in 1966 was the climax of our new group awareness of more positive and emotional issues. Capitol wanted *Shut Down Vol. 5*. They released *Pet Sounds* but they didn't promote it very strongly...". "Mr Positive Thinker" as he called himself had put a 'positive' spin on the album.

THE TOURING GROUP BACK IN FEBRUARY, BRIAN placed their vocals: He had done demos of the lead and harmony parts himself, to such an extent that it was looking like a solo album. The completed 'Caroline No' track was released as a solo early March. Inevitably it flopped once caught up by 'Sloop', issued two weeks later. In the circumstances it probably shocked Capitol as a nice little earner, keeping pace in many markets. One of the album's key tracks but lacking a recognisable "Beach Boy" sound or label, it deserved better according to record-buyers in Canada, Chicago, Los Angeles, the Central Valley, upper New York, Salt Lake City, Milwaukee and Billings, Montana —all places where it entered top 20; the ten in San Jose, Orlando, Boston-New England, the Ohio River Valley in Cleveland and Louisville, and in Wisconsin, where it was broadcast hundreds of miles from clear channel station WSPT, Stevens Pt. Again New York City—where the song was listed at #57 by WMCA—had the casting vote over what America liked and didn't like.

Brian's voice came through too on 'Sloop' (reproduced by Al or Carl in concerts); and 'Wouldn't It Be Nice?' (Carl, live), Mike subsidiary verses or the bridge on each. Brian's original vocal of 'God Only Knows' was excellent but Carl replaced him and made a classic of it. Of the rest, 'Here Today' (a UK cover hit, and in San Bernardino), 'You Still Believe in Me', and 'I Just Wasn't Made for

These Times' appeared on compilations, growing familiar to a broader public. The instrumentals and four other tracks by no means suffer for their lack of fame: 'Don't Talk (Put Your Head on My Shoulder)', Brian emoting in similar fashion to 'You Still Believe in Me' and perhaps not often reissued for that sole reason; his 'Hang On to Your Ego' substituted by Al to better effect as 'I Know There's an Answer'; dynamic 'I'm Waiting for the Day' (Brian again), alternately gentle and commanding with its kettle drums; and 'That's Not Me' (Mike), probably the least commercial song—but with Brian, Carl and Dennis accompanying making it special.

Listened to today the most spectacular rock treatments on the album, 'Wouldn't It Be Nice?' and 'Sloop John B', sound every bit as overtly exciting as Rolling Stones rockers. In fact there is an unmistakable kinship arising from this album. Disregarding the Beach Boys' harmonies, which anyway sound nothing like their usual Four Freshmen-influenced style (on 'Wouldn't It Be Nice?' Brian took six months to get the harmonies to his liking, so exacting had become his aural vision), they and the Stones almost meet in their sheer force of vocal and instrumental drive. Given juxtaposed listening the resemblances seem obvious, posing the likelihood of influence of passages from 'Here Today' on 'Jumpin' Jack Flash', or 'Pet Sounds' on 'Honky Tonk Women'. Certainly, the chording and pacing similarity between the later 'Wild Honey' and 'Street Fighting Man' are striking.

While the Beatles fought it out with the Stones in whipping up fans' adrenaline they looked elsewhere for their music model— continually. In the early days it had been Lonnie Donegan, Elvis Presley, the Everly Bros; by 1963 Carole King, Motown and unnamed "current Americans" obviously including the Beach Boys and probably (judging from results) Burt Bacharach; the following year Bob Dylan. From spring 1966, when John Lennon and Paul McCartney, at Andrew Oldham's residence, listened and relistened to the acetate recording of *Pet Sounds* brought from America by Lou Adler, the most apparent direct influence on them—apart from the ever-present Music Hall tradition—is the Beach Boys. From testimony by Paul McCartney and others who knew the Beatles well, and from internal evidence, they drew on Beach Boy material from 1965, from *Pet Sounds* and from *Wild Honey*. In *McCartney* (1998) Paul's mid-Sixties associate Barry Miles, confirmed by Beatle producer George Martin, says they saw the Beach Boys as their creative rivals: "The real contender was always Brian Wilson... He had managed to reach the top several times in charts dominated by British Invasion groups but commercial success was not his main interest, though it was for the other Beach Boys." Miles does not draw the conclusion nearly far enough. McCartney has for forty years called 'God Only Knows' the greatest song ever written, and he spent four of those years trying to emulate it.

Brian's bass guitar roots specifically brought effusive compliments from Pete Townshend and McCartney: "*Pet Sounds* blew me away. It's still one of my favorite albums. When I first heard it, I thought, 'Wow, this is the greatest record of all time!' Brian took the bass into very unusual places. The band would play in C, and Brian would stay in G. That kind of thing. It gave me great ideas. That musical invention of Brian Wilson was eye-opening, I mean, ear-opening" (from Pritchard & Lysaght, 1998). In Miles' biography, McCartney expresses a kinship with Wilson as a fellow writer of melodic bass lines, and waxes mystical citing him, himself and James Jamerson of Motown as the apex points of a geographical triangle (LA-London-Detroit) of influential bass-players. Father Murry, too, praised his son's bass lines and betrayed fatherly pride in speaking of Brian's "beautiful approach to rock'n'roll", impressed that he had come some way from rock'n'roll to his own preference for "good music"—orchestrated.

McCartney credited *Pet Sounds* as the inspiration for his *Sgt Pepper*—by which time the Beach Boys, or at least Brian Wilson, had pulled further ahead. Others who are said to have called it the best album ever range from Elton John to Tom Petty; and citing it as a major influence: New York City's pioneer of proto-Punk Lou Reed, Sonic Youth, and English favorites Oasis—often called the Nineties' echo of the Beatles.

Britain was in spring 1966 just catching up on the Beach Boy catalog. *Party*, with a timely release for once, exited top ten in April as *Today* (a year late) entered. It is no surprise that, asked a week after *Pet Sounds*' US release in May, British EMI said it had "no plans" for it. It was sheer public pressure that brought the far-advanced, much-feared album into EMI's plans. On grudging release in early July *Pet Sounds,* followed into top ten a week later by *Summer Days*, did all but reach the very top to the company's shock. It seems the UK headquarters had no more insight into (or interest in) great, truly innovative music than its American subsidiary. Three decades later it was voted by a panel of international critics assembled by The Times of London as the best album of the rock era, heading off *Sgt Pepper*. Another belated British accolade was an assessment by New Musical Express (October 2nd 1993) as "Greatest Album of All Time". As a satisfying double, upcoming 'Good Vibrations' would be dubbed by Mojo magazine (1997) "Greatest Single of All Time" heading a list of a hundred. But in May '66 when it counted, British EMI's belief in the Beach Boys' new music, if not a negative entity, was close to zero.

In the States it was a steady mover, taking a year to sell Gold. Number one featured album at WLS, Chicago's premier top 40 station, nationally it peaked on average only one or two chart places short of the Beach Boy albums immediately before and after; in Japan, the next biggest market, it did better than them. It was easily their most successful studio album ever in the UK: six months top ten. At the end of the year all the anti propaganda should have been put to bed by Cash Box's roundup of 1966's Top 100 Albums: 13th best-selling pop/rock album behind *Best of...* compilations from Herman's Hermits, the Animals and Stones, the Mamas & the Papas, *Rubber Soul* (5th), the Stones' *Aftermath, Out of Our Heads* and *December's Children*; four places ahead of *Revolver*, six ahead of *Beach Boys Party* and further back to Simon & Garfunkel's *Sounds of Silence, The Young Rascals*, the Byrds' *Turn! Turn! Turn!* and Lovin' Spoonful's *Daydream*. The leading albums of the Supremes, Four Seasons and Sonny & Cher were nowhere. But the story put about of the failure of new Beach Boy music— almost willed by British EMI and Capitol— simplified the choice between them and the two-forked Brit attack.

Capitol would continue to divert attention from the group's groundbreaking, Beatle-influencing music. In spite of all, 'Wouldn't It Be Nice?'/'God Only Knows' turned out one of the summer's two premier double-sided hits, outdone commercially by the Beatles' 'Yellow Submarine'/'Eleanor Rigby'. Both peaked in late August, the Fabs keeping the Beach Boys' 'God Only Knows' out of the number one spot in the UK. The same happened between the two groups' current albums.

ON APRIL 6TH AS 'CAROLINE' AND 'SLOOP' MADE strides up local charts the Beatles had begun work on *Revolver*, the album that continued the public eclipsing of the Beach Boys. The Fabs had unstoppable career momentum and it made sense when George Martin assigned novice engineer Geoff Emerick to take charge of sound. In the direction Beatles Inc was going it took an inexperienced whizzkid coming in fresh who could devise evermore contrived sounds to include on some of their upcoming albums.

George Martin: "With the new sounds on *Revolver* it was basically an attempt to get more colour into our records. I mean, The Beatles were always looking for new sounds... They didn't know much about instruments, though, which put pressure on me. They needed someone to translate for them. I was there..."

Donovan Leitch: "That was the breakup really with The Beatles, I think. Because Paul is so creative... Paul needed, at that time, somebody like me, who could sit around and jam with him. The Beatles didn't jam at that time. They made records" (both quotes from Pritchard & Lysaght).

It was at the end of summer 1966, three weeks after *Revolver* appeared—the time of their last concert at Candlestick Park, San Francisco—that the Beatles decided they had just done their last tour. Fourteen dates in eighteen days hardly added up to a demanding schedule, especially given their rather perfunctory 30-minute concerts—the idea was just to *see* the Beatles and scream your hardest—but they were exhausted and highly stressed by events unrelated to entertainment. The target of death threats from Japanese traditionalists, hounded out of the Philippines for offending ruling family the Marcoses, in America made to publicly answer for John Lennon's remark that the Beatles were more popular than Jesus: these were among the personal depths they had plumbed in the previous weeks that decided them.

Paradoxically, given the bad press later directed at McCartney for breaking up the Beatles, it was George Harrison who, in his first relaxed moment after the Candlestick concert, declared: "I'm not a Beatle anymore!" According to Beatle publicist Tony Barrow it was Harrison and Lennon who were most vehement against them ever becoming a genuine, performing band again. Brian Epstein, who had made looking after the Beatles his life—and would die within a year of dejection and neglect—knew better than to ever suggest it to them. Such was his state through drugs that he was no longer handling their affairs with his customary aplomb. It was not long, in November, that John and Paul on Mick Jagger's recommendation were seeking out accountant-to-the-rock-stars Allen Klein, wanting him to renegotiate the measly returns on their EMI contract.

Paul embarked on the first Beatle solo project, writing the soundtrack for a Hayley Mills film, *The Family Way*; and by the end of 1966 George had made a spiritual pilgrimage to India to meet the Maharishi Mahesh Yogi of TM fame and learn sitar from Ravi Shankar; and Lennon met self-described *avant garde* Paris-based Japanese artist Yoko Ono. It was the beginning of a great deal of free time—extending through the remains of their career— with little of genuinely outstanding quality to show for it turning up on vinyl. One well-coordinated group project was to grow Zapata moustaches, seen in recent 'spaghetti' Westerns. Uniformly trimmed to identical dimensions as if it was a business policy, they popularized a 'new' look around the world but this time missed out on a merchandising opportunity for Beatle moes.

Over summer the Easy Listening style that the Beatles brought back to popularity moves in on the MOR (Middle of the Road) space formerly reserved for soundtracks of musicals. In America trumpeter Herb Alpert & the Tijuana Brass, just becoming popular in Britain, are unassailable, almost matched by Streisand's *Color Me Barbra*, Sinatra's *Strangers in the Night*, *Dr Zhivago* soundtrack. Chad &

Jeremy, Peter & Gordon, Petula Clark l.p.s are consigned to the lower weekly top forty. The true Brit *avant garde* represented by *Kink Kontroversy* and The Who's *My Generation* miss even the weekly fifty.

Revolver features special Beatle material addressed to their fans — favorites like Harrison's 'Taxman', which leads it off. As unremarkable as this song is, his other two I can't recall ever hearing. It is full of these anonymous songs—and what does a Beatle song amount to when not overplayed on the radio? Disregarding the well known fluff—'Yellow Submarine' and 'Good Day Sunshine' —there are only three good songs on it identifiable by the casual listener: 'Eleanor Rigby', revealing McCartney's reverence for music history; 'Here, There and Everywhere' inspired directly by 'God Only Knows'; and 'Got to Get You Into My Life', said to be inspired by Motown—revealing what Paul thought Soul music was. It was his sole concession on the album to 'rock', of a kind that could easily be sung by Jack Jones, Tony Bennett or Sinatra.

But from here on there is a huge assumption from everyone that a group so famous and popular must be singular and special. In fact, they must be getting better as they go along, so why don't we admire the Emperor's new clothes and go with the flow? *Revolver* has in recent times taken the place for critics of *Rubber Soul* as Best-Beatle-Album-Of-All—a mighty high honor to confer given their status, but an award that somehow keeps changing over the years. Despite its uneven material—the trivial children's nursery rhyme 'Yellow Submarine' was its biggest hit and best loved song —it would go on to the turn of the millennium gaining ascendancy with the highly dubious *White Album* to the top of the Beatle catalogue.

A more realistic UK reception for *Revolver* (300,000 orders and final tally of 500,000) allowed the Beach Boys for the first time to catch up with their rivals. One day after the Beatle release date, August 6th, 'God Only Knows' stormed from #19 to #1 at the number one private station Radio Caroline—ensuring its place as one of the top sellers of the year. It stayed top for a rare second week, defeating 'Yellow Submarine'/'Eleanor Rigby' rising from #14 to #4. The American invaders—who had never played Britain and hadn't set foot on its soil in nearly two years—were keeping pace. *Pet Sounds* had been in UK release five weeks and was improving on the major hits they'd had this year with *Party*, *Today* and *Summer Days*. In another two months the first *Best of...* package would allow Brits to catch up on some more fragments of this puzzle from America.

With 'Tomorrow Never Knows' starting the *Revolver* sessions began Beatle-Corp's fascination with tape loops and the potential of *random* sound. John wrote the first verse and they couldn't come up with anything more. "We had to make it longer somehow and make it different, as well," Paul recalled (Pritchard-Lysaght). 'Inspired' by Stockhausen, "Paul found that by removing the erase head and putting a loop of tape on it, you could actually play a short phrase that would saturate itself. It went round and round and overdubbed itself... When you played it back it was cute to listen to... They each went home and made these funny little loops. I selected eight of them [and] put them all through a mixer... [With the eight tracks] we did many mixes and then decided which was the best one"—George Martin. This track, Martin says, was the start of Beatle psychedelia "and the forerunner of *Sgt Pepper*."

This approach to art wreaks of the convenient artist-can-do-no-wrong-even-subconsciously mentality that would eventually lead to visual/aroma artists defecating and smearing their product on walls, sure in the knowledge that *anything* that came from a self-proclaimed artist with enough sycophants in tow was art. For the worthy *Rubber Soul* Lennon & McCartney had received unbounded praise from all directions—and film director Alfred Hitchcock was deified by Truffaut and others after *Psycho* but hardly ever again produced anything worth watching. Lennon & McCartney did live on to produce golden fragments, Harrison to reveal 'While My Guitar Gently Weeps' and 'Something'. But in recent years the reputation of *Revolver* has even overtaken that of *Rubber Soul*, without justification as listened to with the naked ear.

Looking at the *Revolver* tracks, aficionados plump for 'I'm Only Sleeping' or 'She Said, She Said', or others based on something in their personal lives. And wasn't that the trick?—that the Beatles were so famous and central to Sixties youth culture that people *longed* to find something to relate to? Unbelievably, it was even more covered than *Rubber Soul*, "more than half a dozen other artists recording the songs before the album was on sale, followed by many more versions—all anxious to make or enhance their disc careers with a Beatles song" (Murrells).

Joseph Murrells, pop statistician and unconditional Beatle admirer, apparently ignorant of the roles of George Martin and engineer: "This Beatles album again demonstrates the incredible ingenuity of the group with its new sounds and new ideas. A wide range of musical influences were absorbed in the album including French horn, sitar, trumpet, clavichord, violin, viola and piano... This remarkable LP set a new direction for the pop music field." Murrells wrote off 'Good Vibrations' as a "catchy easy-driving song".

On the last day of 1966 a review panel at Melody Maker, unable to come to a decision, named both *Revolver* and *Pet Sounds* joint top album of the year. From that trade paper's spokesman, it is sobering to read now: "Because of the originality and exploratory character of the collection of Brian Wilson's compositions and productions, there was some reticence to release the album immediately in Britain. But the clamour of Wilson fans grew and finally we were transported by huge orchestral paintings that have never been heard before in pop music" (from Badman, 2004).

To support their Beatle choice Melody Maker was imaginative in avoiding describing the actual music: "After a succession of brilliant previous albums, The Beatles come up with one of their finest in *Revolver*, which contains the new Beatles classic 'Eleanor Rigby'. Every track has something new to say, from the wry humour of 'Taxman' to the weirdness and reverse tapes of 'Tomorrow Never Knows'.

The ongoing, unconditional adoration seemed to affect John Lennon's ego beyond all bounds, growing to divine proportions. He gave a serious interview to London's Evening Standard newspaper that put himself on a plane with Jesus Christ—but more commercially viable at the moment. Soon after the story was picked up by a Birmingham, Alabama radio station it was news around the world. Across the Bible Belt, of course, they destroyed Beatle records but there were already millions of devoted fans in America and there was no going back on their chosen religion. They were willing to swallow any explanation, if one was necessary at all. Surely the unvarnished truth is its own defense and Lennon was just being his honest, incorruptible self by telling the whole truth, no matter how unpalatable to others and coincidentally self-serving. Brian Epstein, however, insisted on a public apology of sorts, for PR purposes.

The press conference Lennon gave in response on the American tour is embarrassing to watch. He squirms right and left, managing to do everything but apologize, talking all around the subject and instead claiming that people had taken what he said wrong and blown it out of proportion—the line taken by the rock press ever since. One pictures this self-defined rebel as a naughty little boy back at Quarry Bank School, looking at his feet and shifting from one to the other trying to explain away his latest attention-getting exercise to the headmaster. Lennon's apologists claim his statement was taken out of context, even that he was being satirical and actually downplaying the Beatles in favor of Christianity. They are among the deluded who read things into Beatle history that just aren't there and stand 180 degrees opposed to historical fact. Here is the offending passage verbatim as quoted by Pritchard & Lysaght (p.217):

"Christianity will go. It will vanish and shrink. I needn't argue about that. I'm right and I'll be proved right. We are more popular than Jesus now. I don't know which will go first, rock and roll or Christianity. Jesus was all right, but his disciples were thick and ordinary."

There is nothing equivocal about this series of sequential, forthright statements. In fact it sounds like a North of England Labour politician railing with all the conviction he can bluff about the ultimate fate of capitalism and its supporters—or a self-appointed guru leading a new religion and nominating himself as co-deity. Lennon's puzzle is that this man who portrayed himself as one of the people was so insecure he had to lift himself above them. And that one who preached so much about love and peace, gave secret support to the Republican Party—who through Nixon and Kissinger waged war by napalming civilians far and wide across Southeast Asia. A citizen of New York City, Lennon was among the élite one quarter of the populace that supported Republican, Establishment policies.

A T THE END OF 1966 *PET SOUNDS*, DISMISSED BY Capitol in America as un-Beach Boy and given a reluctant airing by EMI in the UK after lengthy debate and hand-wringing hesitancy, registered in Britain as 4th biggest rock album of the year after the *Best of...* package, the Stones' *Aftermath* second, and the Beatles' *Revolver* interspersed with two Tijuana Brass and a Seekers'. Named in the official Record Mirror/BBC listings as that year's best-selling artists overall (ahead of Dave Dee, Dozy, Beaky, Mick & Titch and the Kinks), they were also best-charting album artists followed by the Beatles, Walker Bros, Stones and Tijuana Brass. They spent more weeks in the album chart than any other act, and would only be narrowly displaced in 1967 by the Brass and in '68 by Tom Jones and Otis Redding for third. They dominated this three-year period with 308 album-weeks, averaging two albums in the chart (still a top twenty) each week. The Sixties as a whole had the Beatles and Beach Boys as top group for album hits: thirteen.

Hits, an extended-play of '65 songs, set a never-to-be-broken record of 32 weeks at #1 to April 1967 on the soon-defunct e.p. chart. From an era of higher sales 1963's *Twist and Shout* remains highest selling e.p., 670,000 UK. The only Capitol e.p. to ever top in the UK, the Beach Boys' chart run of an extra fifty weeks was outlasted only by the Shadows (Sixties City website). E.p. sales are overlooked comparing Sixties hits with later ones; if counted, 'Barbara Ann' might qualify as a UK gold seller, and 'Help Me Rhonda', 'California Girls' and 'Little Girl I Once Knew' as accordingly bigger hits.

They were again bestselling album rock group in 1967—total chart points by Record Mirror/BBC statistics—with *Best of...* pointing ahead of the Monkees and the Beatles' *Sergeant Pepper*. (By the end of '68 it had only dropped to fourth, its 142-week chart run eventually overtaken by seventies Simon & Garfunkel's *Bridge Over Troubled Water* and Pink Floyd's *Dark Side of the Moon*.) *Best of...* was a household presence still recalled by a younger generation though remarkably only four of 14 tracks had made top twenty and included many obscure to Brit ears (see Appendix II for songs on compilations). *Surfer Girl*, supposed to be four years out of date, pounded surf music onto British shores, and the Beatles had their first lapse, peaking at #7 spot early in the year with the *Collection of Beatles Oldies*.

Yet in the UK the group suffered from the Jim Reeves/Seekers syndrome—selling mountains of records but hardly ever claiming the no.1 weekly spot. The Rolling Stones (eight) and Abba (nine) had soft chart toppers; Beatles too. 'From Me to You' (chart-run sales of 660,000) and 'Hello, Goodbye' (690,000), their ninth-tenth biggest sellers, hardly outsold the Beach Boys' no.2 sellers, yet each stayed an astonishing seven weeks on top. In 1966 the Beach Boys were officially the UK's Bestselling Artists—the Beatles a distant 9th—but who had three chart-topping 45s and album? Despite a continuing stream of no.1s the Beatles and Stones suffered a falling-off of domestic sales. Of the Stones' five biggest songs four are from '64-65; the Beatles' top six were all released '63-65. The Beach Boy top five include none pre-'66 and '68 and '70 releases.

'Good Vibrations' was, claimed an EMI book, "the first Beach Boys single to sell over a million in Britain" (cf. the Stones' top seller 'The Last Time' at about 850,000 with Abba's top, 'Dancing Queen'). Maybe it was taken just over the top by its revival—no.13 NME—ten years later. Then come 'Sloop John B' and 'God Only Knows', about half a million or so at a time of rapidly ebbing UK 45s sales; 'Do It Again', 'Cottonfields' less; 'I Get Around', 'Then I Kissed Her', 'Barbara Ann' Silver Discs; 'Break Away', 'Lady Lynda', 'Heroes & Villains', 'Darlin'', 'I Can Hear Music'…. If 'Wipe Out' (no.2) with the Fat Boys from low-selling 1987 is included it takes over ninth spot.

Through their banner year their world sales of 45s must have come to a ballpark 15 million, albums around half that. Over the next ten years NBC's network station in New York, major Top 40 programmer 66-WNBC, would tabulate their hits from this year as huge in ongoing sales across its 25-million-plus strong catchment. Of all songs from 1966, 'Good Vibrations' came in easily 1st; 'Wouldn't It Be Nice' 2nd only to its massive follow-up; 'Sloop John B' 9th and

'God Only Knows' 11th. A similar wide-ranging 1974 study by Philadelphia station WFIL found 'Vibrations' 3rd seller from 1966 sandwiched between 'Barbara Ann' 2nd and 'Wouldn't It Be Nice' 4th.

But pop culture is a game of immediacy—feeding millions of appetites for instant gratification—and if you don't want to play there are opportunists lining up from here to infinity to claim teen consciousness. The Beach Boys under Brian Wilson's new direction were gearing themselves instead for art appreciation, relying on gradually accruing cultural status. Having withstood the challenge from intellectuals, they were faced with an opposite appeal to juvenilia—the Monkees, promoted by tv, and personality-wise as the Beatles had been. Before long the Monkees' fame worldwide stood with that of the Beatles. But as a nationwide poll of teens demonstrated, fame and popularity were somewhat different things.

'Good Vibrations', released 22nd October, has been assessed world's best-selling record for six weeks until overhauled by 'I'm a Believer', written by Neil Diamond in teenybopper mode for the Monkees and force-fed to audiences the world over via television tube. It marked the Beach Boys' commercial high in France, going to no.1 in most charts early November, staying there through December and slowly descending (Music Media chart—Daniel Lesueur). Here they would be feted for some years to come for the artistry of their recordings, a love affair only the French could bring off without seeming sensually overindulgent.

THIS LATEST BEACH BOY HIT COULDN'T BE IGNORED by EMI in America either, and it became the first non-Beatle Capitol single since the Fabs hit to be awarded a Gold Disc by the RIAA. US sales passed half a million in its first week; the Gold Disc awarded after six weeks, as it hit number one and still had two months to run; chart run total estimated at two million. Japanese, UK and French sales would mount three million. While two sources give a global total of 16 million in six months, half this can be readily established. It was number one trans-Atlantic, trans-English Channel, and most of the rest of the world, and seemingly for evermore would be in an élite handful of most admired tracks.

'Winchester Cathedral', a criminal waste of vinyl, took the Grammy for, unbelievably, "Best Contemorary *Rock'n'Roll* Recording", defeating its famous nominee and sane judgment. If any one event pointed up the folly of the pop industry—and its futility as a field for a serious creative personality such as Brian Wilson—it was this. England's New Vaudeville Band voh-dee-oh-dohed through a megaphone in Twenties-Rudy Vallee style in an upper-crust Noel Coward voice: a drone of a novelty song duly re-recorded by Frank Sinatra (and 400 other acts), giving it his anti-rock seal of approval as he had done for placid Beatle tunes. The Great British Monster the Beatles created three years before turned on them as it became in the US the year's biggest-selling Brit single, steamrolling 'We Can Work It Out', 'Day Tripper', 'Nowhere Man', 'Paperback Writer', 'Eleanor Rigby', 'Yellow Submarine'. The Beatles claimed Song of the Year for 'Michelle'—the one Paul McCartney called a joke. And Paul—not Carl Wilson for 'God Only Knows' or 'Good Vibrations'—got Best Male Solo Vocal: 'Eleanor'.

It was time to look outward, and the superior UK compilation of *Best of...* complemented their first English concert tour. All the Beatles were fans, their repeated unselfish pushing of their rivals' music contributing to mounting sales and credit in Britain—and all four individually greeted the Boys, phoning in to their hotel. The first show was 6th November on touching down—then two shows per evening: London's Finsbury Park, a rest day; Tooting, Leicester, Leeds, Manchester, Cardiff, Birmingham in six days, driving 'Vibrations' to the top. Supporting them were Lulu; the inevitable English duo represented by David & Jonathan, of a lukewarm trans-Atlantic cover of 'Michelle'; and Sounds Incorporated, an instrumental combo that hit in '64 when even the Shadows were going out of date and so missed the Brit-boat to America.

Whirlwind as it was, the tour was a gesture to legions of British fans starting a series over the next four years that would assist mightily to maintain their world status as headliners in the coming lean years at home. Lulu struck up a friendship with Dennis, and later in her autobiography voiced the considered opinion that the Wilson brothers "were too sensitive for this world." This had manifested in their music—and in Dennis's childhood stutter, Brian's late-recovering bedwetting, and Carl's chronic flat mood, interpreted by onlookers as calm beyond his years.

The UK's top pop paper the New Musical Express announced that the showbiz world would "vibrate" with the news that the Beach Boys had been voted into the Beatles' place as World's Outstanding Vocal Group. Over Bruce Johnston's cringing disclaimers, Ringo remarked philosophically, "We're all four of us fans of the Beach Boys... Maybe *we* voted for them." The readers of Record Mirror confirmed they were most popular group in Britain, the new center of cool. Beach Boy stock in rock stood at the pinnacle —Across the rest of Europe too, in France, Germany, Austria as well as in Russia, Japan and the Philippines, they were voted top of the world.

'Vibrations' turned an exceptional year into a truly great one, raising their heads above the maelstrom of competing groups that reached an unprecedented quality in the latter half of 1966: 'Wild Thing', 'Summer in the City', 'Sunshine Superman', 'Sunny Afternoon', 'Black is Black', 'Reach Out', 'What Becomes of the Broken Hearted?', 'Have You Seen Your Mother, Baby?', 'Coming On Strong', 'Rain On the Roof', 'Hazy Shade of Winter', 'You Keep Me Hangin' On', two more by the Beach Boys—and possibly Sinatra's best ever, 'That's Life'.

It won them immense admiration from the general public— even in America. The annual Gilbert Youth Research poll of teens crowned them the nation's favorites. Taken early in 1967 and published in newspapers on March 2nd, it placed them out front, bar none. Their 10.8% vote share was decisive over a trailing clump of Rolling Stones on 7.9%, Monkees 7.6%, Beatles 7.1%. Next came the Supremes. Herman's Hermits at 9th were the only other English group of thirteen named: the Beatles and Stones were the only real survivors from the Brit Invasion after three years. The poll a year before had been swept by the Beatles on 75%!—showing that now Beatlemania was a thing of the past, replaced by Monkeemania. The difference was this time, with all the hype in the world, the hysteria was not so unreasoning as to displace the Beach Boys.

So, after almost five years as highly influential world stars, in a tumultuous decade when most acts that made it at all were history after a hit and a half, the Beach Boys had reached their summit— world's favorites until the Beatles hit back with 'Penny Lane'/ 'Strawberry Fields' and *The Monkees* tv series overcame a void of new Beach Boy material. Total absence from the airwaves—more than nine months between single releases and what seemed like interminable waiting that would extend to 16 months between albums—was an unprecedented hurdle in the context of rapid-fire Sixties pop. A lesser career would not have survived it.

IT'S A SOURCE OF HEAVY IRONY THAT, AS FICKLE fandom in their own country was beginning to sour, the Beatles and Stones more than ever appreciated their American colleagues—both knowing who was really advancing music. Mick Jagger was a longtime fan, taking time off from his Chicago Blues fixation to listen to the Beach Boys intently before the Stones' first tour. Paul McCartney, an admirer long before the Beatles landed, was arguably taken over zombie fashion by *Pet Sounds* and succeeding albums. This is self-evident in the music composed and issued by McCartney as the Beatles' prevailing force from 1966 on. And even in the music written by Jagger and Keith Richards for the Stones? Were the uncharacteristically gentle, psychedelic 'She's a Rainbow' and 'We Love You'—on which Beatles John and Paul provided backing—the Stones' reaction to the Smile Era?

Keith Moon, The Who's wildman, had long ago ceased being a lone herald of 'surf' music. But Pete Townshend, The Who's leader, was now a critic vividly expressing to the press his belief that *Pet Sounds* and 'Good Vibrations' had gone too far for rock'n'roll in their prettiness and studio 'overproduction', humorously accusing Brian Wilson of inhabiting a world "of flowers, butterflies and strawberry flavored chewing gum." For a working class hardman, raised in a musical family, Townshend's maturity lagged behind his creativity. Days after the Beach Boy 45's release in October, his own group coming off classics 'Substitute' and 'I'm a Boy', he ironically called on a group lately lacking in energy: "It needs The Beatles to come out of their hole and make a really simple pop record to sort things out." He got pop as simple as it can get in 'Winchester Cathedral', and later from the Beatles, after exhausting their taste for random electronics, 'All You Need is Love'. Ironically, outdoing pocket symphonies in grandiosity, Townshend would embark on a rock opera.

It was late summer '66 that Scotsman Donovan (Leitch) spearheaded the British Invasion's delayed third wave—actually more of a swell of acts who'd mostly been around in Britain for some time, with the Troggs along with him and The Who and Spencer Davis Group following months later. As close to Dylan as a professional imitator the year before, he transformed into world champion psychedeliac, gold with 'Sunshine Superman' and equally famous 'Mellow Yellow'. Both songs were highlights of the year with the Troggs' 'Wild Thing'. He was always poetic in the best sense but his popularity dipped a little as he got mystical—'There is a Mountain', 'Hurdy Gurdy Man'. His single-handed superiority over 95% of the Brits poses a mystery and travesty: Why does he hardly get a mention today up against the Beatles and Stones, having created music and lyrics more beautiful than either of them?

The steady impetus now came from American musos—Simon & Garfunkel, Hendrix, the Doors, sweeping away the exuberant innocence the Beach Boys stood for. The San Francisco cult bands Jefferson Airplane, Grateful Dead, Moby Grape, Buffalo Springfield, Big Brother & the Holding Company—of spasmodic album releases often betraying erratic ability—took more airspace as drug culture grew a cool image and took on the weight of a philosophy. Creedence Clearwater Revival would be the Beach Boys' replacements... of sorts, lacking whole dimensions.

8: SGT PEPPERS & THE LOST SMILE

'Good Vibrations' and 'Heroes & Villains', the Beach Boys' next pocket symphony long in brewing as a follow-up, stand among the greatest achievements of Sixties music and many say that's too small a claim. If critics thought Wilson's oeuvre had touched creative perfection with Pet Sounds, it was topped off with 'Good Vibrations'. As important was his solo recording of revelatory music that came to be known as Smile, spawning 'Heroes & Villains' but never released in its intended form.

While the Beach Boys retained the Sea and Sun as emblems, coming to celebrate them as conservationists with maybe the best-attuned music of the Rock Era in lyrical tributes to an elemental universe, a new all-pervasive 'wisdom' now directed musicians to shoot up and navel-gaze. Happy to reflect their environment in their songs as few popular artists could claim or even attempt, Beach Boys pursued Eastern mysticism as far as it suited them, reflecting its outer trappings hardly at all—They left Nehru jackets to the fashion-conscious Beatles. In the new arty world introduced by the Beatles as much attention had to be given to an album's cover as the music it contained. The new Western philosophy—and business directive— was: Dress the product up in art's clothing so fashion followers will know what music to buy.

In the absence of Smile, Sgt Pepper's would nullify the Beach Boys as popular challengers to the Beatles. The rejection by members of his own band of this second acknowledged masterpiece hit Wilson so hard that he retreated to an inner, safer world.

SIMULTANEOUS WITH RECORDING *PET SOUNDS*, ON February 18th '66 Brian laid down a basic track for 'Good Vibrations', a song that would take until 1st September to complete and employed six recording studios; takes from four were used on the final track including his favorite Western Recorders (engineered by Chuck Britz) and Gold Star (Larry Levine). While he tried out other majors' studios—Columbia and RCA, where he should have been able to expect support was avoided: Capitol, who had aided the less exacting Beatles on recordings.

Aside from innovative use of a variation on the theremin, whose wailing is heard above the chorus, there was an authentic rock treatment of cello for the first time, rhythmically and rapidly bowed unlike the Beatles' baroque use of it on 'Eleanor Rigby'. Forerunner of the Moog synthesiser, the theremin had been used in thrillers and sci-fi films, spectacularly by Ron Grainer & the BBC Electronic Workshop for tv's *Doctor Who* theme, and would appear prominently on upcoming 'Wild Honey'. The 'Vibrations' tapes, trimmed and seamlessly edited to three minutes and thirty-five seconds—a long track by Beach Boy standards—stamped an ethereal lightness of touch onto rock music. Without resort to raucousness they engendered more excitement than other acts. Maybe the most thrilling of many startling juxtapositions was the crashing snare and tom-tom in unison that came in on the lilting organ pulse. For once, the quality was duly appreciated by both critics and public.

Helping arrange the vigorous cellos for 'Good Vibrations' was former child actor Van Dyke Parks. By the time of its release he had replaced Mike Love as Brian's partner of the moment at the expense of the Beach Boys circle. Mississippi-born Parks had first travelled to California to be a beatnick folk singer, but on seeing the Beach Boys play at Newport Beach in 1962 dumped his career plans and switched to rock. They began work on *Dumb Angel*, said to have been Brian's nickname for brother Dennis, that was quickly shaping into the retitled *Smile*.

Brian attributes his rapid success with Parks to strategic use of uppers: "We were completely different individuals, yet with amphetamines pushing a freight train of ideas through our brains, Van Dyke and I enjoyed a compatibility that was inspiring." He intended to surpass *Pet Sounds* as part of a plan to "create a whole new form of music" in a "teenage symphony to God" (Brian Wilson.com). Grandiose, but who's to say he didn't achieve it? The question was: Would Brian's brothers empathise with his expansive new trip? The simple solution would have been for him to go solo at this point—that is, if he hadn't had the entire Wilson family to support and needed their emotional support in return.

"At a dinner party one evening early in October 1966 I played a handful of acetates including 'Wonderful', 'Holidays', 'Cabin Essence', 'Do You Dig Worms?' and a long, wild, early rendition of 'Heroes & Villains' that engendered such confused reaction I was forced to explain myself." How to justify music?—It either moves you or it doesn't. One of the few Parks lines approved by Mike Love, who thought (rightly, according to precedent) most of Van Dyke's poetic musings too obscure for Beach Boy music, was 'Heroes & Villains''s opening line—because it formed a complete, recognisable sentence.

About 'settlement' of the West, it was a historical theme they would explore repeatedly, speaking up for the native American. (The Shins' 2007 hit 'Phantom Limbs' echoes the theme, and uncannily their lead singer's voice is a perfect distillation of Brian-Al-Carl.) Grammatical or not, it was a radical departure from ad-man Tony Asher, from bushy bushy blonde hairdos, and the self-absorbed complaints of Dylan. Their middle-class-youth hedonism and Mike Love's down-to-earth materialism was pointedly missing. Brian had always been mildly eccentric but now that it had been validated by so much media attention it was as if he was rubbing fairweather fans' noses in his new image as "genius" cultivated by publicist Derek Taylor and New York columnists who'd been to interview him; and they would give him shit back. For Mike the hullabaloo was over the top and he dubbed his cousin's latest collaborations "Brian's ego music." By the time of a 1975 interview with Associated Press's Mary Campbell, Mike had come to see its importance, considering *Pet Sounds* and *Smile* their two greatest albums: "We intend to release *Smile* someday."

Dragged down by flack directed at the poetic obscurity of his lyrics, Parks took his talents as writer/producer to Harper's Bizarre ('Come to the Sunshine')—becoming the California harmony group of 1967 with '59th Street Bridge Song (Feelin' Groovy)', 'Anything Goes', 'Chattanooga Choo Choo'—and Sly Stone's Mojo Men ('Sit

Down, I Think I Love You'): deserting his gift for mystical grandeur for witticisms and Thirties retro.

The two would renew their collaboration in the '90s and again for Parks to create lyrics to complete the redone *Smile*; for now, it was stone dead. The group's insecurities about the new music would harm them before they realised it. Extended returns from France for 'Good Vibrations' and its delayed release in Germany, Italy and many a far-flung corner of the world shored up a false sense of security.

After that first lead-balloon audition of the first *Smile* tapes to friends, the 'Vegetables' sessions beginning in November would go down in legend as co-produced by Brian and Paul McCartney. Roger McGuinn and John Phillips, leaders of the Byrds and the Mamas & the Papas, attended also, to pay homage to the acknowledged uber-leader of California Music. For the first time a bridge had been formed between the highest form pop could aspire to and truly original music. A line had been crossed, and Brian would have hoped there was no going back. But in failing to communicate its importance to the group he believed—probably correctly— he was fatally overestimating listeners in general (H L Mencken: "No one ever lost money *under*estimating public taste.").

With 'Good Vibrations' at its height comes retro Beatle song 'Penny Lane', and finally, Paul's perennial reject the ten-year-old Music Hall number 'When I'm Sixty-Four'—no longer does he need others' approval to record any song. It is months later on April 10th that Paul observes Brian's 'Vegetables' vocal session, participating to the extent that he munches loudly on some for the track. Some might say coincidentally the day after on the flight back to the UK he conceives *Magical Mystery Tour*, beginning recording two weeks later.

The myth went that Brian incinerated the *Smile* tapes in a fit of LSD-induced paranoia on outbreak of a more-than-usual number of fires in conflagration-prone LA through the time the Fire segment of the 'Elements Suite' was being recorded. Directed by Brian and Parks, this session is said to have conjured pictures of a firestorm— doubtfully aided by Brian's request to Marilyn to buy fire helmets for

341

the session musicians. Supposedly, Brian performed a public service by junking thousands of man-hours of work in an effort to halt LA's fires.

Had *Smile* been showcased as intended it might have met a limited audience but it should have equalled or bettered the tremendous influence on rock (but largely kept secret by the media) that *Pet Sounds* had shown, particularly on rock culture's movers and shakers, i.e. the Beatles. Brian's limp later excuse for not pushing all out for *Smile*, "I thought it was inappropriate music for us to make," in the new millennium turned into "Mike Love hated it". Band members might be understood opposing it issued *under the Beach Boys name* but then why agree to the inferior *Smiley Smile?* —what could only be "a bunt instead of a home run," in Carl's words. Brian was now incapable, or unwilling, to push. Why he should have had to when the others had been riding on his train for five years is another question.

Dennis, who continued supporting Brian in his new music, set his gift for hyperbole in full flight: "In my opinion it makes *Pet Sounds* stink, that's how good it is." Some who heard fragments or 'song-bites' of it, and others who heard none of it, wrote the whole project off derisorily as one of history's great might-have-beens, a big-fish tall tale—the one that got away that will be forever spoken about in reverential tones like sighters of the Loch Ness Monster. These taunts would not be conclusively silenced for thirty-seven years, when revelation of any masterpiece in any art—taken well out of social context—would be a comparative anticlimax.

In fairness, with the boom-lowering Brian felt there was mixed in a strong element of cousinly/brotherly protectiveness towards him, who seemed prey to any new idea or drug proffered by hangers-on to the now hip Beach Boy scene. How to gauge what music he was producing was truly good and what might have been products of a dope hangover or random flashbacks—like Ebeneezer Scrooge's indigestible beef morsels after Christmas Eve overindulgence? Mostly, they judged it too big a step beyond current standards acceptable in the pop business. They'd gone far beyond the Beatles many times before and when the gulf deepened to a chasm with *Pet Sounds* they got severely burned for it.

Mike, ripped off of songwriting royalties by Murry and growing wary of Brian's other partners and the limited market for much of his cousin's new music, would come to oppose the Wilson faction, backed up by fellow healthy lifestylers Al and Bruce. He had led the singing on all 12 A-sides up to the end of 1964 but during 1965-69 would solo on just three, 'California Girls', 'Do It Again' and 'Bluebirds Over the Mountain', out of 18: amazingly laid back for a lead singer, even under the band's 'whatever's best for the song' philosophy. Brian, to keep peace and recognizing Mike's drive for group survival, later gave his proxy vote to his cousin. He and Mike had at the start, after all, been the most heavily into music and allies keeping the younger ones in line.

A much fiercer power schism now waged among the Beatles. John remained the nominal leader, but Paul had the drive to professional (and social) success and knew he was a readier composer and musician; he was John's one indispensible partner. George's songs were never in the race; few squeezed through the constant two-way balancing act. Making up recording schedules, Lennon-McCartney realised that while they shared composer royalty per track George's songs were all George's and albums where he had three or four earned him almost as much as each of his elders. McCartney songs won out in proven commerciality, John's more and more relegated to B-sides. By 1966 the other Beatles bitterly resented McCartney's success.

Another newcomer to Brian's world who grated with the Beach Boys circle was David Anderle, heading Brother Records, its mission to nurture artists in a sympathetic non-business atmosphere. Like the Beatles' later Apple, the brotherly side was fatally overdone and Brother would continue as not much more than an imprint on major labels. A promising signing was the Redwoods featuring Danny Hutton—a solo who had cruised on LA charts for years. Brian vetoed their tapes for a claimed propensity to sing off-key—letting them go to Dunhill, which would make millions from them as Three Dog Night, one of the biggest-selling acts 1969-74.

Carl nurtured South African group Flame, who were more impressive a few years later when two members (Blondie Chaplin, bass and vocals for 'Sail On Sailor'; Ricky Fataar, drums, and the

George Harrison character for *The Rutles* satire on the Beatles) lodged in the bosom of the Beach Boys for a couple of years. Dennis persevered with singer-songwriter Charles Manson long past the time it was healthy.

A T A TIME THEY WERE ENTITLED TO FEEL, FINALLY, on top of the world they were suffering through the protracted trauma that was *Smile*, delayed time after time, and they took yet another crippling blow to add to their trials. Days after he turned 20, on 3rd January 1967, Carl appeared in court to defend a charge of draft evasion—the most serious of several attempts on a Beach Boy by the Draft Board; the others obtained a variety of deferments/exemptions. The determination of the authorities to nab a Beach Boy scalp for the Vietnam War was as if the very existence of the United States was in jeopardy but for one Carl Dean Wilson wielding his state-of-the-art 12-string Rickenbacker in combat. Ignominious death in a paddy field had stared these unmatched world ambassadors of music up close in the face. It was not something the Beatles, styling themselves as spokesmen of the Peace Movement, would have to contend with. Times had changed since Elvis, Del Shannon and Gene Vincent went to do their patriotic chore to fight the Cold War in Europe. Vietnam—to see 58,000 Americans and countless others dead for no visible benefit—was not a popular war. Since Bob Dylan, Joan Baez and thousands had protested against it in London's summer of '65 only a growing casualty list was keeping America in the war—until it could withdraw "with honor" as politicians like to call it: a more respectable killing rate dealt out per body bag suffered.

It would be the Seventies before Carl's community service sentence was served to some hawk's satisfaction, maybe fearing he would wreak his pacifism on an unsuspecting public. Later that year Muhammed Ali was stripped of his world boxing title and sent to prison—maybe in the belief that a man who made his living pummelling others couldn't be that hard set against violence. Carl's penance involved hospital work with bedpans and charity appearances by the group, as they originally proposed. A sight more lenient than prison, it was still intentionally degrading unlike the *voluntary* entertaining most stars got away with in WWII while others laid their skins on the line for an incomparably worthier cause.

Just six months after their last visit, starting a new European tour in May, the Beach Boys were forced to play a dismal Ireland concert without Carl, arrested and detained for six days by the FBI until he proved he was a genuine conscientious objector. The group was fully supportive. Mike: "He doesn't mind serving the country but he will never touch a gun." Dennis: "He feels, like me, that there is no reason for anyone to be connected with anything that could kill anyone. Why is there so much hate in the world? The belief of Carl's and mine is nothing to do with religion. It's ourselves. We won't kill."

Carl's draft resistor status was a hot item, and he was provoked at a London Hilton press conference causing him to decamp. On stage Dennis drove to energize the group's performance and presentation. But without sidemen, barred by the UK musicians union, their accompaniment was thin and lacking decibels. Of course, their vocals were as pristine as ever. Helen Shapiro was brought back in support; four years before she had headlined over the Beatles. On the Continental leg German-based Brit Graham Bonney, a big European star, was drafted in (Helsinki and Stockholm), and they were joined by the excellent Small Faces ('All or Nothing', 'My Mind's Eye') for a Berlin show. Asked in Holland why the group did not have a wild stage act like the up-and-coming British acts, they replied as one: "The music is all that counts." It was a natural response from artists but not one designed to send them racing up the popometer scale; one that would totally baffle anyone today in the rock scene.

Not long before the tour, April 25th, Brian appeared solo via a videotaped performance recorded three months earlier as a featured guest on Leonard Bernstein's tv special *Inside Pop: the Rock Revolution*, singing 'Surf's Up' accompanying himself on piano. Recognised for his genius by America's premier 'serious music' personality, it recalled to the minds of Elvis Costello and English critic Barney Hoskyns an impression of Mozart. But the track as recorded by Brian, that has ever since been praised as among his very best, disappeared for four years.

A week and a half later, while the public is distracted and partly mollified five days into a Beach Boy bash of Europe, publicist Derek Taylor, jetsetting between Beatles and Beach Boys, announces *Smile*—already four months late—has been junked. The month before he had met Paul McCartney and roadie Mal Evans flying into LA on Frank Sinatra's Lear Jet—rare in those days—hired out to Brian Epstein by "Old Blue Eyes" presumably in gratitude for the many melodies Paul had written for older generations.

On May 19th at Epstein's home the Beatles' next album is announced to the press, and the race is won. *Sgt Pepper* is fully conceived and directed by Paul, with the idea that he and his group play a lonely hearts club band on the album. In actuality, it is hardly a stretch considering their growing reliance on Music Hall tunes. Throughout, they were 'aided' by LSD—which the Byrds had introduced them to two summers before. In June, soon after the album's release, Paul gives an interview proclaiming his use of LSD and its mind-expanding powers. Reaction around the world is negative, excluding that from other users such as Brian Wilson. By July the Beatles and other British celebrities publish themselves as activists for legalising marijuana. But a month later, keeping up with trends, with Marianne Faithfull and Mick Jagger the group signs up with the Maharishi and accordingly announce their new drug-free lifestyle and come out condemning drug use.

The Beach Boys' first lawsuit issued recently against Capitol over "missing paperwork" and miscounted record sales could only have poured oil on what was an inflammatory relationship. If it was mistimed there could never be a good time to take on a powerful multinational corporation over its business dealings. It was settled by a token payment by Capitol and agreement to distribute what there was of Brother Records. It is now a full year since the American release of the last Beach Boys album. Worse, there is no solution in sight. Amazingly in the circumstances, at the NME Poll Winners Show at Wembley May 7th, the evening following the announcement that *Smile* was a nonevent, the Beach Boys are greeted with easily the most deafening screams of all, in the company of home idols Cream, Cat Stevens, Dusty Springfield, the Troggs, Cliff Richard, Lulu, the

Small Faces and Steve Winwood. Dave Dee, Dozy, Beaky, Mick & Tich, doing a line in Beatle Euro-Pop, were more popular than most. Later across town the Beach Boys, in a respectfully hushed, star-studded select audience, are treated to virtuoso playing by the members of the Jimi Hendrix Experience.

To go with the tour Capitol issued, everywhere but the US and Canada, 'Then I Kissed Her'—a good-enough track but two years old and a remake of a pre-Beatles hit, therefore taboo for anyone wanting to be seen as "with it". The 45 went one place short of top in London amid 'A Whiter Shade of Pale', 'Waterloo Sunset' and 'Silence is Golden' from English groups at their height. It pleased northern Europe where the group played—one of the hits of the year. Through the first half of 1967 judging by album and e.p. sales, the Beach Boys still led the Beatles: 'Penny Lane'/ 'Strawberry Fields' hadn't quite made the top and after their upcoming l.p. there would be no Beatle UK album for another 18 months. But the Monkees had closed in quickly.

During this breathing space as the most popular group in the world the Beach Boys savored a small taste of the adoring allegiance the Beatles had enjoyed for four years. Almost any track from their extensive catalogue could have been selected at random and sold. And that was the problem—for them. The Beatles had come to rely on unquestioning loyalty, undeserving as it often was. In contrast, critics' dire predictions of a rebound on the Beach Boys proved to hold weight: With few exceptions even their big hits would be smaller, never again reaching their 1966 magnitude.

Still fighting Carl's draft battle—used as an excuse to back out — on June 16th came the debacle of the Monterey Pop Festival, the brainchild of the Mamas & the Papas' John Phillips to rival the folk and jazz festivals that had settled on the atmospheric Northern California locale. Set for the height of "The Summer of Love", 30-year-old Phillips and California Music entrepreneur Lou Adler had co-opted Brian Wilson as a figurehead onto the organising board. The Beach Boys were intended to be the cornerstone of the event —*the* headliners—and by appearing might have easily cemented a leadership over alternative music to oppose Beatle overlordship of The Rock Establishment.

As it happened, the Beatles and Music Hall rebounded back to rule under *Sgt Pepper* and simply got new challengers. The Beach Boys saw the instant rock royalty cachet of Monterey conferred on new Blues figures Jimi Hendrix, Janis Joplin and others who had achieved a tiny fraction of older generations of legendary Blues figures. On the first day of the three-day festival the regional San Jose singles chart filled with Joplin's Big Brother & the Holding Company, the Byrds, Country Joe & the Fish, The Who, Grateful Dead, Scott McKenzie, the Association and Janis Ian—setting up a whole new movement. Instantly, albums and FM radio were at the center of the future, allowing longer airplay formats at the cost of singles-driven Top 40. Top in l.p.s in San Jose that day were the Doors, Country Joe and Cream. The previously unknown Hendrix revolutionised guitar technique in one day. And The Who, up to now failed Brit invaders, backstage at Monterey fighting Hendrix for a prime spot to show off their own "auto-destruction" act first, were now almost household names. So the Love Generation audience, clamoring for their new icons, was accordingly treated to Hendrix and The Who competing to see who could wreak most destruction on stage, the latter demolishing their instruments as performance innovation and Hendrix outdoing them—setting a fire, destroying his guitar and simulating humping an amp.

For unreformed white men and challenged leaders of Pop to show their faces in this setting might easily have been interpreted as colossal gall. Brian must have recognised this—but was it his paranoia talking? With such light fare on offer as the Mamas & the Papas, Simon & Garfunkel and the Association, if anything the Beach Boys' customary attire, not their new music, might have encouraged Monterey's Love Generation to hoot them off the stage. Finally, Dennis's ongoing complaints to Brian about their outdated pinstriped uniforms stuck.

To this day to be or not to be—on stage at Monterey—has been hotly debated. What is sure is that their nonappearance traumatised their career, and playing a festival there four years later they were the sensation of the event. Monterey defined the new generation of rock more than *TAMI* had for the earlier scene. On top of everything else, Hendrix's tribute to a seriously ill Dick Dale and mumbling of the possibility of not hearing surf music anymore was publicized as a slight on the absent Beach Boys. More of that paranoia prompted Mike Love to lash out with an unfortunate, comically backfiring retort that Jimi Hendrix "couldn't draw *flies*." Hendrix, who three weeks later joined America's new no.1 group as support act opening the show on a national tour, was in no position (and those in a position to know say he was no snob) to cast aspersions about street cred. He lasted two weeks with pre-teen raves the Monkees, then finally tiring of calls from the crowd during his set for "Davy! Davy!", quit. Two years later Hendrix *was* booed off the stage for trying to play seriously instead of doing his same old auto-destructive thing for the destruction freaks he had attracted.

Not wanting to reduce themselves to appear in a package deal— a charity one at that—the Beatles still used the occasion for promotional purposes, sending all their their love "to all at Monterey from Sgt Peppers Lonely Hearts Club Band" over the public address system. And, of the dozens of festival acts over the three days, George Harrison's musical-spiritual mentor Ravi Shankar was the only one who demanded an appearance fee, a very respectable $3,500 given his dubious box-office draw. Even Indian spirituality only went so far. Still the center of attention, the Beatles stayed in London and gave their blessing to the Monkee machine, attending officially with partners a reception given for the new moptop foursome July 3rd to see their *doppelgangers* gazing back at them.

For the Beach Boys the damage was done. Suddenly seen as over the hill in America, no longer could they compete (there) on the Mount Olympus the Beatles had been raised to. One good thing that came from it was that by nominating Otis Redding as their replacement they raised him to superstar status.

I N 1967 THE RECORD BUSINESS AND THE BEATLES were ready for psychedelia—as a product—boosted by the Beach Boys and now Monterey. 'Strawberry Fields Forever', Beatle psychedelia by John Lennon, and 'Penny Lane', Music Hall with a saving tincture of Beach Boys written-produced by Paul McCartney, were the first songs recorded for *Sgt Pepper*, a five month project. They were taken instead for a new February single. George Martin spliced tapes of two distinct John treatments of 'Strawberry Fields' in different keys and tempos, somehow making them into one track—for the umpteenth time showing his vital place in their recordings and pivotal value to the Beatle legend. Also on this track, John, a fine and probably the best singer on Beatle records 1963 through '66, began to develop a tinny whine on some songs that only got worse.

The Beatle double trip definitely held more charm than most of their 45s—but George Martin immediately regretted the decision to make it the first Beatle 45 ever without a designated A-side, a mistake that was never made again. What is often held up as the greatest double ever delivered a relatively meagre million and a half US sales. The favored side in the UK missed no.1 due to 'Strawberry Fields' getting its share of airplay—what the Beach Boys had suffered innumerable times in their country. It still sold a more than respectable 525,000 (albeit less than half Tom Jones' and Engelbert Humperdinck's hits) but Beatlemania had settled down and objective observers saw Beatle music through the rest of the year could not compete with the radical experimentation of 'Good Vibrations', 'Heroes & Villains', 'Wild Honey'…. The Beatle machine ground on inexorably and with a modicum of imagination and much schoolboy humor produced *Sgt Pepper*, released June 1st.

Martin, who claimed 'Strawberry Fields Forever' as "a new art form" (maybe it was for his part in recording it), showed himself fully into the spirit of *Sgt Pepper's* so-called experimental music, substituting random effects for taste. It was for 'Being for the Benefit of Mr Kite' that Martin and Emerick employed the random-tape-bits-joined technique. He got each Beatle to record his instrument on tape at home. In the studio he reversed the tapes, cut them into fragments, then he and the sound engineer threw them up in the air before picking them in random order to splice together. This has less to do with art than does kids making mudpies, an activity with a direct connection between brain and execution.

Martin: "I wanted to make a mush of noise... And I didn't want any of the notes to be identifiable." This would obviously not have been even contemplated had not Martin and the Beatles known their public would buy literally anything from them. A group of Indian musicians was hired to play for 'Within You, Without You'—again very much by chance, playing whatever they wanted to, with the Beatles stopping them to repeat a 'good' bit for the tape, editing on the run at whim. On an album full of haphazard effects 'A Day in the Life' was a cobbling together of entirely separate John and Paul songs.

Chapple & Garofalo: "[*Sgt Pepper's*], as had *Revolver* before to a lesser extent, helped to popularize acid and Indian music, as well as the less positive, more general trend towards Eastern *kitsch*. The power and popularity the Beatles had assumed in their straighter period was enabling them to lead millions of young people through a series of changes."

Rock gadfly Frank Zappa, a precocious talent as a child and a genuinely original composer, saw through *Sgt Pepper* and within months had issued a parody of it—replicating the celebrated crowd-of-celebs cover superimposed with the new title *We're Only in it for the Money*. English showbiz veterans Joe Brown and Bernard Cribbins saw clearly what it was too, and in a matter of days released faithful covers of 'With a Little Help from My Friends' and 'When I'm Sixty-Four' in their Cockney Music Hall voices.

Red Robinson, a famous Sixties dj (at Vancouver's CFUN 1962-67), quoted in Pritchard & Lysaght: "Interestingly Paul McCartney told me in an interview that his whole inspiration for *Sgt Pepper* was *Pet Sounds* from the Beach Boys. He thought 'Good Vibrations' was the best thing he'd ever heard. I tend to agree with him on that point." Whether Brian Wilson felt ambivalent over inspiring such music is unknown to the writer.

But it was the Beatles, once again cribbing on Beach Boys' work, who went down in history from that moment as responsible for "the second renaissance of rock and roll" in Robinson's words and giving rise to the trend towards FM radio: Their latest work was said to be so uniformly great that the whole album had to be played on the air.

For decades *Sgt Pepper* had acolyte critics' favor as the pinnacle of Sixties music—aside from hype about how nonetheless magnificent the other Beatle albums are. Its magnificence, however, is invisible to someone looking for good rock or even comprehensible songs. Apart from 'Lovely Rita' and 'With a Little Help from My Friends'—fair work that was improved on by interpreters—only 'A Day in the Life' and 'Lucy in the Sky With Diamonds' seem outstanding, the latter for pointing to the much more interesting *Magical Mystery Tour* (though sent up for its supposed drug references by 'Judy in Disguise—with Glasses').

Beatle bumph posing as classic started in earnest with *Revolver* but is even more in evidence on *Sgt Pepper*—the title song, and the previously disregarded 'When I'm Sixty-Four' dredged up from Paul McCartney's teenagerhood, judged not good enough for their *first* album and disproving the general assertion that the Beatles grew exponentially. Stuff of the same character took up much of the *White Album*: 'Ob-La-Di, Ob-La-Da', 'Bungalow Bill', 'Happiness is a Warm Gun', 'Piggies', 'Rocky Raccoon', 'Sexy Sadie'... By the time of *Abbey Road* even the modestly talented Ringo had learnt the formula well enough to be able to produce, single-handed, an 'Octopus's Garden'. For whatever reasons, *Revolver* and the *White Album* are now held to be at least on a par with *Sgt Pepper*.

Outside observers—not Beatle fans—are at a loss to comprehend these everchanging standards and relativities applied to the Beatles' output. As with many other judgments held about the Beatles explanations are deemed superfluous. While proficiency obviously broadened through the Sixties the group lost energy to where such exciting performances as 'Please Please Me', 'Twist & Shout', 'Tell Me Why', 'Help!', 'I'm Down' were limited to 'Revolution' and 'Back in the USSR'.

Acclaim for *Sgt Pepper*, goes the legend, deflated Brian Wilson's hopes and dreams for the best part of a quarter century. It seems simplistic. Here was a compulsively creative personality who had been fighting toe to toe uphill against the Beatles for three and a half years, and on this latest setback he throws it all in? *Smile* was first scheduled for release before Xmas six months previous, and every delay since then had signalled mounting trouble with Brian's usually smooth and dependable creative process and output. What the trouble was has been conjectured about for the forty years since. Only rarely has he begrudged the Beatles their success, and instead he has cited internal, group tensions for his withdrawal.

By the time of *Smiley Smile*'s release Brian Wilson had been going it alone for five years. His increasingly bizarre behavior even by the end of 1964 he was easily able to explain just a couple of years later: "I used to be Mr Everything. I felt I had no choice. I was run down mentally and emotionally because I was running around, jumping on jets from one city to another on one-night stands, also producing, writing, arranging, singing, planning, teaching—to the point where I had no peace of mind and no chance to actually sit down and think or even rest. I was so mixed up and so overworked."

"So what it amounted to was a guilt feeling. I knew I should have stopped going on tours much earlier to do justice to our recordings and business operations. I was also under pressure from my old man, who figured I'd be a traitor if I didn't travel on one-nighters with the other guys... I had a lot of static from everyone outside the group as well as the members. The only way I could do it was by breaking down as I did" (interviewed by veteran journalist/publicist Earl Leaf, 1966, from Tom Nolan, 1972).

The Beatles' numbers held after John's "more popular than Jesus" claim, the self-massaging ego-booster mouthed by English émigré Charlie Chaplin half a century before and other megalomaniac stars fancying themselves deep cultural gurus. Lennon's success in putting this view of himself over says more about star power than pop philosophy. The Beatles ceased touring—their new music was studio-bound electronics, not able to be reproduced on stage—but Lennon's *cachet* among self-appraised intellectuals was enhanced by inaccessibility. Their numbers held but now fewer loved them for their personalities and music, more who kinked-out on power. Was the time ripe for nonsense songs that would appeal to Luv freaks? 'All You Need is Love' filled the bill with its 'philosophy' purveyed by meaningless nonsense wordplay. John wrote it and on June 25th, three weeks after *Sgt Pepper*, the Beatles sang it and played over a four-track tape for a live tv date on *Our World*, a documentary involving an unprecedented link-up as a world event playing to a then astronomical 350 million people.

It seems the hippies, anyway, weren't going for it. Two months later they conducted a mock funeral procession through the streets of the spiritual home of Love, Haight-Ashbury, San Francisco for "The Death of Hippy" protesting commercialisation of the Love-and-Peace Generation. Later came 'Give Peace a Chance', 'Power to the People', with their one lucid line mantraed over and over... And ever since "Lennon"—like Madonna, a single name only is required for the great ones of history—has been taken seriously as a prophet (if not a Jesus) as well as a reliable profit by those influential survivors from the Sixties, pot-headed liberals grown into today's senior executives, and their heirs.

'HEROES & VILLAINS', TRIMMED ALMOST IN HALF from six-plus minutes, and *Smiley Smile* were issued under the Brother tag, the vinyl pressed and distributed (and presumed promoted) by Capitol. An insubstantial group chant, 'You're Welcome', Dennis's voice and Native American tom-tom up front, was put on the flip; minus its charm, it might have been the template for the commercialised 'Give Peace a Chance'.

Giving rising LA station KHJ its world premiere—many had hopes the new 45 might even outdo 'Good Vibrations'—the group and entourage drove in a midnight procession of Rolls Royces *sans chauffeurs* in pomp-deflating Beach Boy fashion. The approach timed precisely according to the muse of Brian's astrologer, the delegation was rebuffed by the duty DJ citing the inviolate playlist. 'Heroes & Villains' was eventually played that night, after a few choice words were shouted down the phone by the station boss, but the moment Brian had savored for nine months dissolved and as if the whammy was put on it that night it would reach a smaller audience than anyone expected. The "You're only as cool as you are current" mentality ruled. Some fans, used to releases every three months, had stopped waiting. It was virtually ignored in San Francisco, Monterey's regional megalopolis and the center of '67 cool; and was a mild toptwentier in Detroit, New York and Chicago. For once there was no scaling of the heights anywhere, though it did better than its national average in Boston (#3), Washington DC, Toronto, parts in between, Charleston, Pittsburgh, Ohio, Indianapolis, Kansas City, Wisconsin, South Dakota, the Twin Cities and the Rockies.

Its nationwide debut August 5th was more than encouraging— the highest new entry at #41 and the group's best-ever sales performance in the part-week of release. Faster than 'Good Vibrations', its second leap took it top twenty. Any and all impulses toward independence banished from his mind, Brian was on the 25th off performing Beach Boy duty in Hawaii—his first real gig in more than two years. The preemptive therapy of playing in paradise might only cover the cracks of the damage done. A performance was taped but the jokey *Lei'd in Hawaii* has only been issued on bootleg under that name.

For those even half as sensitive as the Wilson brothers it was a good time to get away from civilization. Over the past two months the perpetual to-and-froing over the West Bank, Gaza Strip and Golan Heights had begun in the Middle East; the bloody Biafran war for independence against Nigeria had flared; and in late July this summer's race race riots starting in Detroit—where, alone, 43 were killed—spread to a hundred other cities and threatened to mount a depressing new all-time record body count.

It was now at #9 in Cash Box after a fair rise of four places. Two days later on the 27th Brian Epstein was found dead of a drug overdose, leading a shambolic personal life and having suffered depression since realising the Beatles, whom he had made his life for six years, no longer needed him. Though George Harrison proved the only real adherent of Indian spirituality and music the Beatles were on a three-day retreat with the Maharishi in Wales. Thereafter the man who had virtually made the group, to belittle his huge part in their success would be remembered derisively for "putting suits on" (read spoiling) the Beatles.

If the first weekend in September 1961 starts Year Zero for Beach Boy freaks everywhere the beginning of the end of their Sixties career can be pinpointed to the weekend of 2nd September 1967, when 'Heroes & Villains' stopped short before dropping like a stone.

American program directors had begun playing it as a Beach Boy record, then when they realized it was even further out than 'Good Vibrations', stopped. It wasn't the kind of song that would get mass phone-in requests from teen parties—as Bruce Johnston so helpfully pointed out, you couldn't dance to it. The picture was complicated when in Record World it held tight a second week, prevented from easing upwards by an unusually high influx of three high-shooting top ten newcomers that week.

When it settled 'Heroes & Villains' was a media event with a muffled impact: no.8 (low airplay kept it a further four places adrift in Billboard—a trend that would only worsen), same as Britain, better in Canada and New Zealand but lacking that final thrust in Europe. In France a curious fate awaited it—charting still lower but perhaps the only culture that gave it its due, attracting high praise and winning official "Record of the Year" over any and all Eurovision Song Contest entrants.

Founder-editor of New York's new Crawdaddy magazine, Paul Williams, who had interviewed Brian extensively the year before and got some insight into his creative processes, listed the new Beach Boy single in his choice of the best hundred recordings of Twentieth Century popular music. The mix of acclaim and passable success was reportedly no consolation to the highly competitive Wilson. If he couldn't foot it with the Beatles commercially— raw popularity with a mass public—the game was over. His dreams collapsed on an undernourished, wilting psyche.

'Heroes & Villains' featured the same chart weeks as no.1s 'Ode to Billie Joe' and 'The Letter', which claimed tallies of almost three million. Aretha Franklin's 'A Natural Woman', with a chart profile not quite as meteoric as the Beach Boy 45, racked up a mill.

'Gettin' Hungry', rush-released from *Smiley Smile* for "Brian Wilson & Mike Love", was lent a pathetic sympathy vote from Boston and Sioux Falls (their two centers of consistent popularity in 1967) the week 'Heroes' fell. Preteens were getting more disposable cash, and what better way to spend it for impressionable minds than on the Monkees, the Association and Gary Puckett & the Union Gap in place of America's by-now acknowledged musical genius? In cultural history it would be as if the mantle of Western Civilisation passed from Tchaikovsky (to whom the music of the Beach Boys has been repeatedly compared) not to Stravinsky but to... the Beatles' heirs.

M ANY INSIGHTS BETWEEN THEM HOLD THE KEY TO the fate of the Beach Boys' career. One from Marilyn Wilson has been applied to both the *Pet Sounds* and 'Heroes & Villains' fiascos: "But [it] was not a big hit. That really hurt him badly, he couldn't understand it. It's like, why put your heart and soul into something?"

The second, from Jack Rieley, a future manager who in 1971 would lead them in a badly needed new PR direction: "A lot has been made of [Brian's] drug use/abuse, which may indeed have had searing effects upon him. But it was the public failure of 'Heroes' *to wow Capitol and thus wow the world* [my italics] that caused him to withdraw."

Three sources point to industry politics as primary cause. Nick Venet, associated with the group during their first year at Capitol, said in 1972 (Nolan): "Brian had all the odds against him ever having more than two hit records. Brian was a square peg in a round hole. Brian was five years too early with his business thinking, with his creative thinking, and yet he made it. But he suffered for it. And I'm sure he's paying for it today."

Terry Melcher, with them through surf music and in the procession of limos to KHJ to reveal 'Heroes & Villains' to the world, had a more graphic way of putting it: "The guy never asked for any trouble, he just wrote songs about cars and the beach, and everyone nailed the motherfucker to the wall. They really nailed him. That poor motherfucker" (also Tom Nolan, 1972).

"One day I guess he just looked at the world and saw how fucked up it was—He's not a dummy, you know": Carl.

The truly gifted child, good at sports too and wanting to fit in with the mob, is at the mercy of his creative inclinations—the irresistible drive to create something new for the world—and is driven insane by his dim peers' pecking and nagging, alternating bullying and neglect.

The Beatles, cool smoothies in the fashion game, looked around for a solid precedent—in turn skiffle, rock and roll, Brill Building pop, C&W, Latin-Euro Easy Listening, Dylan folk, Beach Boys psychedelia. The one time they didn't—with *Magical Mystery Tour*— was when they were most impressive, and summarily executed by the media. Whatever the diagnosis for the Beach Boys, it was now only the prognosis that mattered.

The Beatles, entering their psychedelic phase months after the Beach Boys, had watched which way the tide was turned by their rivals and taken over with *Pepper's*. The Beach Boys had moved on, deserted Monterey leaving the field clear for the Beatles, Stones, The Who, Hendrix and the San Francisco bands to fight the youth subcultural battle. Brian and the group's second-best effort was to adapt some of the cast-off *Smile* tracks to simpler, more easily digestible arrangements. Given group insecurities at this time maybe it was all they could do together.

Smiley Smile, when it finally came in September, was nectar to psychedeliacs though anathema to a lot of traditional Beach Boy fans—reflected by its unprecedented low Billboard rating. Pick of the week on stations from Denver to Dayton, it went to the top in Phoenix and was played on New York City FM radio. Shooting to top 20 in the two other US majors, with less than half its five-month run counted it made Cash Box's top-selling fifty rock l.p.s of 1967 and might have approached the 450,000 first-run US units Capitol planned for *Smile* but fell short of the million projected. November 11th it peaked in the UK's New Musical Express top half dozen as *Best of...* I-II sat above and below.

Possibly, if the Beach Boys had been the Beatles the music would have been acclaimed without a second (or first) thought. But the less imaginative fans who had rejected *Pet Sounds* weren't in the mood for another tweaking of their mindsets. News filtered out that it was being used as therapy in mental health clinics. *Smiley Smile* and *Wild Honey* more than matched the Beatles' two albums that year in creativity but the Fabs' media machine won out over the Beach Boys' lack of one.

A little-known fact—precisely because of the manoeuvring determining who gets to be a superstar and who remains a nobody in pop culture—is that a month after *Smiley Smile*, Van Dyke Parks' solo album *Song Cycle* was released to near unanimous critical acclaim: album of the year for august magazines for sophisticated urbanites, The New Yorker, Time and Esquire. It sold less than *15,000* but, backed by the artistic indulgence of Warner Bros, Parks continued through the eighties to produce and release full-length works. The same reverse market logic decreed that some of the most critically admired Beach Boy albums—*Friends, Sunflower, The Beach Boys Love You*—be rejected by the public. To paraphrase popular sixties DJ Cousin Brucie, cherishing his heyday from a distance of thirty years, if you dumb music down so that everyone can hum it, it takes on a "magic" and becomes a hit.

Given a spanking by the US media for attempting to take the public well past *Pet Sounds*, even with an eviscerated version of *Smile*, a chastened, emasculated Brian, started immediately to repair bridges by partnering cousin Mike on almost every song for *Wild Honey*, generally credited for leading "a return to basics".

9: OLD SURFERS NEVER DIE, THEY JUST FADE AWAY

The Sixties, despite its explosion of brilliance, like any era of pop culture was an age of trivia given significance—gimmicks posing as originality: the Beatles and mod fashions, Herman Hermit with little-boy grin and pouting lower lip, Mick Jagger with both perpetually pouting lips, Sonny & Cher's animal skins, Jimi Hendrix picking his teeth with guitar strings and lighting fires on stage, Pete Townshend and The Who destroying instruments and the stage in the name of... something, and surf adopted by the media as a genre of music. At the beginning, in rock's early days, the tags were harmless—youth symbols for those longing to belong. After the Summer of Love soured they were held to have some level of social and artistic significance, especially by the business that perpetrated them, and those who slavishly followed their heroes far down destructive back alleys.

The Beach Boys didn't rate in the race for the most sensational new look. The early surfer-outsider image of Dennis and Dave was baby-softened into a marketing tool to sell them to the public—healthy sun-tanned fun-loving California. A Disney lamb suit was thrust on them as horns and gigantic ram cajones inevitably burst through. Dennis's recurring violent episodes; Brian's mental illness and long drug addiction; substance abuse by the other Wilsons; paternity suits against Mike and Dennis; Dennis's involvement with mass murderer Charles Manson; his marriage to Mike's out-of-wedlock teenage daughter in the last year of his life; and alcohol-related drowning—have all come and gone with no effect on the music's reception. It's the ultimate testament to the strength of their and Brian Wilson's artistry—their ability to create a dream world in which his music is set, in the way that a successful novelist creates an imaginary setting for heroic characters.

Disdainful of hype, the Beach Boys distanced themselves from it as they matured into the late Sixties—even divorcing themselves from pop culture. Wilson had in summer '64 ceased to write about popular subjects of instant appeal but the world only noticed two years later with Pet Sounds—*and the others continued his thrust as they came to compose. While the Stones, Bee Gees and most of the Beatles carried on writing songs about the politics of "romance" the Beach Boys still composed their music as a direct transfer of emotions onto tape.*

According to the bean counters who rule the pop music industry and demand a rapid turnover of product, five years at the top was all anyone could expect. First they had to face yet another surge of energy coming from the other side of the Atlantic.

S IMON FRITH (*ROCK FILE 5*, 1978) ON DECADE 1967-77 of 'progressive' music when the market had turned from pop to *rock*: "Twenty-five has continued to be the cut-off age for rock interest and involvement, and rather than developing their musical tastes, most rock fans' tastes freeze at the age of eighteen. 'Progessive' rock taste has turned out to mean buying another Led Zeppelin or Rolling Stones record every year and the most successful rock groups base their success on *not* progressing. The supergroups which emerged at the beginning of the decade still dominated album sales and concert receipts at the end." It is depressing to see how little has changed in the thirty years since.

The Beach Boys, experimenting to their commercial detriment, were not among these successful 'progressive' ones but were truly progressive. Their success to mid-1967 had been qualified only in terms of the Beatles' overlaying fame. In the turmoil of the Sixties, seeing a far quicker turnover of acts than any other decade, it was a marvel. Given sponsorship from Capitol it was a miracle. They had seen off all from the Brit Invasion but the Beatles and Stones—the two essential elements in this world production of the "Punch & Judy Show". The Stones set the definitive template of rowdy misbehaving for rock acts to follow to the present day.

The Dave Clark Five, Herman's Hermits and the rest—names on America's lips and the choice of record-buyers months before— were in snob circles by summer '67 only fit to be denigrated and under your breath in case you were overheard to even know them. The Beach Boys would never descend to this level of obscurity— Instead, they were castigated, held up as poster boys showing what *not* to be in the cool world, and held down as whipping boys by those begrudging the group's continuing semi-divine standing among peers. Tasteful snobs were seen leaving record shops with Beach Boy product, tucked under their arm in a brown paper bag.

They survived too the Mamas & the Papas, the Monkees and even Donovan—*the* force of the British Invasion's third wave, who had justly threatened to usurp Bob Dylan's place in Rock's pantheon but was soon consigned to oblivion. While still scoring passably popular hits at home, the group's centre of gravity had shifted and would align along a European-Far East-Pacific axis, into the Seventies their records doing best along this narrowing sliver of the globe. They were recognized by those in the know as one of the three great groups of Rock—*the* American group leaving others behind qualitatively. Theirs was an excellence sparked by genius, fulsomely conceded by their three English rivals—counting The Who now coming into their own. It can only be imagined what might have been achieved had they stumbled upon an ounce of luck after their uptake by Capitol in May '62 or had there been even occasional patches of smooth sailing in their personal and business lives from May '66.

As Presley (and Lennon) biographer Albert Goldman relates of '67, Elvis, confined to his screen musicals, was something of a joke in rock circles while "the British Invasion of 1965 [sic] had now been echoed by a tremendous upsurge of pop music right under Elvis's nose on the West Coast. Jim Morrison and the Doors, Grace Slick and Jefferson Airplane, Janis Joplin with Big Brother and the Holding Company, the Byrds, the Beach Boys, the Grateful Dead, the first concerts and light shows at the Fillmore West—all signaled the onset of the most feverishly creative period in American pop music since the midfifties." It had all started with the Beach Boys.

Early Sixties figures burnt out in a firestorm. Wilson's energy lasted '61-7, Lennon's '63-66, McCartney's '62-9, Jagger-Richards' intermittently '65-9. Lennon & McCartney would not be remotely the same forces as individuals. It says it all that nursery rhymes 'Imagine' and 'Ebony and Ivory', made immeasurably worse by their grade-school lyrics of political correctness, are held up as classics from their solo careers. The Beach Boys' real problem was that the more profound their music and lyrics the more irrelevant they grew in youth culture. Simon Frith said it: the others stayed popular by *not* progressing.

Only now recognized in America were The Who: 'Happy Jack', 'I Can See for Miles', more popular with 'Call Me Lightning', 'Magic Bus', and in 1969 rock opera *Tommy* about "that deaf, dumb and blind kid" who "sure plays a mean pinball": 'Pinball Wizard', 'I'm Free', 'The Seeker', 'See Me, Feel Me'. A three-piece 'blues fusion' group, they were closest to the Stones in roots but not really close in approach. Their high-pitched backing vocals were reminiscent of the Beach Boys—hear the chiming of 'Substitute' and the humming introduction and bridge of 'I'm a Boy'. Forging a link was Pete Townshend's "wildly propulsive rhythm guitar influenced heavily by Beach Boy Carl Wilson..." among others (Dave Marsh, *Rolling Stone Illustrated History of Rock & Roll*, 1976). Owing so much Eddie Cochran too, their remake of 'Summertime Blues' had to follow the Beach Boys', as they had on 'Barbara Ann' and 'Bucket T' from the hotrod era. Keith Moon's drumming owed his formative, favorite surf music, overlapping from Denny Wilson's rhythmic pounding on 'Surf Jam'. While Townshend was called by Marsh "the greatest auteur of pure rock'n'roll" the Beach Boys didn't recognize boundaries, their credo Whatever is good for the song, do it whether rock'n'roll, jazz, classical.

The new iconic figures of the moment though, from late '67 for a year on, were Cream, with their huge-selling *Disraeli Gears*— under New York producer Felix Pappalardi, continuing the custom of the best Brit rock recordings emerging with American input, gearing them up to Stateside expectations in what was after all a thoroughly American musical idiom. From it came Blues-Rock standards 'Sunshine of Your Love', 'Strange Brew', 'Tales of Brave Ulysses' and 'SWLABR'.

Early admirer Eric Clapton might very well have been influenced by 'Heroes & Villains' to write a similarly narrative epic in 'Ulysses', but young record buyers didn't know it and weren't interested. Low airplay and growing media apathy cemented the Beach Boys' descent. The high-toned New York columnists had deserted them and they looked out of place in teen magazines with Kurt Russell and Billy Mumy. Billboard, placing weight on weekly airplay, was lent prestige by the media that exist by airplay; the other major charts were attuned to disc sales. From 'Heroes & Villains' through '71 every hit 45 went substantially higher in Cash Box and Record World than in Billboard and every album went much higher in Record World, Cash Box less consistently. Plainly, the group retained high US popularity for years after going out of fashion.

T WO WEEKS AFTER EPSTEIN'S PASSING THE BEATLES were filming *Magical Mystery Tour* for tv—their first project without his guidance and their first knockback at home. While the double-e.p. that went with it climbed to #2 of UK singles and sold very well (620,000), the album conceived by Capitol-US only made #31 from a total of 100,000 shipped from UK factories —a fact virtually expunged from Beatle history. Possibly the best Beatle album of all—seriously disfavored by critics because not a 'concept' album—it contains several of their best tracks ever, maybe more than *Help!* or *Rubber Soul*, its only serious competition. The studio musicians are especially admired by critics.

Issued November 27th 1967 in North America—three weeks before the Beach Boys' *Wild Honey*, it went on to sell six million to date, as many as *Rubber Soul* and more than any other of their soundtracks. The cobbled-together *Magical Mystery Tour* album includes both 'Penny Lane' and 'Strawberry Fields Forever'; further explorations in psychedelia in 'I Am the Walrus' and 'Baby You're a Rich Man'; McCartney's delicately created 'Fool on the Hill'; massively iconic singles and nonsense songs 'All You Need is Love' and 'Hello, Goodbye', like them or loathe them; and 'Magical Mystery Tour' and 'Your Mother Should Know'—both Music Hall but less offensive than the average of their ilk. At the time, even the light fare of 'I Am the Walrus' (#46), 'Magical Mystery Tour' and 'Baby You're a Rich Man' (#34), heavy with John Lennon word-play lyrics, seemed to carry a weight totally lost in retrospect. Yet the overall effect is imaginative and uplifting. Of an economical 11-track album, this left only 'Blue Jay Way' and 'Flying' as fillers.

When the BBC screened *Magical Mystery Tour*, a 50-minute tv film, it attracted scathing reviews—questioning whether that government department would ever have passed it had it not been the Beatles. The 'plot' was pretty much the Beatles travelling around on a bus, but it was the avant-garde surreal presentation and its message that was supposed to matter. A "parody of mass communication", the Beatles were deflating their own phenomenon but the fans and idol-makers didn't want to know (Keith Dewhurst in Salewicz). The flack ricocheted on what was some genuinely distinguished music on the album, delivering the Beatles their one and only resounding chart flop in their own country. In America they were appreciated as ever, the album grossing $8 million in ten days and the film $2 million from college rentals alone (Salewicz).

Wild Honey had been masterminded by Brian and Mike with Carl's voice and production substituted brilliantly. But the attempt at catch-up in public favor failed. It remains an exciting excursion into minimalism, featuring piano and/or organ up front, used to carry melody and drive the rhythm, augmented by heavy bass. Coming out of left field just as the record-buying world was splitting between Monkee madness and heavy Hendrix, it was poised to be vastly underrated. But the group's turn to basic sounds in rock gave *carte blanche* to the Beatles and Stones to venture into heavier realms, reinstating themselves following the year and a half both English groups spent not touring—just reflecting, evidently mesmerized by *Pet Sounds*. Now they ruminated on *Smiley Smile* and *Wild Honey*.

The new album cleared a path to late-Sixties rock, leading to CCR. It raised eyebrows and gapped mouths in shock that the Beach Boys, in the current climate the hated "Whitey", could put across a heavier sound so convincingly. It did better than the last but was still not the blanket success they'd been used to. The pick album of the week in Cincinnati, it streaked to top in Milwaukee, San Bernardino and other outposts of Beach Boy loyalty; held out in Phoenix only by *Magical Mystery Tour*, #5 in St Louis. Typical of the harder sound were 'Here Comes the Night', sung in r&b style by Brian; and the frenetically paced 'How She Boogalooed It' (Carl)—ahead of its time, a far-advanced harbinger of Punk and appreciated as a 45 in Sweden. Other outstanding tracks were 'Country Air', 'Let the Wind Blow' and Carl's reworking of Stevie Wonder's 'I Was Made to Love Her'—an amazing achievement of spare instrumentation—all lost in the media rush to pointedly ignore the group. In the UK some were heard on *Best of...*s.

A forecast hit pick almost everywhere but suffering low airplay, the title song was the single that broke the Beach Boys' five-year string of Billboard top 20 hits, shunned in all but US *sales* charts, the Far East and Australasia. In one of those cruel messages from fans to artists, telling them they were stretching the leash, even their usually staunch British and Dutch patrons rejected it. In America it didn't help that the most influential station on the airwaves, New York's WABC, didn't rate it higher than #58—though top twenty at archrival WMCA. In Washington DC it was huge—#2 for three weeks, pipped by an all-new Beatles called the Monkees; runner-up too in Akron, Ohio; #4 the Twin Cities, #5 in Portland, West Coast Mecca of r&b; #6 in blues center Kansas City and in Phoenix, Arizona. It was as well liked as 'California Girls' in down-to-earth Detroit, #9; top ten across Pennsylvania, in Cleveland, Vancouver, almost in Houston and Charleston, West Virginia. KOL-Seattle's annual vote-in a year later found 'Wild Honey' a popular song still, ranking with 'Lady Madonna', 'I Want to Hold Your Hand', 'Sgt Pepper' and 'Here, There and Everywhere'. Where its r&b wasn't appreciated it was dismissed as un-Beach Boy. So ultimately they couldn't win either way.

It was just the opening required by trendy Jann Wenner, all-powerful founding editor of Rolling Stone magazine, new HQ of the San Francisco Counter Culture. Wenner wrote an excoriating article dismissing the richness of Beach Boy music, claiming they were vainly trying to catch up with the Fabs, in a reversal of logic that the Beatles themselves knew was false. But enough mud stuck and after this it was highly uncool in American critical circles to give the Beach Boys any weight at all.

Regardless, they continued to markedly influence not only their peers the Beatles but now the new leaders in rock. In the Summer of Love America came up with its version of the Stones, the Doors.

Gothic themes threading their music, 'Light My Fire' and 'Hello, I Love You' could be used on a horror soundtrack while later 'Love Her Madly' and 'Riders on the Storm' take exploration of the mind's secrets a step further, hinting at encroaching madness, a descent into incurable insanity or suicide as an alternative lifestyle— an all-pervading pessimism that has held a fascination for young music buyers ever since. Opposite in mood to most Beach Boy hits, the downbeat Brian songs and early Dennis compositions (alternating with rocking-out faster songs) bear some relation to Doors music in its sombre-gothic tone.

The coolest new figure of the new scene, a new Mick Jagger, Doors leader Jim Morrison after his early death went on to rival Hendrix as an image on posters and lavatory mats. For now, he went on record as admiring the new Beach Boys album to distraction. It was a stance diametrically opposing Jann Wenner—a man subject to unfounded biases and easily swayed by personal relations in his supposed critiques, according to sometime associate English rock writer Barney Hoskyns (interview on Radio New Zealand, 2007). Morrison risked personal image and career status in aligning his taste with that of an ebbing supergroup, hoisting his colors to a slowly sinking ship.

The follow-up single from *Wild Honey*, 'Darlin'', more tuneful than the title song and more exciting than the run of r&b, hit the top ten fringe trans-Atlantic to bring the group back to some form but no longer in the Beatle class of chart-topping. Some of their best-ever recordings—and great, innovative r&b by any standards —had gone begging, dissed alike by 'surf' fans and r&b fans intolerant of the icons of 'white' American music. At *them* was directed a backlash on behalf of Black artists deprived of their rightful place in pop culture over the previous four years by the dominance of British looks and sounds. It would take Reverend Jesse Jackson to publicly acknowledge in the new millennium the Beach Boys' contribution to black music (presumably mentoring Blondie Chaplin and Ricky Fataar) for them to be 'forgiven'. While neither 'Wild Honey' or 'Darlin'' were granted a look in at such influential r&b stations as KATZ-St Louis (both made top 30 at local KXOK), such imaginary r&b acts as Dionne Warwick and the Supremes were welcomed. Even more strangely, the Beatles were given space along with Lulu's 'To Sir With Love', presumably for its association with black movie star Sidney Poitier. Of white American acts the Rascals and few others were given a hearing.

THE UK WAS SLOW CATCHING ON TOO. SEPTEMBER '67 showed what was left of the once energized Brit Invasion—the Stones, rising no higher than the Beach Boys. The Tremeloes emulate the Beach Boys' old "good time" style; the Flowerpot Men give an especially sincere imitation:

1. The Last Waltz—Engelbert Humperdinck
2. Fall in Love—Tom Jones
3. San Francisco—Scott McKenzie
4. Excerpt From a Teenage Opera—Keith West
5. Let's Go to San Francisco—the Flowerpot Men
6. Itchycoo Park—the Small Faces
7. Even the Bad Times Are Good—the Tremeloes
8. Heroes & Villains—the Beach Boys
9. Just Loving You—Anita Harris
10. We Love You/Dandelion—the Rolling Stones

By the time 'Darlin'' peaks six months to the day later (March 17th '68), jockeying nine weeks under top ten, the Beach Boys are almost Heavy Metal compared to the most popular songs:

1. Cinderella Rockafella—Esther & Abi Ofarim
2. Legend of Xanadu—Dave Dee, Dozy, Beaky, Mick & Titch
3. Fire Brigade—The Move
4. Rosie—Don Partridge
5. Jennifer Juniper—Donovan
6. Delilah—Tom Jones
7. Green Tambourine—the Lemon Pipers
8. The Mighty Quinn—Manfred Mann
9. Dock of the Bay—Otis Redding

10. Me, the Peaceful Heart — Lulu

Similarly, Stateside just in the Cash Box top ten, 'Darlin'' is rivaled for funk only by Aretha Franklin's cookin' 'Chain of Fools'. Long term it was especially liked by record buyers along the Eastern Seaboard, where (in 1976) it tabulated 11th from its year in a wide-ranging sales-and-votes survey conducted by New York's NBC station. In contemporary charts it did best in Los Angeles (#2), top at Santa Barbara; top five in Washington DC, Boston-Springfield-New Haven, Honolulu, Milwaukee; #6 in San Diego and Fresno; #7 Portland, Louisville, Columbus; #9 Toronto. It barely made Billboard's top twenty, again brought down by diminishing airplay, now threatening a radio-fulfilling prophecy.

The Beatles instantly went out harder on 'Lady Madonna', closely resembling 'Darlin'' in slow motion, in its undulating bass and piano pulse; then 'Revolution' and their all-pretences-dropped Beach Boy soundalike, 'Back in the USSR'. This left the Beach Boys precisely nowhere—an independent voice whose ideas are appropriated and corrupted by those backed by big music industry politics. Curiously, the Stones had stopped public performances the same time as the Beatles—summer '66—as if part of the same organism. Kick-started afresh by American producer Jimmy Miller in spring '68, 'Jumpin' Jack Flash' and 'Street Fighting Man' got them back into their element after a long bout of hazy psychedelia. As albums became more important the Stones continued popular, selling at about a third of the rate of the Beatles but by 1970 a multiple of the Beach Boys' new low in American sales.

ONCE UPON A TIME IT HAD BEEN SO SIMPLE. THE Beach Boys met a post-War Hollywood that, at times cutthroat, was straightforward. Before rock music was for ego gratification— before the *act* was more important than the music— when it was still a giving, not a taking thing, the Beach Boys were outdistanced by an industry of growing hype and spin. Every year of the mid-60s brought a new look, sound, fads to be emulated and discarded. Only those with well-defined images (rarely musical styles) survived. The boys were backstabbed and casually misunderstood too many times and struggled to maintain innocence. It is vastly to their credit that they sustained a fresh creative outlook so long.

Their early surfing theme arose spontaneously. Carl stated in a Seventies radio interview that the music would have been the same without surf lyrics. Can any form of music relate to a sport? But the label stuck. When they wrote about personal themes it was still called surf music. Something akin to Schubert, who wrote many beerhall songs, being written off as king of 'boozing music'.

In his then-prestigious book *The Sound of the City* (1970) Charlie Gillett asserted that "For Wilson and Love, the surf scene was a genuine interest, probably the only subject they could have written songs about with any conviction." One sentence, two statements— both wrong, bringing to mind Frank Zappa's apt quote on rock journalists: "people who can't write interviewing people who can't talk for people who can't read." Chuck Berry, in writing songs about cars and girls, was hailed by critics as a classic chronicler of the American way of life, a true artist and cultural treasure. Mike Love, not.

If anyone was, the Beach Boys were imaginative cultural reporters: glorifying teen trends without being sucked in. The band was never touched by British fashion *or* British music. Soon after the Beatles hit Dennis's hair was longer, but never Beatle-cut. On tv performing 'Surfin' USA' in early spring '63—ten months before the Beatles were known in America—he was tressed in surfer mode, long on top and sides but fringe swept casually off the forehead: by the standards of the day sorely in need of a haircut. He carried on his own way, getting a crewcut for the summer of '67: daring iconoclasm for that time. In the late Sixties Dennis, the coolest of an uncool band, was mocked by the 'beautiful people' of London —fashion lickspittles—for being seen in tennis shoes.

As they aged their visage was a deliberate non-event—*It was the music that counted*. But in gathering new fans, who wanted Kingston Trio lookalikes when you could have the Jefferson Airplane and Grateful Dead?—by their clothes and attitudes, at least, celebrants of nonconformity.

Around the time of *Pet Sounds* Derek Taylor's mission was to push the 'eccentric genius' angle in competition with the Beatles' and Stones' supercool-dudes image. An obvious problem with the genius approach was that people who were interested already knew Brian was a genius and those who weren't (i.e. radio listeners, who were getting younger all the time) wouldn't have cared if he was Mozart and Einstein rolled into one—it was the era of Don Kirshner's zany-cutesie Monkees, after all.

As it was, even with Capitol's neglect in having their sales audited, in 1968, in celebrating its first ten years the Recording Industry Association of America named the most prolific winners of Gold Discs as the Beatles, Elvis Presley, tv veteran Mitch Miller, the Beach Boys and Frank Sinatra. Exhausted to a standstill up against the Beatles and the rest of the Establishment, the group took time to navel-gaze. Mike Love found a solution of sorts, in *joining* the Beatles, Donovan and Mia Farrow (and various relatives memorialised in 'Jennifer Juniper' and 'Dear Prudence') in the foothills of the Himalayas to meditate with the Maharishi. Dennis had introduced himself to the yogi in Paris the previous December after a UK tour as the Beach Boys prepared for a UNICEF concert. Prompted by some foreboding the Maharishi gave Dennis, just turned 23, an insightful warning, hinting at a life to be cut short: "Live your life to the fullest" (*Dennis Wilson: Dreamer* website, Dan Addington).

Far from the Beatles' cultivated air of Eastern mysticism, Mike was disappointed to hear them asking about levitation, as a party trick. A month later they would 'expose' the guru for making advances to young white women, issuing a collective statement that the Maharishi had been "a public mistake"—meaning a much more embarrassing one than their usual missteps, carefully stifled by minders before the public got wind of them. In their second turnaround in as many months they went back to their druggy lifestyle. By now the Beatles were so exalted their public swallowed anything they did as imbued with cosmic love. But much in the way they pulled their laddish Liverpool humor on fans at concerts, it is impossible not to believe (what other explanation is there?) that the same hardass leg-pulling is responsible for studio products 'Yellow Submarine' and 'Sergeant Pepper' and, no less celebrated in the history of so-called Rock, the mind-numbingly repetitive 'Hey Jude', its second half comprising "nah" chanted 175 times.

Attempting to substitute idealism for showbiz, the Beach Boys brought TM to the stage—Step right up, the one and only Maharishi, fresh from SRO in the Rishikesh…. For a week, even assuming his strong accent was intelligible to Americans, audiences withstood a pre-show 90-minute dose of transcendental meditation from the guru that scared thousands of music fans away. It reeked of "Take your medicine first—Then you can enjoy yourself…" Of all the nerve, it was the Maharishi who bowed out… without notice. The Beach Boys, sadly, wouldn't go on without him, even when they were guaranteed thousands more in attendance to what would have been the last concert.

Their latest single, the gentle 'Friends' in its 3/4 Waltz-shuffle, turned out an unprecedented international flop—hardly heard in Europe. It had made steady progress by mid-April to top 30 in Houston, Chicago #37 and New York City #33 on May 1st, then mostly disappeared. Word about the Beach Boys' new act spread to LA, where, rising to #17, the new song vanished. It did best along the Ohio River Valley, surfacing top ten St Louis, Louisville, Pennsylvania tri-cities, Boston #20, settling mid-thirties nationally—a further a decile down in Billboard as usual.

That month John and Paul flew to New York to announce the advent of Apple Corps (pronounced "core"), their own company, on *The Tonight Show*. It was an invitation to scam artists worldwide, more than recording artists, to drain the Beatles' new-found funds on any scheme that sounded arty and was guaranteed to bring in no income. And it is now, barely four months after announcing his official engagement to Jane Asher, that he begins 'dating' Linda Eastman (not that Paul had *ever* been faithful to Jane—Salewicz), photographer and girlfriend to rock stars. To get over his dumping by Jane, Paul whisks yet another girlfriend off on a Mediterranean vacation. In May, new A-list socialite coupling Paul & Linda dine with Andy Williams and sit through his London concert. The group's next major recording session, under Paul, is in July—'Ob La Di, Ob La Da'. Even Andy wouldn't have been caught recording anything so twee.

A SERIES OF VIOLENT DEATHS THROUGH SPRING symbolized the end of Sixties innocence: the destruction in a routine test flight of cosmonaut Yuri Gagarin, who at 27 had been the first space hero; the assassination of Martin Luther King, sparking riots in nearly two hundred cities, and of Robert Kennedy, lost as a civil rights champion who looked like a winner over Nixon in the upcoming election. Liberal experiments began in Czechoslovakia under premier Alexander Dubcek, and Canada —led by glam-intellectual Pierre & Margaret Trudeau, an echo of the Kennedys' Camelot to challenge Paul & Linda and John & Yoko among the magazine cover set.

By summer '68 Brian Wilson had given in. Lately anything that could go wrong did. He described *Friends* many years later on his Internet website as "our best production to date. It had perfect instrumental tracking with no mistakes. I used the Beach Boys and many studio musicians as well." Dennis's drumming is recognizable on his 'Little Bird' and others. It absolutely bombed in the US; rose just outside top ten UK and a quite lucrative ranking inside it in Japan.

Short of relocating to Louisville—their most consistent market for singles lately—or Japan, there seemed little the group could do. Meantime others were capitalising on their style. Rhode Island family group the Cowsills—who always sounded like the Mamas & the Papas trying to sing Beach Boys—had taken the organ pulse of 'Good Vibrations' a year later and set it to the similarly themed 'The Rain, the Park & Other Things', their biggest hit ever. Through July their upbeat pop disc 'Indian lake' was a top tenner and Beach Boys to a tee in all but name. In Britain former Ivy League members and ex-Beatle and Who associates John Carter and Ken Lewis had done better than any other Englishmen emulating them with 'Let's Go to San Francisco', and the adventurous Paul & Barry Ryan went from 'Keep it Out of Sight', Spectorish down to the booming *baion* beat and castanets, to pocket symphony 'Eloise', following the new Brian Wilson structure, even to its middle harmony break.

Their sound was so universally known and admired by now the Beatles would soon pay open tribute with 'Back in the USSR'. Instead of the out-and-out collaboration McCartney suggested to Lennon, they made a fair imitation on their own. That is, with coaching from Mike Love. Witnessing Paul composing the song in March in India, Mike saw the style it was taking on and, joining in the creative process, advised Paul how to further Beach Boys-ize the song. In return the Beatles wrote a dismal "happy birthday" song for Mike, singing it to him to celebrate his 27th. In perhaps the heaviest irony of the Beatles vs Beach Boys dichotomy, the resulting recording is a cross between 'Help Me Rhonda' and 'California Girls', in a style the Beach Boys had outgrown three years before. Yet, it has ever since been justly hailed by *Beatle* fans as one of their heroes' best ever records.

It would be a shame to kick sand in all those admirers' faces, including the Beatles'. So, once again prompted by Mike, Brian and he wrote 'Do It Again', ostensibly about a day Mike spent surfing with a friend but really about him reclaiming commercial ground for himself and the group, even down to referencing their past milestone hit 'California Girls'.

Recall to surf music thrilled The Establishment: These cleancut kids, annoyingly so unpredictable, were back in place in vanilla suits, if worn too flamboyantly to be 'one of us'. And why is the lead singer heavily bearded like some hermit, and the drummer half-bearded—a bum from a spaghetti western? None of the group smiled anymore for publicity shots. Since 'Vibrations' airplay had been moderate at best. Play was no better now—in the Hot 100 even lower than 'Darlin''— but they were welcomed back with open arms by television. This was a comeback. Sales were high— Chicago #1, Calgary #2, LA #3, San Diego and Kentuckiana #4, Toronto and Ft Knox #5, Boston #6, Washington DC and tri-cities Pennsylvania #7, New York City, Detroit and Cincinnati #8—but it was Johnny Carson, doyen of intellectual tv Dick Cavett and Mike Douglas, all out of New York, who brought them back before a big public, followed in October by their third, and last, Sullivan show: They played the new hit and 'Vibrations' with psychedelic effects and mirrored Dennis and Bruce images: the two handsomest guys in the band—and sang over tracks specially recorded.

Their status as national icons held, just. Boston-New England, Salt Lake City, Phoenix would stay freakishly devoted. Southern California—after a year and a half of apathy—had come back with a rush to their new music '66-70. Detroit, always ambivalent, supported them better now than in their '65-66 heyday. New Yorkers too came to the party, but peered closely at reviews for each new single. Miami dropped them like a hot brick after 'Vibrations', as did San Francisco, backing its counter-culture bands' album tracks under the FM format. About now the Northwest and Canada's RPM chart (hardly reflecting the group's frequent triumphs in the biggest cities) began to freeze-dry on them. Markets would peel off several at a time across the continent, after harsh decisions by radio chain owners.

Top of the UK heap for 31st August 1968:

1. Do It Again – the Beach Boys
2. I Gotta Get a Message to You – the Bee Gees
3. This Guy's in Love With You – Herb Alpert
4. Mony Mony – Tommy James & the Shondells
5. Help Yourself – Tom Jones
6. Fire – the Crazy World of Arthur Brown

Second week at peak in Record World, September 21st, overtaken by the Beatles and early Deep Purple, a psychedelic take on Joe South:

1. Harper Valley PTA – Jeannie C Riley
2. Hey Jude/Revolution – the Beatles
3. 1-2-3 Red Light – 1910 Fruitgum Company
4. People Got to Be Free – the Rascals
5. Hush – Deep Purple

6. The House That Jack Built — Aretha Franklin
7. Do It Again — the Beach Boys
8. Born to Be Wild — Steppenwolf
9. Fool on the Hill — Sergio Mendes & Brasil '66
10. Slip Away — Clarence Carter

The group had reclaimed commercial respectability around the world—#8 Cash Box, topping UK and Australia, almost in Germany and many other countries—while remaining irrelevant to the sociopolitical environment: a concern central to the music business if you wanted to be taken as serious 'musicians' in the late Sixties. Muso-politicos would have liked nothing better than songs-to-sway-slowly-to documenting: the Red Army crushing democracy in Czechoslovakia, late August; Mayor Daley's Chicago police crushing democratic protest outside the Democrat Party convention; Democrats voting pro-Vietnam War, choosing Hubert Humphrey as compromise candidate against Nixon over 'dangerous liberal' George McGovern and 'radical lefty' Eugene McCarthy.

Late summer when Vietnam bled freest and civil unrest was rife at home, Capitol included on the third *Best of...* such demeaning trivialities as 'Frosty the Snowman', decrepit prototype 'Surfin''; dated '409' and 'Dance Dance Dance'; and bygone ballads 'She Knows Me Too Well' and 'Girl Don't Tell Me'. 'Sloop John B', 'Caroline No', 'Wouldn't It Be Nice?', 'Wild Honey', 'Friends', 'Do It Again'... would have been ideal but were ignored—some were included on the UK edition. Given the charitable interpretation of mere gross incompetence by Capitol, it was worse than a commercial turkey and the group was unhumorously roasted.

Any life left in their career was severely prejudiced too by *Stack 'O Tracks*—fifteen Beach Boy hits shorn of their singing, useful only for *karaoke*, not yet invented. By way of overkill, stomping (and maybe pissing) on the ashes, the label reissued a clipped *Surfin' USA* album as *Close Up*, its name implying this ancient surf music—six years old, buried under six strata of Sixties music—was indeed the essence of the Beach Boys. Paleontologists ensured sales more apocalyptic than the disaster of *Best of... III*. This was selling the group as a sworn enemy might, rather than a committed business partner. From this sort of treatment the Beatles themselves could never have recovered.

10: IF WE SING IN A VACUUM CAN YOU HEAR US?

A *social revolution propelled by world events swirled.* *While Lennon and others protested against the war and famine in Biafra, the Beach Boys played benefits for 'positive' causes. Their peers—the Beatles, Stones, The Who—still admired them beyond bounds but they lost cred with youth in an era that defined hip as simplistic social stance. But even then instead of Carl's draft resisting attracting credit, London police busting John & Yoko at Ringo's home for possessing marijuana was the style of photo-op media event that oppressed youth empathised with.*

'Do It Again', their last big hit for two decades, was proof positive there was no way out for Brian & the Beach Boys. They could do surf music and succeed, or innovate and fail. But after six years as world stars their music confirmed in many minds that they were survivors and deserved to be. In Seattle, in the annual KOL listener vote taken as 'Do It Again' peaked, 'Surfer Girl' and 'In My Room' were hailed the two most popular songs from 1963, overtaking previous favorites 'Rhyhm of the Rain', 'End of the World' and 'Wipe Out'.

Longevity said little in pop currency. A new plateau in US sales in fall '68 meant a top three 45 could ship two million units (e.g. 'Love Child', 'Stoned Soul Picnic') and the most popular— 'Harper Valley PTA', 'Hey Jude', 'I Heard It Through the Grapevine'—four million in as many months. Gold 45s in 1969 multiplied 1965's total by six, though more money in teens' pockets saw the album about to overtake the single. Riding high were Easy Rider *classic 'Born to Be Wild' with Jose Feliciano's Latin remake of 'Light My Fire' and the Doors' 'Hello, I Love You'. Cream's 'Sunshine of Your Love', Deep Purple and Arthur Brown represented a hard rock British Infusion—far more skilled than the original, with no accompanying mania.*

OUT OF MEDITATION CAME FLOURISHING COMMERCIAL inspiration from the Beatles. Mary Hopkin, spotted on tv by famous model Twiggy and passed on to Paul McCartney, provided the Music Hall basis for their Apple Corps—up to now consisting mainly of their London fashion boutique. 'Lady Madonna' was their last single on Parlophone/Capitol and in going to 'only' no.4 in Billboard after four years of cast-iron no.1s they must have felt the red carpet they had been treated to wearing a little thin. The "White" double album began its long recording schedule in May '68. Two months later an animated film about them, *Yellow Submarine*— by the makers of *The Beatles* cartoon tv series—debuted. The Beatle industry ground on.

It was during the making of the *White Album* that the Beatles visibly unravelled. Each would bring his own projects conceived in India into the studio expecting the others to participate on the spot coming in cold. It wasn't as if any, apart from Paul to some degree, had the ability of a Beach Boy to tape himself doing a part for a song and later splice it in. Entering the studio one day, John Lennon was openly insulting, understandably, of Paul's ska tune 'Ob-La-Di, Ob-La-Da' and then and there improvised the suitably derisory Colonel Blimp intro for it on piano. By introducing girlfriend Yoko Ono to recording sessions with no beg-pardons John had brought more tension to his creative and personal relationship with Paul, already stretched to breaking point. Now, egged on to more and more 'artistic independence' by Yoko and scorning Paul's discipline that had always brought him back in line, John was turning from musician (though never in Paul's class) to middle-aged hellraiser. No longer collaborating, the song sketches brought to the table by each suffered. John-Yoko as a single entity would spend more and more time away from music, borrowing Ringo's house to get addicted to heroin (Chis Salewicz) and only coming out for their highly publicised international Peace projects. Soon busted for marijuana possession, Yoko miscarried their baby due to the stress.

George Harrison's solo 'While My Guitar Gently Weeps' was a rare highlight on what should have been a bonanza of brilliance, given their reputations. In fact, Harrison (the *Wonderwall* film soundtrack) and John-Yoko (*Two Virgins*) projects were released just three and two weeks before the group double album in early November. *Two Virgins*, best known for its 'artistic' cover of the nude couple, was a flop on both sides of the Atlantic. Ringo would come out with a solo album (*Sentimental Journey*) before long, then another (*Beaucoups of Blues*) hopefully recorded in Nashville. Though impacting not at all on the massive earnings coming from the group effort, they were clear signals that at least three Beatles had other plans.

That month, November, 'Hey Jude' completed its nine-week run at number one and US release of the *Yellow Submarine* movie brought them to ebb tide just as group relations were going into meltdown. Fully melded to Yoko, John and fiancée appeared at the Royal Albert Hall in December dressed in a giant white bag. They wittily dubbed this new movement—after their nudism promoted on the *Two Virgins* cover—Bagism. Beatle followers either affectionately indulged these egocentric symptoms or considered them stretching the boundaries of art. Many others were growing tired of people who seemed to draw no limits on grabbing attention: the new Sonny & Cher, but lacking their humor.

Apple business was going great guns, the virginal Mary introduced to America by Ed Sullivan. Billboard rated her Gypsy-Music Hall number (actually Russian in origin) 'Those Were the Days' runner up under 'Jude', the other major trades multiple weeks on top—moving over five million worldwide by year's end. But her rapid falling off ('Goodbye' was pure Music Hall and a near sequel) had to be taken up by the Beatles themselves, as always ready with a good, easily memorable singalong for the old folks home—though with a style up to a hundred years old many would have to strain.

'Revolution 9' was typical of their arty approach to composition as it developed post-*Rubber Soul*. Lennon described his track as "an abstract sound picture" though only those enthralled by the Emperor could see his new clothes. The technique was legitimised by terms from the visual arts—collage, montage. The creative process: From EMI's London library were copied bits of old tapes from various sources, chopped further or run backwards. Lennon, once the down-to-earth Liverpudlian who would take crap from no one, was now arty-farty-full-of-it: "There are many symbolic messages going on in it, but it just happened. You know, cosmic meandering." His once macho baritone had degenerated to something ponderous and faltering on tracks like 'Across the Universe', then a reedy little voice almost duplicating Yoko-squeaking by the time of 'Stand By Me' (1976).

When the Beatles understandably lost interest in 'Helter Skelter' it was left to a stand-in newcomer—Chris Thomas, who produced at least ten tracks—and a new engineer to speed up the track and improvise an ending. Against George Martin's wishes, the *White Album* was extended to thirty tracks—more than double the usual. From the fact that he took a three-week holiday in the middle of the project, and from his later comments, it is impossible not to see through his gentlemanly politeness total disillusionment. It was later he realised the Beatles were rushing to deliver a quota of tracks to EMI so they could begin a new contract at a higher royalty rate. Knowing it would be unacceptable from any other group, the Beatles spewed out a new track every two days under a green producer unable to control them. Even Beatle George assessed the album could readily have been culled to their standard fourteen tracks.

Writer Chris Salewicz, a Beatle supporter: "The White Album was something of a failure. In the main, it consisted of rough sketches of songs that sounded as though they had been conceived for separate solo records."

So much for this particular Beatle masterpiece. Needless to say, released on the fifth anniversary of JFK's assassination, it proved their biggest ever seller with nearly two million advance US sales: If you're going to pull a hoax pull it big and barefaced, and so believable. Beatle 'mysticism', a.k.a. sleight of hand, had triumphed again. The Beach Boys openly stated that *Party* was knocked off in a rush to meet the contract, urging fans not to take it seriously. The Beatles let fans believe that their knock-off was weighty indeed.

'Helter Skelter' was inspiration to one Charles Manson, new resident of Southern California of no fixed abode—until he gave his parole officer Dennis Wilson's address as his own. Manson, through his twisted senses, saw the song as a personal love call—an incitement to race war.

R ECORDING OF MOST OF THE UPCOMING *20 / 20* WAS completed in November as the *White Album* was released. Lennon's 'Revolution', that is, anti it, was a rallying call to conservatives, hippies and staid pacifists alike. Seemingly the voice of eminent reasonableness, it found an audience for its solid rock values, a ripping guitar intro by John, and Ringo's thumping bass-laden shuffle beat. It outdid 'Do It Again', included on *20 / 20*— whose strongest tracks after all might be 'Cabinessence' and 'Our Prayer' (making a distinguished appearance on the soundtrack of a new German film in November 2007), both adapted from *Smile*.

In hopes as a 45 the Beach Boys acquiesced to Bruce Johnston's urging to issue a danceable song, and revived Ersel Hickey rockabilly from ten years before—not a well advised career move but in accord with their devotion to rock'n'roll. 'Bluebirds Over the Mountain' had been a minor hit too for the Echoes in 1962 and was minor yet again. Thanks to guitar work from session man Ed Carter it sounded like a white version of Hendrix—no competition for current classic 'Crosstown Traffic'. Riding on their recent surfin' success, it did best in Record World—by 25 places over Billboard—and top twenty in the sales surveys of Los Angeles, San Diego, Detroit, Boston-New England, Columbus, Minneapolis and Missouri; San Francisco and Birmingham just outside. In key cities New York, ChiTown, Philadelphia and large chunks of the rest of America, the group, an expired commodity to the radio industry, were missing presumed dead.

In Canada too it continued a steep slide. But in the Chicago Daily Herald of November 22nd, seven years into the group's recording career, a Japanese teen spokesperson just arrived in the country announced: "Oh, Japanese teens love the Monkeys [sic], the Beatles and the Beach Boys."

Early in the Xmas-UK tour season rivals the Supremes scored a Royal Command Performance. They had missed Billboard's top twenty twice in the past year and would repeat that average this coming year. The last noticeable hit for the Four Seasons was eight months before, a knockout reworking of 'Will You Still Love Me

Tomorrow?'. The upcoming Beach Boy hit would post worldwide, in US sales charts just below The Who's 'Pinball Wizard', above Elvis's 'Memories', the Doors, as cool as you could get on 'Wishful, Sinful (Wicked You)', and Cream's 'Badge', co-written by George Harrison, faltering in the 60s of the Hot 100.

The Boys would two years later be commanded to play for a Royal: Princess Margaret; but Paul & Linda were soon escorting her on a state visit to the set of *The Magic Christian* to see movie stars Ringo, Peter Sellers and Marlon Brando. They went ahead with their Euro-tour enhanced by $600,000 in new sound equipment and three sidemen with them for years to come—Darryl Dragon on keyboards, Ed Carter guitar and Mike Kowalski percussion, plus a four-piece horn section. Supports included Barry Ryan of the impressive 'Eloise', and Vanity Fare—typical Britpop, coming off a mediocre remake of Murry Wilson's 'I Live for the Sun'.

The *Live in London* album, recorded at the Astoria on December 8th, saw them in good form—beginning a superlative live reputation sustained through the mid seventies. It flopped none the less and wasn't released at home until their next comeback. Still rock royalty, the day after the show they were invited to visit the Beatles' Apple offices by Derek Taylor, now back home with his original charges and soon embarking on that famous John & Yoko lie-in in Montreal. Gifted copies of the *White Album*, it must have felt strange indeed to see Beach Boy memorabilia mirrored back at them—'Back in the USSR', 'Wild Honey Pie'.... With the Beatles' Northern Songs granted Europe publishing rights for 'Bluebirds', inter-group ties became yet closer when it was rumored ludicrously that its composer Ersel Hickey was Paul McCartney. Still, it was perceived, the Fabs were doing *them* a favor hanging out.

The Beatles were now visibly responding too to free radicals Jimi Hendrix and Cream to delve heavier into a blues approach by introducing the keyboard playing of Billy Preston, the young Little Richard/Sam Cooke veteran—contributing electric piano and organ to many of the Liverpudlians' best late-Sixties hits—to finally redeem their lack of funk apparent to all but their fans all along. Compare the licks on 'Don't Let Me Down' to Hendrix's earlier 'The Wind Cries Mary'. This was maybe the last straw for Beatle Corp in its previous cover-all cross-generational dominance of the UK market, tainted as they were now by genuine black music. Their singles in particular took a dive in UK sales through their last two years, only the big McCartney ballads reappearing to tug young and old Music Hallers' heartstrings.

The Beatles had sorted their label problems, in Apple. The idea was "to make business fun", get recordings out without the grind of routine. As the Beach Boys had discovered 18 months before with Brother, dollars and cents inevitably get in the way. But with a huge double album and double 45 underway, Mary Hopkin off the ground, soon James Taylor and Billy Preston as a solo, Beatle business was booming. Having conquered pop culture, the world of commerce looked in the bag.

On January 30th 1969, two and a half years after ceasing touring and maybe nostalgic for the old days, the Beatles set up their equipment on top of the Apple Building in Savile Row and, joined by Billy Preston on electric piano, played for the public for the last time, for free—an episode replayed by the B-sharps on *The Simpsons*, frequently living out its obsession with Beatle lore. They had only got through 'Get Back' (Paul) and its flip 'Don't Let Me Down' (John) when police stopped the show in response to disgruntled office workers complaining about "the noise". Despite their live performance improving out of sight since their early recording days— only now catching up to the Beach Boys' *TAMI Show* standard of performance—the most famous rock band in the world were treated with no more respect than a group of anonymous Hawthorne kids who had upset cranky neighbors in 1961— maybe saying it all about what inroads rock'n'roll hadn't made into the Establishment through the decade and where the real power doesn't lie.

Recorded five months before, 'I Can Hear Music' promoted *20 / 20*. The first single Brian hadn't participated in, its quality stands as a tribute to the surviving band and particularly Carl, who produced it and took the impressive contralto lead vocal. The best 'girl group' recording of 1969, a video clip played on the BBC's *Top of the Pops* April 3rd opposite Marvin Gaye and Joe South ('Games People Play') and some of Britain's most popular artists including Cliff Richard, Lulu, the Hollies and Foundations, was sufficient exposure to drive it to top ten. With this, as with 'Do It Again', they helped pioneer the rock video, promo clips of both distributed internationally. These extended their European presence and they impressed enough industry people in Germany to prompt huge conglomerate Deutsche Grammophon to express interest in taking over from the Capitol tenure about to end.

Carl's superior remake—called the definitive version by the Ronettes, who sang the original—impacted the world over but despite good sales across the States—#5 Boston, #7 New York and Chicago, top ten Los Angeles, San Diego, Seattle, Vancouver, Houston, across Ohio (top in Akron), almost in Detroit—it couldn't break the hoodoo of American radio, Billboard peaking it at 24. *20 / 20* emphasized the media greylisting that was confined to America. Under-promoted by Capitol as their last album, the label knowing it would get no flow-on benefits, it was still their biggest in Britain since *Pet Sounds* and bar none in Japan.

A syndicated contemporary review of *20 / 20* by David F Wagner: "The Beach Boys, as Crawdaddy once pointed out, were the first to return to simplicity (even before Dylan, so dig it)... Dennis Wilson saved it all for the pounding 'All I Want to Do' (rock musicologists insist this is what the form is all about, and the Stones didn't invent it either). Unfortunately, the very young find the Beach Boys old, and too many 'hip' people are now-ists, so the group has slipped in popularity."

The Dennis song was their best rocking of the late sixties. Mike was inspired to sing all-out in Dennis style, while the composer saved his energy for the fading tag—"I just want to do it to you girl, all night long! Oh come on, come on, come on baby!"—as he, setting a new mark for rock drummers to aspire to, and a woman friend performed for real in the studio, complete with grunts and gasps.

Attrition by media had telling effects. In a field whose prevailing principle was to milk a paying product to its last drop, the US industry preempted the judgment of the public and doomed the group to a shallow grave. But all the neglect couldn't prevent a telltale hand popping above ground every so often. Two years before in the Gilbert Youth Research survey of the nation the Beach Boys had been voted America's favorites—decisively ahead of the Stones, Monkees and Beatles, the Supremes following. In the poll of New Year '69 they still ranked high—on par with Jimi Hendrix Experience, the Doors, Temptations and Fifth Dimension—but below an upper level of Beatles, Simon & Garfunkel, Rascals and (rapidly fading) the Association.

Regardless, Dennis was at his creative peak and began recording 'San Miguel', 'Got to Know the Woman' and 'Forever' for the intended *Sunflower*. Progress was slow, most work coming down to the two remaining Wilsons, the hardest workers too on *20 / 20*. No one could have predicted midyear that the final showdown with Capitol would postpone *Sunflower* a year. As with the Beatles the Beach Boys' power vacuum found form in an unwieldy democracy — each getting two or so of his songs per new album, sometimes irrespective of quality. The majority (having Brian's proxy vote) had developed little creative power thus far to back its authority. Mike Love, able from the start to be Brian's lyricist and sometime musical editor, would rarely stand alone or as senior partner with satisfactory results. Often, disparate personalities would neuter each other instead of enhancing a group effort, the whole collapsing in paralysis for want of a cohesive sum of parts. Dennis wisely put some of his best songs aside, until he could direct them as solo recordings, even if coming to collaborate with the others later. Dennis's restless temperament wouldn't allow him to dally in the studio convincing everyone. Brian—also past that point but straining against inertia—provided most new material, the others between them producing just half a dozen or so commercial enough songs between album release dates: an interval now expanding to a year, the impetus that once allowed them to produce an album every three or four months a thing of the past.

The Beatle film *Let It Be* had also begun in the New Year of '69, meant as a tv show where the band would play new tracks but emerging a year and a half later as a painstakingly crafted album and an unfinished documentary of a project that never eventuated.

APPLE BECAME VERY MUCH MORE RATIONALIZED and businesslike—and a lot less fun—once American tycoon Allen Klein appeared. Going back to the early Sixties as accountant or business manager for Bobby Darin, Bobby Vinton, the Shirelles and Sam Cooke, he handled British Invaders Dave Clark Five, the Animals and Hermans Hermits before moving on to the Rolling Stones, whom he co-managed with Andrew Oldham. After nearly three years experiencing his services the Stones recommended Klein to the Beatles, who signed him in spring 1969 to control their finances—all but Paul, who aligned his business affairs with the Eastman family headed by Paul's father-in-law, New Yorker Lee Eastman. Paul had married Linda Eastman—followed eight days later by John, now in obsessive competition with Paul in every sphere, marrying Yoko Ono. The visual artist had become a constant presence in John's life and a contentious one at recording sessions. For the most part the contest between John and Paul had been a healthy fertile one. But through this period, stated one staffer central to events, Lennon impressed him as being off his rocker—made unstable by the tension caused when he thrust Yoko on the others. Even before Klein arrived Apple was no ideal business, with Lennon and McCartney casually countermanding each other's orders to staff.

But the move was bound to alienate McCartney, who had after all contributed most to the group's musical career—and most to their image as friendly all-round good guys, come to that. From the time they had stopped touring John and George had kicked over the carcass of the band, Paul being the gung ho one for staying together. With others staying as a convenience, and now facing what must have seemed like a personal betrayal, it was just a matter of time until Paul handed in his walking papers. He would make it official in court on New Year's Eve 1969.

It was in early May that the bubble burst. All Beatle minder-confidants were cast aside by the new regime. Alistair Taylor, who considered himself a close friend since coming aboard with Brian Epstein, was top of Klein's hitlist. Nicknamed 'Mr Fixit', up to now he had been first port of call for all the dirty work, including making paternity suits go away. Desperate, Taylor tried to phone them all. But the Beatles had developed the knack, long before superstardom, of switching their engaging personalities off—even from friends—when they wanted to be aloof. According to Stafford Hildred, ghost writer for one of Taylor's three books on the Beatles, Taylor, the man who knew too much, was airbrushed out of Beatle history as one witness too many. Taylor claims to have been the senior collaborator over Paul in writing 'Hello Goodbye', not exactly an outrageous boast. And perennial mate/road manager Mal Evans says he too collaborated significantly with Paul on 'Sgt Pepper' and 'Fixing a Hole' (in Salewicz)—and who can doubt him? Prevailed upon not to spoil the Lennon-McCartney brand on the credits, he was given royalties.

It would be three years or so, after Klein had been indicted for tax evasion, before the three admitted they were seriously taken in. The consensus of those on hand is that Yoko was prime but not sole factor in the Beatles' looming breakup. Under Yoko's influence John got pushier at Apple; and Allen Klein, to get around John, was said to defer to Yoko's opinions and ambitions. Yoko was so intent on being a dominant personality she ridiculously denied ever having heard of the Beatles previous to meeting John

Meantime, John & Yoko did their Montreal bed-in for peace—and the press. Timed immaculately four days into their prone protest the self-mythologizing 'Ballad of John & Yoko' dented top ten. Paul's 'Get Back', released a few weeks earlier, was a much bigger hit. Both were excellent tracks—but John&Yoko wasn't the same person as just John, and wasn't as popular. Recorded a few days later, stalling outside the top discs, came 'Give Peace a Chance', hardly music—a droning chant hauled out for peace demonstrations ever since. Its follow-up, 'Cold Turkey', was exactly that. Cooing Paul love ballads 'Hey Jude', 'Let It Be', 'Long and Winding Road' were their only songs guaranteed to top the charts—in the US, no longer at home. Their albums were as big as ever—bigger with the rapidly growing market for long-players. To the end of '68 it was estimated (Chapple & Garofalo) that the group had sold, worldwide, discs worth $154 million. Sales of their next release would mount over five million globally in three months; and even as they broke up their last l.p. topped 3,700,000 US in just over two weeks.

By summer the Beatles had been sidetracked to *Abbey Road*. George Martin thought long and hard before working with them again after his experience on *Let It Be* early that year: "They were becoming unpleasant people—to themselves as well as to other people. And I really thought we'd finished" (Pritchard & Lysaght). As always, Paul was the peacemaker in persuading Martin and rounding up the others. And this time he brought Linda McCartney to the studio to balance against the John-Yoko faction. The counter force of Linda, guilty of taking John's 'first love'—as John later described Paul—brought out a physically violent jealousy in John on more than one occasion (Salewicz).

The resulting album was very much the sort of compromise the Beach Boys too had become used to—first side the gospel according to John; a second side according to Paul, also heavily involving Martin. Its big double was 'Come Together'/'Something', both well-crafted and commercial songs. 'Oh! Darling', 'Here Comes the Sun' and 'She Came in Through the Bathroom Window' were others worthwhile. The usual cutesie wordplay songs were kept to a minimum in 'Mean Mr Mustard' and 'Polythene Pam'. There was enough rock to make it interesting but the Music Hall of 'Maxwell's Silver Hammer' (which John condemned as "Paul's granny music") and Ringo's 'Octopus's Garden' is seriously offputting and 'Golden Slumbers'/'Carry That Weight' slumber-inducing. Released late September, it wasn't as lucrative as the double album, maybe indicating they were bought less for rock now and more for their 'mystique'.

The Beach Boys had not only an internal schism in common with the Beatles but business fragility. Victims of creative accounting as the Beatles had suffered, it was coincidentally April Fools Day that the Beach Boys announced they were suing Capitol again for $2 million of unpaid royalties. There was another settlement. The June 1969 shock heard around the world of "Beach Boys near bankruptcy", as melodramatically reported by Brian Wilson was the last nail in the coffin of any hope of rivalling the Beatles. Brian's rush of blood to the head blew a marginal business squeeze into a real loss of confidence from potential backers of the group.

EUROPEAN TOURS WERE NOW A TWICE-ANNUAL IM-perative but their May-June '69 shows boosted their own morale and American goodwill as first by a rock group behind the Iron Curtain. Guest of honor on the Czech leg was Alexander Dubcek, hero of the "Prague Spring" liberalisation deposed by the Soviet invasion the previous summer. The Beach Boys may have come close to causing an international incident in dedicating their show to this officially disfavored member of the audience. They gave more shows in Hungary and Finland, also neglected by the rock world. Sound engineer Steve Desper has told how, with a 50,000-Watt system, he could barely make the band heard over the screaming at their Prague shows—the kind of Beachboymania they weren't experiencing at home lately. Germany, France—a return to the Paris Olympia where they had scored so heavily five years before—Belgium and Holland were also included.

It had started in the UK and Bruce Johnston (in Badman) was right that, to advance the new image of the Beach Boys it would have needed a group like the seriously creative Fairport Convention in support rather than American tv stars Paul Revere & the Raiders, unknown in Britain. Highlight was a long, impromptu, unplugged show they gave on their own for hundreds in the nurses home at Leeds Infirmary performed as a personal favor for compere Jimmy Savile, a UK radio & tv institution. Giving a performance hard to imagine from the Beatles, three on acoustic guitars and Dennis beating on a packing case and waving a tambourine filled the bill.

The upcoming single was well received in performance, especially in Eastern Europe where the title was symbolic. Intended as a facile bonding initiative from Murry Wilson, his father-son 'Break Away' co-writing project worked less well than the Brian-Mike makeup attempts. Brian predicted publicly, "It'll either be a big hit or a gigantic miss—You can never tell in this business." Both eventualities turned out right, on separate continents, not that a single hit would pull them out of the mire.

With the explosion of black music (confined to America) via Atlantic/Stax—and blues-based Brits Cream and Led Zeppelin on the label—Motown, the Sound of Philadelphia and San Francisco's Sly & the Family Stone, the Beach Boys were off the pace. Their nominal peaks were lower than ever. Widespread shunning now by radio forced them to the margins, independent stations that hadn't heard the word or had not much to lose by playing them: #4 in Council Bluffs, Iowa serving Omaha across Old Man River; #11 in Columbus, #17 in Fargo, North Dakota; barely top twenty New England and California's Central Valley, Sacramento to Fresno; in the twenties at spots through the Midwest and into Canada; #27 in Chicago, #35 in New York. It settled in the 30s in national sales but Billboard's placing thirty down meant barely audible airplay. "Summer music" now meant Sly & the Family Stone's 'Hot Fun in the Summertime'— said to be a satirical comment on the country's race riots. In the UK 'Break Away' did well through July, 8-7-6-8-11, blocked by 'In the Ghetto', 'Ballad of John & Yoko', 'Honky Tonk Women', 'Give Peace a Chance'.

A hit single no longer had the weight to sustain stardom. It was the era of the supergroup—Blind Faith, incorporating stars from Cream, Traffic and the Spencer Davis Group, gave its first concert in Hyde Park, London—and the multi-day "pop" festival: It wasn't called rock until the seventies, when it took on a degraded definition. During summer Jimi Hendrix, Joe Cocker, Creedence Clearwater Revival, Ike & Tina Turner, the Byrds and Jethro Tull played at Newport, where Led Zeppelin were about to debut; The Band, Steppenwolf and Blood, Sweat & Tears at Toronto; Janis Joplin and Canned Heat in

Atlanta. To the Beach Boys stardom meant calling your own terms. There was no going back to package deals, at the mercy of a promoter.

At the end of June their seven-year contract with Capitol expired and Carl, group spokesman, was free to remark on the now former relationship: "They were against *Pet Sounds* and all the albums that came after. They wanted us to stick with surfing and hot-rod records. But we said 'We don't want to do that. We're doing other music now.' But they really weren't going for it. And so they had all these hundreds of people in their organisation pushing another thing, and people were bound to get the wrong impression about the group." Six years later Mike added that when they "made the transition in 1965-66... Capitol Records thought we were overstepping our nice Southern California sunnysideup profile... Capitol wouldn't promote us as a group with an evolving consciousness" (Mary Campbell, Associated Press).

Exploitation is the classic complaint of artists; from Michelangelo vs the Pope, to Chuck Berry whose suspicion of promoters was legendary, to George Michael vs Sony. Michelangelo, we know, was under constant pressure of supporting his father and brothers—and of pleasing the Establishment. The Beatles, on the same label as the Beach Boys, also had reason to complain of exploitation by many from Brian Epstein outwards. After years of Mike complaining of suffering scams by his uncle it might have surprised only Brian that, just months after initiating the co-writing project to help his kids, Murry, seeing them on the career skids and figuring there would be very little made from Beach Boy songs not on the radio, saw an instant solution. Boss of his and Brian's publishing house, Sea of Tunes, he solved his own cashflow problems by selling off all of Brian's copyrighted songs up to 1967 to A&M Records for a bargain basement $700,000. The artist truly traumatised at losing his children, this was one occasion when Brian did escape to his room for days. Though he bore the loss, full recovery from this latest betrayal was measured in, not days or months or years, but generations.

The Deutsche Grammophon offer was withdrawn, warned off by the public statements of the chief Beach Boy, and rumored deals with American majors fizzled. Concert dates were drying up and promoters willing to bankroll them offered less. Then through the good offices of Van Dyke Parks, high enough in the flat, progressive Warner-Reprise chain of command, they signed for a better-than-expected quarter-million up front per album. As an annuity this was hardly going to keep them afloat. When they started they had earnings from four albums a year, boosted by growing concert returns. Now they were starting all over again, almost from scratch.

I~F~ THEY SURVIVED CHARLES MANSON THEY COULD survive anything. Denny Wilson, warming to the Maharishi's veiled prophecy, didn't need any encouragement to "live life to the fullest". He drank deep from the cup of life because his cup runneth over with all kinds of temptations. The few he didn't seek out found him. Among many hellion outlets bordering on the helter-skelter— including a Golden Penetrators Club with pals Terry Melcher and Greg Jakobson—he took to hanging out with fellow hotrod rebel Steve McQueen, on the success of *Bullitt* the world's hottest movie star. The association fuelled Dennis's wild creative instinct and steered it towards films. He had said that if the Beach Boys hadn't happened he would have liked to be a writer—a serious one, a novelist. Before long the one Beach Boy with a salable, projecting screen persona would be, like new pal McQueen, a movie star—in *Two Lane Blacktop* directed by Monte Hellman, an up-and-coming *auteur* in the Roger Corman/Jack Nicholson circle.

Dennis's drive to improve his composing and record-producing skills led him into dark places in the music business. His first meeting with a wannabe songwriter, white supremacist and soon-to-be mass-murder guru should have been a sharp warning—when in summer 1968 a shadowy figure confronted him on a dark night as he returned home at Pacific Palisades. Presciently, Dennis's first words to him were, "Are you going to hurt me?" It was a simple enquiry from the fearless Dennis, who would later beat up Charles Manson more than once, almost to a pulp for threatening beloved stepson Scotty. But Dennis had something in common with him, having picked up some of Manson's female zombies hitch-hiking. Manson, glib in sixties hippy-speak, was for the moment reassuringly plausible.

It was at this time that LA's Turtles wrote and recorded 'Surfer Dan' in ripping surf-music style as B-side of 'Elenore', obviously chronicling the life and times of Surfer Denny. The Beach Boys on the strength of 'Do It Again' were topical again; Denny had never ceased to be: "Everybody's talkin' 'bout Surfer Dan... in his Chevy sedan... He's a friendly Maharishi in his baggies and beads. Surfer's got surfer job down to his knees... Movin' so fast you can't see him go by. He's so ripped he can't see you go by... Surfer Dan—someone that everyone knows—Twenty-seven girls follow wherever he goes!" and so on.

Failing to latch on to the Beatles, thrilled by imaginary racist, helter-skelter messages he read into the *White Album*, Manson proceeded to leech off Dennis as the local equivalent. Dennis was impressed with his dark folk music and mastery of the dark arts—and the lifestyle of Manson's 'Family', which included free-flowing sex in Denny's direction—and agreed to plug the self-styled messiah's songs to his brothers, his partners in Brother Records.

Late that summer Manson recorded—in Brian's studio, it is said with assistance from Brian and Carl—an album Dennis intended for release. One Manson song, creepily titled 'Cease to Exist', was adapted by Dennis from gothic folk into the full-scale production 'Never Learn Not to Love', the B-side of 'Bluebirds Over the Mountain'. He later explained deleting Manson's credit in return for the liberation of much of Dennis's wealth including his accumulation of Gold Discs and collection of luxury cars. In another collaboration that also turned up on *20 / 20*, 'Be With Me', Dennis took Manson's words and wrote the music in its entirety. It was haunting, and would have been better without the lyrics—more of the "Give up your world—Come on and be with me"/"Be a part of me—It would set you free" mind-control theme.

The last straw in their association fell in the wrecking of Dennis's Ferrari, going the way of his trashed house, Rolls Royce, Mercedes and AC Cobra by Manson's right-hand slaughterman Tex Watson and the evil witches in his personal coven. Up to then, to suit both parties, a fair proportion of the Family camped on Dennis's large property at the ocean end of Sunset Boulevard; Manson, a habitual criminal, used the wayward Beach Boy's as his home address to impress his parole officer. As mother Audree would 'explain', Dennis never could refuse people in trouble.

Dennis, Melcher and Jakobson encouraged Manson's fledgling career for some time but after Melcher rejected some of his songs for publication The Wizard's (as Dennis in his fascination had called him) psychedelic charisma began to wear off to show more conventional sociopathic rage. Dennis moved to Pacific Palisades and then to Jakobsen's house in Benedict Canyon. Manson tracked him down— not surprising since, always prey to his sex addiction, Dennis had taken more than a dozen of Manson's sick, clap-ridden harem with him.

It was in August '69 that police started hunting for the mass-murderers of two households in the Los Angeles hills: eight-months-pregnant starlet Sharon Tate, young wife of *avant garde* director Roman Polanski (2003 Oscar-winner for *The Pianist*), and her friends including Dennis and Brian's erstwhile hair stylist Jay Sebring and Abigail Folger, heiress to the coffee empire of the same name; and the La Biancas, a couple living nearby. Since known as the Tate-La Bianca murders, the bloody mess made of these people is on the public record. Three weeks after the first Moon landings, it drove all thoughts of Neil Armstrong and "one giant leap for mankind" instantly out of people's heads. It has been offered that, far from motiveless butchery dressed up as occult ritual, the Los Angeles drug trade had everything to do with it.

Three days after the massacres and long before Manson was found out—though his rock associates were instantly suspicious— Dennis turned him down for two 'loans', prompting a bullet through the mail and a death threat to Scotty. The Family had entered Terry Melcher's home at night and moved the furniture around, to let him know.... Now, one night, Dennis and fiancée Barbara woke from an uneasy sleep to see knife-wielding figures looming over them, melting back into the darkness. When it broke, the front-page story in the LA Times about Dennis's association with Manson infuriated other Beach Boys and bemused fans. Dennis pointed out not entirely innocently, "If I'd known anything I would have been up on that stand."

ONE THING THE BEACH BOYS COULD BE THANKFUL for was they were not as newsworthy as the top British bands—and so escaped a Manson backlash. Not that they had much of a career left to save, in America anyway. The Stones and Beatles were marked for drug busts, Mick and Marianne Faithfull victims of the vice squad early in summer. While a certain amount of scandal was good for the Stones image, the Beatles had to be careful. Cushioned by minders and facilitators every step of the way, their people could make potential scandals go away.

The Stones' devoted following was looking shaky, first faltering —unjustly—in fall '68 with a none the less great 'Jumpin' Jack Flash' soundalike, 'Street Fighting Man', culminating in their total absence from the US 100 from the last strains of 'Honky Tonk Women' on the radio in fall '69 for twenty months until 'Brown Sugar', yet another soundalike. Trauma came—apparently relief for others in the band— when chronically self-involved Brian Jones left the Stones in early June. Within a month he was dead, drowned in his swimming pool— attributed to misadventure until a millennium deathbed murder confession by his then builder. Immersing himself in a new film acting career, Jagger was accidentally shot on the set of *Ned Kelly* in Australia. Faithfull, with him on set, attempted suicide. There was worse to come at Altamont towards the end of the year. For now, they played a respectful memorial for Jones in Hyde Park, attended by 150,000. In a fiasco typical of the Stones' ever-inflating superstar self-indulgence, thousands of white butterflies intended for symbolic release died in overheated cages.

In mid August two events: the "half a million strong" Woodstock be-in in upstate New York near Dylan's home, and the Beatles last recorded together, captured on *Abbey Road*. Two weeks later came Britain's second Isle of Wight festival, headlining Bob Dylan and The

Band. Elvis Presley, like the Beach Boys for now rejecting festivals, performed live for the first time since 1961 —booked for a season in Las Vegas. It was not a venue the Beach Boys, intent on rock credibility, would consider.

John & Yoko were exhibiting two art films in London and appeared September 13th with a mates' band—Eric Clapton, Klaus Voormann—at Toronto's Rock'n'Roll Revival. The other acts included Little Richard, Chuck Berry, Bo Diddley, Jerry Lee Lewis and Gene Vincent—all of whom had striven to revive real rock'n'-roll for the duration of Beatlemania's rule; so far the only converts were Creedence Clearwater Revival. A lowlight in entertainment value was Yoko getting pelted off the stage by projectiles from Beatle fans blaming her for their imminent break-up. Three weeks later, despite all, the Beatles released another two number ones in 'Something'/'Come Together'. It was obvious only a wanton act of self-destruction could defeat them. The Beach Boys, also near foundering as far as the American media and the public knew, four days after the Toronto event once again supplanted the Stones in a UK poll: second among World Vocal Groups. Two days later Paul McCartney produces a version of 'Que Sera Sera' by Mary Hopkin— against the young songbird's wishes, she claims—blander than Doris Day's.

It might have been intended as Detroit's revenge on the Beatles — but the rumor started by a Motor City DJ that Paul had been dead for two years, replaced by a stand-in, backfired. Clear, unmistakable signs were there on album covers and on vinyl tracks for anyone who wanted to see and hear. As their latest double rose up the charts, the belief grew from a cult to a major publicity coup—one more negative that turned into a positive for the group that had made a world-beating career out of me-first exploiters, useful, loyal connections and felicitous happenstance.

The coincidences that 'proved' Paul's death are too numerous and labyrinthine to go into here, but they enhanced the mystique of his group if that was possible. This was the same old Beatlemania in fantasy fiction form. Popular music was one thing, and popular mythology, mainly what the self-perpetuating Beatle publicity machine dealt in, another.

By early November '69 Led Zeppelin, made up from the bones of the Yardbirds, were on their second album and third American tour, commencing at Carnegie Hall; the Stones on their first for three years; The Who were attempting to play *Tommy* at the Fillmore, New York; King Crimson debuted in the US; and Rod Stewart joined the Faces. It was looking very much like a real British infusion, this time of seriously good music.

At the end of the year John Lennon sent back his MBE medal to the Queen in protest at the Biafran War and, he said as an out-of-place joke, the failure of his single 'Cold Turkey'. He and Yoko were stars at a Toronto press conference for peace. And another rope-em-all-in show in London had Eric Clapton, George Harrison, Keith Moon and other names.

The Stones, finally getting what they wished for, found their reputation at rock bottom even among rock aficionados as they played on through the murder of a teen fan in the crowd, in tune with their dark anarchism, beaten to death by Hells Angels 'security' thugs hired for the Stones-Grateful Dead gig at Altamont Raceway east of San Francisco. The event was popularised by the movie *Gimme Shelter*.

To top it all off, in a deathly spirit of Sixties Past, on Xmas Eve the Manson Family trial began—not resolved for another fifteen months, and even then the Manson victims still on his hitlist couldn't rest knowing they could be targeted on orders from prison. Dennis and those close to him suspected, from a sudden personality change, he was got to by spiked cigarette.

As the Beatles began their court case, Paul versus the rest— April 1970 it was announced to the world that they had officially broken up—the loyalty of Australasian Beach Boy fans was repaid by a tour. They remained extremely popular in Sydney, largest city and surf-center, and Auckland, where international pariahs 'Friends', 'Bluebirds' and 'Break Away' had found top twenty, 'I Can Hear Music' had gone close to top and under Stateside/Warner 'Add Some Music to Your Day'/'Slip On Through', 'Don't Go Near the

Water'/'Student Demonstration Time' and 'California Saga'/'Sail On Sailor' would resume their old habit of double-siders getting good airplay—in this part of the world. But it had cost the group $200,000 to launch the tour, and given the limited Australia-New Zealand market it was doubtful they recouped this.

FIRST THE FANS STOP BUYING YOUR RECORDS AND then, as it should be, the radio stations ease off playing them—a natural mellowing of a career, so that a top act's last hits will score better in airplay than sales as station programmers cling to who they know, often for years. For the Beach Boys the pattern was reversed, showing a preemptive, conscious decision by radio to drop them. After three years of this treatment public apathy to the Beach Boys in America reached a level so low that sales levels measured by Cash Box and Record World finally plummeted to their airplay (Billboard) ratings. The Byrds—incidentally having switched producer from one surf music veteran, Terry Melcher, to another, Gary Usher—and the Rascals suffered too, targeted by radio as payback for specific crimes against the industry (daring to insist on integrated shows in the South). While the Beatles, after the Kinks, complained about the taxman taking all their dough the Byrds lampooned "plastic ware" and radio's star-making industry —a serious no-no.

Radio fulfilled its aim and a commercial treasure was taken out of play by an industry that didn't know what was in its best interests. The fact that the Beach Boys were uncontrollable, unpredictable artists worked against them in a business long since rationalized into a few privately owned networks driving for hit predictability and risk averse to the point of ever-narrowing the number of tunes they played. Regional 'top 40s', once ennumerated down to seventy or eighty at some stations, were mostly down to twenty or less, album lists coming to dominate.

A small triumph was Capitol's reissue of 'Good Vibrations' going straight to no.1 in Boston. Confirmation that there was no real forgiveness from America was the cold February reception given

'Add Some Music to Your Day'—an outpouring of love in rock-ballad form that went unrequited. Orders for the single were reported as very big—but the newly important program directors of FM stations decided *en masse* that the Beach Boys would no longer be played, no matter how good. At a time when their world popularity was confirmed yet again by the New Musical Express for the umpteenth time, led only by the Two-Headed Brit Monster —seven months after their last single and nearly a year since *20 / 20*—their currency with the US media had shrunk from the margins last year to just pockets. The song entered the major top 30s from New York to Boston, Los Angeles and Utah, but apart from top ten in St Louis there was no media momentum to carry it further. Again they were halted in Billboard mid-sixties, just in top 40 in Record World, just out in Canada.

Long, showy guitar and drum solos from Led Zeppelin, Santana, Blind Faith, Black Sabbath, Deep Purple, the Allman Bros Band, Grand Funk Railroad, Yes and Emerson, Lake & Palmer were what the newly important FM stations craved. The Boys were out at most AM stations, too. Loyal Brother retainer Fred Vail, now co-manager, tells how he approached the programming boss of a premier top 40 station—Jay Cook, WFIL-Philadelphia—asking for 'Add Some Music' to be put on the playlist and was told that no matter how good/important the Beach Boys were they were not hip anymore (Badman). This from someone who had, as a lesson in hip, 'Love Grows (Where My Rosemary Goes)' topping his chart on March 23rd and Vegas crooners Elvis Presley and Bobby Sherman,, Easy Listening darlings the Fifth Dimension, the Sandpipers, Marmalade, Ray Stevens ('Everything is Beautiful') and fading teen idol Gary Pucket on his platter rack that week.

The paradox was that two years later the same stations would be falling over themselves to play the softer, anticlimactic California 'rock' of the Eagles and America and non-rock of Carole King, Carly Simon and a host of others. There had been great hopes for 'Add Some Music' pre-release and it still sounds like it should have been a rock anthem of the day, urging as it did peace and a coming together through music, more eloquent and stirring than most such hymns.

How dire things were was evidenced by it remaining their biggest American hit for close to half a decade until reissue of 'Surfin' USA'. The signs were ominous for upcoming *Sunflower*.

Just days after the latest Beach Boy issue, in early March 'Let It Be' was released and swamped all thoughts of the Beatles' rivals. Their absence from the airwaves was now so pronounced many casual listeners in America assumed they too had broken up—and this as live performances of their new music were acclaimed critically and popularly in Europe and around the world. America had hardened its heart. The Beach Boys, again with a leader barely out of his teens, would spend their twenties trying to regain favor from compatriots who were dissing and deserting them for the umpteenth time.

On the New Zealand-Australia tour they muttered to the press about resettling in this part of the world—getting away from the politicized, big business-ruled, polluted atmosphere of America. Dennis: "I don't like America. The land is OK, it's the government. I don't like seeing wealth [ab]used... while people are starving in the ghettos. I don't have the power to control this but I don't have to stay amongst it." Mike, in the mid-seventies, would say "I'm very nasty, snide and caustic about America's faults and failings but we're a most positive and creative country." Mostly they settled for relocating out of smog-filled LA; Dennis would stay on to rub shoulders, and share drinks, with urban down-and-outers.

On big bro Brian's retreat they kept his spirit alive by reprising the 'Heroes & Villains' aura, hymning a nation on a historic timeline—a new-old, unique distillation of an American Dream. Again bringing out folk themes for Brian to interpret on vinyl, as he had with 'Sloop John B', it was Al Jardine who introduced bluesman Leadbelly's 'Cottonfields', adapted by Brian on *20 / 20*. Al sang it at concerts through the following year. Too laid back and unfinished for a 45, Al's own thorough reworking of it was released this April. Aired on tv's *Something Else*, hosted by comic impressionist John Byner, it made top tens as few and far between as Manchester, New Hampshire and Tucson, Arizona, but 'Cottonfields' somehow managed the national sales hundred. Though the spirit was of "back in Louisiana, just about a mile from Texarkana, in them old cotton fields back home!"—oozing a folksy Americana—it was their loyal world audience who hugged them to their bosom.

To America's embarrassment, excluded on the US pressing of *Sunflower*, it sold two million-plus overseas. Despite a yawning ten-month singles gap, it made runner-up in the UK's Melody Maker —as high as 'Let It Be' and spending twice as long in the upper sales zone, kept out only by mega-novelty 'In the Summertime'. Setting a personal best UK four-month run, it was listed by New Musical Express as the kingdom's 10th biggest seller of the year. No.1 in Australia, Scandinavia and South Africa—almost in Japan, Spain and Ireland—it marked the end of the group's eight-year run of world hits.

Let It Be, mostly recorded a year or more before, was finally released May 8th 1970. Paul McCartney, especially, and George Martin, were deeply dissatisfied at the results of John Lennon calling in Phil Spector, who augmented the existing tracks with massed strings, choruses and horns—obviously to leave his mark, as required of a signature producer. Five days later the film premiered in London to mixed reviews—some said Allen Klein, with his pervasive hands-on approach to all Beatle business, ruined it. The *Let It Be* movie premiere, held jointly in London and Liverpool, was attended by no Beatles. At two to three week intervals previous, Ringo and Paul had debuted with solo albums, ever expanding the Beatle legend while the Beatles as a band imploded. For some years yet every time John, Paul, George or Ringo released an album or appeared in public it was treated by the media as a Beatle event, not merely something involving an *ex*-Beatle.

But as they called it a day—just in time to promote *Let It Be*— even as their earning power increased through the movie and album, and the Stones and The Who maintained popularity parallel with and outlasting Hendrix, the Beach Boys were cast adrift on their own timeless wave moving at cross purposes to the new mainstream of pop culture.

'The Long and Winding Road', the usual stupendous McCartney ballad unnecessarily sweetened by Spectorian overproduction, was the last Beatles single. Released only in America, it sold 1,200,000 in two days and left the charts late July. *Hey Jude*, a compilation assembled by George Martin also for the huge American market, sold nearly four million through to October, going up against the long-awaited *Sunflower*. *Let It Be* moved four million in a record two weeks and lingered for a year, as distraught Beatle fans realised they were getting the last tastes of the dysfunctioning band that was left. This ghost of a group won a Grammy for Best Original Score. The future for the Beach Boys looked dismal, pitted against a corpse revered by a world media in shock and denial as just the first stages of a generations-long grieving process.

Ironically, there had been growing, now emphatic, signs that Britain, where Beatlemania was sown seven years before, was no longer in its grip. Beatle 45s were once regarded as extraspecial events commanding a million orders UK. And the radio industry had proved it was still in love with them when Paul received an Ivor Novello Award for 'Ob La Di, Ob La Da' as most played song of the year in the UK. But from 'Paperback Writer' spring '66 the norm was just over a half-million all up, 'Hello Goodbye' and 'Hey Jude' exceptions around three-quarters. 'Lady Madonna' pitched another quantum lower, 300,000—repeated by 'Ballad of John & Yoko' and 'Let It Be'; 'Something'/'Come Together' 200,000 flat. This explains why no UK issue for 'Long and Winding Road'. Imagine an embarrassing anticlimax instead of the career topper the dwindling number of British Beatle followers needed to perpetuate the myth of invincibility.

As Beatles all launched solo into a series of pop singles it appeared the former drummer—now Ringo was primarily a singer and writer of sorts—might be most successful and even have most potential careerwise from the all-star *Magic Christian*. Apple protegés Badfinger, who emerged in the film, were obliged to perform the McCartney composition 'Come and Get It' and then did much better with their self-penned (McCartney lookalike Pete Ham) 'No Matter What', 'Day After Day', 'Baby Blue'.

The Sixties ended as, on September 18th, Jimi Hendrix, *the man* of hard rock, died in his London flat choking on drug-induced vomitus—his female counterpart, Janis Joplin, to follow in two weeks or so. In between the two disasters Andrew Lloyd Webber & Tim Rice's 'rock' musical *Jesus Christ Superstar* was released, spelling curtains for the age of organic rock groups and individual styling. From now on so-called rock would increasingly be a theater industry based on choreography and nightly projection of fixed, on-stage characters, eschewing all spontaneity. Hendrix's loss was a tragedy for *music*. Having shown incomparable guitar ability coupled with ideally keyed songwriting, who knows what he was capable of had he survived past 27?—It is impossible to envision decline through reggae, country and soppy ballads like Clapton. A day later 'Cottonfields'—competing with a basic, dull version from Creedence Clearwater Revival—appeared for the last time in the UK chart. And a week after that the Beach Boys took a giant step into the unknown as *Sunflower* charted in the mighty Billboard and would reap more praise from critics in America and Britain than any of their work since *Pet Sounds*. It showed the way to the best rock to come, greatly influencing, as was their habit, the biggest stars for the next decade.

AFTERWORD

John, Paul, George and Ringo became soloists with a captive audience, miraculously remaining gods of rock though the quality fell drastically, George excepted (though he too was overrated— 'All Those Years Ago'). The loss on breaking up was lamented by former rock journalist turned rock producer Charlie Gillett in his better reasoned (1977) essay 'In praise of the professionals' in *Rock File 5*: "I... yearn for a return of the energy that was captured by the Beatles under George Martin's watchful eye but never recaptured by any of them on their own without him.... For some artists, the long-term aim is to become their own producers, having learned all they can from working under a&r men, managers, engineers... Brian Wilson of the Beach Boys was far ahead of most artists in achieving this goal, writing, arranging, and producing Beach Boys records from 1965 [it was 1961] onwards, and it may have been a determination by some of the individual Beatles to achieve comparable autonomy that caused them to break apart and stay apart; John Lennon and George Harrison both started strongly and then lost momentum, while Paul McCartney gradually revealed himself to be a 'stayer' with apparently limitless ingenuity and perseverance."

For ten years after *Pet Sounds* there is not a single recorded track released by the Beach Boys that can be pointed to that has as its goal a sale in a record store, and many were determinedly uncommercial— until 1976 when the anti-Wilson faction overbalanced its commercial asset into a tangible taint. The result was the Beach Boys, on every second album, were ordinary for the first time in their career, on these outings repeating themselves through advancing middle age in a pointless, doomed effort to recapture the Sixties. Positives were that Dennis, then Carl, and finally a recovered Brian, were spurred to follow their own creative inclinations, materialising in solo albums— and Dennis's solo single, 'Sound of Free', a revelation, emerging at the end of 1970 but only in the UK. The best Beach Boy tracks had long since been solo-directed anyway, leaving such dire results as 'Loop de Loop' to emerge from group efforts.

But over 1970-73 the Beach Boys faced the reputations of former Beatles and fashioned another of the very few strands of Rock that endures. It is evident that in the latter year—maybe catalysed by Murry's death—they too stopped going forward (as a group). They were enjoying high praise for live performances and had pulled off an album revival. In 18 months *Surf's Up, Carl & the Passions* and *Holland* made Billboard's top 50—something they hadn't achieved once since 1967—and the upcoming *Beach Boys in Concert* would do even better. Three of the releases were hailed. But that summer a cut-price album of their old hits went to the top of the budget charts and the following summer all was settled by *Endless Summer*, a huge double album no.1 containing no hits newer than 1965—and a majority of the group, desiring something predictable to hang their hat on, cast the Beach Boys as an oldies act. To cement in the policy in successive summers came sister double album *Spirit of America* (and then *20 Golden Greats*, a two-million seller in Britain)—and *15 Big Ones*, ostensibly their first album of new material in three years but containing mostly remakes of oldies and originals written long before.

The late seventies brought two rewarding albums, *The Beach Boys Love You* (1977) and *The Light Album* (1979). Carl retained his loyalty to rock by refusing to play Vegas-Tahoe style venues, and Dennis refused to record disco. Both issued very good to truly great solo l.p.s. Mike Love, going with the audience, led a back-to-the-sixties drive, Al Jardine going along remaking 'Peggy Sue', 'Come Go With Me', 'California Dreamin''…. In the eighties a dwindling group—Dennis drowned at the end of 1983 after a year as a walking shell, and Brian was only half there—was adopted as Reagan and Bush family favorites to become "America's Band".

The presidential favoritism they enjoyed dissipated to the point that in 2000 they were referred to on a record review website as: "unjustly forgotten. Their mid-'60s hits have become a part of our collective unconscious, but the author of those magic A-sides— Brian Wilson—is an obscure figure, remembered more his mental illness, drug abuse, and hermit-like existence than for his musical achievements" (Wilson & Alroy). Disregarding Wilson's acclaim since resuming touring and recording, it's a summation that overrates currency. After all, what is McCartney remembered for? A succession of wives according to most media coverage today, much less for his musical achievements; Lennon, for Yoko Ono and the slippery halo conferred by the media on his demise.

In summer 1988 Brian delivered his first official solo album—critically welcomed but hardly a commercial success going up against the platinum 'Kokomo' single initiated and co-written by Mike Love. Amid a series of solo albums, Brian's real renaissance came at 60 in 2002 when he began touring with a 13-piece band— Britain and the Continent, Japan and Australasia, even America, performing *Pet Sounds* and then in 2004, *Smile.*

In the August 2005 issue of UK rock magazine *GQ* a panel of 42 contributors voted a top 100 albums of the rock era. For the first time just a sprinkling of Sixties albums made the upper reaches of the list—one from Bob Dylan, one from the Beatles, of course *Pet Sounds*—Brian's first real solo album—and a sensational #1 in Van Dyke Parks' *Song Cycle* (1968), hardly known to the public; at #18, Dennis's *Pacific Ocean Blue* (1977). It seems that finally the Wilson "family" is reaping due appreciation.

Beatlemania had exploded late in 1963. Fashion followers styled their hair, bought (or made) their clothes and modified their accents to Beatle mode. Groups looked and sounded like them, superficially. But this all passed. The Beatles as musicians founded no new tradition, no school as musical stylists. By the late Sixties the teen audience had been through Herman's Hermits and the Monkees and was captured in turn by the Archies' bubblegum, David Cassidy/the Partridge Family and the Osmonds. Trite mush oozing Tin Pan Alley clichés had been ensured perpetuation by the Beatles' precedent.

To Beach Boys followers the Beatles were *clever* (no ethereal genius here), better at presenting themselves, music and lyrics synonymous with the spirit of the times, looking good in movies. As the Beach Boys never encroached on Beatle territory, the Beatles couldn't capture the fresh, exhilarating Beach Boy feel experienced by listeners on a primal level, their sublime sound and treatment of a song at times touching a spiritual chord. The overall strength of Brian

Wilson's group became obvious on his withdrawal with the younger Wilsons' dynamic but uncommercial music emerging as a shining light. Imagine the consequences if the Beatles had lost their guiding genius, Lennon-McCartney-Martin, in 1967. With the loss of Brian Epstein and partial withdrawal of Martin, the Beatles were already losing creative impetus.

As Dennis said in 1970 on the breakup of the Beatles: "Because of the attitude of a few mental dinosaurs intent on exploiting our initial success, Brian's huge talent has never been fully appreciated in America and the potential of the group has been stifled... If the Beatles had suffered this kind of misrepresentation they would never have got past singing 'Please Please Me' and 'I Want to Hold Your Hand' and leaping around in Beatle suits."

Both groups (and for a time, The Who) produced bodies of work that stand supreme in the Sixties and therefore above everything since. Brian Wilson and his group were shortchanged, unable to compete with the media-driven acclaim for the Beatles. For what should have been rock's crowning glory through 1966-67 there was no media machine waiting for the Beach Boys. What was left of Wilson's acknowledged musical gems dribbled out, tucked away on underselling albums.

On an everyday theme, compare the sheer vitality—*joie de vivre* —of 'Amusement Parks USA' with the forced, lumbering 'Magical Mystery Tour' two years later. (Of course, Beatle-siders would characterise the first as light, the latter as weighty.) This is not to say—necessarily—that the Beatles tracked the Beach Boys as deliberately as the Stones had the Beatles, but 'Help!' following close on the heels of 'Help Me Rhonda', 'Girl' on 'Girl Don't Tell Me', 'Oh Darlin'' after 'Darlin'', and spookily 'Wild Honey Pie' emerging months after 'Wild Honey'...? They could have used the Beach Boys first hand when it came to recording 'Back in the USSR' but turned out a sincere tribute to their precursors.

The personality-appeal of the Beatles would forever elude the Beach Boys—not because they didn't understand it in terms of showbiz success, but they couldn't relate to its importance to musical success. What America had seen at that first press conference at JFK was the kind of naïve self-belief to the point of arrogance that Americans were known for around the world. Reflected back at them with charm added it was irresistible. In "youngsters" the overconfidence was attractive, and probably justifiable but for different reasons. As a collective entity they had survived the mean streets of Liverpool intact—after that, conquering America was a quiet nosh of Lancashire Hotpot "int' snoog".

Interviewed on *Larry King Live* in 2001, Ringo, less attractive in his overconfidence at 60, would barely allow for an element of luck in Beatle success, to the visible incredulity of King, who opened the door for some humility by citing the example of Paul Newman admitting there were actors who ran rings around him but never got the breaks. Yet, backed by a world-beating corporation back in '62, Oprah-like (if short of the mindless moxy of Judge Judy), they had already decided their fate—and became their own cheering section when morale needed boosting: John would ask rhetorically, "Where are we going, lads?" and the answer came, "To the toppermost of the poppermost!"—playfully in a Goons style, but not even half-joking.

A few years later, in a flatter fest with Paul McCartney, BBC celebrity interviewer Michael Parkinson spent a whole hour giving the former Beatle feeder lines designed for him to tell the world exactly how great he was. If anyone was expecting them, there were no modest disclaimers. Asked what separated them from the hundreds of other hopeful groups of the Sixties, Paul said it might be to do with cleverness—he had got right up there in high school and John had been to art school. When Parkinson singled out 'Yesterday' for particular praise as a song that would live for hundreds of years, Paul half-smiled charmingly, or was it a cheeky smirk with his tongue planted in his cheek, worried that if he opened his mouth at all he might let the cat out of the bag? There should be no doubting now that Sir Paul, for one (and Sir Mick for another), will take the whole truth of his myth to his grave.

Beyond that the Brit-style rock-without-finesse of the Beatles— 'Twist & Shout' or 'I Wanna Be Your Man' might say it best— and (perpetuated by) the Rolling Stones is responsible for a philistine redefinition of rock that holds stronger than ever today. Once, pre-

Beatles and running parallel with them through the Sixties, rock included all possible nuances of expression: roaring, rasping, shouting, pleading, whispering, trilling, wailing and weeping, often all in one song. Now *screaming* at the top of one's lungs with no expression but strident anger is admired as the epitome of a rock song: a monotone, dumbed-down excuse for a genre. Otherwise, as one new she-screamer said derisively, it is *pop*.

APPENDIX: BEACH BOYS HIT ALBUMS (1962-1970)

*****INSPIRED   ****EXCELLENT   ***COULD DO BETTER
**LACKING   *INEXCUSABLE

SURFIN' SAFARI (rel Oct 1 '62, charted to Aug '63)
Billboard#32 Cash Box#26 Japan#6
** Showcasing 'Surfin' Safari'/'409', including debut 'Surfin'', it lacks impact apart from these classics and 'Ten Little Indians'.

SURFIN' USA (rel Mar 25 '63, charted to Oct '64)
Billboard#2 Cash Box#2 Jap#5 UK#17
Billboard: *1st best-charting rock album of 1963*
*** One of the first major rock albums, again the double-sided hit furnishes the highlights: 'Surfin' USA'/'Shut Down'. Still has (instrumental) filler, but more listenable: 'Surf Jam', and fuller harmonies on 'Lonely Sea', 'Farmer's Daughter', 'Lana'.

SHUT DOWN (with Various Artists) (rel Aug '63)
Billboard#7
Cash Box: *5th best-charting rock album of 1963*
         19th best-charting rock album of 1964

SURFER GIRL (rel Sept 16 '63, charted to Nov '64)
Billboard#7 C/Box#10 Jap#9 UK#13
Cash Box: *32nd best-charting rock album of 1964*
**** The first album officially credited as a Brian Wilson production, it marked another advance through the title track, 'In My Room', 'Little Deuce Coupe', 'Catch a Wave' and 'Hawaii': all good enough to be A-sides of singles.

LITTLE DEUCE COUPE (rel Oct 7 '63, charted to Sept '64)
Billboard#4 Cash Box#6 Japan#10
Billboard: *6th best-charting rock album of 1963*

Cash Box: *8ᵗʰ best-charting rock album of 1964*
**** Car songs '409', 'Shut Down' and 'Little Deuce Coupe' repeated but fitting into a spirited album of high overall quality. Essaying the all-American dream lifestyle, the group stakes its claim as America's band.

SHUT DOWN 2 (rel Mar 2 '64, charted to Jan '65)
Billboard#13 Cash Box#11 Record World#12 Japan#3
Cash Box: *4ᵗʰ best-charting rock album of 1964*
**** Boasting all-time classics 'Fun Fun Fun', 'Don't Worry Baby' and 'Warmth of the Sun', for a reputedly uneven album 'Why Do Fools Fall in Love?', 'Keep an Eye on Summer', 'In the Parking Lot' and 'Pom Pom Play Girl' were still worthwhile.

ALL SUMMER LONG (rel Jul 13 '64, charted to Jul '65)
Billboard#4 Cash Box#4 Record World#3 Japan#7 UK#4
Billboard: *9ᵗʰ best-charting rock album of 1964*
Cash Box: *20ᵗʰ best-charting rock album of 1965*
***** Their first go at 'matching' the Beatles. 'I Get Around', 'Little Honda' and 'Wendy' qualify as classics, while 'All Summer Long', 'Girls on the Beach', 'Hushabye', 'Don't Back Down' and 'Drive-In' are reissue favorites. Filler is cut to three tracks.

BEACH BOYS CONCERT (rel Oct 19 '64, charted to Jan '66)
Billboard#1 Cash Box#1 Record World#1 Japan#10
Billboard: *4ᵗʰ best-charting rock album of 1964*
Cash Box: *3ʳᵈ best-charting rock album of 1965*
*** Faithful renditions of 'In My Room', 'Fun Fun Fun' and 'I Get Around', and an energetic 'Johnny B Goode' made it their best-selling album to date. Taken from two concerts in December 1963 and August 1964, it could have done with 'Surfin' USA' from *The TAMI Show* instead of 'Papa-Oom-Mow-Mow' and 'Long Tall Texan'.

BEACH BOYS CHRISTMAS (rel Nov 9 '64)
Billboard#6   Record World#84   Japan#10
** Slushy strings, enlivened only by the comparatively rocking 'Little St Nick' and 'Merry Christmas, Baby'. Some of the ballads—Brian's 'Blue Christmas', Al's 'Christmas Day', the group harmonies on 'We Three Kings'—are bearable muzak in the right mood.

BEACH BOYS TODAY (rel Mar 8 '65, to Mar '66)
Billboard#4   Cash Box#3   Record World#4   Japan#3   UK#3
Cash Box: *4th best-charting rock album of 1965*
***** Foreshadowing *Pet Sounds*, the rocking side has 'When I Grow Up', 'Dance Dance Dance' and 'Do You Wanna Dance?', and prototype 'Help Me Ronda'. Matching it is the reflective side with 'Please Let Me Wonder', 'Kiss Me Baby', 'She Knows Me Too Well', an improved Spector's 'I'm So Young' and Dennis's lead on 'In the Back of My Mind'.

SUMMER DAYS (rel Jul 5 '65, charted to Mar '66)
Billboard#2   Cash Box#4   Record World#2   Japan#7   UK#4
Billboard: *13th best-charting rock album of 1965*
UK: *16th best-charting album of 1966*
***** The last and perhaps most evocative of their fun image, with four international hits: 'California Girls', 'Help Me Rhonda', 'Then I Kissed Her' and 'Amusement Parks USA'. 'You're So Good to Me' and 'Girl Don't Tell Me' have been bolstering *Best of...* albums ever since; 'The Girl From New York City' and 'Salt Lake City' are no slouches either. 'Let Him Run Wild' with its piano pulse keeping the medium-tempo beat and Brian's pleading vocal slipping in and out of falsetto, pointed to shapes of things to come.

BEACH BOYS PARTY (rel Nov 8 '65, to May '66)
Billboard#6   Cash Box#7   Record World#5   Japan#11   UK#3
Cash Box: *19th best-charting rock album of 1966*
UK: *15th best-charting album of 1966*

*** The atmosphere is created in the studio with suitably little serious music, including the big hit lifted from the album, 'Barbara Ann'. The only performance of any note: Dennis's rendering of 'You've Got to Hide Your Love Away', more soulful than John Lennon's.

PET SOUNDS (rel May 16 '66, charted to Feb '67)
Billboard#10 Cash Box#8 Record World#6   Japan#5 UK#2
Cash Box: *13th best-charting rock album of 1966*
UK: *4st best-charting rock album of 1966 (8th overall)*
****** Enough said

BEST OF BBs... (rel Jul 11 '66, charted to Jan '68)
Billboard#8 Cash Box#8 Record World#4   Japan#7 UK#2
US edition: Surfin' USA. Catch a Wave, Surfer Girl, Little Deuce Coupe, In My Room, Little Honda; Fun Fun Fun, The Warmth of the Sun, Louie Louie, Kiss Me Baby, You're So Good to Me, Wendy
Cash Box: *27th best-charting rock album of 1966*

UK edition: Surfin' Safari, Surfin' USA, Little Deuce Coupe, Fun Fun Fun, I Get Around, All Summer Long, In My Room; Do You Wanna Dance, Help Me Rhonda, California Girls, Barbara Ann, You're So Good to Me, Sloop John B, God Only Knows
1st best-charting album of 1966
1st best-charting rock album of 1967 (2nd overall)
4th best-charting rock album of 1968 (5th overall)

BEST OF... VOL.2 (rel Aug 31 '67, to Jan '68)
Billboard#50 Cash Box#25 Record World#24 Japan#7 UK#3
US edition: Barbara Ann, When I Grow Up, Long Tall Texan, Please Let Me Wonder, 409, Let Him Run Wild; Don't Worry Baby, Surfin' Safari, Little Saint Nick, California Girls, Help Me Rhonda, I Get Around

UK edition: Surfer Girl, Don't Worry Baby, Wendy, When I Grow Up, Good to My Baby, Dance Dance Dance, Then I Kissed Her; The Girl from New York City, Girl Don't Tell Me, The Little Girl I Once Knew, Mountain of Love, Here Today, Wouldn't It Be Nice, Good Vibrations
6th best-charting rock album of 1967

SMILE (unreleased)
***** What would come to be called the Smile Tapes, taking on almost a Nixonian pall of intrigue, were nixed by the band only to be repeatedly plundered for group use on Brian's retreat. The highlights of what were released disembowelled: 'Good Vibrations' (the Air segment of The Elements Suite, 'Cool Cool Water' (Water), 'Vegetables' (Earth) and 'Mrs O'Leary's Cow' (Fire); 'Heroes & Villains'/ 'Bicycle Rider', 'Surf's Up'/ 'The Child is Father of the Man', 'Wind Chimes', 'Cabinessence', 'Our Prayer' and 'Wonderful'. The other less well known tracks were 'Indian Wisdom', 'Who Ran the Iron Horse?', 'Grand Coulee Dam', 'Old Master Painter', 'You Are My Sunshine', 'You're Welcome', 'Barnyard', 'Holidays', 'I'm in Great Shape'. Despite its reworking and issue in 2004 we can only imagine its treatment and power if it had come pre-Sgt Pepper.

SMILEY SMILE (rel Sept 18 '67, charted to Feb '68)
Billboard#41 Cash Box#19 Record World#17 Japan#9 UK#6
Cash Box: *50th best-charting rock album of 1967*
**** 'Good Vibrations', 'Heroes & Villains', 'Gettin' Hungry' (issued by Brian & Mike) and mainly dregs from the SMILE project—still a lot, taken track by track.

WILD HONEY (rel Dec 18 '67, charted to Apr '68)
Billboard#24 Cash Box#19 Record World#15 Japan#12 UK#7
**** Shows their ultimate artistry, able to turn their hand to any genre (in this case r&b) and make it their own. Highlights: 'Wild

Honey', 'Darlin'', 'Here Comes the Night', 'Let the Wind Blow', 'Country Air' and their take on 'I Was Made to Love Her'.

FRIENDS (rel Jun 24, charted to Aug '68)
Billboard#126 Cash Box#58 Record World#54 Japan#6 UK#13
*** Appreciated more now than it was then, mainly notable for Dennis Wilson's emerging talents—'Little Bird' and 'Be Still' delivered with perfectly gauged emotional expression. The fragmentary 'Meant for You' leading in to 'Friends' is one of their all-time great openings to an album, but after that there is much meandering.

*BEST OF… VOL.*3 (rel Aug 26, charted to Oct '68)
Billboard#153 Cash Box#87 Record World#68 Japan & UK#8
US edition: God Only Knows, Dance Dance Dance, 409, The Little Girl I Once Knew, Frosty the Snowman, Girl Don't Tell Me; Surfin', Heroes & Villains, She Knows Me Too Well, Darlin', Good Vibrations
UK edition: Do It Again, The Warmth of the Sun, 409, Catch a Wave, Lonely Sea, Long Tall Texan, Wild Honey; Darlin', Please Let Me Wonder, Let Him Run Wild, Country Air, I Know There's an Answer, Friends, Heroes & Villains

'20 / 20' (rel Feb 10, charted to May '69)
Billboard#68 Cash Box#71 Record World#60 Japan#2 UK#3
**** A collection of oddments—and all the better for it! Inclusion of singles 'Do It Again', 'Bluebirds Over the Mountain' and 'I Can Hear Music' made it commercial everywhere but America. 'Our Prayer' and 'Cabinessence' were included, and for ghouls that notorious Charles Manson song 'Cease to Exist' diplomatically renamed.

LIVE IN LONDON/BEACH BOYS'69 (rel '69 UK, '76 US)
Billboard#75 Record World#81
*** Recorded in December 1968, heading into their best-ever live
form (c.1970-74) which was captured somewhat better on their live
double album of 1973.

BEACH BOYS GREATEST HITS (rel June '70)
United Kingdom #5   Japan #10
UK: *18th best-charting rock album of 1970*

BIBLIOGRAPHY

ABBOTT, Kingsley *The Beach Boys Pet Sounds: The Greatest Album of the 20th Century* Helter Skelter, 2001

BADMAN, Keith *The Beach Boys: the definitive diary of America's greatest band on stage and in the studio* Backbeat 2004

BENSON, Ross *Paul McCartney: behind the myth* Victor Gollancz 1992

BOOTH, Stanley *The True Adventures of the Rolling Stones* Heinemann 1985

BUCKLEY, Jonathan & ELLINGHAM, Mark editors *Rock: The Rough Guide* Rough Guides Ltd/Penguin 1996

CHAPPLE, Steve & GAROFALO, Reebee *Rock and Roll is Here to Pay: the History and Politics of the Music Industry* Nelson Hall 1977

EHNERT, Gunter *Hit Guide: US Chart LPs 1964-1982* Taurus Press, 1985

FREUND, Charles Paul *Reason* magazine, June 2001 issue, article 'Still Fab: Why we still listen to the Beatles'

GILBERT, Eugene—Gilbert Youth Research surveys 1962-66

GILBERT, Nancy—Gilbert Youth Research surveys 1967 & 1969

GILLETT, Charlie & FRITH, Simon editors *Rock File 4* Panther 1976; *Rock File 5* Panther 1978

GRIEG, Charlotte *Girls Talk* BBC Radio, 1998

GUINNESS Company *The Top 10 of Everything* Guinness, 1996

GURALNICK, Peter *Careless Love: The Unmaking of Elvis Presley* Little, Brown & Co, 1999

HANBOO & John2000 & Dane *The Beatles Sales Thread* website on UKMix.org

HECHLER, Mattias editor 'Mount Vernon & Fairway' website, 2002

HOFFMANN, Frank *The Cash Box Singles Charts (1950-1981)* Scarecrow, 1983

JASPER, Tony *The Top Twenty Book: the Official British Record Charts (1955-1982)* Blandford, 1983

LANG, Barbara editor 'The Beach Boys Journal' website, 2002

MERCER, Derrik *Chronicle of the 20th Century* International, 1988

MILLER, Jim editor *The Rolling Stone Illustrated History of Rock and Roll* Rolling Stone, 1976

MURRELLS, Joseph *The Book of Golden Discs* Barrie & Jenkins, second edn 1978

NOLAN, Tom 'The Beach Boys: a California Saga' in *The Beach Boys Complete* Amsco, 1973

OLDHAM, Andrew Loog *Stoned* Vintage, 2001

PFEIFFER, Gary & SCHWOB, John, et al *Airheads Radio Survey Archive (ARSA)* website

PRITCHARD, David & LYSAGHT, Alan *The Beatles: an Oral History—inside the one and only lonely hearts club band*—various contributors Allen & Unwin 1998

SALEWICZ, Chris *McCartney: The Biography* Queen Anne Press, 1986

SCARUFFI, Piero 'History of Rock Music' website (1999)

SMITH, Steve & The Diagram Group *Rock Day By Day* Diagram Visual Information, 1987

STEBBINS, Jon *The Beach Boys*

TOBLER, John *The Beach Boys* Hamlyn, 1977

UNITED PRESS INTERNATIONAL (UPI) weekly chart surveys 1962-1966

WEBB, Adam *The Life and Music of Dennis Wilson: Dumb Angel* Creation, 2001

WHITE, Timothy *The Nearest Faraway Place* 1996

WILLIAMS, Paul   *Brian Wilson & the Beach Boys: How Deep is the Ocean?* Omnibus, 1997

WILLIAMS, Richard   *Out of His Head: The Sound of Phil Spector* Abacus, 1972

Printed in the United States
115036LV00008B/3/A

9 781601 453174